Lecture Notes in Computer Science   11430

Commenced Publication in 1973
Founding and Former Series Editors:
Gerhard Goos, Juris Hartmanis, and Jan van Leeuwen

More information about this series at http://www.springer.com/series/7408

Jonathan P. Bowen · Zhiming Liu ·
Zili Zhang (Eds.)

Engineering Trustworthy Software Systems

4th International School, SETSS 2018
Chongqing, China, April 7–12, 2018
Tutorial Lectures

Editors
Jonathan P. Bowen ⓘ
London South Bank University
London, UK

Zhiming Liu ⓘ
Southwest University
Chongqing, China

Zili Zhang
Southwest University
Chongqing, China

ISSN 0302-9743   ISSN 1611-3349 (electronic)
Lecture Notes in Computer Science
ISBN 978-3-030-17600-6   ISBN 978-3-030-17601-3   (eBook)
https://doi.org/10.1007/978-3-030-17601-3

LNCS Sublibrary: SL2 – Programming and Software Engineering

Cover illustration: Academic supervisor tree for Alan Turing. LNCS 11430, p. 213, used with permission.
Photograph on p. xiii: The photograph of the group was taken by Hui Xiang, used with permission.

This Springer imprint is published by the registered company Springer Nature Switzerland AG
The registered company address is: Gewerbestrasse 11, 6330 Cham, Switzerland

Preface

The 4th School on Engineering Trustworthy Software Systems (SETSS 2018) was held during April 7–12, 2018, at Southwest University, Chongqing, China. It was aimed at PhD and Master students in particular, from around China and elsewhere, as well as being suitable for university researchers and industry software engineers. This volume contains tutorial papers related to a selection of the lecture courses and evening seminars delivered at the school.

SETSS 2018 was organized by the School of Computer and Information Science, in particular the Centre for Research and Innovation in Software Engineering (RISE), at Southwest University, providing lectures on leading-edge research in methods and tools for use in computer system engineering. The school aimed to enable participants to learn about state-of-the-art software engineering methods and technology advances from experts in the field.

The opening session was chaired by Prof. Guoqiang Xiao. A welcome speech was delivered by the Vice President of Southwest University, Prof. Yanqiang Cui, followed by an introductory briefing for SETSS 2018 by Prof. Zhiming Liu. The session finished with a photograph of participants at the school.

The following lecture courses (each consisting of six hour-long lecture sessions, with breaks) were delivered during the school, chaired by Jonathan Bowen, Zhiming Liu, Zhendong Su, and Shmuel Tyazberwicz:

- Mark Utting: An Introduction to Software Verification with Whiley
- Wang Yi: Model-Based Design of Real-Time Systems: From Timed Automata to Di-Graph and Back
- Zhendong Su: Randomized and Systematic Testing of Software
- Lijun Zhang: Omega-Automata Learning Algorithms and Its Application
- Jorge Cuellar: Securing the Future IoT Application
- Nikolaj Bjørner: Programming Constraint Services with Z3

    In addition, there were two evening seminars:

- Yu Jiang: Fuzzing Testing in Theory and Practice
- Jonathan P. Bowen: From Alan Turing to Formal Methods

    These additional presentations complemented the longer lecture courses.

Courses

An Introduction to Software Verification with Whiley

Lecturer: Dr. Mark Utting, University of the Sunshine Coast, Australia

Biography: Mark Utting is a senior lecturer in ICT at the University of the Sunshine Coast (USC), in Queensland, Australia. Prior to joining USC, he worked at UQ, QUT, and Waikato University in academic positions, and he has also worked in industry, developing next-generation genomics software and manufacturing software. Mark is passionate about designing and engineering good software that solves real-world problems, and has extensive experience with managing software development projects and teams both in academia and industry. He is author of the book *Practical Model-Based Testing: A Tools Approach*, as well as of more than 50 publications on model-based testing, verification techniques for object-oriented and real-time software, and language design for parallel computing.

Overview: This course introduced students to the fundamental ideas of software verification for imperative programming. It covered basic specification techniques, how to use preconditions and postconditions, the relationship between specifications and code, techniques for verifying conditional code, loops, arrays, records, and functions. The course included a series of hands-on verification exercises using the Whiley programming language and its online verification tool.

Model-Based Design of Real-Time Systems: From Timed Automata to Di-Graph and Back

Lecturer: Prof. Wang Yi, Uppsala University, Sweden

Biography: Wang Yi received a PhD in Computer Science from Chalmers University of Technology in 1991. He was appointed Professor of Embedded Systems at Uppsala University, Sweden, in 2000, and Distinguished Professor at North Eastern University, China, in 2007. He is a fellow of the IEEE and member of the Academy of Europe. His interests include embedded systems and formal verification. He was the recipient of the CAV 2013 Award for the development of UPPAAL, Best Paper Awards at RTSS17, RTSS15, RTSS09, ECRTS15, DATE13, and Outstanding Paper Award at ECRTS12. He is a board member of ACM SigBed and Award Committee Chair of the ACM SigBed Caspi Dissertation Award. He is a Steering Committee Co-chair of EMSOFT, and Steering Committee member of ESWEEK, FORMATS, LCTES, and SETTA. He is editor for the journals *ACM Transactions on Embedded Computing and Systems*, *IEEE Embedded Systems Letters*, *IEEE Design and Test*, and the *Journal of Computer Science and Technology*. Recent keynote talks were given at ETAPS15, SIES16, APSEC17, and ICFEM17.

Overview: The first part of my lecture focused on modeling and verification of real-time systems in the framework of timed automata, covering the theoretical foundation, modeling, and specification languages, as well as the central algorithms of UPPAAL, a tool developed jointly by Uppsala and Aalborg University. The second part of my lecture was based on our recent work on real-time scheduling and timing analysis. I presented a new graph-based model for timed systems, that allows us to precisely capture the timing behavior of real-time software and yet keep the analysis problems tractable. For the theoretically intractable cases of interest, we presented a refinement technique, which allows for effective guidance to significantly prune away the global search space and to efficiently verify the desired timing properties in real applications.

Randomized and Systematic Testing of Software

Lecturer: Prof. Zhendong Su, ETH Zürich, Switzerland

Biography: Zhendong Su received his PhD from the University of California, Berkeley, and until recently he was a professor and chancellor's fellow at the University of California Davis, before taking up a professorial position at ETH Zürich, Switzerland. His research focuses on methodologies, techniques, and tools for improving software quality and programming productivity. His work has been recognized with best paper awards from EAPLS, SIGSOFT, OOPSLA and PLDI, CACM Research Highlight, NSF CAREER Award, UC Davis Outstanding Engineering Faculty Award, and industrial research awards (Cisco, Google, IBM, Microsoft, Mozilla). He served as Associate Editor for ACM TOSEM, program (co-)chair SAS (2009), ISSTA (2012), and FSE (2016), and serves on the Steering Committees of ESEC/FSE and ISSTA.

Overview: Random testing (aka fuzzing) has been remarkably successful in finding important software flaws and vulnerabilities. There is also much exciting recent progress in developing more advanced systematic techniques and adapting them to different domains. This set of lectures introduced and highlighted several of these important advances, including EMI and SPE testing for compilers and interpreters, and mathematical execution for solving floating-point constraints and analyzing numerical software. It also discussed key open technical challenges and promising new applications.

Omega-Automata Learning Algorithms and Its Application

Lecturer: Prof. Lijun Zhang, State Key Laboratory of Computer Science, Institute of Software Chinese Academy of Sciences, China

Biography: Lijun Zhang is a research professor at State Key Laboratory of Computer Science, Institute of Software Chinese Academy of Sciences. Before this he was an associate professor at the Language-Based Technology section, DTU Compute, Technical University of Denmark. He was a postdoctoral researcher at the University of Oxford and obtained gained a diploma degree and a PhD (Dr. Ing.) at Saarland University. His research interests include: probabilistic models, simulation reduction, decision algorithms for probabilistic simulation preorders, abstraction, and model checking. His recent work is in combining automata learning techniques with model checking. He is leading the development of the model checker IscasMC.

Overview: Learning-based automata inference techniques have received significant attention from the community of formal system analysis. In general, the primary applications of automata learning in the community can be categorized into two groups: improving efficiency and scalability of verification and synthesizing abstract system model for further analysis. Most of the results in the literature focus on checking safety properties or synthesizing finite behavior models of systems/programs. On the other hand, Büchi automaton is the standard model for describing liveness properties of distributed systems. Unlike the case for finite automata learning, learning algorithms for Büchi automata are very rarely used in our community. In this talk, we present algorithms to learn a Büchi automaton from a teacher who knows an omega-regular language. The algorithm is based on learning a formalism named family of DFAs (FDFAs) recently proposed by Angluin and Fisman. The main catch is that we use a classification tree structure instead of the standard observation table structure. The worst-case storage space required by our algorithm is quadratically better than the table-based algorithm. We implement the first publicly available library ROLL (Regular Omega Language Learning), which consists of all omega-regular learning algorithms available in the literature and the new algorithms proposed in this paper. Further, with our tool, we demonstrate how our algorithm can be exploited in classic automata operations such as complementation checking and in the model-checking context.

Securing the Future IoT Application

Lecturer: Prof. Dr. Jorge Cuellar, Siemens AG and University of Passau, Germany

Biography: Jorge Cuellar is a principal research scientist at Siemens AG. He was awarded the DI-ST Award for the best technical achievement for his work on modeling of operating systems and transaction managers. He has worked in several topics, including performance analysis, on learning algorithms, hand-writing recognition, formal verification of distributed system design, and security and he has co-authored 50 publications. He has done technical standardization work on privacy and security protocols at the IETF, 3GPP, and the Open Mobile Alliance. He has worked in several EU-funded research projects, mostly on security topics. He regularly serves in Program Committees for international conferences and he has held many short-term visiting teaching positions, in different universities around the world.

Overview: In the near future, computing devices – belonging to different owners with competing expectations and diverse security goals – will be embedded into all sort of commonplace objects, including smart surfaces or devices in buildings and at home, wearables, city and transportation infrastructure, etc. The IoT promise is that those "things" will talk to each other and will create self-configuring systems. There is a need to negotiate compromises ("contracts") that manage their interactions and interoperate the security policies and functionality goals.

We require a formal language for specifying the possible interactions and contracts and to enforce the agreements reached. We propose to use Petri nets, smart contracts, and a public ledger (like a blockchain or a Merkle tree). The system resembles in some aspects Bitcoins, Etherum, or other cryptocurrencies, but instead of coins, the tokens represent mostly permissions ("authorization tokens") or information. To allow verification, we avoid Turing-complete contracts, but construct smart contracts using Petri nets based on building blocks with cryptographic functionality (secure or fair interactions) or guarded commands.

In this short course, we reviewed how to construct and to use authorization tokens for IoT, how to create workflows as Petri nets, how to define and implement basic cryptographic building blocks, how to use them to create more complex smart contracts, and how to use a public ledger for common information and for resolving disputes.

Programming Constraint Services with Z3

Lecturer: Dr. Nikolaj Bjørner, Microsoft Research, USA

Biography: Nikolaj Bjørner is a principal researcher at Microsoft Research, Redmond, USA, working in the area of automated theorem proving and network verification. His current main line of work with Leonardo de Moura, Lev Nachmanson, and Christoph Wintersteiger is on the state-of-the-art theorem prover Z3, which is used as a foundation of several software engineering tools. Z3 received the 2015 ACM SIGPLAN Software System Award, most influential tool paper in the first 20 years of TACAS in 2014, and the 2017 Skolem Award for the 2007 paper on *Efficient E-matching for SMT Solvers*. Another main line of activity is focused on network verification with colleagues in Azure, Karthick Jayaraman, and academia, George Varghese. Previously, he developed the DFSR, Distributed File System Replication, part of Windows Server since 2005, and before that worked on distributed file sharing systems at a startup, XDegrees, and program synthesis and transformation systems at the Kestrel Institute. He received his Master's and PhD degrees in computer science from Stanford University, and spent the first three years of university at DTU and DIKU in Denmark.

Overview: Many program verification, analysis, testing, and synthesis queries reduce to solving satisfiability of logical formulas. Yet, there are many applications where satisfiability, and optionally a model or a proof, is insufficient. Examples of useful additional information include interpolants, models that satisfy optimality criteria, generating strategies for solving quantified formulas, enumerating and counting solutions. The lectures describe logical services from the point of view of the Satisfiability Modulo Theories solver Z3. We cover their foundations, algorithmics, and ways to put these features to use.

As an overview, we provide a few types of queries below.

Type of Query	Query in symbolic form
Satisfiability	$\varphi \rightsquigarrow$ sat, unsat, timeout
Certificates	$\varphi \rightsquigarrow$ model, proof, unsat core
Interpolation	$\varphi[x,y] \rightarrow I[x] \rightarrow \psi[x,z]$
Optimization	max $x \mid \varphi$
Consequences	$\varphi \rightarrow \varphi_1 \wedge \ldots \wedge \varphi_n$
Sat subsets	$\psi_1 \wedge \psi_2, \psi_1 \wedge \psi_3$
Unsat cores	$\neg(\psi_1 \wedge \psi_2), \neg(\psi_1 \wedge \psi_3)$
Model counting	$|\{x \mid \varphi\}|$
All models	$Ideal(\varphi), M_1 \models \varphi, M_2 \models \varphi, \ldots$
Model probability	$\ldots$

The first type of query is the most typical query posed to SMT solvers: whether a formula φ is satisfiable and a corresponding yes/no/don't know answer. This conveys some information, but applications typically need to retrieve additional output. At the very least they may need a certificate. An assignment of values to variables for satisfiable formulas, e.g., a model is very commonly used. Dually, proofs or cores for unsatisfiability can be used for unsatisfiability formulas. Other queries include asking to find models that optimize objective values, finding formulas that are consequences, count or enumerate models.

Seminars

Fuzzing Testing in Theory and Practice

Lecturer: Dr. Yu Jiang, Tsinghua University, China

Biography: Yu Jiang received his PhD degree in computer science from Tsinghua University in 2015, worked as a postdoc at the University of Illinois at Urbana-Champaign in 2016, and is currently an assistant professor at Tsinghua University in Beijing, China. His research focuses on safety and security assurance of modern software systems such as deep learning systems and big data systems, and proposed systematic methods for the reliability analysis and testing of those systems, which has been applied in the design and mass production of train control system (MVB/WTB) of CRRC. He has published 40+ papers in international journals (TPDS, TC, TCPS, etc.) and conferences (ICSE, ASE, ICCAD, etc.). He won the China Computer Association Outstanding Doctoral Dissertation Award in 2015, and the Excellent Guide Teacher Award for a national software test competition in 2017.

Abstract: Fuzzing is a widely used software testing technique for bug and vulnerability detection, and the testing performance is greatly affected by the quality of initial seeds and the effectiveness of mutation strategy. In this presentation, we introduced some basic concepts about fuzzing and then presented SAFL, an efficient fuzzing testing tool augmented with qualified seed generation and efficient coverage-directed mutation. After conducting thoroughly repeated evaluations on real-world program benchmarks against state-of-the-art versions of fuzzing tools, we also presented the obstacles encountered in industrial practice, and how we finally solved these obstacles to detect real-world vulnerabilities. Finally, we described some potential domains where fuzzing can be applied and customized.

From Alan Turing to Formal Methods

Lecturer: Prof. Jonathan P. Bowen, Southwest University, China

Biography: Jonathan Bowen, FBCS FRSA, is Adjunct Professor in the Centre for Research and Innovation in Software Engineering (RISE) at Southwest University, Chongqing, China. He is also Chairman of Museophile Limited (founded in 2002) and Emeritus Professor of Computing at London South Bank University in the UK, where he established and headed the Centre for Applied Formal Methods from 2000. Previously, he worked at Imperial College London, the Oxford University Computing Laboratory, the University of Reading, and Birmingham City University, as well as in industry. He has been a visitor at the United Nations University (Macau) and East China Normal University (Shanghai). His interests have ranged from software engineering, formal methods, safety-critical systems, the Z notation, provably correct systems, rapid prototyping using logic programming, decompilation, hardware compilation, software/hardware co-design, linking semantics, and software testing, to the history of computing, museum informatics, and virtual communities. In 2017, he co-authored *The Turing Guide*, a book on the work of the computing pioneer Alan Turing.

Abstract: Alan Turing (1912–1954) has been increasingly recognized as an important mathematician and philosopher, who despite his short life developed ideas that have led to foundational aspects of computer science and related fields, such as the Turing machine and the Turing test. This seminar talk provided an overview of the diverse aspects related to Turing's remarkable achievements, in the context of the production of a book, *The Turing Guide*, a collected volume of 42 chapters, published by Oxford University Press in 2017. In particular, the talk considered Turing's foundational work with respect to the development of formal methods. Although the story of Turing is partly one of tragedy, with his life cut short while still at the height of his intellectual powers, just short of his 42nd birthday, from a historical viewpoint Turing's contribution to science and even culture has been triumphant.

From the courses and seminars, a record of the school has been distilled in five chapters in this volume as follows:

- David J. Pearce, Mark Utting, and Lindsay Groves: An Introduction to Software Verification with Whiley
- Yong Li, Andrea Turrini, Yu-Fang Chen, and Lijun Zhang: Learning Büchi Automata and Its Applications
- Prabhakaran Kasinathan and Jorge Cuellar: Securing Emergent IoT Applications
- Nikolaj Bjørner, Leonardo de Moura, Lev Nachmanson, and Christoph M. Wintersteiger: Programming Z3
- Jonathan P. Bowen: The Impact of Alan Turing: Formal Methods and Beyond

For further information on SETSS 2018, including lecture material, see:
http://www.swu-rise.net.cn/SETSS2018

SETSS 2018 was supported by IFIP Working Group 2.3 on Programming Methodology. The aim of WG 2.3 is to increase programmers' ability to compose programs, which fits very well with the themes of SETSS.

We would like to thank the lecturers and their co-authors for their professional commitment and effort, the reviewers for their help in improving the papers in this volume, the strong support of Southwest University, and the enthusiastic work of the local organization team, without which SETSS 2018 and these proceedings would not have been possible. Finally, we are grateful for the support of Alfred Hofmann and Anna Kramer of Springer's *Lecture Notes in Computer Science* (LNCS) in the publication of this volume.

February 2019
Jonathan P. Bowen
Zhiming Liu
Zili Zhang

Group photograph at SETSS 2018. Front row, left to right: Zhiping Shi (attendee), Bo Liu (organizer), Weiwei Chen (attendee), Zhiming Liu (organizer), Jonathan Bowen (organizer, lecturer), Yanqiang Cui (Vice President, SWU), Zili Zhang (Dean, SWU), Mark Utting (lecturer), Jorge Cuellar (lecturer), Shmuel Tyazberwicz (organizer), Guogiang Xiao (Dean, SWU), Maoling Zhang (attendee)

Organization

School Chairs

Zili Zhang   Southwest University, China
Guoquiang Xiao   Southwest University, China

Academic Instructors

Jonathan P. Bowen   RISE, Southwest University, China
     and London South Bank University, UK
Zhiming Liu   RISE, Southwest University, China

Organizing Committee

Bo Liu (Chair)   RISE, Southwest University, China
Rao Dan   RISE, Southwest University, China
Huazhen Liang   RISE, Southwest University, China
Xiao Qin   RISE, Southwest University, China
Shmuel Tyszberowicz   RISE, Southwest University, China
     and Tel Aviv University, Israel
Qing Wang   RISE, Southwest University, China
Xia Zeng   RISE, Southwest University, China
Tingting Zhang   RISE, Southwest University, China
Yukun Zhang   RISE, Southwest University, China
Hengjun Zhao   RISE, Southwest University, China

School Academic Committee

Michael Butler   University of Southampton, UK
Yixiang Chen   East China Normal University, China
Zhi Jin   Peking University, China
Zhiming Liu   RISE, Southwest University, China
Cong Tian   Xi'Dian University, China
Ji Wang   National University of Defence Science and Technology,
     China
Yi Wang   Uppsala University, Sweden
     and Northeast University, China
Jim Woodcock   University of York, UK
Jianhua Zhao   Nanjing University, China

Paper Reviewers

Troy Astarte	Newcastle University, UK
Nikolaj Bjørner	Microsoft Research, USA
Jorge Cuellar	Siemens AG, Germany
	and University of Passau, Germany
Bo Liu	RISE, Southwest University, China
Andrea Turrini	Institute of Software, China
Shmuel Tyszberowicz	RISE, Southwest University, China
	and Tel Aviv University, Israel
Mark Utting	University of the Sunshine Coast, Australia
Hengjun Zhao	RISE, Southwest University, China

Contents

An Introduction to Software Verification with Whiley

David J. Pearce[1]⊙, Mark Utting[2(✉)]⊙, and Lindsay Groves[1]

[1] Victoria University of Wellington, Wellington, New Zealand
{david.pearce,lindsay}@ecs.vuw.ac.nz
[2] University of the Sunshine Coast, Sunshine Coast, QLD, Australia
utting@usc.edu.au

Abstract. This tutorial introduces the basic ideas of software specification and verification, which are important techniques for assuring the quality of software and eliminating common kinds of errors such as buffer overflow. The tutorial takes a practical hands-on approach using the Whiley language and its verifying compiler. This verifying compiler uses an automated proof engine to try to prove that the code will execute without errors and will satisfy its specifications. Each section of the tutorial includes exercises that can be checked using the online Whiley Labs website.

1 Background

In our modern world, software is a trusted part of many aspects of our lives. Unfortunately, the impact and significance of software failures has increased dramatically over the last decade [15,40]. A study into software problems between 1980–2012 concluded *"About once per month on average, the news reports death, physical harm, or threatened access to food or shelter due partly to software problems"* [40]. One study found that more than one-third of water, gas and electricity failures were caused by software faults [53]. A modern automobile has an estimated 100M lines of computer code [14], which makes them vulnerable to software faults. In 2003, a blackout caused by software failure lasted 31 hours and affected around 50 million people in the US/Canada [58]. In 2015, a software bug was discovered in the Boeing 787 despite over a decade of development by that point and ≈300 planes in operation [35]. To mitigate the risk of catastrophic mid-flight failure, the US Federal Aviation Administration issued a directive, instructing airlines to reboot the control units on all Boeing 787s at least once every 248 days. Other similar examples include: the Therac-25 computer-operated X-ray machine, which gave lethal doses to patients [47]; the 1991 Patriot missile which hit a barracks, killing several people [32]; and the Ariane 5 rocket which exploded shortly after launch, costing the European Space Agency an estimated $500 million [1].

Software is also important for our privacy and security. *Black hats* are hackers who break into computer systems for criminal purposes, such as stealing credit

© Springer Nature Switzerland AG 2019
J. P. Bowen et al. (Eds.): SETSS 2018, LNCS 11430, pp. 1–37, 2019.
https://doi.org/10.1007/978-3-030-17601-3_1

card numbers. Many attacks on computer systems are enabled because of hidden software bugs. One such example was the infamous Heartbleed bug disclosed in 2014 [10,25]. This was a relatively simple software bug (in fact, a buffer overrun) found in the widely used OpenSSL cryptography library. There was concern across the internet for several reasons: firstly, a large number of people were affected (at the time, around half a million secure web servers were believed to be vulnerable); secondly, OpenSSL was an open source project but the bug had gone unnoticed for over two years. Joseph Steinberg of Forbes wrote, *"Some might argue that [Heartbleed] is the worst vulnerability found (at least in terms of its potential impact) since commercial traffic began to flow on the Internet"* [55].

Given the woeful state of much of the software we rely on every day, one might ask what can we as computer scientists do about it? Of course, we want to ensure that software is correct. But how? To answer this, we need to go back and rethink what software development is. When we write a program, we have in mind some idea of what this means. When we have finished our program, we might run it to see whether it appears to do the right thing. However, as anyone who has ever written a program will know: *this is not always enough!* Even if our program appears to work after a few tests, there is still a good chance it will go wrong for other inputs we have not yet tried. The question is: *how can we be sure our program is correct?*

2   Specification and Verification

In trying to determine whether our program is correct, our first goal is to state precisely what it should do. In writing our program, we may not have had a clear idea of this from the outset. Therefore, we need to determine a *specification* for our program. This is a precise description of what the program should and should not do. Only with this can we begin to consider whether or not our program actually does the right thing. If we have used a modern programming language, such as Java, C# or C++, then we are already familiar with this idea. These languages require a limited specification be given for functions in the form of *types*. That is, when writing a function in these languages we must specify the permitted type of each parameter and the return. These types put requirements on our code and ensure that certain errors are impossible. For example, when calling a function we must ensure that the argument values we give have the correct type. If we fail to do this, the compiler will complain with an error message describing the problem, which we must fix before the program will compile.

Software verification is the process of checking that a program meets its specification. In this chapter we adopt a specific approach referred to as automated software verification. This is where a tool is used to automatically check whether a function meets its specification or not. This is very similar to the way that compilers for languages like Java check that types are used correctly. The tool we choose for this is a programming language called Whiley [52], which allows us to write specifications for our functions, and provides a special compiler which will attempt to check them for us automatically.

This chapter gives an introduction to software verification using Whiley. Whiley is not the only tool we could have chosen, but it has been successfully used for several years to teach software verification to undergraduate software engineering students. Other tools such as Spark/ADA, Dafny, Spec#, ESC/-Java provide similar functionality and could also be used with varying degrees of success.

3   Introduction to Whiley

The Whiley programming language has been in active development since 2009. The language was designed specifically to help the programmer eliminate bugs from his/her software. The key feature is that Whiley allows programmers to write *specifications* for their functions, which are then checked by the compiler. For example, here is the specification for the `max()` function which returns the maximum of two integers:

```
1  function max(int x, int y) => (int z)
2  // must return either x or y
3  ensures x == z || y == z
4  // return must be as large as x and y
5  ensures x <= z && y <= z:
6      // implementation
7      if x > y:
8          return x
9      else:
10         return y
```

Here, we see our first piece of Whiley code. This declares a function called max which accepts two integers `x` and `y`, and returns an integer `z`. The body of the function simply compares the two parameters and returns the largest. The two `ensures` clauses form the function's post-condition, which is a guarantee made to any caller of this function. In this case, the max function guarantees to return one of the two parameters, and that the return will be as large as both of them. In plain English, this means it will return the maximum of the two parameter values.

3.1   Whiley Syntax

Whilst a full introduction to the Whiley language is beyond this tutorial, we provide here a few notes relevant to the remainder. A more complete description can be found elsewhere [51].

- **Indentation Syntax.** Like Python, Whiley uses indentation to identify block structure. So a colon on the end of a line indicates that a more heavily indented block of statements must follow.

- **Equality.** Like many popular programming languages, Whiley uses a double equals for equality and a single equals for assignment. But in mathematics and logic, it is usual to use a single equality sign for equality. In this paper, we shall use the Whiley double-equals notation within Whiley programs (generally typeset in rectangles) and within statements S in the middle of Hoare triples $\{P\}\ S\ \{Q\}$, but just a single-equals for equality when we are writing logic or maths.
- **Arrays.** The size of an array `aa` is written as `|aa|` in Whiley, and array indexes range from `0` upto `|aa|-1`.
- **Quantifiers**. In Whiley, quantifiers are written over finite integer ranges. For example, a universal quantifier `all {i in a..b | P}` ranges from the lower bound `a` up to (but not including) the upper bound `b`. For example, we can specify that every item in an array `aa` is positive with `all {i in 0..|aa| | aa[i] > 0}`.

When verification is enabled the Whiley compiler will check that every function meets its specification. For our `max()` function, this means it will check that the body of the function guarantees to return a value which meets the function's postcondition. To do this, it will explore the two execution paths of the function and check each one separately. If it finds a path which does not meet the postcondition, the compiler will report an error. In this case, the `max()` function above is implemented correctly and so it will find no errors. The advantage of providing specifications is that they can help uncover bugs and other, more serious, problems earlier in the development cycle. This leads to software which is both more reliable and more easily maintained (since the specifications provide important documentation).

4   Writing Specifications

Specifying a program in Whiley consists of at least two separate activities. Firstly, we provide appropriate specifications (called *invariants*) for any data types we have defined (we will discuss this further in Sect. 4.4). Secondly, we provide specifications in the form of *preconditions* and *postconditions* for any functions or methods defined—which may involve defining additional data types and properties. In doing this, we must acknowledge that precisely describing a program's behaviour is extremely challenging and, oftentimes, we want only to specify some *important aspect* of its permitted behaviour. This can give us many of the benefits from specification without all of the costs.

4.1   Specifications as Contracts

A specification is a contract between two parties: the *client* and *supplier*. The client represents the person(s) using a given function (or method or program), whilst the supplier is the person(s) who implemented it. The specification ties the *inputs* to the *outputs* in two ways:

- **Inputs.** The specification states what is *required* of the inputs for the function to behave correctly. The client is responsible for ensuring the correct inputs are given. If an incorrect input is given, the contract is broken and the function may do something unexpected.
- **Outputs.** The specification states what outputs must be *ensured* by a correctly behaving function. The supplier is responsible for ensuring all outputs meet the specification, assuming that correct inputs were provided.

From this, we can see that both parties in the contract have obligations they must meet. This also allows us to think about *blame*. That is, when something goes wrong, *who is responsible?* If the inputs to our function were incorrect according to the specification, we can blame the client. On the other hand if the inputs were correct, but the outputs were not, we can blame the supplier.

An interesting question arises about who the client and supplier are, exactly. A common scenario is where they are different people. For example, the supplier has written a library that the client is using. However, this need not be the case and, in fact, they can be the same person. For example, consider a program with one function f() that calls another g(), both of which were written by the same person. In this case, that person acts as both client and supplier: first as a client of g() (i.e. because their function f() calls g() and relies on its specification); second, they are a supplier of g() because they implemented it and are responsible for it meeting its specification. Finally, we note the special case of the top level function of a program (e.g. main())) which is called the language runtime. If this function has a precondition, then it is the responsibility of the runtime to ensure this is met. A good example of this is when an array of strings are passed to represent command-line arguments. In such case, there may be a precondition that the array is not null.

Example. As an example, let us consider a function for finding the maximum value from an array of integers. Here is an *informal* specification for this function:

```
1   // REQUIRES: At least one item in items array
2   // ENSURES: Item returned was largest item in items array
3   function max([int] items) -> (int item)
```

We have specified our function above using comments to document: firstly, the requirements needed for the inputs—that the array must have at least one element; and, secondly, the expectations about the outputs—that it returns the largest element in the array. Thus, we could not expect the call `max([])` to operate correctly; likewise, if the call `max([1,2])` returned `3` we would say the implementation was incorrect.   ∎

4.2   Specifying Functions

To specify a function or method in Whiley we must provide an appropriate *precondition* and *postcondition*. A precondition is a condition over the input parameters of a function that is required to be true when the function is called.

The body of the function can use this to make assumptions about the possible values of the parameters. Likewise, a postcondition is a condition over the return values of a function that is required to be true *after* the function body is executed.

Example. As a very simple example, consider the following specification for our function which finds the maximum value from an array of integers:

```
1  function max([int] items) => (int item)
2  // At least one item in items array
3  requires |items| > 0
4  // Item returned as large as largest in items array
5  ensures all { i in 0 .. |items| | items[i] <= item }
6  // Item returned was in items array
7  ensures exists { i in 0 .. |items| | items[i] == item }
```

Here, the `requires` clause gives the function's precondition, whilst the `ensures` clauses give its postcondition. This specification is largely the same as that given informally using comments before. However, we regard this specification as being *formal* because, for any set of inputs and outputs, we can calculate precisely whether the inputs or outputs satsify these specifications.

For example, consider the call `max([])`. We can say that the inputs to this call are incorrect, because `|[]| > 0` evaluates to `false`. For the informal version given above, we cannot easily evaluate the English comments to determine whether they were met or not. Instead, we rely on our human judgement for this—but, unfortunately, this can easily be wrong! ∎

When specifying a function in Whiley, the `requires` clause(s) may only refer to the input parameters, whilst the `ensures` clause(s) may also refer to the return parameters. Note, however, that the `ensures` clause(s) always refers to the values of the parameters on entry to the function, not those which might hold at the end.

Exercise: Absolute Value.
Give suitable precondition(s) and postcondition(s) for the following Whiley function, which returns the absolute value of `x`. To check the answer, use the online Whiley Labs system at http://whileylabs.com.

```
1  function abs(int x) -> (int r)
2  requires ???
3  ensures ???:
4      //
5      if x < 0:
6          return -x
7      else:
8          return x
```

4.3 Contractual Obligations

The main benefit of adding specification clauses (`requires` and `ensures`) to a function is that it gives us a precise contract that acts as an agreement between the client and the supplier of the function. We can now be more precise about the obligations and benefits for both parties.

- **The client**, who calls the function, must make certain that every input value satisfies the `requires` conditions (*Obligation*); and, can assume every output of the function satisfies the `ensures` conditions (*Benefit*).
- **The supplier**, who implements the function, must ensure all returned values satisfy the `ensures` conditions (*Obligation*); but, may assume that every input will satisfy the `requires` conditions (*Benefit*).

In both cases, the Whiley verifying compiler will check these obligations and display an error message such as **"postcondition may not be satisfied"** if its automatic prover cannot prove that the obligation is satisfied. This could mean either that:

- the proof obligation is false, so the code is incorrect; or
- the automatic prover is not powerful enough to prove the obligation.

In general, software correctness proofs are undecidable, especially when they involve non-trivial multiplications or other non-linear functions, so the automatic prover has a timeout (typically 10 s) after which it reports that it cannot prove the proof obligation. So when the Whiley compiler reports an error, it could mean an error in the code, or just that something is too hard to prove automatically. To help decide which is the case, one can ask the Whiley verifier to generate a *counter-example*. If it is able to generate counter-example values, then this can be inspected to see why the proof obligation is false - it could be due to an error in the code or in the specification. If the Whiley verifier cannot find any counter-example values, then it is possible that the proof obligation is too complex for the verifier to be able to prove within its timeout limit. In this case one can: increase the timeout; or, simplify the code and specifications to make the proof obligation more obvious; or, mark this proof obligation as needing further inspection and verification by humans.

Exercise: Specify Binary Minimum.
Add specifications to the following `min()` function that determines the minimum of its two arguments, by completing the `ensures` predicate.

```
1  function min(int x, int y) -> (int r)
2  ensures ???:
3      if x < y:
4          return x
5      else:
6          return y
```

Exercise: Generate Counterexample.
The following function contains a bug and fails verification. Using the counterexample feature of Whiley, identify an input which illustrates the problem.

```
1  // Read an item from the buffer, or null if it doesn't exist
2  function read(int[] buffer, int index) -> (int|null r):
3      if index < 0 || index > |buffer|:
4          return null
5      else:
6          return buffer[index]
```

4.4   Specifying Data Types

In Whiley, a *data type* is simply a set of values. Practically, the usual structured types are supported (arrays and records), as well as various primitive types such as integer and boolean. In addition, the Whiley type system allows users to specify *data invariants* as part of a type definition. For example, we could define a type called `pos` that is the strictly positive integers, or a type `percent` that can range only from $0 \ldots 100$. The following example shows how we can define a `rectangle` type that is restricted to only allow non-empty rectangles.

```
1  type pos is (int x) where x > 0
2  type Rectangle is { int x, int y, pos width, pos height }
3
4  function area(Rectangle r) -> (pos a):
5      return r.width * r.height
```

Exercise: Rectangle Containment.
Complete the implementation of the following function by writing its code body. Use multiple simple **if** statements that return true or false. To make the exercise more challenging, check one condition at a time, and do not use logical conjunction or disjunction operators.

```
1  type pos is (int x) where x > 0
2  type Rect is { int x, int y, pos width, pos height }
3
4  // Does rectangle a contain rectangle b?
5  function contains(Rect a, Rect b) -> (bool r)
6  ensures r == ( a.x <= b.x &&
7                  b.x + b.width <= a.x + a.width &&
8                  a.y <= b.y &&
9                  b.y + b.height <= a.y + a.height):
10     return true // TODO: code this using if-else statements.
```

5 Verifying Loop-Free Code

In this section we will practice verifying simple non-looping programs that contain just: *assignment statements, variable declarations, if-else conditionals, return statements,* and *assertions.* A key challenge here lies in understanding how the automated verification tool works. To help, we will introduce some theory—called *Hoare logic*—which provides a mathematical background for verification [34]. Whilst the verification tools can be used without understanding all the details of this theory, it is recommended to work through Sects. 5.1 to 5.4 to get a deeper understanding.

5.1 Motivating Example

We shall start with a brain teaser. Here is some Whiley code (adapted from an example by Back and von Wright [4, page 97–98]) that does some kind of transformation of two values. Try to work out what it does, and write a specification of its input-output behavior by completing the ensures predicate.

```
1  function f(int x, int y) -> (int r, int s)
2  ensures r == ??? && s == ???:
3      x = 2 * x + y
4      y = x - y
5      x = x - y
6      return x, y
```

This example shows that it can be quite complex to reason about a sequence of assignments. It is not always obvious what state the variables should be in between two statements. In fact, the specification of this code is remarkably simple and this will become apparently shortly. But this probably was not obvious from the rather convoluted code, which was designed to swap two variables (and double one of them) without using any temporary storage – such code was useful when embedded computers had extremely limited memory, but is rarely needed these days.

Software verification tools can sometimes immediately verify our code, even when it does have a complex sequence of assignments like this. But when there is a problem, we will sometimes need to 'debug' our program or our verification, step by step, which requires that we understand the intermediate states. So we need intermediate predicates between statements to say what should be true at that point. Whiley provides two kinds of statements which can help:

- assert e to check if e is true at that point. The verifier will attempt to prove that e is satisfied at that point and will give an error if it is not provable. Adding assertions makes the verifier work a little harder, but will never destroy the soundness of the verification.

– assume e to add an (unproven) assumption. The verifier will *not* attempt to prove e, but will simply assume that it is true at that point, and will use it to help verify subsequent proof obligations. Assumptions can be useful for performing 'what if' experiments with the verifier, or for helping the verifier to overcome difficult proofs that it cannot do automatically. However, assumptions allow one to override the usual verification process, so care must be taken not to introduce unsound verifications by adding incorrect assumptions.

By inserting assertions and assumptions at various points in our program, we can check our understanding of what should be true and, if necessary, can prove one scenario at a time. For example, we could use assume statements to focus on particular input values such as $x == 10$ and $y == 11$, and an assert statement to check that we have done the correct calculation for those values.

```
1  function f(int x, int y) -> (int r, int s):
2  assume x == 10
3  assume y == 11
4  //
5  x = 2 * x + y
6  y = x - y
7  x = x - y
8  //
9  assert x == 11 && y == 2 * 10
10 return x, y
```

But how can we find, or design, these intermediate assertions? This is where Hoare logic comes in. But, before we get to that, here is the solution for our brain teaser.

```
1  function f(int x, int y) -> (int r, int s)
2  ensures r == y && s == 2 * x:
3      x = 2 * x + y
4      y = x - y
5      x = x - y
6      return x, y
```

Now let's investigate the three ways that we can calculate intermediate assertions for complex sequences of code.

5.2 Hoare Logic

Hoare Logic [34] is a well-known system for proving the correctness of programs. Figure 1 presents Hoare Logic rules for the basic statements in Whiley. Note that $p[e/x]$ means replace all free occurrences of the variable x in p by the expression *e*. Unlike Hoare's original logic, Fig. 1 includes [assert] and [assume] statements, and loops have explicit loop invariants.

The rules are presented in terms of *correctness assertions* (also known as *Hoare triples* of the form: $\{p\}\ s\ \{q\}$, where p is a precondition, s is a Whiley statement, and q is a postcondition. A Hoare triple is true if whenever the precondition is true, then executing the statement establishes the postcondition. For example, consider the following Hoare triple:

$$\{x \geq 0\}\ x = x + 1\ \{x > 0\}$$

Here we see that, if $x \geq 0$ holds immediately before the assignment then, as expected, it follows that $x > 0$ holds afterwards. However, whilst this is intuitively true, it is not so obvious how this triple satisfies the rules of Fig. 1. For example, as presented it does not immediately satisfy H-ASSIGN. However, rewriting the triple is helpful here:

$$\{x + 1 > 0\}\ x = x + 1\ \{x > 0\}$$

The above triple clearly satisfies H-ASSIGN since $(x > 0)[x + 1/x]$ simplifies to $x + 1 > 0$, which is the same as our precondition. Furthermore, we can obtain the original triple from this triple via H-CONSEQUENCE (i.e. since $x + 1 > 0 \implies x \geq 0$).

5.3 Calculating Backwards Through Assignments

The rules of Fig. 1 naturally give rise to an approach where we calculate preconditions from postconditions. Whilst this may seem unnatural at times, it is rather convenient. We can take this further and consider the *weakest precondition* that can be calculated. This is the weakest condition p that guarantees that *if* it is the case that statement s terminates, then the final state will satisfy q. The rule H-ASSIGN for assignment statements demonstrates this most clearly. Consider the following:

$$\{???\}\ x = y + 1\ \{x > 0\}$$

To apply rule H-ASSIGN here, we simply substitute all occurrences of x in the postcondition with $y + 1$ (i.e. the expression being assigned) to give:

$$\{y + 1 > 0\}\ x = y + 1\ \{x > 0\}$$

At this point, we have a simple mechanism for calculating the weakest precondition for a straight-line sequence of statements.

$$\frac{p \implies e}{\big\{p\big\} \text{ assert } e \big\{p\big\}} \text{ (H-ASSERT)} \qquad \frac{}{\big\{p\big\} \text{ assume } e \big\{p \wedge e\big\}} \text{ (H-ASSUME)}$$

$$\frac{}{\big\{p[e/x]\big\} \ x = e \ \big\{p\big\}} \text{ (H-ASSIGN)} \qquad \frac{\big\{p\big\} \ s_1 \ \big\{r\big\} \ \big\{r\big\} \ s_2 \ \big\{q\big\}}{\big\{p\big\} \ s_1 \ s_2 \ \big\{q\big\}} \text{ (H-SEQUENCE)}$$

$$\frac{\big\{p_1\big\} \ s \ \big\{q_1\big\}}{p_2 \implies p_1 \quad q_1 \implies q_2 \quad \text{(H-CONSEQUENCE)}}{\big\{p_2\big\} \ s \ \big\{q_2\big\}} \qquad \frac{\big\{p \wedge e_1\big\} \ s_1 \ \big\{q\big\}}{\big\{p \wedge \neg e_1\big\} \ s_2 \ \big\{q\big\}}{\big\{p\big\} \ \text{if}(e_1) \ (s_1) \ \text{else} \ (s_2) \ \big\{q\big\}} \text{ (H-IF)}$$

$$\frac{\big\{e_1 \wedge e_2\big\} \ s \ \big\{e_2\big\}}{\big\{e_2\big\} \ \text{while}(e_1) \ \text{where} \ e_2 \ (s) \ \big\{\neg e_1 \wedge e_2\big\}} \text{ (H-WHILE)}$$

Fig. 1. Extended rules of Hoare Logic.

Exercise: Calculating Backwards.

Work backwards from the through the following sequence of Hoare triples calculating the weakest precondition before each assignment. Upon reaching the start, one should find the precondition simplifies to **true**.

$$\big\{???\big\} \ a = (2 * x) + y \ \big\{???\big\} \ b = a - y \ \big\{(a - b) == y \wedge b == 2 * x\big\}$$

Variable Versions. Since Whiley is an imperative language, it permits variables to be assigned different values at different points. Whilst the rules of Hoare logic accomodate this quite well, there are some limitations. In particular, we often want to compare the state of a variable *before* and *after* a given statement. The following illustrates this:

```
1  function increment(int x) -> (int y)
2  ensures y > x:
3      x = x + 1
4      return x
```

We can express the above program as a straight line sequence of Hoare triples where the return x is represented as y = x (i.e it is treated as an assignment to the return variable):

$$\big\{???\big\} \ x = x + 1 \ \big\{x > x\big\} \ y = x \ \big\{y > x\big\}$$

However, there must be a problem since the intermediate assertion $x > x$ is clearly false. *So what went wrong?* The problem lies in our formulation of the postcondition in the final assertion. Specifically, in the final assertion, x refers to the value of variable x *at that point*. However, in the ⌐ensures⌐ clause, ⌐x⌐ refers to the value of ⌐x⌐ *on entry*.

In order to refer to the value of a variable on entry, we can use a special *version* of it. In this case, let x_0 refer to the value of variable x on entry to the function. Then, we can update our Hoare triples as follows:

$$\{x + 1 > x_0\} \; x = x + 1 \; \{x > x_0\} \; y = x \; \{y > x_0\}$$

By assuming that $x = x_0$ on entry to the function, we can see the weakest precondition calculated we've calculated above is satisfied.

5.4 Calculating Forwards Through Assignments

An alternative approach is to propagate predicates *forward* through the program. For a given precondition, and a statement s, we want to find the strongest postcondition that will be true after s terminates. This turns out to be a little more challenging than calculating weakest preconditions. Consider this program:

$$\{0 \le x \le y\} \; x = 1 \; \{???\}$$

From the precondition to this statement, one can infer that y is non-negative. But, how to update this and produce a sensible postcondition which retains this information? The problem is that, by assigning to x, we are losing information about its original value and relationship with y. For example, substituting x for 1 as we did before gives $0 \le 1 \le y$ which is certainly incorrect, as this now implies y cannot be zero (which was permitted before). The solution is to employ Floyd's rule for assignments [30]:

$$\{p\} \; x = e \; \{\exists v.(p[v/x]) \wedge x = e[v/x]\}$$

This introduces a new variable v to represent the value of x before the assignment and, hence, provide a mechanism for retaining all facts known beforehand. For above example, this looks like:

$$\{0 \le x \le y\} \; x = 1 \; \{\exists v.(0 \le v \le y) \wedge x = 1\}$$

With this postcondition, we retain the ability to infer that y is non-negative. Unfortunately, the postcondition seems more complex. To simplify this, we can employ the idea of variable versioning from before:

$$\{0 \le x \le y\} \; x = 1 \; \{0 \le x_0 \le y \wedge x = 1\}$$

Here, x_0 represents the value of x before the assignment. We are simply giving a name (x_0) to the value that Floyd's Rule claims to exist. Technically this is called 'skolemization'. Observe that, with multiple assignments to the same variable, we simply increment the subscript of that variable each time it appears on the left-hand side of an assignment statement. The following illustrates this:

$$\left\{0 \leq x\right\} x = x+1 \left\{0 \leq x_0 \wedge x = x_0+1\right\} x = 0 \left\{0 \leq x_0 \wedge x_1 = x_0+1 \wedge x = 0\right\}$$

Exercise: Calculating Forwards.
Work forwards through the following Hoare triples for a sequence of assignment statements, calculating the strongest postcondition after each assignment.

$$\left\{\texttt{true}\right\} x = (2 * x) + y \left\{???\right\} y = x - y \left\{???\right\} x = x - y \left\{???\right\}$$

Doing this, it should be possible to establish the postcondition for the function $\boxed{\texttt{f()}}$ above.

This approach of strongest postconditions with variable versions is essentially how the Whiley verifier analyzes each path through the Whiley code. In fact, when looking at a counter-example from the verifier for a proof that fails (for whatever reason), one will sometimes see numbered versions of some variables, referring to their intermediate values. One reason for using this strongest postcondition approach in preference to the weakest precondition approach is that the strongest postcondition approach typically generates multiple smaller proof obligations rather than one large proof obligation, which helps to make error messages more precise and helpful.

5.5   Reasoning About Control-Flow

Reasoning about conditional code, such as if-else statements, is similar to reasoning about a single sequence of code, except that we now have two or more possible execution sequences. So we must reason about each possible sequence. To do this, we use the following three principles:

- Within the **true branch** the condition is known to **hold**;
- Within the **false branch** the condition is known to **not hold**;
- Knowledge from **each branch** can be combined afterwards using **disjunction**.

The following illustrates what assertions are true at each point in the code. Note how the assertion after the whole if-else block is simply the disjunction of both branches, and from this disjunction we are able to prove the desired postcondition $z \geq 0$.

```
1    assume y >= 0
2    //
3    if x >= 0:
4        // {x ≥ 0 ∧ y ≥ 0}
5        z = x + y
6        // {x ≥ 0 ∧ y ≥ 0 ∧ z == x + y}
7    else:
8        // {x < 0 ∧ y ≥ 0}
9        z = y - x
10       // {x < 0 ∧ y ≥ 0 ∧ z == y − x}
11   //
12   // {(x ≥ 0 ∧ y ≥ 0 ∧ z == x + y) ∨ (x < 0 ∧ y ≥ 0 ∧ z == y − x)}
13   assert z >= 0
```

A **return** statement terminates a function and returns to the calling function. Since execution does not continue in the function after the return, our reasoning about sequences of code also stops at each return statement. At that point, we must prove that the postcondition of the whole function is satisfied. The following example illustrates this:

```
1    function abs(int x) -> (int r)
2    ensures r >= 0:
3        //
4        if x >= 0:
5            // {x ≥ 0}
6            return x
7        //
8        // {x < 0}
9        return -x
```

Exercise: Return Statement.
Answer the following questions about this Whiley program. (After having written the answers, sample solutions are available in Appendix A.)

```
1    function inc(int x) -> (int r)
2    ensures x < r:
3        x = x + 1
4        return x
```

– **Q)** What knowledge do we have at the **point of return**?

– **Q)** Is this enough to **establish the postcondition**?

5.6   Reasoning About Expressions

Our next example (see Fig. 2) illustrates a more complex function example that uses conditionals and recursion to sum an array of integers. Note that variable declarations in Whiley are typed like in Java and C, so int x = ... declares and initializes the variable x.

One issue that arises in this example is that whenever the code indexes into an array, we need to check that the index is a valid one. Checks like this ensure that buffer overflows can never occur, thereby eliminating a major cause of security vulnerabilities. To ensure that the array access in line 14 is valid, we must prove that at that point the index $\boxed{\texttt{i}}$ is within bounds. This introduces the following proof obligation—or *verification condition*—for our program (we use a bold **implies** to clearly separate the assumptions of the proof obligation from the conclusions):

$$0 \leq \texttt{i} \leq |\texttt{items}| \wedge \texttt{i} \neq |\texttt{items}| \quad \textbf{implies} \quad 0 \leq \texttt{i} < |\texttt{items}|$$

The Whiley verifier can easily prove this verification condition holds true and, hence, that the array access is within bounds.

More generally, many inbuilt functions have preconditions that we need to check. For example, the division operator a/b is only valid when $b \neq 0$. And user-defined functions have preconditions, which must be satisfied when they are invoked, so the verifier must generate verification conditions to check their arguments. Here is a list of the verification conditions that Whiley generates and checks to verify code:

1. Before every **function call**, the function's precondition is true;
2. Before every **array access**, arr[i], the index i is within bounds;
3. Before every **array generator**, [v; n], the size n is non-negative;

```
1    function sum(int[] items, int i) -> (int r)
2    // All elements of items are natural
3    requires all { k in 0..|items| | items[k] >= 0 }
4    // Index is at most one past bounds of array
5    requires 0 <= i && i <= |items|
6    // Result is natural
7    ensures r >= 0:
8        // {0 ≤ i ≤ |items| ∧ ∀k.(0 ≤ k < |items| ⟹ items[k] ≥ 0)}
9        if i == |items|:
10           // {i == |items| ∧ ...}
11           return 0
12       else:
13           // {0 ≤ i < |items| ∧ i ≠ |items| ∧ ∀k.(0 <= k < |items| ⟹ items[k] ≥ 0)}
14           int x = items[i]
15           // {x ≥ 0 ∧ 0 ≤ i < |items| ∧ i ≠ |items| ∧ ∀k.(...)}
16           int y = sum(items,i+1)
17           // {y ≥ 0 ∧ x ≥ 0 ∧ 0 ≤ i < |items| ∧ i ≠ |items| ∧ ∀k.(...)}
18           return x + y
```

Fig. 2. A recursive function for summing an array of integers

4. Before every integer **division** a/b, it is true that b $\neq$ 0;
5. Every **assert** statement is true;
6. in assignment statements, each right-hand-side result satisfies the type constraints of the corresponding left-hand-side variable;
7. At each **return**, the **ensures** conditions are true.

These conditions apply to the recursive invocation of sum(...) on Line 16 as well. We must prove that the precondition of sum(...) is satisfied just before it is called. In this case this means proving:

– $0 \leq i \leq |\text{items}| \land i \neq |\text{items}|$ **implies** $0 < i+1 \leq |\text{items}|$
– $\forall k. \big(0 \leq k < |\text{items}| \implies \text{items}[k] >= 0\big)$ **implies**
  $\forall k. \big(0 \leq k < |\text{items}| \implies \text{items}[k] >= 0\big)$.

Note that if we wanted to prove termination, to ensure that this function does not go into infinite recursion, we would also need to define a decreasing *variant* expression and prove that each recursive call strictly decreases the value of that expression towards zero. However, the current version of Whiley only proves partial correctness, so does not generate proof obligations to ensure termination. This may be added in the future.

5.7 Reasoning About Function Calls

Correctly reasoning about code which calls another function can be subtle. In our recursive sum example we glossed over this by simply applying the postcondition for sum(int[],int) directly. Sometimes we need to reason more carefully. It is important to understand that the verifier never considers the body of functions being called, only their specification. This makes the verification *modular*. Consider the following simple function:

```
1  function id(int x) -> (int r):
2  return x
```

This is the well-known *identity* function which simply returns its argument untouched. However, even with this simple function, it is easy to get confused when reasoning. For example, we might expect the following to verify:

```
1  assert id(0) == 0
```

Whilst it is easy to see this must be true, the verifier rejects this because the specification for id() does not relate the argument to its return value. Remember, the verifier is ignoring the *body* of function id() here. This is because the details of *how* the specification for id() is met should not be important (and the implementation can change provided the specification is still met). However, the verifier will accept:

```
1  assert id(0) == id(0)
```

This may seem confusing since it appears that the verifier is considering the body of function id(). However, in fact, it is only reasoning about the property of *pure functions*—namely, that given the same input, they produce the same output.

Exercise: Specification versus Implementation.
Consider these two functions:

```
1    function increment(int x) -> (int y)
2    ensures y > x:
3        return x+1
4
5    function test(int x):
6        int z = increment(x)
7        assert z == x + 1
```

Check that this program fails to verify and use the counterexample feature to find values which illustrate the problem. Answer the following questions:

– **Q)** Do these values satisfy the *specification* of increment()?
– **Q)** Do these values satisfy the *implementation* of increment()?

Finally, weaken the assert statement so that it establishes the strongest property regarding the relationship between variable x and z.

6   Verifying Loops

Verifying looping code is more complex than verifying non-looping code, since execution may pass through a given point in the loop many times, so the assertions at that point must be true on every iteration. Furthermore, we do not always know beforehand how many times the loop will iterate – it could be zero, one, or many times.

To make loops more manageable, the usual technique is to introduce a *loop invariant* predicate. For example, in the following simple program, one property that is clearly always true as we execute the loop is `i >= 0`.[1] Another loop invariant is `prod == i * n`, since `n` is added to `prod` each time that `i` is incremented. Yet another loop invariant is `i <= n`. However, `i < n` is not a loop invariant since the last iteration of the loop will increment `i` to be equal to `n`.

```
1    function sq(int n) -> (int r)
2    requires n > 0
3    ensures r == n * n:
4        int i = 0
5        int prod = 0
```

---
[1] This holds because integers are unbounded in Whiley.

```
 6       //
 7       while i < n:
 8           i = i + 1
 9           prod = prod + n
10       //
11       return prod
```

If we use all three of these loop invariants to analyze this program, and note that when the loop exits the guard must be `false`, which means that `i >= n`, then we have both `i >= n` and `i <= n`. This implies that `i == n`. Combining this with the third loop invariant `prod == i * n`, we can prove the postcondition of the whole function: `r == n * n`.

Let us define this concept of loop invariant more precisely, so that we can understand how tools like the Whiley verifying compiler use loop invariants to prove loops correct.

6.1   Loop Invariants

A loop invariant is a predicate which holds before and after each iteration of the loop. The three rules about loop invariants are:

1. Loop invariants must hold before the loop.
2. Loop invariants must be restored. That is, within the loop body, the loop invariant may temporarily not hold, but it must be re-established at the end of the loop body.
3. The loop invariant and the negated guard are the *only* properties that are known to be true after the loop exits, so they must be sufficiently strong to allow us to verify the code that follows the loop.

The following diagram illustrates these three rules graphically, for a loop occurring within a function body.

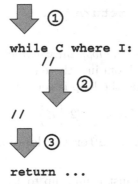

```
function f() requires R ensures E:
```
①
```
while C where I:
    //
```
②
```
    //
```
③
```
    return ...
```

We can explain the three loop invariant loops more precisely, using the notation of Hoare triples.

1. **Loop Invariants must hold before the loop.**

    function f() requires R ensures E:

    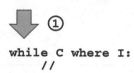

    while C where I:
    //

    Informally: Information known at the start of loop **must imply** the loop invariant. Formally, we can express this as:

    $$\{R\}\, S1\, \{P\} \quad \text{implies} \quad (P \implies I)$$

    where $S1$ represents all statements **before the loop**.

2. **Loop Invariants must be maintained.**

    while C where I:
    //

    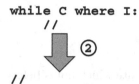

    //

    Informally: Assuming only the loop invariant I and the loop condition C hold at the start of the loop body, the information known at the end of the loop body **must imply** the loop invariant I. Formally:

    $$\{I \wedge C\}\, S\, \{P\} \quad \text{implies} \quad (P \implies I)$$

    where S represents the **loop body**.

3. **Loop Invariants hold after the loop.**

    //

    return ...

    Informally: We can assume that the *loop invariant* and the *negated condition* hold after the loop terminates. From just those two assumptions, we must be able to prove that the code after the loop is correct. Formally:

    $$\{I \wedge \neg C\}\, S2\, \{E\}$$

    where $S2$ represents all statements **after the loop**; and E is the **postcondition**.

    The following function, which just counts up to 10, illustrates a very simple loop invariant that captures some information about the range of the loop variable i.

```
1   function g(int i) => (int r)
2   //
3   requires i >= 0
4   ensures r >= 10:
5
6       // {i ≥ 0}
7       while(i < 10) where i >= 0:
8           // {i < 10 ∧ i ≥ 0}
9           i = i + 1
10          // {i ≥ 0}
11
12      // {i ≥ 10 ∧ i ≥ 0}
13      return i
14  }
```

To help relate the Whiley code to the Hoare triples that we are discussing, we show various intermediate assertions that would appear in the Hoare triples for this program. Such intermediate assertions are not normally written in a Whiley program (because the Whiley verifier calculates them automatically), so we show them here as Whiley comments. This provides an outline of a Hoare-style verification that this function meets its specification. Note that this does not prove the function terminates (although we can see that it does) and, in general, this is not our concern here.

Here is another example of a simple loop that sums two arrays pair-wise into an output array. What would be a suitable loop invariant for the loop in this function?

```
1   function sum(int[] v1, int[] v2) -> (int[] v3)
2   // Input vectors must have same size
3   requires |v1| == |v2|
4   // Result has same size as input
5   ensures |v1| == |v3|
6   // Each element of result is sum of corresponding elements in inputs
7   ensures all { i in 0..|v1| | v3[i] == v1[i] + v2[i] }:
8       //
9       int i = 0
10      int[] old_v1 = v1
11      //
12      while i < |v1|
13      where ??? TODO: relate v1 to old_v1 and v2 somehow ???:
14          v1[i] = v1[i] + v2[i]
15          i = i + 1
16      //
17      return v1
```

6.2   Ghost Variables and Loop Invariants

A **ghost variable** is any variable introduced specifically to aid verification in some way, but is unnecessary to execute the program. In the vector sum example above, variable $\boxed{\texttt{old\_v1}}$ is a **ghost variable**, because we can **implement** the solution without it, but we cannot **verify** the solution without it! Here is the loop invariant for the vector sum example, showing how we need to use $\boxed{\texttt{old\_v1}}$ in the loop invariant to refer to the original contents of the $\boxed{\texttt{v1}}$ vector:

```
1    //
2    while i < |v1|
3    where 0 <= i && i <= |v1|
4    where |v1| == |old_v1|
5    where all { j in 0..i | v1[j] == old_v1[j] + v2[j] }
6    where all { j in i..|v1| | v1[j] == old_v1[j] }:
7        v1[i] = v1[i] + v2[i]
8        i = i + 1
9    //
```

Recall that Rule 3 for loops says that the *only* thing known after a loop is the loop invariant and the negated loop guard. In theory, this means that our loop invariant should include *all known facts about all the variables* in the function. So perhaps we should add predicates like $\boxed{\texttt{|v2| == |old\_v1|}}$ into the loop invariant above, even though neither of these variables are changing within the loop? This would become very verbose and tedious - it is a very common case that some variables are not changed at all within a loop.

Fortunately, Whiley uses an extended form of Rule 3 for variables **not modified** in a loop: all information about them from before loop is **automatically retained**. This generally includes all ghost variables (since they typically just capture the previous values of some variable), but also variables like $\boxed{\texttt{v2}}$ in the vector sum example above, because there is no assignment to it in the loop. So for a predicate that does not mention any variables changed by the loop, it is not necessary to include that predicate in the loop invariant, as it will automatically be preserved across the loop.

6.3   Example: Reversing an Array (Implementation)

Now that we have all the necessary tools, such as loop invariants and ghost variables, let us consider what loop invariant is needed to verify the following program, which reverses the contents of an array in-place.

```
1    // In-place reverse of items in an array
2    function reverse(int[] xs) -> (int[] ys)
3
4    ensures |xs| == |ys|
5    // All items in return array in reversed order
6    ensures all { i in 0..|xs| | xs[i] == ys[|xs|-(i+1)]}:
7        int i = 0
8        int j = |xs| - 1
9        while i < j
10       where ???:
```

```
11        int tmp = xs[i]
12        xs[i] = xs[j]
13        xs[j] = tmp
14        j = j - 1
15        i = i + 1
16     return xs
```

To help visualize the required invariant, imagine that we are half way through reversing the array. The region between i and j remains to be reversed.

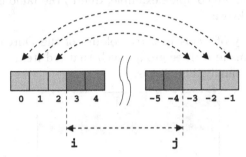

Exercise: Reversing Array Invariant.
Find a suitable loop invariant to verify this **reverse** function, using as few of the following hints as possible:

1. start with a loop invariant that is a weakened version of the postcondition;
2. weaken it so it applies to just the part of the array that has been reversed;
3. add lower and upper bounds for i and j, since they are changing;
4. remember to say that the *unprocessed* region of the array is unchanged—that is, is still equal to the original array;
5. introduce a ghost variable for the initial value of the xs array;
6. remember to say that the *length* of xs is the same as its original length.

Exercise: Find the index.
Verify the following indexOf() function, by finding a suitable loop invariant.

```
1  function indexOf(int[] items, int item) -> (int r)
2  ensures r >= 0 ==> items[r] == item
3  ensures r >= 0 ==> all { i in 0 .. r | items[i] != item }
4  ensures r < 0 ==> all { i in 0 .. |items| |
5                          items[i] != item }:
6      //
7      int i = 0
8      while i < |items|:
9          if items[i] == item:
```

```
10          return i
11       i = i + 1
12    //
13    return -1
```

6.4 Example: Dutch National Flag

We now consider a more complex example, due to the famous Dutch computer scientist Edsger Dijkstra:

> "Given a quantity of items in three colours of the Dutch National flag, partition the items into three groups such that red items come first, then white items and, finally, blue items."

This can be thought of as a special case of sorting, and is very similar to the "split/partition" part of quicksort. Unlike the real Dutch flag, we don't know how many of each colour there are, so we can't use that to predetermine where the three regions should be. Also, we are required to do this in-place, without using additional arrays.

Rather than give the algorithm and then show how to verify it, we will use this problem to illustrate the approach to programming advocated by Dijkstra, in which programs are constructed from their specifications in a way that guarantees their correctness. In particular, loops are designed by first choosing a loop invariant, by weakening the postcondition of the loop, and then designing the loop body so as to maintain the loop invariant while making progress towards termination. This *refinement* approach to developing programs [48] develops the code step-by-step guided by the specifications, so it typically leads to code that is easier to verify than code just written directly by a programmer without considering the specifications. As functions become larger and more complex, we recommend that a refinement approach should be used, which is why we demonstrate this approach in this final example of this chapter.

In this case, our postcondition is that the array be a permutation of the original, and that it be arranged into three regions containing red, white and blue elements, respectively. Let us introduce two markers, `lo` and `hi` to mark the ends of these regions—more specifically, to mark the first and elements of the white region. Thus, the final state looks like this (we will explain `mid` shortly):

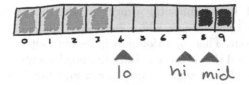

We can describe this more formally using Whiley syntax:

```
1    0 <= lo && lo <= hi && hi <= |cols|
2    all { i in 0..lo | cols[i] == RED }
3    all { i in lo..hi+1 | cols[i] == WHITE }
4    all { i in hi+1..|cols| | cols[i] == BLUE }
```

The first line specifies the ranges of `lo` and `hi`. The remaining lines say that each of the three regions contains only values of the appropriate colour. We will omit the permutation condition, since it is easy to verify, and focus on these conditions. The precondition is that the array initially contains only three distinct values:

```
1    all { i in 0..|cols| |
2        cols[i] == RED || cols[i] == WHITE || cols[i] == BLUE }
```

Our algorithm needs to build these three regions incrementally as it inspects each element of the array. So at an arbitrary point in the process, we will have three regions containing the red, white and blue elements we've already seen. We will also have a fourth region containing the elements we haven't inspected yet.

The algorithm will consist of a loop in which elements are successively taken from the "unseen" region and added to one of the other regions according to its colour. We could keep the "unseen" region to the left of the red region, between the red and white or white and blue regions, or to the right of the blue regions. We will make an arbitrary choice, and keep it between the white and blue regions, and introduce another marker, `mid`, to mark the start of the "unseen" region, which means that `cols[mid]` is the next element to be put into the correct region.

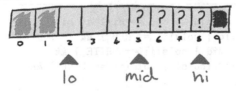

Again, we can describe this situation formally using Whiley notation:

```
1    0 <= lo && lo <= mid && mid <= hi+1 && hi < |cols|
2    all { i in 0..lo | cols[i] == RED }
3    all { i in lo..mid | cols[i] == WHITE }
4    all { i in hi+1..|cols| | cols[i] == BLUE }
```

Again, the first line defines the ranges of the marker variables, and the remaining lines say that the red, white and blue regions only contain values of the appropriate colour. This condition now gives our loop invariant. We can now design the loop around this invariant. Initially, no elements have been inspected, so the red, white and blue regions are empty, and the "unseen" region is the whole array.

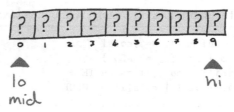

So, our initialisation must establish the condition:

```
1    lo == 0 && mid == 0 && hi == |cols|-1
```

This is the precondition for the loop, and we can easily verify that it implies the loop invariant.

```
1    lo == 0 && mid == 0 && hi == |cols|-1
2  implies
3    0 <= lo && lo <= mid && mid <= hi+1 && hi < |cols| &&
4    all { i in 0..lo | cols[i] == RED } &&
5    all { i in lo..mid | cols[i] == WHITE } &&
6    all { i in hi+1..|cols| | cols[i] == BLUE }
```

The algorithm will terminate when the "unseen" region is empty, i.e. when mid is greater that hi (as shown in the first diagram), so the loop guard is $mid \leq hi$.

We can easily check that the postcondition will hold when the loop invariant is true and the loop guard is false:

```
1     0 <= lo && lo <= mid && mid <= hi+1 && hi < |cols| &&
2     all { i in 0..lo | cols[i] == RED } &&
3     all { i in lo..mid | cols[i] == WHITE } &&
4     all { i in hi+1..|cols| | cols[i] == BLUE } &&
5     !(mid <= hi)
6  implies
7     0 <= lo && lo <= hi && hi <= |cols| &&
8     all { i in 0..lo | cols[i] == RED } &&
9     all { i in lo..hi+1 | cols[i] == WHITE } &&
10    all { i in hi+1..|cols| | cols[i] == BLUE }
```

Notice that we have already proved two of the correctness conditions for the loop, and we haven't even written the loop body yet! Now let us consider the loop body. The loop body has to reduce the size of the "unseen" region—this guarantees that we make progress towards termination. We will take the easy approach of reducing by one. Thus, we need to reduce `hi-lo`, which may happen either by increasing `lo` or by decreasing `hi`.

The key part of the algorithm is now to determine how we can take the next element from the "unseen" part of the array and add it to one of the other three regions, according to its colour. We want to write something like:

```
1  if mid[i] == RED:
2    add cols[i] to red region
3  else if cols[i] == BLUE:
4    add cols[i] to blue region
5  else:
6    add cols[i] to white region
```

Adding `cols[i]` to the white region is simple: is it already in the next available place for white, so we just need to increment `mid`. Adding `cols[i]` to the blue region is also quite easy. We need to put it just to the left of the existing blue region, in the last location of the "unseen" region. But what do we do with the element that is there? We need to swap with the element at `cols[i]`, since that location is about to be "vacated". So in this case we make progress by decreasing `hi`.

The last case is to add `cols[i]` to the red region. This is a bit harder, because (in general), the space to the right of `lo` is already part of the white region. But if we swap `cols[i]` with that element, this will add `cols[i]` to the red region, and effectively move the white region one place to the right, so we can increment both `lo` and `mid`.

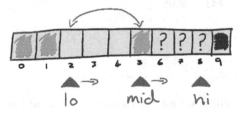

And we are done, the final algorithm is given in Fig. 3. Note: on the Whiley Labs website there is a time limit of 10 s for the whole verification. This program may take a little longer than that to verify, so you might need to verify this program on your own computer with a longer timeout.

```
1  function partition(Color[] cols) -> (Color[] ncols)
2  // Must have at least one colour in the input array
3  requires |cols| > 0
4  // Output array same size and input array
5  ensures |ncols| == |cols|
6  // Resulting array is sorted
7  ensures all { k in 1..|ncols| | ncols[k-1] <= ncols[k] }:
8      nat lo = 0
9      nat mid = 0
10     int hi = |cols|
11     // copy output to input
12     ncols = cols
13     //
14     while mid < hi
15     // size of cols does not change
16     where |cols| == |ncols|
17     // invariants between markers
18     where lo <= mid && hi <= |cols|
19     // All elements up to lo are RED
20     where all { i in 0 .. lo | ncols[i] == RED }
21     // All elements between lo and mid are WHITE
22     where all { i in lo .. mid | ncols[i] == WHITE }
23     // All elements from hi upwards are BLUE
24     where all { i in hi .. |ncols| | ncols[i] == BLUE }:
25         //
26         if ncols[mid] == RED:
27             ncols[mid] = ncols[lo]
28             ncols[lo] = RED
29             lo = lo + 1
30             mid = mid + 1
31         else if ncols[mid] == BLUE:
32             hi = hi - 1
33             ncols[mid] = ncols[hi]
34             ncols[hi] = BLUE
35         else:
36             mid = mid + 1
37     //
38     return ncols
```

Fig. 3. Algorithm for solving the Dutch National Flag problem

Exercise: Palindrome.

The following program returns true if the given array of characters contains a *palindrome*. That is, a word that has the same sequence of characters reading from left to right as it does reading from right to left. So the word reversed is the same as the original word.

Verify this program by writing a suitable loop invariant.

```
1  function isPalindrome(int[] chars) -> (bool r)
2  ensures r <==> all { k in 0..|chars| |
3                  chars[k] == chars[|chars|-(k+1)] }:
4      int i = 0
5      int j = |chars|
6      while i < j:
7          j = j - 1
8          if chars[i] != chars[j]:
9              return false
10         i = i + 1
11     return true
```

7   Related Work

We discuss several related tools which provide similar functionality and operation to Whiley. In addition, we examine some of the techniques that underpin these tools.

7.1   Tools

ESC/Java & JML. The Extended Static Checker for Java (ESC/Java) is one of the most influential tools in the area of verifying compilers [28]. The ECS/Java tool was based on earlier work that developed the ESC/Modula-3 tool [23]. The tool provides a verifying compiler for Java programs whose specifications are given as annotations in a subset of JML [12,41]. The following illustrates a simple method in JML which ESC/Java verifies as correct:

```
1  /*@ requires n >= 0;
2   @ ensures \result >= 0;
3   @*/
4  public static int method(int n) {
5      int i = 0;
6      /*@ maintaining i >= \old(i); */
7      while(i < n) { i = i + 1; }
8      return i;
9  }
```

Here, we can see preconditions and postconditions are given for the method, along with an appropriate loop invariant. Recalling our discussion from Sect. 6.2, \old(i) refers to i on entry to the loop and, hence, we have \old(i)==0 holds in this case.

The ESC/Java tool makes some unsound assumptions when verifying programs. In particular, arithmetic overflow is ignored and loops are treated unsoundly by simply unrolling them for a fixed number of iterations. The tool also provides limited support for reasoning about dynamic memory through the use of ownership annotations and `assignable` clauses for expressing frame conditions. ESC/Java has been demonstrated in some real-world settings. For example, Cataño and Huisman used it to check specifications given for an independently developed implementation of an electronic purse [11]. Unfortunately the development of JML and its associated tooling has stagnated over the last decade, although has more recently picked up again through the OpenJML initiative [17,18,54].

Spec#. This system followed ESC/Java and benefited from many of the insights gained in that project. Spec# added proper support for handling loop invariants [6], for handling safe object initialisation [26] and allowing temporary violations of object invariants through the `expose` keyword [45]. The latter is necessary to address the so-called *packing problem* which was essentially ignored by ESC/Java [7]. Another departure from ESC/Java was the use of the BOOGIE intermediate language for verification (as opposed to guarded commands) [5], and the Z3 automated theorem prover (as opposed to Simplify) [49]. Both of these mean that Spec# is capable of verifying a wider range of programs than ESC/Java.

Although the Spec# project has now finished, the authors did provide some invaluable reflections on their experiences with the project [6]. Amongst many other things, they commented that:

> "Of the unsound features in ESC/Java, many were known to have solutions. But two open areas were how to verify object invariants in the presence of subclassing and dynamically dispatched methods (...) as well as method framing."

A particular concern was the issue of method re-entrancy, which is particularly challenging to model correctly. Another interesting insight given was that:

> "If we were to do the Spec# research project again, it is not clear that extending an existing language would be the best strategy."

The primary reason for this was the presence of constructs that are difficult for a verifier to reason about, and also the challenge for a small research group in maintaining compatibility with a large and evolving language.

Finally, the Spec# project lives on in various guises. For example, VCC verifies concurrent C code and was developed by reusing much of the tool chain from Spec# [16]. VCC has been successfully used to verify Microsoft's Hyper-V hypervisor. Likewise, Microsoft recently introduced a *Code Contracts* library in .NET 4.0 which was inspired by the Spec# project (though mostly focuses on runtime checking).

Dafny. This is perhaps the most comparable related work to Whiley, and was developed independently at roughly the same time [43,44]. That said, the goals of the Dafny project are somewhat different. In particular, the primary goal of Dafny to provide a proof-assistant for verifying algorithms rather than, for example, generating efficient executable code. In contrast, Whiley aims to generate code suitable for embedded systems [50,56,57]. Dafny is an imperative language with simple support for objects and classes without inheritance. Like Whiley, Dafny employs unbound arithmetic and distinguishes between pure and impure functions. Dafny provides algebraic data types (which are similar to Whiley's recursive data types) and supports immutable collection types with value semantics that are primarily used for ghost fields to enable specification of pointer-based programs. Dynamic memory allocation is possible in Dafny, but no explicit deallocation mechanism is given and presumably any implementation would require a garbage collector.

Unlike Whiley, Dafny also supports generic types and dynamic frames [38]. The latter provides a suitable mechanism for reasoning about pointer-based programs. For example, Dafny has been used successfully to verify the Schorr-Waite algorithm for marking reachable nodes in an object graph [44]. Finally, Dafny has been used to successfully verify benchmarks from the VSTTE'08 [46], VSCOMP'10 [39], VerifyThis'12 [36] challenges (and more).

7.2 Techniques

Hoare provided the foundation for formalising work in this area with his seminal paper introducing Hoare Logic [34]. This provides a framework for proving that a sequence of statements meets its postcondition given its precondition. Unfortunately Hoare logic does not tell us how to *construct* such a proof; rather, it gives a mechanism for *checking* a proof is correct. Therefore, to actually verify a program is correct, we need to construct proofs which satisfy the rules of Hoare logic.

The most common way to automate the process of verifying a program is with a verification condition generator. As discussed in Sect. 5.4, such algorithms propagate information in either a forwards or backwards direction. However, the rules of Hoare logic lend themselves more naturally to the latter [31]. Perhaps for this reason, many tools choose to use the weakest precondition transformer. For example, ESC/Java computes weakest preconditions [28], as does the Why platform [27], Spec# [8], LOOP [37], JACK [9] and SnuggleBug [13]. This is surprising given that it leads to fewer verification conditions and, hence, makes it harder to generate useful error messages (recall our discussion from Sect. 5.4). To workaround this, Burdy *et al.* embed path information in verification conditions to improve error reporting [9]. A similar approach is taken in ESC/Java, but requires support from the underlying automated theorem prover [22]. Denney and Fischer extend Hoare logic to formalise the embedding of information within verification conditions [21]. Again, their objective is to provide useful error messages.

A common technique for generating verification conditions is to transform the input program into *passive form* [8,23,28,33]. Here, the control-flow graph of each function is converted using standard techniques into a reducible (albeit potentially larger) graph. This is then further reduced by eliminating loops to leave an acyclic graph, before a final transformation into *Static Single Assignment form (SSA)* [19,20]. The main advantage is that, after this transformation, generating verification conditions becomes straightforward. Furthermore, the technique works well for unstructured control flow and can be tweaked to produced compact verification conditions [2,3,29,42].

Dijkstra's *Guarded Command Language* provides an alternative approach to the generation of verification conditions [24]. In this case, the language is far removed from the simple imperative language of Hoare logic and, for example, contains only the sequence and non-deterministic choice constructs for handling control-flow. There is rich history of using guarded commands as an intermediate language for verification, which began with the ECS/Modula-3 tool [23]. This was continued in ESC/Java and, during the later development of Spec#, a richer version (called Boogie) was developed [5]. Such tools use guarded commands as a way to represent programs that are in passive form (discussed above) in a human-readable manner. As these programs are acyclic, the looping constructs of Dykstra's original language are typically ignored.

Finally, it is worth noting that Frade and Pinto provide an excellent survey of verification condition generation for simple WHILE programs [31]. They primarily focus on Hoare Logic and various extensions, but also explore Dijkstra's Guarded Command Language. They consider an extended version of Hoare's While Language which includes user-provided loop invariants. They also present an algorithm for generating verification conditions based on the weakest precondition transformer.

8   Conclusions

In this chapter we have introduced the basic ideas of verifying simple imperative code. With just the executable code, a verifying compiler does not know what the program is intended to do, so all it can verify is that the code will execute without errors such as: array indexes out of bounds, division by zero.

But if we add some *specification* information, such as preconditions to express the input assumptions and postconditions to express the desired results, then the verifying compiler can check much richer properties. If the postconditions are strong enough to express the complete desired behavior of the function, then the verifying compiler can even check full functional correctness.

In practice, the reasoning abilities of verifying compilers are gradually improving with time, and at the current point in time it is usually necessary to annotate our programs with extra information to aid verification, such as loop invariants and data invariants. One can argue that it is good engineering practice to document these properties for other human readers anyway, even if the verifying compiler did not need them. But in the future, we envisage that verification tools will become smarter about inferring obvious invariants, which will gradually reduce the burden on human verifiers.

Acknowledgements. Thanks to all the students and researchers who have contributed to the development of Whiley. The slides used to present this tutorial at SETSS were based on David Pearce's slides for the SWEN224 (Software Correctness) course at Victoria University of Wellington, 2015-2016. Thanks to the students of those classes for their feedback and comments. Thanks to Professor Zhiming LIU for organising SETSS 2018.

Appendix A: Sample Answers to Selected Exercises

This appendix gives sample solutions to the exercises that cannot be checked using the online Whiley Labs website.

Answer: Return Statement.
- **Q1)** What knowledge do we have at the **point of return?**
- **A1)** At the point of return the final value of x is returned, so we know that $r == x_0 + 1$, where x_0 is the initial value of the input parameter x.

- **Q2)** Is this enough to establish the postcondition?
- **A2)** Yes, because $r == x_0 + 1$ implies $r > x_0$, which is equivalent to the desired postcondition.

Answer: Specification versus Implementation.
- **Q1)** Do these values satisfy the *specification* of increment()?
- **A1)** Yes. For example x=0, y=2 satisfies the ensures clause.

- **Q2)** Do these values satisfy the *implementation* of increment()?
- **A2)** No. The counterexample values are do not satisfy y=x+1, even though that is what the implementation does. This is because the verifier only uses the published *specification* properties of the function to help verify function calls, not the extra details of the function implementation. This separation of concerns makes modular verification possible.

References

1. European Space Agency: Ariane 5: Flight 501 failure. Report by the Enquiry Board (1996)
2. Babić, D., Hu, A.J.: Exploiting shared structure in software verification conditions. In: Yorav, K. (ed.) HVC 2007. LNCS, vol. 4899, pp. 169–184. Springer, Heidelberg (2008). https://doi.org/10.1007/978-3-540-77966-7_15
3. Babić, D., Hu, A.J.: Structural abstraction of software verification conditions. In: Damm, W., Hermanns, H. (eds.) CAV 2007. LNCS, vol. 4590, pp. 366–378. Springer, Heidelberg (2007). https://doi.org/10.1007/978-3-540-73368-3_41

4. Back, R.J.R., von Wright, J.: Refinement Calculus: A Systematic Approach. Graduate Texts in Computer Science. Springer, New York (1998). https://doi.org/10.1007/978-1-4612-1674-2
5. Barnett, M., Chang, B.-Y.E., DeLine, R., Jacobs, B., Leino, K.R.M.: Boogie: a modular reusable verifier for object-oriented programs. In: de Boer, F.S., Bonsangue, M.M., Graf, S., de Roever, W.-P. (eds.) FMCO 2005. LNCS, vol. 4111, pp. 364–387. Springer, Heidelberg (2006). https://doi.org/10.1007/11804192_17
6. Barnett, M., Fähndrich, M., Leino, K.R.M., Müller, P., Schulte, W., Venter, H.: Specification and verification: the Spec# experience. Commun. ACM 54(6), 81–91 (2011)
7. Barnett, M., DeLine, R., Fähndrich, M., Leino, K.R.M., Schulte, W.: Verification of object-oriented programs with invariants. J. Object Technol. 3(6), 27–56 (2004)
8. Barnett, M., Leino, K.R.M.: Weakest-precondition of unstructured programs. In: Proceedings of the Workshop on Program Analysis for Software Tools and Engineering (PASTE), pp. 82–87. ACM Press (2005)
9. Burdy, L., Requet, A., Lanet, J.-L.: Java applet correctness: a developer-oriented approach. In: Araki, K., Gnesi, S., Mandrioli, D. (eds.) FME 2003. LNCS, vol. 2805, pp. 422–439. Springer, Heidelberg (2003). https://doi.org/10.1007/978-3-540-45236-2_24
10. Carvalho, M., DeMott, J., Ford, R., Wheeler, D.: Heartbleed 101. IEEE Secur. Priv. 12(4), 63–67 (2014)
11. Cataño, N., Huisman, M.: Formal specification and static checking of gemplus' electronic purse using ESC/Java. In: Eriksson, L.-H., Lindsay, P.A. (eds.) FME 2002. LNCS, vol. 2391, pp. 272–289. Springer, Heidelberg (2002). https://doi.org/10.1007/3-540-45614-7_16
12. Chalin, P., Rioux, F.: JML runtime assertion checking: improved error reporting and efficiency using strong validity. In: Cuellar, J., Maibaum, T., Sere, K. (eds.) FM 2008. LNCS, vol. 5014, pp. 246–261. Springer, Heidelberg (2008). https://doi.org/10.1007/978-3-540-68237-0_18
13. Chandra, S., Fink, S.J., Sridharan, M.: Snugglebug: a powerful approach to weakest preconditions. In: Proceedings of the ACM conference on Programming Language Design and Implementation (PLDI), pp. 363–374. ACM Press (2009)
14. Charette, R.: This car runs on code. IEEE Spectr. 46, 3 (2009)
15. Charette, R.N.: Why software fails. IEEE Spect. 42(9), 42–49 (2005)
16. Cohen, E., et al.: VCC: a practical system for verifying concurrent C. In: Berghofer, S., Nipkow, T., Urban, C., Wenzel, M. (eds.) TPHOLs 2009. LNCS, vol. 5674, pp. 23–42. Springer, Heidelberg (2009). https://doi.org/10.1007/978-3-642-03359-9_2
17. Cok, D.R.: OpenJML: JML for Java 7 by extending OpenJDK. In: Bobaru, M., Havelund, K., Holzmann, G.J., Joshi, R. (eds.) NFM 2011. LNCS, vol. 6617, pp. 472–479. Springer, Heidelberg (2011). https://doi.org/10.1007/978-3-642-20398-5_35
18. Cok, D.R.: OpenJML: Software verification for Java 7 using JML, OpenJDK, and eclipse. In: Proceedings of the Workshop on Formal Integrated Development Environment (F-IDE), vol. 149, pp. 79–92 (2014)
19. Cytron, R., Ferrante, J., Rosen, B., Wegman, M., Zadeck, F.K.: An efficient method of computing static single assignment form. In: Proceedings of the ACM symposium on the Principles Of Programming Languages (POPL), pp. 25–35 (1989)
20. Cytron, R., Ferrante, J., Rosen, B.K., Wegman, M.N., Zadeck, F.K.: Efficiently computing static single assignment form and the control dependence graph. ACM Trans. Program. Lang. Syst. 13(4), 451–490 (1991)

21. Denney, E., Fischer, B.: Explaining verification conditions. In: Meseguer, J., Roşu, G. (eds.) AMAST 2008. LNCS, vol. 5140, pp. 145–159. Springer, Heidelberg (2008). https://doi.org/10.1007/978-3-540-79980-1_12
22. Detlefs, D., Nelson, G., Saxe, J.B.: Simplify: a theorem prover for program checking. J. ACM **52**(3), 365–473 (2005)
23. Detlefs, D.L., Leino, K.R.M., Nelson, G., Saxe, J.B.: Extended static checking. SRC Research Report 159, Compaq Systems Research Center (1998)
24. Dijkstra, E.W.: Guarded commands, nondeterminacy and formal derivation of programs. Commun. ACM **18**, 453–457 (1975)
25. Durumeric, Z., et al.: The matter of heartbleed. In: Proceedings of Internet Measurement Conference (IMC), pp. 475–488. ACM Press (2014)
26. Fähndrich, M., Leino, K.R.M.: Declaring and checking non-null types in an object-oriented language. In: Proceedings of the ACM conference on Object-Oriented Programming, Systems, Languages and Applications (OOPSLA), pp. 302–312. ACM Press (2003)
27. Filliâtre, J.-C., Marché, C.: The Why/Krakatoa/Caduceus platform for deductive program verification. In: Damm, W., Hermanns, H. (eds.) CAV 2007. LNCS, vol. 4590, pp. 173–177. Springer, Heidelberg (2007). https://doi.org/10.1007/978-3-540-73368-3_21
28. Flanagan, C., Leino, K., Lillibridge, M., Nelson, G., Saxe, J.B., Stata, R.: Extended static checking for Java. In: Proceedings of the ACM conference on Programming Language Design and Implementation (PLDI), pp. 234–245 (2002)
29. Flanagan, C., Saxe, J.B.: Avoiding exponential explosion: generating compact verification conditions. In: Proceedings of the ACM symposium on the Principles Of Programming Languages (POPL), pp. 193–205. ACM Press (2001)
30. Floyd, R.W.: Assigning meaning to programs. In: Proceedings of Symposia in Applied Mathematics, vol. 19, pp. 19–31. American Mathematical Society (1967)
31. Frade, M.J., Pinto, J.S.: Verification conditions for source-level imperative programs. Comput. Sci. Rev. **5**(3), 252–277 (2011)
32. Software problem led to system failure at dhahran, saudi arabia, gao report #b-247094 (1992)
33. Grigore, R., Charles, J., Fairmichael, F., Kiniry, J.: Strongest postcondition of unstructured programs. In: Proceedings of the Workshop on Formal Techniques for Java-like Programs (FTFJP), pp. 6:1–6:7. ACM Press (2009)
34. Hoare, C.A.R.: An axiomatic basis for computer programming. CACM **12**, 576–580 (1969)
35. Holzmann, G.J.: Out of bounds. IEEE Softw. **32**(6), 24–26 (2015)
36. Huisman, M., Klebanov, V., Monahan, R.: Verifythis verification competition 2012 - organizer's report (2013)
37. Jacobs, B.: Weakest pre-condition reasoning for Java programs with JML annotations. J. Log. Algebr. Program. **58**(1–2), 61–88 (2004)
38. Kassios, I.T.: Dynamic frames: support for framing, dependencies and sharing without restrictions. In: Misra, J., Nipkow, T., Sekerinski, E. (eds.) FM 2006. LNCS, vol. 4085, pp. 268–283. Springer, Heidelberg (2006). https://doi.org/10.1007/11813040_19
39. Klebanov, V., et al.: The 1st verified software competition: experience report. In: Butler, M., Schulte, W. (eds.) FM 2011. LNCS, vol. 6664, pp. 154–168. Springer, Heidelberg (2011). https://doi.org/10.1007/978-3-642-21437-0_14

40. Ko, A.J., Dosono, B., Duriseti, N.: Thirty years of software problems in the news. In: Proceedings of the 7th International Workshop on Cooperative and Human Aspects of Software Engineering, CHASE 2014, Hyderabad, India, 2–3 June 2014. ACM Press (2014)

41. Leavens, G.T., Cheon, Y., Clifton, C., Ruby, C., Cok, D.R.: How the design of JML accommodates both runtime assertion checking and formal verification. Sci. Comput. Program. **55**(1–3), 185–208 (2005)

42. Leino, K.R.M.: Efficient weakest preconditions. Inf. Process. Lett. **93**(6), 281–288 (2005)

43. Rustan, K., Leino, M.: Developing verified programs with Dafny. In: Joshi, R., Müller, P., Podelski, A. (eds.) VSTTE 2012. LNCS, vol. 7152, p. 82. Springer, Heidelberg (2012). https://doi.org/10.1007/978-3-642-27705-4_7

44. Leino, K.R.M.: Dafny: an automatic program verifier for functional correctness. In: Clarke, E.M., Voronkov, A. (eds.) LPAR 2010. LNCS (LNAI), vol. 6355, pp. 348–370. Springer, Heidelberg (2010). https://doi.org/10.1007/978-3-642-17511-4_20

45. Leino, K.R.M., Müller, P.: Using the Spec# language, methodology, and tools to write bug-free programs. In: Müller, P. (ed.) LASER 2007–2008. LNCS, vol. 6029, pp. 91–139. Springer, Heidelberg (2010). https://doi.org/10.1007/978-3-642-13010-6_4

46. Leino, K.R.M., Monahan, R.: Dafny meets the verification benchmarks challenge. In: Leavens, G.T., O'Hearn, P., Rajamani, S.K. (eds.) VSTTE 2010. LNCS, vol. 6217, pp. 112–126. Springer, Heidelberg (2010). https://doi.org/10.1007/978-3-642-15057-9_8

47. Leveson, N., Turner, C.: An investigation of the Therac-25 accidents. IEEE Comput. **26**(7), 18–41 (1993)

48. Morgan, C.: Programming from Specifications, 2nd edn. Prentice Hall, Upper Saddle River (1994)

49. de Moura, L., Bjørner, N.: Z3: an efficient SMT solver. In: Ramakrishnan, C.R., Rehof, J. (eds.) TACAS 2008. LNCS, vol. 4963, pp. 337–340. Springer, Heidelberg (2008). https://doi.org/10.1007/978-3-540-78800-3_24

50. Pearce, D.J.: Integer range analysis for Whiley on embedded systems. In: Proceedings of the IEEE/IFIP Workshop on Software Technologies for Future Embedded and Ubiquitous Systems, pp. 26–33 (2015)

51. Pearce, D.J.: The Whiley Language Specification (Updated, 2016)

52. Pearce, D.J., Groves, L.: Whiley: a platform for research in software verification. In: Erwig, M., Paige, R.F., Van Wyk, E. (eds.) SLE 2013. LNCS, vol. 8225, pp. 238–248. Springer, Cham (2013). https://doi.org/10.1007/978-3-319-02654-1_13

53. Rahman, H.A., Beznosov, K., Martí, J.R.: Identification of sources of failures and their propagation in critical infrastructures from 12 years of public failure reports. Int. J. Crit. Infrastruct. **5**(3), 220–244 (2009)

54. Sánchez, J., Leavens, G.T.: Static verification of PtolemyRely programs using OpenJML. In: Proceedings of the Workshop on Foundations of Aspect-Oriented Languages (FOAL), pp. 13–18. ACM Press (2014)

55. Steinberg, J.: Massive internet security vulnerability - here's what you need to do (2014). https://www.forbes.com/sites/josephsteinberg/2014/04/10/massive-internet-security-vulnerability-you-are-at-risk-what-you-need-to-do. Accessed 12 Jan 2019

56. Stevens, M.: Demonstrating Whiley on an embedded system. Technical report, School of Engineering and Computer Science, Victoria University of Wellington (2014). http://www.ecs.vuw.ac.nz/~djp/files/MattStevensENGR489.pdf

57. Weng, M.H., Pfahringer, B., Utting, M.: Static techniques for reducing memory usage in the C implementation of Whiley programs. In: Proceedings of the Australasian Computer Science Week Multiconference, ACSW 2017, pp. 15:1–15:8. ACM, New York (2017). https://doi.org/10.1145/3014812.3014827
58. White, D., Roschelle, A., Peterson, P., Schlissel, D., Biewald, B., Steinhurst, W.: The 2003 blackout: solutions that won't cost a fortune. Electr. J. **16**(9), 43–53 (2003)

Learning Büchi Automata and Its Applications

Yong Li[1,2], Andrea Turrini[1,3(✉)], Yu-Fang Chen[4], and Lijun Zhang[1,2,3]

[1] State Key Laboratory of Computer Science,
Institute of Software, Chinese Academy of Sciences, Beijing, China
{turrini,zhanglj}@ios.ac.cn
[2] University of Chinese Academy of Sciences, Beijing, China
[3] Institute of Intelligent Software, Guangzhou, China
[4] Institute of Information Science, Academia Sinica, Taipei, Taiwan

Abstract. In this work, we review an algorithm that learns a Büchi automaton from a teacher who knows an ω-regular language; the algorithm is based on learning a formalism named *family of DFAs* (FDFAs) recently proposed by Angluin and Fisman. We introduce the learning algorithm by learning the simple ω-regular language $(ab)^{\omega}$: besides giving the readers an overview of the algorithm, it guides them on how the algorithm works step by step. Further, we demonstrate how the learning algorithm can be exploited in classical automata operations such as complementation checking and in the context of termination analysis.

1 Introduction

Model checking is a widely used technique in the verification of hardware and software systems, scaling from case studies in academic publications to real systems in industry; the importance of model checking has been recognized by means of the 2007 Turing award, which has been assigned to Edmund M. Clarke, E. Allen Emerson, and Joseph Sifakis for "their roles in developing model checking into a highly effective verification technology, widely adopted in the hardware and software industries".

Large systems are usually obtained by developing several small components that interact concurrently with each other so to globally achieve the desired functionality. The main obstacle in applying model checking to concurrent systems is the well-known state explosion problem [31]. The number of global states of such systems can be enormous: it is actually of the form n^p where p is the number of processes and n is the number of states in each process. There have been several approaches proposed in literature to combat the state explosion problem, such as symbolic model checking based on BDDs [78], bounded model checking [18], and learning-based compositional verification [34]. The latter approach, the learning-based compositional verification, tries to learn models of the single components that are smaller than the original processes while preserving their behavior. The learning algorithm used in [34] is the well-known L* algorithm proposed by Dana Angluin [8], which allows one to learn deterministic finite automata (DFAs).

© Springer Nature Switzerland AG 2019
J. P. Bowen et al. (Eds.): SETSS 2018, LNCS 11430, pp. 38–98, 2019.
https://doi.org/10.1007/978-3-030-17601-3_2

Automata learning algorithms have received significant attention from the verification community in the past two decades. Besides being used to improve the efficiency and scalability of compositional verification, automata learning has also been successfully applied in other aspects of verification: among others, it has been used to automatically generate interface models of computer programs [7], to learn a model of the traces of the system errors for diagnosis purposes [27], to find bugs in the implementation of network protocols [88], to extract behavior model of programs for statistical program analysis [29], and to do model-based testing and verification [81,107]. Later in 2017, Frits Vaandrager [103] surveyed the concept of *model learning* used in the above applications.

In order to be of practical use, the learning algorithms have to be computationally efficient and easily adaptable to the different learning scenarios. On the one hand, with more complex tasks at hand, some researchers have proposed several optimizations to improve the efficiency of finite automata learning, such as learning algorithms based on *classification trees* [59,63], efficient counterexample analysis for learning algorithms [87], learning algorithm NL^* for nondeterministic finite automata (NFAs) [20], and learning algorithms for alternating finite automata [10].

On the other hand, due to the demands from the different verification tasks, some researchers also develop and apply learning algorithms for richer models. For example, there are learning algorithms for I/O automata [2], event-recording automata [50], register automata [57,58], timed systems [75], probabilistic systems [43], and nominal automata [79]. Specially, van Heerdt *et al.* in [53] proposed an automata learning framework based on category theory which unifies the learning of several automata including DFAs and weighted automata.

However, aforementioned learning algorithms are all designed for the automata accepting finite words; those automata are used to model the finite behaviors of the systems, which are usually characterized by safety properties expected to hold. For instance, one can use a DFA to recognize all possible bad behaviors, i.e., behaviors leading in a finite number of steps to a state violating a safety property. Instead, for characterizing the infinite behaviors of the systems, generally corresponding to liveness properties, automata accepting infinite words are used.

In his seminal work [25], Büchi introduced automata accepting infinite words to prove the decidability of a restricted *monadic second order* (MSO) logic; now such automata are widely known as Büchi automata (BA). A Büchi automaton has the same structure as an NFA, except that it operates on infinite words: instead of accepting a finite word if it leads the run of the automaton to end in an accepting state, a BA accepts an infinite word if it leads the automaton to visit an accepting state infinitely often. Büchi automata are nowadays very popular in the model checking field, in particular when the specification is given by a linear temporal logic (LTL) formula; see the introductory paper by Vardi [104] on the use of BAs for LTL analysis.

Besides being used in LTL verification and synthesis, Büchi automata have been also used as a standard model to describe the liveness properties of distributed systems [6]. Therefore, in order to verify whether a concurrent system satisfies a liveness property, one can model every process of the system as a Büchi automaton. It follows that if one can learn smaller Büchi automata for the processes, then performing compositional verification on the given concurrent system can become less expensive, similarly to the DFA case. Motivated by that, Farzan et al. presented in [42] the first learning algorithm for the complete-class of ω-regular languages represented as Büchi automata; the algorithm is able to extract automatically a Büchi automaton as an assumption from a component of concurrent systems for compositional verification. Note that already in 1995 Maler and Pnueli [76] introduced the first learning algorithm for Büchi automata, but it learns Büchi automata accepting only a proper subset of ω-regular languages. In 2014, Angluin and Fisman proposed in [11] a learning algorithm for the ω-regular languages by means of a formalism called a *family of DFAs* (FDFAs). Later in [73], Li et al. proposed to use classification trees to learn FDFAs rather than observation tables used by Angluin and Fisman. Learning algorithms based on classification trees usually need less runtime memory and can be much more efficient when compared to its observation table based counterparts [59]. Further, Li et al. presented in [73] a more efficient learning algorithm for Büchi automata based on FDFAs and classification trees compared to the learning algorithm in [42].

There are already a few learning algorithms for Büchi automata available in the literature, yet the learning algorithms are not widely used in the model checking community. One reason for this is that the learning algorithms are quite technically demanding and not so easy to follow and understand; in this paper we give a simple presentation of one BA learning algorithm, with simple but complete examples, to introduce the reader to such learning framework. Another reason is that there are fewer learning libraries available for Büchi automata compared to those implemented for learning automata accepting finite words: for instance, for learning automata accepting finite words there are robust and publicly available libraries such as libalf [21] and LearnLib [60]. To the best of our knowledge, there is, however, only one publicly available library for learning Büchi automata named ROLL [73] which implements also the BA learning algorithm described in this paper.

In this paper, we review the BA learning algorithm proposed in [73] by learning the simple ω-regular language $(ab)^\omega$: besides giving the reader an overview of the algorithm, it guides them on how the algorithm works step by step. Our main goal in this work is to give an intuitive explanation of the different learning algorithms for both finite and ω-regular languages; in this way the reader can get the ideas underlying the learning algorithms before getting involved in their formalism, presented in the related literature; we achieve this by means of the examples we carefully chose so to be simple but still exposing the different challenges the learning algorithms for Büchi automata face and the solution techniques that have been adopted.

Further, we discuss two possible interesting applications of the BA learning algorithms. The complementation problem for Büchi automata is a challenging problem in the research community both in theory and practice. We show that the BA learning algorithm can be easily applied to complement Büchi automata. Experimental results show that the learning-based complementation algorithm of Büchi automata can yield much smaller complement automata for some cases than classical algorithms. Lastly, we discuss how the learning algorithms can be also applied in proving the termination of C programs. Heizmann *et al.* in [55] proposed a novel termination analysis algorithm based on Büchi automata. Interestingly, the efficiency and scalability of this termination analysis algorithm highly depend on getting smaller complement automata of Büchi automata, where one naturally can use the learning based complementation algorithm.

Organization of the Paper. We first set up some notions and notations for this work in Sect. 2. We then introduce some basic operations on Büchi automata in Sect. 3, together with their complexity analysis, before turning to the learning algorithms in the following sections. In order to ease the presentation, we first present the learning algorithm for DFAs in Sect. 4 and then move onto the learning of Büchi automata in Sect. 5. After that, we show how to apply our learning algorithm to the complementation problem of Büchi automata in Sect. 6. Before concluding the paper in Sect. 8, we consider the application of BA learning algorithm to program termination analysis in Sect. 7.

2   Preliminaries

Let X and Y be two sets; we use $X \ominus Y$ to denote their *symmetric difference*, i.e., the set $(X \setminus Y) \cup (Y \setminus X)$. We use $[i \cdots j]$ to denote the set $\{i, i+1, \ldots, j\}$.

Let Σ denote a finite non-empty set of letters called *alphabet*. A *word* is a finite or infinite sequence $w = w_1 w_2 \cdots$ of letters in Σ; we denote by $|w|$ the length of the word w, i.e., the number letters in w. If w is infinite, then $|w| = \infty$, and we call it an *ω-word*. We use ε to denote the word of length 0, i.e., the empty word. We denote by Σ^* and Σ^ω the sets of all finite and infinite words, respectively. Moreover, we use Σ^+ to represent the set $\Sigma^* \setminus \{\varepsilon\}$.

We denote by $w[i]$ the i-th letter of a word w. We use $w[i..k]$ to denote the subword of w starting at the i-th letter and ending at the k-th letter, inclusive, when $i \leq k$ and the empty word ε when $i > k$. For $u \in \Sigma^*$, we denote by $\mathrm{Pref}(u)$ the set of its prefixes, i.e., $\mathrm{Pref}(u) = \{\varepsilon, u[1], u[1..2], \ldots, u[1..|u|]\}$. Similarly, we denote by $\mathrm{Suf}(u)$ the set of its suffixes, i.e., $\mathrm{Suf}(u) = \{u[1..|u|], u[2..|u|], \ldots, u[|u|], \varepsilon\}$. Given a finite word $u = u_1 \cdots u_k$ and a word w, we denote by $u \cdot w$ the *concatenation* of u and w, i.e., the finite or infinite word $u \cdot w = u_1 \cdots u_k w_1 \cdots$. We may just write uw instead of $u \cdot w$.

Definition 1. *An* acceptor automaton *is a tuple* $A = (\Sigma, Q, \bar{q}, \delta, F)$ *consisting of the following components: a finite alphabet* Σ, *a finite set* Q *of states, an initial state* $\bar{q} \in Q$, *a transition relation* $\delta \subseteq Q \times \Sigma \times Q$, *and an accepting condition* F.

For convenience, we also use $\delta(q, a)$ to denote the set $\{q' \in Q \mid (q, a, q') \in \delta\}$.

In the remainder of the paper, we assume that all automata share the same alphabet Σ, which we may omit from their definitions.

A *run* of an acceptor automaton on a finite word $v = a_1 a_2 a_3 \cdots a_n$, $n \geq 1$, is a sequence of states $q_0, q_1, \ldots, q_n$ such that $q_0 = \bar{q}$ and $(q_i, a_{i+1}, q_{i+1}) \in \delta$ for every $0 \leq i < n$; similarly, a *run* of an acceptor automaton on an infinite word $w = a_1 a_2 a_3 \cdots$ is a sequence of states $q_0, q_1, \ldots$ such that $q_0 = \bar{q}$ and $(q_i, a_{i+1}, q_{i+1}) \in \delta$ for each $i \in \mathbb{N}$. The run on a word is *accepting* if it satisfies the accepting condition F. A word is accepted by an acceptor automaton A if A has an accepting run on it.

A *finite language* is a subset of Σ^* while an ω-*language* is a subset of Σ^ω; the language of an acceptor automaton A, denoted by $\mathcal{L}(A)$, is the set $\{\, u \in \Sigma^* \cup \Sigma^\omega \mid u \text{ is accepted by } A \,\}$.

A *deterministic acceptor automaton* is an acceptor automaton such that $|\delta(q, a)| \leq 1$ for any $q \in Q$ and $a \in \Sigma$. For deterministic acceptor automata, we may write $\delta(q, a) = q'$ instead of $\delta(q, a) = \{q'\}$. The transition relation of a deterministic acceptor automaton can be lifted to finite words by defining $\delta(q, \varepsilon) = q$ and $\delta(q, av) = \delta(\delta(q, a), v)$ for each $q \in Q$, $a \in \Sigma$, and $v \in \Sigma^*$. We also use $A(v)$ as a shorthand for $\delta(\bar{q}, v)$.

A *finite automaton* (FA) is an acceptor automaton where $F \subseteq Q$ and a finite word v is accepted if there is a run $q_0, q_1, \ldots, q_n$ on v such that $q_n \in F$; no infinite word is accepted. A *deterministic finite automaton* (DFA) is a FA which is also a deterministic acceptor automaton. A complement DFA A^C of a DFA A is a DFA such that $\mathcal{L}(A^C) = \Sigma^* \setminus \mathcal{L}(A)$. Complementing a DFA is easy: it is enough to add an accepting sink state collecting all missing transitions and complement the original set of accepting states. Let A and B be two FAs; one can construct a product FA, denoted by $A \times B$, accepting the language $\mathcal{L}(A) \cap \mathcal{L}(B)$ using a standard product construction; see, e.g., [56].

A *Büchi automaton* (BA) is an acceptor automaton where $F \subseteq Q$ and an infinite word w is accepted if there is a run $\rho = q_0, q_1, \ldots$ on w such that for each $i \in \mathbb{N}$, there exists $j > i$ such that $\rho[j] \in F$; no finite word is accepted. Intuitively, an infinite word w is accepted by a BA if there exists a run on w visiting at least one accepting state in F infinitely often. A *deterministic Büchi automaton* (DBA) is a BA which is also a deterministic acceptor automaton.

A BA is a *limit deterministic Büchi automaton* (LDBA) if its set of states Q can be partitioned into two disjoint sets Q_N and Q_D, such that (1) $\delta(q, a) \subseteq Q_D$ and $|\delta(q, a)| \leq 1$ for each $q \in Q_D$ and $a \in \Sigma$, and (2) $F \subseteq Q_D$. It is trivial to note that each DBA is also an LDBA, by taking $Q_N = \emptyset$ and $Q_D = Q$.

Example 1. As examples of Büchi automata, consider the two automata shown in Fig. 1. The automaton A is a DBA with alphabet $\Sigma = \{a, b\}$, set of states $Q = \{q_0, q_1\}$, initial state $\bar{q} = q_0$ (marked by the small incoming arrow), transition relation $\delta = \{(q_0, a, q_1), (q_0, b, q_0), (q_1, a, q_1), (q_1, b, q_0)\}$, and $F = \{q_1\}$ (denoted as a double-circled state). The language accepted by A is the ω-regular language $\mathcal{L}(A) = \{\, w \in \Sigma^\omega \mid w \text{ has infinitely many } a\text{'s} \,\}$.

$$\mathcal{L}(A) = \{\, w \mid w \text{ has infinitely many } a\text{'s}\,\} \quad \mathcal{L}(B) = \{\, w \mid w \text{ has finitely many } a\text{'s}\,\}$$

Fig. 1. Examples of Büchi automata and their accepted languages

The automaton B is an NBA that accepts the language $\mathcal{L}(B) = \{\, w \in \Sigma^\omega \mid w \text{ has finitely many } a\text{'s}\,\}$, which is the complement of $\mathcal{L}(A)$. Note that B is also a limit deterministic Büchi automaton, where the corresponding partition of Q is given by $Q_N = \{q_0\}$ and $Q_D = \{q_1\}$.

We call the language of an FA a *regular* language. An ω-language $L \subseteq \Sigma^\omega$ is ω-*regular* if there exists a BA A such that $L = \mathcal{L}(A)$. Words of the form uv^ω, where $u \in \Sigma^*$ and $v \in \Sigma^+$, are called *ultimately periodic* words. We use a pair of finite words (u, v) to denote the ultimately periodic word $w = uv^\omega$. We also call (u, v) a *decomposition* of w; note that an ultimately periodic word can have several decompositions: for instance (u, v), (uv, v), and (u, vv) are all decompositions of uv^ω. For an ω-language L, let $\mathrm{UP}(L) = \{\, uv^\omega \in L \mid u \in \Sigma^*, v \in \Sigma^+ \,\}$ denote the set of all ultimately periodic words in L. Note that the set of ultimately periodic words of an ω-regular language L can be seen as the fingerprint of L, as stated by the following theorem.

Theorem 1 (Ultimately Periodic Words of ω-Regular Languages [25, 26]**).** *(1) Every non-empty ω-regular language L contains at least one ultimately periodic word. (2) Let L, L' be two ω-regular languages. Then $L = L'$ if and only if $\mathrm{UP}(L) = \mathrm{UP}(L')$.*

We refer interested reader to [25, 26] for the proof of Theorem 1. An immediate consequence of Theorem 1 is that, for any two ω-regular languages L and L', if $L \neq L'$ then there must exist some ultimately periodic word $uv^\omega \in \mathrm{UP}(L) \ominus \mathrm{UP}(L')$.

3   Operations on Büchi Automata

In this section we present how nondeterministic Büchi automata support the standard set operations on their languages, namely, union, intersection, and complementation, as well as derived operations and decision problems. The main result is that nondeterministic Büchi automata are closed under such operations, e.g., giving two Büchi automata A_0 and A_1, we can construct another Büchi automaton A such that $\mathcal{L}(A) = \mathcal{L}(A_0) \cap \mathcal{L}(A_1)$. Deterministic Büchi automata, however, are strictly less expressive than nondeterministic ones, since there are ω-regular languages accepted by a nondeterministic BA for which there does not exist a deterministic BA accepting them; DBAs are also *not* closed under complementation, i.e., there is a DBA whose complement language can only be accepted by a nondeterministic BA.

There are several resources available in literature for the readers interested in more details on ω-languages and their automata; see, e.g., [30, 32, 49, 62, 94, 96, 97].

3.1 Union of Büchi Automata

Given two Büchi automata A_0 and A_1, it is rather easy to construct a Büchi automaton $A_{0 \cup 1}$ such that $\mathcal{L}(A_{0 \cup 1}) = \mathcal{L}(A_0) \cup \mathcal{L}(A_1)$. In fact, since by definition of language of a Büchi automaton, a word w belongs to its language if there exists an accepting run on w, it is enough to create an automaton having all runs of A_0 and A_1: this can be easily achieved by just considering A_0 and A_1 as a single automaton, up to some minor adaptation on the initial state.

Proposition 1. *Given two Büchi automata* $A_0 = (Q_0, \bar{q}_0, \delta_0, F_0)$ *and* $A_1 = (Q_1, \bar{q}_1, \delta_1, F_1)$ *such that* $Q_0 \cap Q_1 = \emptyset$, *let* $A_{0 \cup 1} = (Q, \bar{q}, \delta, F)$ *be the Büchi automaton whose components are defined as follows:*

- *$Q = Q_0 \cup Q_1 \cup \{\bar{q}\}$ where $\bar{q}$ is a fresh state such that $\bar{q} \notin Q_0 \cup Q_1$,*
- *$\delta = \delta_0 \cup \delta_1 \cup \{ (\bar{q}, a, q_0) \mid q_0 \in \delta_0(\bar{q}_0, a) \} \cup \{ (\bar{q}, a, q_1) \mid q_1 \in \delta_1(\bar{q}_1, a) \}$, and*
- *$F = F_0 \cup F_1$.*

Then, $\mathcal{L}(A_{0 \cup 1}) = \mathcal{L}(A_0) \cup \mathcal{L}(A_1)$ with $|Q| = |Q_0| + |Q_1| + 1$.

The proof of the above proposition is rather trivial: given an ω-word w, except for the initial state $\bar{q}$, a run on w of the automaton $A_{0 \cup 1}$ is identical to a run on w of either A_0 or A_1.

Note that the requirement that A_0 and A_1 must have disjoint sets of states can be easily fulfilled by simply renaming their states, since actual state names play no role in accepting a word. Moreover, if we would have allowed a set of initial states instead of a single initial state, then the union automaton would be just the component-wise union of the two given Büchi automata.

3.2 Intersection of Büchi Automata

The construction of a Büchi automaton accepting the intersection of the languages of A_0 and A_1 is slightly more involved than their union. The main idea underlying the intersection construction is to run on the input word in parallel in both A_0 and A_1, by means of a product construction similar to the one for the intersection of finite automata; as accepting condition, we require that we reach the accepting states of A_0 and A_1 in an alternating mode, i.e., every time we reach an accepting state in A_c for $c \in \{0, 1\}$, then we have to reach an accepting state in A_{1-c}. If we can alternate infinitely often, then both automata accept the input word, i.e., it is in the intersection of their languages; if we alternate only finitely often, this means that the BA where we get stuck is not accepting such a word, so the intersection automaton must reject the word as well. This is different from the accepting condition for finite automata, where a product state is accepting if both states in the pair are accepting: in fact, for infinite words it does not matter whether the two BAs reach an accepting state exactly at the same moment, since it can also be the case that both automata accept an ω-word w but A_0 reaches an accepting state only once every ten times A_1 has reached an accepting state.

Proposition 2. *Given two Büchi automata $A_0 = (Q_0, \bar{q}_0, \delta_0, F_0)$ and $A_1 = (Q_1, \bar{q}_1, \delta_1, F_1)$, let $A_{0 \cap 1} = (Q, \bar{q}, F, \delta)$ be the Büchi automaton whose components are defined as follows:*

- $Q = Q_0 \times Q_1 \times \{0, 1\}$;
- $\bar{q} = (\bar{q}_0, \bar{q}_1, 0)$;
- $\delta = \{ ((q_0, q_1, c), a, (q'_0, q'_1, next(q_0, q_1, c))) \mid q'_0 \in \delta_0(q_0, a), q'_1 \in \delta_1(q_1, a) \}$
  where $next \colon Q_0 \times Q_1 \times \{0, 1\} \to \{0, 1\}$ is defined as

$$next(q_0, q_1, c) = \begin{cases} 1 - c & \text{if } q_c \in F_c, \\ c & \text{otherwise}; \end{cases}$$

- $F = F_0 \times Q_1 \times \{0\}$.

Then, $\mathcal{L}(A_{0 \cap 1}) = \mathcal{L}(A_0) \cap \mathcal{L}(A_1)$ with $|Q| = 2 \cdot |Q_0| \cdot |Q_1|$.

The above construction is based on the transformation of generalized Büchi automata to Büchi automata. Generalized BAs differ from BAs only on the fact that they have multiple accepting sets; an ω-word w is accepted if there exists a run on w reaching a state in each accepting set infinitely often. Since generalized BAs have the same expressive power as ordinary BAs and are not used in this work, we refer the interested reader to, e.g., [32] for more details.

3.3 Complementation of Büchi Automata

Complementing Büchi automata is the most difficult operation on their languages. First of all, the usual subset construction used for converting nondeterministic finite automata to equivalent deterministic finite automata and then easily complement the resulting DFAs can not be adapted to Büchi automata since DBAs are strictly less expressive than BAs:

Proposition 3 (cf. [68]). *There exists an ω-regular language L that is recognizable by a BA but not by a DBA.*

This means that for such a language L, we can find a BA A such that $\mathcal{L}(A) = L$ but there does not exist a DBA D such that $\mathcal{L}(D) = L$. As a consequence, applying a subset construction to A does not lead to a DBA accepting the same language.

Note that the language witnessing the correctness of the above result is rather simple: $L = \Sigma^* \cdot b^\omega$, that is, L is the language of all words having only b occurring infinitely often. For $\Sigma = \{a, b\}$, this language is recognized by the BA B shown in Fig. 1; its complement, i.e., the language whose words contain infinitely many a, is easily recognized by the DBA A also shown in Fig. 1. This means that DBAs are *not* closed under complementation, while BAs are indeed closed, as witnessed by the several complementation algorithms that have been proposed in literature.

Before presenting such algorithms, we want to introduce the main result about the complexity of complementing Büchi automata.

Proposition 4 (cf. [90]). *Given a BA A with n states, it is possible to construct a BA A^C such that $\mathcal{L}(A^C) = \Sigma^\omega \setminus \mathcal{L}(A)$ whose number of states is in $\Omega(tight(n - 1))$ and $\mathcal{O}(tight(n + 1))$, where $tight(n) \approx (0.76n)^n$.*

In practice, the above is the best known complexity result for the complementation of Büchi automata, where the lower- and upper-bounds about the number of states of the complement Büchi automaton have a minor gap lying in $\mathcal{O}(n^2)$.

There are mainly four types of complementation algorithms, according to the classification proposed in [19,98]: Ramsey-based [24,25,93], rank-based [46,51, 65,90], determinization-based [44,82,89,91], and slice-based [5,61,98,106] complementation. A complementation construction unifying the rank-based and slice-based approaches can be found in [45]. All these algorithms construct the complement Büchi automata based on the transition structures of the input Büchi automata. Besides the complementation algorithm proposed for nondeterministic Büchi automata, there are also complementation algorithms specialized for limit deterministic Büchi automata [19,28] and for deterministic Büchi automata [66].

Given the highly demanding technicalities involved in the above complementation algorithms for Büchi automata, we refer the interested reader to the cited literature for more details on the different approaches and algorithms.

3.4   Difference of Büchi Automata

The BA language difference operation is tightly connected to the complementation operation, from which it derives its super-exponential complexity, as stated by the following proposition.

Proposition 5. *Given two BAs A_0 and A_1 with n_0 and n_1 states, respectively, it is possible to construct a BA $A_{0\setminus 1}$ such that $\mathcal{L}(A_{0\setminus 1}) = \mathcal{L}(A_0) \setminus \mathcal{L}(A_1)$ whose number of states is in $\Omega(n_0 \cdot tight(n_1 - 1))$ and $\mathcal{O}(n_0 \cdot tight(n_1 + 1))$.*

The language difference operation is based on the complementation operation: in order to get an automaton $A_{0\setminus 1}$ such that $\mathcal{L}(A_{0\setminus 1}) = \mathcal{L}(A_0) \setminus \mathcal{L}(A_1)$, it is enough to construct the automaton for the language $\mathcal{L}(A_0) \cap \mathcal{L}(A_1^C)$. Thus, the complexity result follows from Propositions 2 and 4.

Note that we can not improve the complexity of the language difference operation to be better than $\Omega(tight(n_1 - 1))$, since otherwise we would be able to improve the complexity of the complementation operation as well, since trivially we have that $\mathcal{L}(A_1^C) = \Sigma^\omega \setminus \mathcal{L}(A_1)$ where Σ^ω is the language of the BA A_0 having exactly one state, the initial state, being accepting with only self-loops as transitions, so in Proposition 8 we would have $n_0 = 1$.

3.5   Decision Problems on Büchi Automata

Besides the three main operations presented above, namely union, intersection, and complementation, there are three main decision problems relative to the languages of Büchi automata: emptiness, universality, and language inclusion.

Given a BA A, the emptiness problem is relative to decide whether $\mathcal{L}(A) = \emptyset$ while the universality problem refers to the equality $\mathcal{L}(A) = \Sigma^{\omega}$. Finally, the language inclusion problem requires to decide whether $\mathcal{L}(A_0) \subseteq \mathcal{L}(A_1)$ for the given BAs A_0 and A_1. These problems have different complexity results, which are summarized by the following propositions. The corresponding proofs can be found in the cited papers or in [32, Sect. 4.4].

Proposition 6 (cf. [40,41,93]). *Given a BA A, the emptiness problem $\mathcal{L}(A) = \emptyset$ is decidable in linear time and is NLOGSPACE-complete.*

The proof of the linear time complexity is based on finding a strongly connected component, i.e., a set of states each one reachable from each other, which is reachable from the initial state and contains a state in F. This can be easily done by a simple graph exploration based on depth-first visit. In theory, we can also nondeterministically find an accepting state and the accepting run of A visiting the accepting state infinitely often, which is in NLOGSPACE. In fact, it is enough to guess an accepting state $q_f \in F$ and two paths: a stem path from $\bar{q}$ to q_f and a lasso path from q_f to q_f itself, both of them with length at most $|Q|$. Clearly storing $q_f \in F$ requires a space that is logarithmic in $|Q|$; for the paths, it is enough to store the current state q and a counter cnt to keep track of the length of the path so far; both require logarithmic space.

The algorithm works as follows: initially, $q = \bar{q}$ and the following steps are repeated to find a stem path from $\bar{q}$ to q_f: (1) from q, a successor is chosen nondeterministically and cnt is increased; (2) if cnt exceeds $|Q|$, then "no" is returned; (3) if $q = q_f$ and $cnt \leq |Q|$, then the algorithm turns to look for a lasso path. Starting with $q = q_f$, the following steps are repeated to find a lasso path from q_f to q_f itself: (1) from q, a successor is chosen nondeterministically and cnt is increased; (2) if cnt exceeds $|Q|$, then "no" is returned; (3) if $q = q_f$ and $cnt \leq |Q|$, then "yes" is returned. We refer interested reader to [40,41,93] for the proof of the NLOGSPACE-hardness result.

Proposition 7 (cf. [93]). *Given a BA A, the universality problem $\mathcal{L}(A) = \Sigma^{\omega}$ is decidable in exponential time and is PSPACE-complete.*

The universality problem is decided by means of a reduction to the emptiness problem: in order to decide $\mathcal{L}(A) = \Sigma^{\omega}$, it is enough to check $\mathcal{L}(A^{\mathcal{C}}) = \emptyset$, where $A^{\mathcal{C}}$ is the complement BA of A. Since $A^{\mathcal{C}}$ is exponentially larger than A, the complexity results follow from Proposition 6.

Proposition 8 (cf. [93]). *Given two BAs A_0 and A_1, the language inclusion problem $\mathcal{L}(A_0) \subseteq \mathcal{L}(A_1)$ is decidable in exponential time and is PSPACE-complete.*

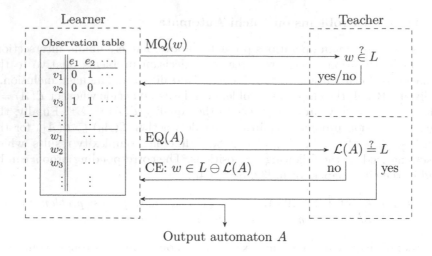

Fig. 2. DFA active automata learning framework

The language inclusion problem is decided by means of a reduction to the emptiness problem: in order to decide $\mathcal{L}(A_0) \subseteq \mathcal{L}(A_1)$, it is enough to check whether $\mathcal{L}(A_0) \cap \mathcal{L}(A_1^{\mathcal{C}}) = \emptyset$, where $A_1^{\mathcal{C}}$ is the complement BA of A_1. Since $A_1^{\mathcal{C}}$ is exponentially larger than A_1, the complexity results follow from Propositions 2 and 6.

4   Learning Finite Automata

In this section, we present a variant of the learning algorithm for finite automata used in [11]. In 1987, in her seminal work [8], Angluin proposed the L* algorithm to learn a DFA accepting a target regular language; L* belongs to the class of *active automata learning algorithms* [103], in which the learner can interact with an oracle until the correct automaton is constructed.

4.1   Overview of the DFA Learning Algorithm

As depicted in Fig. 2, in the active automata learning setting presented in [8], there is a *teacher* and a *learner*. The teacher knows the target language L which can be a regular language or an ω-regular language. The learner wants to learn the target language, represented by an automaton, from the teacher by means of two kinds of queries: *membership queries* and *equivalence queries*. A membership query $MQ(w)$ asks whether a word w belongs to L while an equivalence query $EQ(A)$ asks whether the conjectured automaton A accepts L. Depending on whether the conjectured automaton A is correct, the teacher replies with either "yes" or "no". In case of a positive answer, the learner outputs A and completes his job. For the negative answer, the teacher provides as well a witness $w \in L \ominus \mathcal{L}(A)$ which allows the learner to further refine the conjectured automaton A.

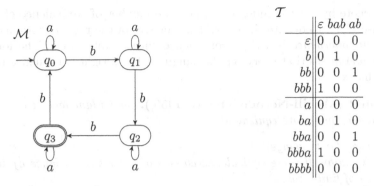

$$T$$

	ε	bab	ab
ε	0	0	0
b	0	1	0
bb	0	0	1
bbb	1	0	0
a	0	0	0
ba	0	1	0
bba	0	0	1
$bbba$	1	0	0
$bbbb$	0	0	0

$R = \{\, u \in \{a,b\}^+ \mid \text{the number of } b \text{ in } u \text{ is } 4n+3, \text{ for some } n \in \mathbb{N} \,\}$

Fig. 3. A DFA $\mathcal{M}$, its regular language R, and an observation table T for R

In this paper, the learner uses a data structure called *observation table* to store all answers to the membership queries, since it is easy to present and understand. We remark that observation tables have been originally adopted by Angluin for her L^* algorithm [8]. Instead of observation tables, the learner can use a tree-based data structure called *classification tree* to store such answers, which is usually more compact than observation tables; we refer the interested reader to [59, 63, 73] for the details on classification trees.

In the following, we play the role of the learner to learn a regular language represented by a DFA from a teacher. Regular language learning is actually a procedure for a learner to gradually identify the states in the minimal DFA $\mathcal{M}$ recognizing the target language. As an example, consider the regular language R accepted by the DFA $\mathcal{M}$ shown in Fig. 3, where $R = \{\, u \in \{a,b\}^+ \mid$ the number of b in u is $4n + 3$ for some $n \in \mathbb{N} \}$. We observe that for any pair of words $u_1, u_2 \in \{a,b\}^*$, $\mathcal{M}(q_0, u_1) \neq \mathcal{M}(q_0, u_2)$ if there exists some word $v \in \{a,b\}^*$ such that $\mathcal{M}(q_0, u_1 v) = q_3$ while $\mathcal{M}(q_0, u_2 v) \neq q_3$. That is, in the DFA $\mathcal{M}$, for any pair of words $u_1, u_2 \in \{a,b\}^*$, if there exists some word $v \in \{a,b\}^*$ such that $u_1 v \in \mathcal{L}(\mathcal{M})$ while $u_2 v \notin \mathcal{L}(\mathcal{M})$, then $\mathcal{M}(q_0, u_1)$ and $\mathcal{M}(q_0, u_2)$ must be two different states. Our goal is to develop a learner who can identify the states in the DFA $\mathcal{M}$; using such a word extension v to distinguish words u_1 and u_2 is a good means to identify two different states in $\mathcal{M}$.

4.2 Right Congruences and Myhill-Nerode Theorem

This idea of distinguishing words by extensions is formalized by the notion of *right congruence*. A right congruence is an equivalence relation $\backsim$ on Σ^* such that $x \backsim y$ implies $xv \backsim yv$ for every $x, y, v \in \Sigma^*$. The right congruence relation is the theoretical foundation for the DFA learning algorithms to discover the states in a target DFA $\mathcal{M}$.

We denote by $|\smallsmile|$ the index of $\smallsmile$, i.e., the number of equivalence classes of $\smallsmile$. We use $\Sigma^*/_\smallsmile$ to denote the equivalence classes of the right congruence $\smallsmile$. A *finite right congruence* is a right congruence with a finite index. The following theorem guarantees that every regular language has a right congruence relation of finite index.

Theorem 2 (Myhill-Nerode Theorem [56]**).** *For a language R over Σ, the following statements are equivalent:*

1. *R is a regular language.*
2. *R is the union of some equivalence classes of a right congruence equivalence relation of finite index.*
3. *The right congruence relation $\smallsmile_R$ is of finite index, where $x \smallsmile_R y$ if and only if for each $v \in \Sigma^*$, $xv \in R \iff yv \in R$.*

The theorem basically states that given a regular language R over Σ, the whole set of finite words Σ^* can be partitioned into a finite number of equivalence classes by the right congruence relation $\smallsmile_R$. For a word $u \in \Sigma^*$, we denote by $[u]_\smallsmile$ the equivalence class of the right congruence $\smallsmile$ u belongs to.

Given a right congruence relation $\smallsmile_R$ for the language R, we can construct an automaton accepting R by means of $\smallsmile_R$: as set of states Q, we just use the equivalence classes induced by $\smallsmile_R$; the initial state $\bar{q}$ is simply the class of the empty word ε; the transition relation just considers as the a-successor of the class of u the class of ua; finally, the accepting states F are the classes of the words in R.

Definition 2 (DFA induced by $\smallsmile_R$). *Given a right congruence relation $\smallsmile_R$ for the language R, the corresponding DFA $A_{\smallsmile_R}$ is the tuple $A_{\smallsmile_R} = (Q, \bar{q}, \delta, F)$ where*

- $Q = \Sigma^*/_{\smallsmile_R}$;
- $\bar{q} = [\varepsilon]_{\smallsmile_R}$;
- *for each $u \in \Sigma^*$ and $a \in \Sigma$, $\delta([u]_{\smallsmile_R}, a) = [ua]_{\smallsmile_R}$; and*
- $F = \{\, [u]_{\smallsmile_R} \in Q \mid u \in R \,\}$.

As an example, consider the regular language R shown in Fig. 3; we have four equivalence classes in $\Sigma^*/_{\smallsmile_R}$, namely $[\varepsilon]_{\smallsmile_R}$, $[b]_{\smallsmile_R}$, $[bb]_{\smallsmile_R}$, and $[bbb]_{\smallsmile_R}$, which intuitively correspond to how many b's have been seen so far, modulo 4; in particular, the regular language R is exactly the equivalence class $[bbb]_{\smallsmile_R}$. The automaton constructed from $\smallsmile_R$ is $\mathcal{M}$, whose states q_0, q_1, q_2, and q_3 represent the four equivalence classes $[\varepsilon]_{\smallsmile_R}$, $[b]_{\smallsmile_R}$, $[bb]_{\smallsmile_R}$, and $[bbb]_{\smallsmile_R}$, respectively.

We can use the word bab to distinguish the words in the equivalence class $[b]_{\smallsmile_R}$ from the words in the other three equivalence classes $[\varepsilon]_{\smallsmile_R}$, $[bb]_{\smallsmile_R}$, and $[bbb]_{\smallsmile_R}$. For instance, $\varepsilon \cdot bab \notin R$ while $b \cdot bab \in R$, hence $\varepsilon \not\smallsmile_R b$. One can check, as hinted by the column headers of the table in Fig. 3, that it is enough to use the word extensions ε, bab, and ab to distinguish the words from the four equivalence classes in $\Sigma^*/_{\smallsmile_R}$. We can use any other word as extension, as long as it distinguishes words: for instance, we could use $(aba)^{12}$ instead of ε

or $a(ababa)^{300}b$ instead of ab. Note however that longer extensions slow down the learning algorithm, whose complexity depends also on the length of the distinguishing words (cf. Theorem 4).

Assume that we want to design a learner to learn the regular language $R = \{\, u \in \{a, b\}^+ \mid$ the number of b in u is $4n+3$, for some $n \in \mathbb{N} \,\}$, i.e., to discover all states in the target automaton $\mathcal{M}$ as shown in Fig. 3. By Theorem 2, we know that the right congruence relation $\backsim_R$, by means of word extensions, can help us to distinguish the equivalence classes of Σ^* generating R, which intuitively correspond to the states of $\mathcal{M}$. However, we do not know R and we also do not know $\backsim_R$; in order to learn them, the idea is to ask for a few words whether they belong to R, and use the obtained information to conjecture a DFA which is supposed to accept R. Yet there are still several things we are missing:

1. How does an observation table organize the results of membership queries we have collected so far?
2. How can we build a DFA from an observation table correctly?
3. How can we update an observation table and discover new states from the returned counterexample if the conjectured DFA is incorrect?

The answers to the three questions are the key cornerstones of the DFA learning algorithm. In the following, we first show how an observation table organizes the results of membership queries. Then we show how to build a DFA from an observation table. Afterwards we explain how to analyze a returned counterexample to update an observation table so to discover new states in target DFA $\mathcal{M}$. At last, we present our DFA learner for regular languages.

4.3 Observation Tables

An observation table is a tuple $\mathcal{T} = (U, V, T)$ where U is a prefix-closed set of words called *access strings*, V is a set of words called *experiments*, and $T\colon (U \cup U\Sigma)V \to \{0, 1\}$ is a total mapping.

As the name suggests, an observation table $\mathcal{T}$ is represented by a table, where rows and columns are labelled with words taken from $U \cup U\Sigma$ and V, respectively, and the table entries are the value assigned by T to them. Consider for instance the observation table $\mathcal{T} = (U, V, T)$ shown in Fig. 3; the labels of the four rows in the upper part of the table correspond to the set $U = \{\varepsilon, b, bb, bbb\}$; the labels of the five rows in the bottom part of the table are those in $U\Sigma \setminus U$, so $U \cup U\Sigma$ is exactly the set of labels of the rows of the table; the labels of the three columns in the table correspond to the set $V = \{\varepsilon, bab, ab\}$. The entry value of row u and column v represents the value assigned by $T(\cdot)$ to the word uv, i.e., $T(uv)$; such a value is 1 if $uv \in R$ and 0 otherwise. As depicted in Fig. 3, the entry value of row b and column bab is $T(bbab) = 1$ since $b \cdot bab \in R$, while the entry value of row b and column ab is $T(bab) = 0$ since $b \cdot ab \notin R$.

Given an observation table for a language R with right congruence $\backsim_R$, like the one in Fig. 3, we can see that every equivalence class $[u]_{\backsim_R}$ of $\Sigma^*/_{\backsim_R}$ has a representative word u in U. Therefore we also use the representative word such as ε to represent the equivalence class $[\varepsilon]_{\sim_R}$. A word in V is a word extension or experiment used to distinguish the words belonging to different equivalence classes. For instance, consider the column ab in Fig. 3: the entry value at row ε is 0 while the entry value at row bb is 1, which indicates that the words from those two equivalence classes can be distinguished by the word ab. Hence any two rows with different entry values in the table are classified to be different equivalence classes while any two rows with the same entry values are seen as one equivalence class. For instance, in Fig. 3, row b in the upper table and row ba in the lower table are seen as one equivalence class since they have the same entry values for each experiment.

We remark that those rows which are currently seen as one equivalence class may later be classified into different equivalence classes, as result of a counterexample returned by the teacher.

The domain of the mapping T also contains the set $U\Sigma$, i.e., there are also some rows labelled by the words from $U\Sigma$ in the table. The existence of this set $U\Sigma$ of rows in the table makes it possible for the learner to look for the next equivalence class or the successor state $[ua]_{\sim_R}$ in the DFA construction after reading a letter $a \in \Sigma$ at the equivalence class or state $[u]_{\sim_R}$, where $u \in U$. For example, suppose that we want to compute the a-successor of state ε in Fig. 3: the expected successor is $\varepsilon \cdot a$. In order to find its actual representative, we first look for the row $\varepsilon \cdot a$ in the table and then get the successor state $\varepsilon \in U$ which has the same entry values as row $\varepsilon \cdot a$. From the table we see that the row $\varepsilon \cdot a = a$ has entry values 000; the same entry values occur for the row $\varepsilon \in U$, thus the a-successor of ε is ε itself.

In order to efficiently check whether two rows represent the same equivalence class, we formally define the rows as the total function $row\colon (U \cup U\Sigma) \to (V \to \{0,1\})$. To a word $u \in U \cup U\Sigma$ we assign a total function $row(u)\colon V \to \{0,1\}$ such that $row(u)(v) = T(uv)$ for each $v \in V$. We call such a function a row of T and we denote by $Rows(T)$ the set of rows of T; similarly, we denote by $Rows_{upp}(T) = \{\, row(u) \mid u \in U \,\}$ the set of rows in the "upper" part of the table and $Rows_{low}(T) = \{\, row(u) \mid u \in U\Sigma \setminus U \,\}$ the set of rows appearing in the "lower" part. Consider again the observation table in Fig. 3: we have $Rows_{low}(T) = \{row(a), row(ba), row(bba), row(bbba), row(bbbb)\}$, where, e.g., $row(a)$ is the constant function $row(a)(v) = 0$ for each $v \in V$. In practice, we can identify each function $row(u)\colon V \to \{0,1\}$ with the content of T in the row labelled by u.

In the learning framework depicted in Fig. 2, the learner can ask the teacher two types of queries, namely, membership and equivalence queries. In order to pose an equivalence query, the learner has to generate a DFA from the information stored in the observation table, which has to contain all information that is needed to build such a DFA. As Angluin proposed in [8], a table has such a needed information when it is *closed* and *consistent*.

A table T is *closed* if for any $u \in U$ and $a \in \Sigma$, there exists $u' \in U$ such that $row(ua) = row(u')$; similarly, a table is *consistent* if for any $u_1, u_2 \in U$ and $a \in \Sigma$, $row(u_1) = row(u_2)$ implies $row(u_1 a) = row(u_2 a)$. Intuitively, the

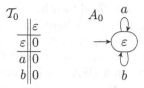

Fig. 4. Table T_0 and DFA A_0

closeness of a table makes sure that every successor of a state is in the set of discovered states while the consistency of a table ensures that those words which have been classified into the same equivalence class should behave consistently, i.e., they have the same successor equivalence classes, when extended with the same letter.

We now present how the learner proceeds in the learning algorithm to learn the target language R represented by a DFA. Let the alphabet be $\Sigma = \{a, b\}$. At the beginning, the learner has no information, so he initializes both U and V to $\{\varepsilon\}$ and defines $T(uv)$ for every $u \in U \cup U\Sigma$ and $v \in V$ according to the results of membership queries, that is, he asks the teacher the membership queries $MQ(\varepsilon)$, $MQ(a)$, and $MQ(b)$; the teacher answers "no" to all of them, so the learner sets $T(\cdot)$ to be the constant function 0. The result is shown as T_0 in Fig. 4. Since T_0 is closed and consistent, we can build the DFA A_0, also depicted in Fig. 4, according to Definition 3.

In case the current T is not closed, the learner makes it closed by repeatedly updating T as follows: he looks for a word $u \in U\Sigma$ such that there is no $u' \in U$ with $row(u) = row(u')$; then moves u to U and for every $a \in \Sigma$, he adds ua to $U\Sigma$ whenever needed while setting $T(uav)$ for each $v \in V$ by means of membership queries. According to [11], whenever T is closed, it is also consistent since by construction there do not exist $u_1, u_2 \in U$, $u_1 \neq u_2$, with $row(u_1) = row(u_2)$.

Instead of moving a single word u from $U\Sigma$ to U when T is not closed, the learner can also add all its prefixes $Pref(u)$ to U just as the L^* algorithm does in [8]. This may result in a quicker growth of T, which anyway does not change the correctness (cf. Theorem 3) and complexity (cf. Theorem 4) of the DFA learning algorithm.

4.4   DFA Construction from an Observation Table

Definition 3 answers the second question about how to build a conjecture DFA A from an observation table correctly.

Definition 3 (DFA of a Table). *Let T be a closed and consistent observation table. We can construct a DFA $A = (Q, \bar{q}, \delta, F)$ from T as follows.*

- $Q = Rows_{upp}(T) = \{row(u) \mid u \in U\}$,
- $\bar{q} = row(\varepsilon)$,
- $\delta(row(u), a) = row(ua)$, *and*
- $F = \{ row(u) \in Rows_{upp}(T) \mid row(u)(\varepsilon) = 1 \}$.

Consider the observation table $\mathcal{T}_0$ shown in Fig. 4. The learner can construct from $\mathcal{T}_0$ the DFA $A_0 = (Q_0, \bar{q}, \delta_0, F_0)$ where $Q_0 = \{row(\varepsilon) = 0\}$, $\bar{q} = row(\varepsilon)$, $F_0 = \emptyset$, and δ_0 as depicted in Fig. 4. Note that in the whole paper we use the representative words $u \in U$ instead of the row functions $row(u)$ defined in Definition 3 to mark the states in a DFA; for instance, we mark the single state of A_0 with the representative word ε instead of the row function $row(\varepsilon)$. In this way, it is easier for the reader to relate the equivalence classes to the states in the conjectured automaton.

Now the conjectured DFA A_0 is constructed and the learner can pose the equivalence query $\mathrm{EQ}(A_0)$ to the teacher. A_0 is clearly not the right conjecture, so the teacher answers "no" together with a counterexample, say $bbab \in \mathcal{L}(\mathcal{M}) \ominus \mathcal{L}(A_0)$. In the following we provide the answer to the third question, that is, how to update the observation table from the received counterexample.

4.5 Counterexample Analysis

On receiving the counterexample w, the learner has to analyze w in order to update the observation table; this would then allow the learner to expand the conjectured DFA by adding new states to correctly classify the received counterexample. To discover new states in $\mathcal{M}$, we essentially need new experiments for the table; the following lemma provides a way to find such new experiments.

Lemma 1. *Let R be the target language and A be the conjectured DFA. On receiving a counterexample $v \in R \ominus \mathcal{L}(A)$, we can always find an experiment $v' \in Suf(v)$, words $u, u' \in U$, and letter $a \in \Sigma$ such that $row(ua) = row(u')$ and $uav' \in R \iff u'v' \notin R$.*

As a notation, we use $\mathrm{MQ}(s, w)$ to denote the membership query $\mathrm{MQ}(s \cdot w)$ in order to give a clear presentation of the analysis procedure on the returned counterexample v as explained in the following. On receiving a counterexample $v \in R$ and $v \notin \mathcal{L}(A)$, the learner can check whether the membership queries return different results for v and $\tilde{v}$ where $\tilde{v} = A(v)$. Let $n = |v|$ and for $i \in [1 \cdots n]$, let $s_i = A(v[1..i])$ be the state reached after reading the first i letters of v. Recall that $s_i \in U$ is the representative word of that state in the upper part of the observation table. In particular, $s_0 = \varepsilon$. Therefore, $\tilde{v} = s_n$ and there is a sequence of membership queries $\mathrm{MQ}(s_0, v[1..n] = v)$, $\mathrm{MQ}(s_1, v[2..n])$, $\mathrm{MQ}(s_2, v[3..n])$, and so on, up to $\mathrm{MQ}(s_n, \varepsilon) = \mathrm{MQ}(\tilde{v}, \varepsilon)$. This sequence has different results for the first and the last query since $s_0 \cdot v \in R$ while $\tilde{v} \cdot \varepsilon \notin R$ by the assumption. It follows that there exists an experiment $v[i+1..n]$ for the earliest $1 \le i \le n$ distinguishing $s_{i-1}a'$ from s_i. Let $u = s_{i-1}$, $u' = s_i$, $a = a'$, and $v' = v[i+1..n]$. According to Definition 3, we have $row(ua) = row(u')$ since $A(s_{i-1}a) = A(ua) = u' = s_i$ and $uav' \in R$ while $u'v' \notin R$. The handling for the other case when $v \notin R$ and $v \in \mathcal{L}(A)$ is symmetric.

According to Lemma 1, on receiving a counterexample $bbab \in R \ominus \mathcal{L}(A_0)$, the learner poses a sequence of membership queries $\mathrm{MQ}(s_0 = \varepsilon, bbab)$, $\mathrm{MQ}(s_1 =$

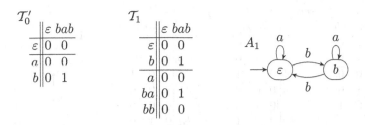

T_0'

	ε	bab
ε	0	0
a	0	0
b	0	1

T_1

	ε	bab
ε	0	0
b	0	1
a	0	0
ba	0	1
bb	0	0

Fig. 5. Tables T_0', T_1, and DFA A_1

ε, bab), MQ($s_2 = \varepsilon, ab$), MQ($s_3 = \varepsilon, b$), and MQ($s_4 = \varepsilon, \varepsilon$); it is easy to check that the experiment $v[2..4] = bab$ distinguishes $s_0 b = b$ from $s_1 = \varepsilon$. Therefore, the learner adds bab into the set V and updates the mapping T via membership queries, until obtaining the observation table T_0' shown in Fig. 5. As T_0' is not closed since there is no $u \in U$ such that $row(u) = row(b)$, the learner moves the row b to the upper table, i.e., to the set U, and adds the rows ba and bb—the one letter extensions of b—to the lower part of the table as mentioned before. The learner then fills the missing entry values by means of membership queries; the resulting observation table is T_1 shown in Fig. 5. As T_1 is closed and also consistent, the learner can build the DFA A_1 from T_1, depicted in Fig. 5.

We remark that instead of finding just one experiment $v' \in \text{Suf}(v)$, our learner may also add all its suffixes $\text{Suf}(v)$ into V just as the algorithm does in [76]. This may also result in a quicker grown of T, which anyway does not change the correctness (cf. Theorem 3) and complexity (cf. Theorem 4) of the DFA learning algorithm we are presenting.

The learner poses now the equivalence query EQ(A_1) to the teacher; since $\mathcal{L}(A_1) \neq R$, the teacher returns "no" and a counterexample, say again $bbab \in \mathcal{L}(\mathcal{M}) \ominus \mathcal{L}(A_1)$. Similarly to the previous counterexample analysis, the learner asks the sequence of membership queries MQ($s_0 = \varepsilon, bbab$), MQ($s_1 = b, bab$), MQ($s_2 = \varepsilon, ab$), MQ($s_3 = \varepsilon, b$), and MQ($s_4 = \varepsilon, \varepsilon$), which allows the learner to find the experiment $w[3..4] = ab$ to distinguish $s_1 b = bb$ from $s_2 = \varepsilon$. The learner adds ab into the set V and updates T by further membership queries, resulting in the observation table T_1' shown in Fig. 6.

T_1' is not closed, since there is no row in the upper part corresponding to $row(bb)$, so the learner moves bb to the upper part, adds bba and bbb to the lower part, and fills the content of the table by means of membership queries. The result of these operations is table T_1'' which is still not closed since there does not exist $u \in U$ such that $row(bbb) = row(u)$. Therefore, as before, the learner moves bbb to the upper part, adds the missing words $bbba$ and $bbbb$ to the lower part, and fills the content, obtaining the table T_2 depicted in Fig. 6, which is now closed. The DFA A_2 constructed from T_2 is depicted in Fig. 6 and the learner gets the answer "yes" from the teacher after posing the equivalence query EQ(A_2), which means that he has completed his learning task.

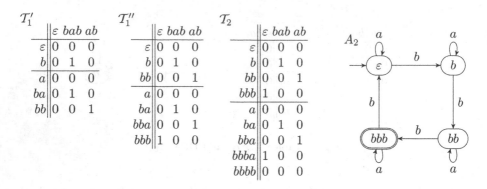

Fig. 6. Tables T_1', T_1'', T_2, and DFA A_2

Algorithm 1. The DFA Learner

---

1 Initialize table $T = (T, U, V)$ with $U = \{\varepsilon\}$ and $V = \{\varepsilon\}$;
2 $CloseTable(T, MQ(\cdot))$ and let $A = Aut(T)$;
3 Let (a, v) be the teacher's response on EQ(A);
4 **while** $a = $ *"no"* **do**
5 | $V = V \cup FindDistinguishingExperiment(v)$;
6 | $CloseTable(T, MQ(\cdot))$ and let $A = Aut(T)$;
7 | Let (a, v) be the teacher's response on EQ(A);
8 **return** A;

4.6 The Learner

In the previous part of this section we have introduced a regular language learning algorithm by means of a running example. We now give the formal definition of the learner by means of Algorithm 1 for completeness of presentation; we can see that it agrees with the learning procedure we presented above. The function *CloseTable* is responsible for closing a table T, so it needs to perform membership queries MQ$(\cdot)$ to fill the missing entry values in T. Moreover, as we have seen, it may repeatedly move rows from the lower to the upper part of the input table and add new rows to the lower part, until the table becomes closed. All conjectured DFAs are constructed from the table T by calling the function $Aut(T)$ based on Definition 3. On receiving a counterexample v, the function *FindDistinguishingExperiment*(v) gets a new experiment which is later added into the set V. The refinement loop of the conjecture A terminates once we get a positive answer from the teacher.

The soundness and completeness of Algorithm 1 is guaranteed by Theorem 3.

Theorem 3. *Assume that R is the target regular language. Algorithm 1 terminates and returns a DFA A such that $\mathcal{L}(A) = R$.*

The returned DFA A from Algorithm 1 is a correct conjecture automaton simply because the teacher has approved it. The remaining problem is how we show the termination of Algorithm 1. The reason why Algorithm 1 terminates is that: (1) by Lemma 1, we can discover new states, i.e., new equivalence classes in $\Sigma^*/_{\backsim_R}$, whenever receiving a counterexample from the teacher and (2) the index of $\backsim_R$ is finite according to Theorem 2. It follows immediately the complexity result in Theorem 4.

Theorem 4. *Let R be the target regular language and $n = |\backsim_R|$; let m be the maximum length of any counterexample returned by the teacher.*

1. *Algorithm 1 terminates on receiving at most n counterexamples.*
2. *The number of membership queries is in $\mathcal{O}(n^2 \cdot |\Sigma| + n \cdot m)$.*

5   Learning Büchi Automata

After presenting the DFA learning algorithm in Sect. 4, we are now ready to introduce the learning algorithm for Büchi automata. Throughout this section, except stated otherwise, we let the ω-regular language L be the target language.

We have seen that, for learning a regular language R, the right congruence relation $\backsim_R$ plays an important role in identifying the equivalence classes in $\Sigma^*/_{\backsim_R}$, so we could consider to extend such an approach to the ω-regular language setting. It would be easy to learn ω-regular languages by means of BAs if we can characterize them by a right congruence relation $\backsim_L$ of finite index for each given ω-regular language L. There are, however, few questions to be answered for such an extension:

- How can we use finite memory to represent an ω-word, which has infinite length?
- Is there a right congruence relation $\backsim_L$ of finite index for a given ω-regular language L?

The answer to the first question is easy: we only need to learn the set of ultimately periodic words UP(L) for a given ω-regular language L, since by Theorem 1 the set UP(L) is the fingerprint of L; given that every ultimately periodic word w can be written as a pair of finite words (u, v) with $w = uv^\omega$, only finite memory is needed for storing w.

5.1   Right Congruences for ω-Regular Languages

In contrast, the answer to the second question is more tricky: a first proposal for extending the right congruence relation $\backsim_R$ with respect to the ω-regular language L replaces the extension $v \in \Sigma^*$ with the ultimately periodic extension xy^ω for $x \in \Sigma^*$ and $y \in \Sigma^+$.

Definition 4. *Let u_1 and u_2 be words in Σ^*. $u_1 \backsim_L u_2$ if and only if for every $x \in \Sigma^*$ and $y \in \Sigma^+$, $u_1xy^\omega \in L \iff u_2xy^\omega \in L$.*

Based on the right congruence $\backsim_L$, Maler and Pnueli [76] introduced a learning algorithm to learn a strict subset of ω-regular languages. Nonetheless, the right congruence relation $\backsim_L$ is in general not enough to learn an ω-regular language L, as the following example shows.

Example 2. Assume $L = \{a, b\}^* \cdot b^\omega$. The index of $\backsim_L$ is 1 and the only equivalence class is $[\varepsilon]_{\backsim_L}$. This follows from the fact that for any $u \in \Sigma^*$, we have $u \cdot xy^\omega \in L$ if $y^\omega = b^\omega$, otherwise $u \cdot xy^\omega \notin L$. Therefore, we only have one state with self-loops in the conjectured BA A which certainly does not recognize the target language L, since A accepts either Σ^ω or $\emptyset$, depending on whether the single state is accepting or not, respectively.

The reason why it is so difficult to learn ω-regular languages via Büchi automata is that there is a lack of right congruence for Büchi automata compared to DFAs and regular languages. Farzan *et al.* in [42] proposed the first learning algorithm to learn the complete class of ω-regular languages by means of Büchi automata; their algorithm circumvents the lack of right congruence by first using L^* to learn the DFA $D_\$$, as defined in [26], and then transforming $D_\$$ to a BA. Basically, the DFA $D_\$$ captures the set of ultimately periodic words of L by means of the regular language $\mathcal{L}(D_\$) = \{ u\$v \mid u \in \Sigma^*, v \in \Sigma^+, uv^\omega \in L \}$, where $\$ \notin \Sigma$.

Another way to solve the lack of right congruence is to define a Myhill-Nerode like theorem for ω-regular languages. Inspired by the work of Arnold [12], Maler and Staiger [77] proposed the notion of *family of right-congruences* (FORC for short) and presented a "Myhill-Nerode" theorem for ω-languages. The idea underlying the definition of FORC is based on the fact that every ω-regular language L can be written in the form of an ω-regular expression $\bigcup_{i=1}^n U_i \cdot V_i^\omega$ for some $n \in \mathbb{N}$, where for any $i \in [1 \cdots n]$, U_i and V_i are regular languages. So the intuition of using FORC is to first define a right congruence $\backsim$ to distinguish all finite word prefixes, and then define a right congruence $\approx_u$ for the finite word periods for each equivalence class $[u]_\backsim$ of the finite word prefixes. Hence we see that $[u_i]_\backsim = U_i$ with $u_i \in U_i$ being an equivalence class in $\Sigma^*/_\backsim$ and $[v_i]_{\approx_{u_i}} = V_i$ being an equivalence class in $\Sigma^*/_{\approx_{u_i}}$ such that $u_i \cdot V_i^\omega \subseteq L$.

5.2 Family of Deterministic Finite Automata

Based on this idea of FORC, Angluin and Fisman [11] recently proposed to learn ω-regular languages via a formalism called *family of DFAs* (FDFA for short), in which every DFA corresponds to a right congruence of finite index. Further, Angluin *et al.* [9] suggest to use FDFAs as language acceptors of ω-regular languages. The BA learning algorithm described in this section first learns an FDFA and then transforms it to a BA. The formal definition of an FDFA is as follows.

Definition 5 (Family of DFAs [9]). *A family of DFAs $\mathcal{F} = (M, \{A^q\})$ consists of a leading DFA $M = (Q, \bar{q}, \delta, \emptyset)$ and a set of progress DFAs $\{ A^q = (Q_q, \bar{q}_q, \delta_q, F_q) \mid q \in Q \}$.*

Fig. 7. An example of an FDFA $\mathcal{F} = (M, \{A^\varepsilon\})$

An example of FDFA $\mathcal{F}$ is depicted in Fig. 7 where the leading DFA M has only one state ε and the progress DFA corresponding to the state ε is A^ε.

Each FDFA $\mathcal{F}$ characterizes a set of ultimately periodic words $\text{UP}(\mathcal{F})$ by the acceptance condition defined as follows.

Definition 6 (Acceptance condition of FDFA). *Let $\mathcal{F} = (M, \{A^q\})$ be a FDFA and w be an ultimately periodic word. We say that*

- *w is accepted by $\mathcal{F}$ if there exists a decomposition (u, v) of w accepted by $\mathcal{F}$;*
- *a decomposition (u, v) is accepted by $\mathcal{F}$ if $M(uv) = M(u)$ and the decomposition (u, v) is captured by $\mathcal{F}$; and*
- *a decomposition (u, v) is captured by $\mathcal{F}$ if $v \in \mathcal{L}(A^q)$ where $q = M(u)$.*

Consider the FDFA $\mathcal{F}$ in Fig. 7: $(ab)^\omega$ is accepted by $\mathcal{F}$ since there exists the decomposition (a, ba) of $(ab)^\omega$ such that $M(a \cdot ba) = M(a) = \varepsilon$ and $ba \in \mathcal{L}(A^{M(a)}) = \mathcal{L}(A^\varepsilon)$. Note that the decomposition (ab, ab) of $(ab)^\omega$ is not accepted by $\mathcal{F}$ since (ab, ab) is not captured by $\mathcal{F}$, i.e., $ab \notin \mathcal{L}(A^{M(ab)}) = \mathcal{L}(A^\varepsilon)$.

In the following, we recall the definition of the complement of an FDFA $\mathcal{F}$.

Definition 7 (Complement of FDFA [9]). *Given an FDFA $\mathcal{F} = (M, \{A^q\})$, the complement $\mathcal{F}^C$ of $\mathcal{F}$ is the FDFA $\mathcal{F}^C = (M, \{(A^q)^C\})$.*

It is easy to see that the complement FDFA $\mathcal{F}^C$ captures every decomposition (u, v) in $\Sigma^* \times \Sigma^+$ which is not captured by $\mathcal{F}$.

It is shown in [11] that for every ω-regular language L, there exists an FDFA $\mathcal{F}$ such that $\text{UP}(\mathcal{F}) = \text{UP}(L)$. More precisely, Angluin and Fisman [11] suggest to use three kinds of FDFAs as canonical representations of ω-regular languages, namely *periodic FDFAs*, *syntactic FDFAs*, and *recurrent FDFAs*. In this work, we only consider the periodic FDFAs to simplify the presentation of the BA learning algorithm; we refer the interested reader to [11,73] for more details on the other two canonical FDFAs.

The definition of periodic FDFAs provided in [11] is given in terms of right congruences.

Definition 8 (Periodic FDFA [11]). *Let L be an ω-regular language.*

Given $u \in \Sigma^*$, the periodic right congruence $\approx_P^u$ is an equivalence relation on Σ^* such that for each $x, y \in \Sigma^*$, $x \approx_P^u y$ if and only if for each $v \in \Sigma^*$, it holds $u(xv)^\omega \in L \iff u(yv)^\omega \in L$.

The periodic FDFA $\mathcal{F}$ of L is the FDFA $\mathcal{F} = (M, \{A^u\})$ where:

- *the DFA $M = (\Sigma^*/_{\backsim_L}, [\varepsilon]_{\backsim_L}, \delta, \emptyset)$ is the leading DFA, where $\delta([u]_{\backsim_L}, a) = [ua]_{\backsim_L}$ for each $u \in \Sigma^*$ and $a \in \Sigma$;*

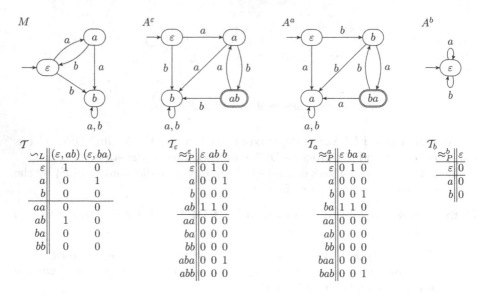

Fig. 8. A periodic FDFA $\mathcal{F} = (M, \{A^\varepsilon, A^a, A^b\})$ with $\mathrm{UP}(\mathcal{F}) = (ab)^\omega$

– for each $[u]_{\frown_L} \in \Sigma^*/_{\frown_L}$, the DFA $A^u = (\Sigma^*/_{\approx_P^u}, [\varepsilon]_{\approx_P^u}, \delta_u, F_u)$ is a progress DFA, where $\delta_u([v]_{\approx_P^u}, a) = [va]_{\approx_P^u}$ for each $v \in \Sigma^*$ and $a \in \Sigma$, and $F_u = \{[v]_{\approx_P^u} \in \Sigma^*/_{\approx_P^u} \mid uv^\omega \in L\}$.

As shown in [11], given an ω-regular language L, $\frown_L$ and $\approx_P^u$ for any $u \in \Sigma^*$ are all right congruences of finite index, so DFAs can be built from them.

We remark that the set of ultimately periodic words $\mathrm{UP}(\mathcal{F})$ accepted by the periodic FDFA $\mathcal{F}$ is consistent with those characterized by the regular language $\mathcal{L}(D_\$)$ defined in [26].

Consider the periodic FDFA $\mathcal{F}$ depicted in Fig. 8 where $\mathcal{F}$ characterizes the ω-regular language $L = (ab)^\omega$. The leading DFA M of $\mathcal{F}$ has three states, namely ε, a, and b which correspond to the equivalence classes $[\varepsilon]_{\frown_L}$, $[a]_{\frown_L}$, and $[b]_{\frown_L}$, respectively, given by the upper part U of $\mathcal{T}$. The set of experiments V contains decompositions of ultimately periodic words, which play the role of x and y in Definition 4 introducing $\frown_L$. As shown in table $\mathcal{T}$ for M, the experiments (ε, ab) and (ε, ba) are enough to distinguish the equivalence classes in $\Sigma^*/_{\frown_L}$. In fact, for any $u_1, u_2 \in \Sigma^*$, an experiment xy^ω for which $xy^\omega \neq ((ab)^+)^\omega$ and $xy^\omega \neq ((ba)^+)^\omega$ cannot distinguish u_1 and u_2, since for sure we have $u_1 \cdot xy^\omega \notin L$ and $u_2 \cdot xy^\omega \notin L$. Since the leading DFA has three states ε, a, and b, there are three progress DFAs in $\mathcal{F}$ associated to them, namely A^ε, A^a, and A^b, respectively.

In the following, we show how the periodic FDFA $\mathcal{F}$ corresponds to the ω-regular expression $\varepsilon(ab)^* \cdot ((ab)^+)^\omega \cup a(ba)^* \cdot ((ba)^+)^\omega \cup \{b, a(ba)^*a\}\{a, b\}^* \cdot \emptyset$, where for clarity of presentation we use $\cup$ instead of the usual symbol $+$ to distinguish the different ω-regular expressions.

Let us consider the first part of the ω-regular expression, i.e., $\varepsilon(ab)^* \cdot ((ab)^+)^\omega$, which corresponds to the state ε of M and its progress DFA A^ε, whose language is clearly $\mathcal{L}(A^\varepsilon) = (ab)^+$. Let the components of M be $(Q, \varepsilon, \delta, \emptyset)$ and consider the DFA $M^\varepsilon = (Q, \varepsilon, \delta, \{\varepsilon\})$ obtained by setting the accepting set of M to $\{\varepsilon\}$. It is easy to see that $\mathcal{L}(M^\varepsilon) = \varepsilon(ab)^*$. Let $U_1 = \mathcal{L}(M^\varepsilon) = \varepsilon(ab)^*$ and $V_1 = \mathcal{L}(A^\varepsilon) = (ab)^+$. It follows that the expression $U_1 \cdot V_1^\omega$ is exactly $\varepsilon(ab)^* \cdot ((ab)^+)^\omega$. Similarly we can get the other two ω-regular expressions $a(ba)^* \cdot ((ba)^+)^\omega$ and $\{b, a(ba)^*a\}\{a,b\}^* \cdot \emptyset$ from the remaining two states a and b of M and their corresponding progress DFAs A^a and A^b, respectively. Note that $\varepsilon(ab)^* \cdot ((ab)^+)^\omega \cup a(ba)^* \cdot ((ba)^+)^\omega \cup \{b, a(ba)^*a\}\{a,b\}^* \cdot \emptyset = (ab)^\omega$, that is, the induced ω-regular expression corresponds to the language accepted by $\mathcal{F}$. In general, we can construct from the periodic FDFA $\mathcal{F}$ accepting L a unique ω-regular expression representing L.

We remark that by fixing a state of M, say state ε, the right congruence $\approx_P^\varepsilon$ is actually the same as the right congruence $\backsim_R$ for the regular language $R = V_1$. Recall that the idea underlying FORC is to first define a right congruence $\backsim$ distinguishing all finite word prefixes, and then define, for each equivalence class $[u]_\backsim$ of the finite word prefixes, a right congruence $\approx_u$ for the finite word periods. Thus after fixing the equivalence class $[\varepsilon]_{\backsim_L}$ for the finite word prefixes of L, we can define the right congruence $\backsim_R$ for the regular language $R = V_1$ of finite word periods defined as $\{ v \in \{a,b\}^+ \mid \varepsilon \cdot v^\omega \in L \}$ and call it $\approx_P^\varepsilon$. These right congruences allow for the development of a learning algorithm for ω-regular languages represented by FDFAs, where the FDFA learner can be seen as a procedure to simultaneously run an instance of the DFA learner for each DFA in the FDFA. In the remaining part of this section we first introduce a periodic FDFA learner and then present the learning algorithm for BAs.

5.3 Learning a Family of DFAs

In order to present the periodic FDFA learner, we need first introduce the observation tables for each internal DFA learner. In this work, we often use FDFA learner as a shorthand for the periodic FDFA learner since we only consider periodic FDFAs. We remark that the FDFA learner introduced in this section is specialized for the periodic FDFAs which differs from the FDFA learner specified in [11,73] by requiring the received counterexamples satisfying Definition 9.

Observation Tables for a Family of DFAs. An observation table $\mathcal{T}$ for the leading DFA learner, called *leading table*, has the same structure (U, V, T) as the one for the DFA learner presented in Sect. 4.3 except that T and V are adapted to handle ω-regular words: V is a set of decompositions rather than a set of finite words; $T: (U \cup U\Sigma)V \rightarrow \{0,1\}$ is still a mapping but the entry value of row u and column (x,y), denoted by $T(u,(x,y))$, is 1 if $uxy^\omega \in L$ and 0 otherwise. Consider for instance the leading table $\mathcal{T}$ shown in Fig. 8: we have that $V = \{(\varepsilon, ab), (\varepsilon, ba)\}$ is the set of experiments and $T(a, (\varepsilon, ab)) = 0$ since $a \cdot \varepsilon \cdot (ab)^\omega \notin L$ while $T(a, (\varepsilon, ba)) = 1$ since $a \cdot \varepsilon \cdot (ba)^\omega \in L$. The *row* function

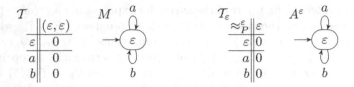

Fig. 9. The initial FDFA $\mathcal{F}_0$ and its corresponding tables while learning $(ab)^\omega$

remains unchanged, thus we still have $row\colon (U \cup U\Sigma) \to (V \to \{0,1\})$ being a total function such that for each word $u \in U \cup U\Sigma$, $row(u)\colon V \to \{0,1\}$ is a total function defined as $row(u)(x,y) = T(u,(x,y))$ for each $(x,y) \in V$.

For every $u \in U$ of the leading table T, there exists an observation table T_u for the progress DFA learner called *progress table*. T_u has the same structure (U_u, V_u, T_u) as the one for the DFA learner (cf. Sect. 4.3) except that the entry value of row x and column v, denoted by $T_u(x,v)$, is 1 if $u \cdot (xv)^\omega \in L$ and 0 otherwise. Consider for instance the table T_a shown in Fig. 8: $T_a(\varepsilon, ba) = 1$ since $a \cdot (\varepsilon ba)^\omega \in L$ while $T_a(\varepsilon, a) = 0$ since $a \cdot (\varepsilon a)^\omega \notin L$.

Unless stated otherwise, all remaining notions for the table of a DFA learner can be also directly applied to the leading table and progress tables, such as the DFA construction from a table and the closeness and consistency of a table.

The Learning Procedure of the FDFA Learner. After the introduction of the observation tables for the FDFA learner, we are now ready to give the intuition about how the FDFA learner works by learning the ω-regular language $L = (ab)^\omega$ over $\Sigma = \{a,b\}$.

As for the DFA learner, at the beginning the FDFA learner has no information so he initializes the components U and V of the leading table T to $\{\varepsilon\}$ and $\{(\varepsilon, \varepsilon)\}$, respectively. Then he turns to fill the content of T, so for each $u \in U \cup U\Sigma$ and $(x,y) \in V$, he makes a membership query $\mathrm{MQ}(u \cdot x, y)$ whose answer is stored as $T(u,(x,y))$; the membership query $\mathrm{MQ}(f,g)$ is used to asks the FDFA teacher whether the word fg^ω belongs to L.

Once T is fully defined, the learner checks whether T is closed; if it is not closed, he repeatedly moves rows from the lower part to the upper part, adds the new rows in $U\Sigma$ as needed, and fills T, as done by the DFA learner (see Sect. 4.3), until T becomes closed.

As soon as T is closed, the learner constructs the corresponding leading DFA M and then turns to the progress tables: for each $u \in U$ of T, he first creates a progress table T_u and then initializes both U_u and V_u to $\{\varepsilon\}$. For every $x \in U_u \cup U_u\Sigma$ and $v \in V_u$, $T_u(x,v)$ is defined according to the result of the membership query $\mathrm{MQ}(u, xy)$. Then the learner makes sure that each progress table T_u is closed before constructing the corresponding progress DFA A^u. Once all DFAs are constructed, he is ready to pose the first equivalence query $\mathrm{EQ}(\mathcal{F}_0)$ for the conjectured $\mathcal{F}_0$ to the FDFA teacher; $\mathcal{F}_0$ is shown in Fig. 9 together with its corresponding tables.

On receiving $EQ(\mathcal{F})$, the teacher has to decide whether the conjectured FDFA $\mathcal{F}$ is an appropriate periodic FDFA of the target language L. $\mathcal{F}_0 = (M, \{A^\varepsilon\})$ is clearly not the right conjecture so she answers "no" and provides a counterexample, say the decomposition (ε, ab). Note that the counterexample (x, y) returned by the teacher is not just an ultimately periodic word $xy^\omega \in UP(\mathcal{F}) \ominus UP(L)$, but it needs to satisfy additional requirements given in the following definition, in order to be useful for the learner to refine the conjectured FDFA.

Definition 9 (Counterexample for the FDFA learner). *Let L be the target language and $\mathcal{F}$ be the conjectured FDFA. We say that a counterexample (u, v) is*

- positive *if (u, v) is not captured by $\mathcal{F}$ and $uv^\omega \in UP(L)$, and*
- negative *if (u, v) is captured by $\mathcal{F}$ and $uv^\omega \notin UP(L)$.*

Remark 1. Besides the periodic FDFAs, Angluin and Fisman [11] introduced also the recurrent and the syntactic FDFAs, which make use of a different definition of right congruence. Similarly to the periodic case, also for these two FDFAs it is possible to define positive and negative counterexamples, which are however more involved. We refer the interested reader to [73] for more details on these two other types of FDFAs.

Refinement of the Conjectured FDFA $\mathcal{F}$. In order to decide which DFA in the conjectured $\mathcal{F}$ has to be refined, the learner acts differently depending on whether the received counterexample (u, v) is positive or negative.

If (u, v) is a positive counterexample, the learner proceeds as follows: let $\tilde{u} = M(u)$; if $\tilde{u} \cdot v^\omega \in UP(L)$, then the progress DFA $A^{\tilde{u}}$ is refined, otherwise the leading DFA M is refined. In case (u, v) is a negative counterexample, the learner just acts symmetrically: if $\tilde{u} \cdot v^\omega \in UP(L)$, then M is refined, otherwise $A^{\tilde{u}}$ is refined.

Consider again the conjectured FDFA $\mathcal{F}$ shown in Fig. 9 and the returned counterexample (ε, ab): (ε, ab) is clearly a positive counterexample so the conjectured progress DFA A^ε has to be refined since $\tilde{u} = \varepsilon = M(\varepsilon)$ and $\varepsilon \cdot (ab)^\omega \in UP(L)$.

Refinement of the Progress DFA $A^{\tilde{u}}$. Assume that (u, v) is a positive counterexample: by definition we have that $\tilde{u} \cdot v^\omega \in UP(L)$ and $A^{\tilde{u}}$ has to be refined so to accept v.

The counterexample analysis is similar to Lemma 1 due to the close relation of $\approx_P^u$ with $\frown_R$: let $n = |v|$ and for each $i \in [1 \cdots n]$, let $s_i = A^{\tilde{u}}(v[1..i])$ be the state in $A^{\tilde{u}}$ after reading the first i letters of v; recall that $s_0 = \varepsilon$. There exists a sequence of membership queries $MQ(\tilde{u}, s_0 \cdot v[1..n])$, $MQ(\tilde{u}, s_1 \cdot v[2..n])$, and so on, up to $MQ(\tilde{u}, s_n \cdot \varepsilon)$. By assumption we have $\tilde{u} \cdot (s_0 \cdot v[1..n])^\omega \in L$ while $\tilde{u} \cdot (s_n \cdot \varepsilon)^\omega \notin L$ due to the fact that (u, v) is not captured by $\mathcal{F}$ and thus s_n is not an accepting state. Recall that by Definition 8, the accepting set $F_{\tilde{u}}$ of the progress DFA $A^{\tilde{u}}$ is the set of equivalence classes $\{ [v]_{\approx_P^{\tilde{u}}} \mid \tilde{u} \cdot v^\omega \in$

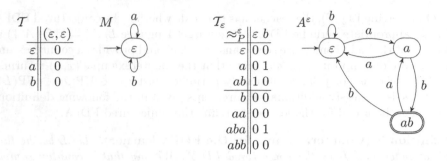

Fig. 10. The refined FDFA $\mathcal{F}_1$ and its corresponding tables while learning $(ab)^\omega$

L}. Therefore, the learner can find the first experiment $v[j+1..n]$ such that $\tilde{u} \cdot (s_{j-1}v[j] \cdot v[j+1..n])^\omega \in L$ while $\tilde{u} \cdot (s_j \cdot v[j+1..n])^\omega \notin L$; this means that $s_{j-1}v[j]$ and s_j do not represent the same equivalence class and must be split.

Consider again the conjectured FDFA $\mathcal{F}_0$ shown in Fig. 9 that has to be refined by means of the positive counterexample (ε, ab), which requires to refine the progress A^ε: from the sequence of membership queries $\mathrm{MQ}(\varepsilon, \langle s_0 = \varepsilon \rangle \cdot ab)$, $\mathrm{MQ}(\varepsilon, \langle s_1 = \varepsilon \rangle \cdot b)$, and $\mathrm{MQ}(\varepsilon, \langle s_2 = \varepsilon \rangle \cdot \varepsilon)$, the learner finds the experiment b distinguishing $\varepsilon \cdot a$ from ε. So he first adds b to V_ε of table $\mathcal{T}_\varepsilon$, then fills the missing entries, makes the table $\mathcal{T}_\varepsilon$ closed, and constructs from $\mathcal{T}_\varepsilon$ a new FDA A^ε, resulting in a new conjectured FDFA $\mathcal{F}_1$, shown in Fig. 10.

With $\mathcal{F}_1$ at hand, the learner can ask the teacher the equivalence query $\mathrm{EQ}(\mathcal{F}_1)$; she answers "no" with for instance the counterexample (ε, bab). According to Definition 9, (ε, bab) is a negative counterexample, since it is captured by $\mathcal{F}_1$ but clearly $\varepsilon(bab)^\omega \notin L = (ab)^\omega$. The learner has to refine again the progress DFA A^ε: after asking the sequence of membership queries $\mathrm{MQ}(\varepsilon, \langle s_0 = \varepsilon \rangle \cdot bab)$, $\mathrm{MQ}(\varepsilon, \langle s_1 = \varepsilon \rangle \cdot ab)$, $\mathrm{MQ}(\varepsilon, \langle s_2 = a \rangle \cdot b)$, and $\mathrm{MQ}(\varepsilon, \langle s_3 = ab \rangle \cdot \varepsilon)$, he finds the experiment ab distinguishing $\varepsilon \cdot b$ from ε. In general, on receiving a negative counterexample (u, v), the sequence of membership queries has different results for the first query $(\tilde{u}, \varepsilon \cdot v)$ and the last query $(\tilde{u}, A^{\tilde{u}}(v) \cdot \varepsilon)$. This is because $\tilde{u} \cdot (\varepsilon \cdot v)^\omega \notin L$ by assumption while $\tilde{u} \cdot (A^{\tilde{u}}(v) \cdot \varepsilon)^\omega \in L$ since $A^{\tilde{u}}(v)$ is an accepting state. The learner thus uses the experiment ab to update the table $\mathcal{T}_\varepsilon$ as seen before and constructs a new progress DFA A^ε out of $\mathcal{T}_\varepsilon$, which are shown in Fig. 11.

The learner is ready to ask the equivalence query $\mathrm{EQ}(\mathcal{F}_2)$ obtaining yet another time "no" as answer, together with a counterexample, say (a, ab), which is again a negative counterexample. Since $\tilde{u} = M(a) = \varepsilon$ and $\varepsilon \cdot (ab)^\omega \in L$, the learner this time has to refine the leading DFA M.

Refinement of the Leading DFA M. Assume that the learner has received a negative counterexample (u, v); the case of positive counterexamples is symmetric and thus omitted here. Let $\tilde{u} = M(u)$; by definition we have $uv^\omega \notin L$ while $\tilde{u}v^\omega \in L$. Let $n = |u|$ and for every $i \in [1 \cdots n]$, let $s_i = M(u[1..i])$ be the state

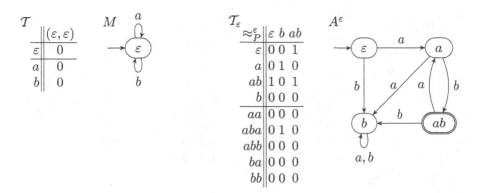

Fig. 11. The intermediate FDFA $\mathcal{F}_2$ and its corresponding tables while learning $(ab)^\omega$

in M after reading the first i letters of u. In particular, $s_0 = \varepsilon$. As in the previous analyses, there is the sequence of membership queries $\mathrm{MQ}(s_0 \cdot u[1..n], v)$, $\mathrm{MQ}(s_1 \cdot u[2..n], v)$, and so on, up to $\mathrm{MQ}(s_n \cdot \varepsilon, v)$. This sequence has different results for the first and the last query since $s_0 \cdot u[1..n] \cdot v^\omega \notin L$ while $s_n \cdot \varepsilon \cdot v^\omega \in L$. Therefore, the learner can find the first experiment $(u[j+1..n], v)$ such that $s_{j-1} \cdot u[j] \cdot u[j+1..n] \cdot v^\omega \notin L$ while $s_j \cdot u[j+1..n] \cdot v^\omega \in L$, which means that the experiment $(u[j+1..n], v)$ can be used to distinguish $s_{j-1} \cdot u[j]$ from s_j.

Consider again the FDFA $\mathcal{F}_2$ shown in Fig. 11 and the negative counterexample (a, ab): the learner finds the experiment (ε, ab) to distinguish $\varepsilon \cdot a$ from ε. As usual, after updating the leading table $\mathcal{T}$ by adding the experiment (ε, ab) and closing $\mathcal{T}$, the learner constructs a new conjecture leading DFA M, which is depicted in Fig. 12. Moreover, for every new state $u \in U$ of $\mathcal{T}$, he initializes a new progress table $\mathcal{T}_u$ and builds the corresponding progress DFA A^u as before; see for example the progress table $\mathcal{T}_a$ and the progress DFA A^a depicted in Fig. 12.

The learner asks the teacher whether $\mathcal{F}_2$ is correct. Assume that the teacher answers "no" with the counterexample (bb, ab) which is negative. By following the same procedure as above, he finds the experiment (b, ab) to distinguish $\varepsilon \cdot b$ from a, which is used to update the leading table $\mathcal{T}$ with experiment (b, ab) and to add the new progress DFA A^b for the state b of M, obtaining the FDFA $\mathcal{F}_4$ shown in Fig. 13.

By comparing the leading DFA M in $\mathcal{F}_4$ in Fig. 13 with the one in Fig. 7, we can see that they are the same, so M is not going to be changed anymore since it is already consistent with the one induced by $\backsim_L$ in Definition 8. However, the progress DFA A^a is still not correct so the teacher answers "no" to the equivalence query $\mathrm{EQ}(\mathcal{F}_4)$ posed by the learner. Assume that the teacher returns the counterexample (a, ba) which is positive. The learner then finds the experiment a to refine the progress DFA A^a and finally he generates the new conjectured FDFA $\mathcal{F}_5$ depicted in Fig. 14.

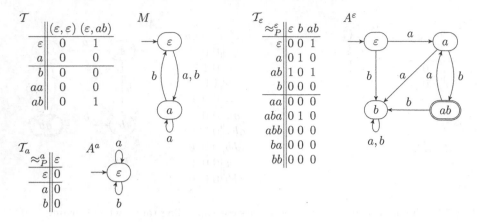

Fig. 12. The intermediate FDFA $\mathcal{F}_3$ and its corresponding tables while learning $(ab)^\omega$

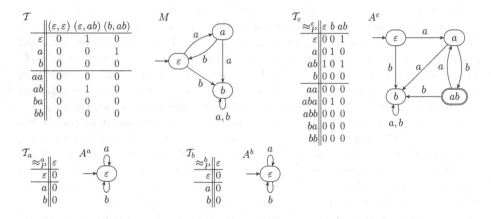

Fig. 13. The FDFA $\mathcal{F}_4$ and its corresponding tables while learning $(ab)^\omega$

The FDFA $\mathcal{F}_5$ is still not the right conjecture and the teacher answers again "no" to the equivalence query for it. Assume that the returned counterexample is (a, aba) which is clearly negative. As before, the learner refines the progress DFA A^a and gets a new conjecture FDFA $\mathcal{F}_6$ shown in Fig. 15.

The teacher now answers "yes" to the equivalence query $EQ(\mathcal{F}_6)$ and the learner has completed his job.

The FDFA Learner. By means of the previous example, we have introduced informally the ω-regular language learning algorithm, which is formalized in Algorithm 2 as the periodic FDFA learner. We can note that the learning procedure we described in the running example follows exactly the steps of the algorithm. In Algorithm 2 we have functions acting on DFAs that are specialized for the leading DFA M (whose with subscript l) and functions specialized

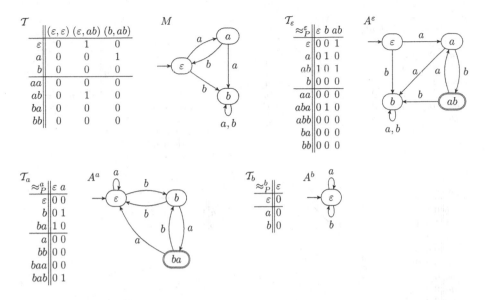

Fig. 14. The intermediate FDFA $\mathcal{F}_5$ and its corresponding tables while learning $(ab)^\omega$

for the progress DFAs (whose with subscript p). Since for the refinement of the progress DFA $A^{\tilde{u}}$ the learner does not need the word u but just $\tilde{u}$, function $FindDistinguishingExperiment_p$ takes the parameter instance $\tilde{u}$ instead of u.

The soundness and completeness of Algorithm 2 are guaranteed by Theorem 5.

Theorem 5. *Assume that L is the target ω-regular language. Algorithm 2 terminates and returns a periodic FDFA $\mathcal{F}$ capturing the set of decompositions $\{\,(u,v) \in \Sigma^* \times \Sigma^+ \mid uv^\omega \in L\,\}$.*

Clearly, the FDFA $\mathcal{F}$ returned by Algorithm 2 is a correct conjecture because the teacher has approved it; Algorithm 2 terminates because: (1) we can discover new states, i.e., new equivalence classes in $\Sigma^*/{\backsim_L}$ or in $\Sigma^*/{\approx_P^{\tilde{u}}}$, whenever receiving a counterexample (u,v) from the teacher, where $\tilde{u} = M(u)$ (cf. [72]); and (2) $\backsim_L$ and $\approx_P^{\tilde{u}}$ for any $u \in \Sigma^*$ are all right congruences of finite index (cf. [11]).

The complexity of Algorithm 2 is stated in Theorem 6; let the length of a decomposition (u,v) be the sum of the lengths of u and v, i.e., $|(u,v)| = |u| + |v|$.

Theorem 6. *Given a target ω-regular language L, let n be the sum of the indexes of the right congruences, i.e., $n = |{\backsim_L}| + \sum_{[u]_{\backsim_L} \in \Sigma^*/{\backsim_L}} |{\approx_P^u}|$, and m be the maximum length of any counterexample (u,v) returned by the teacher.*

1. *Algorithm 2 terminates on receiving at most n counterexamples.*
2. *The number of membership queries is in $\mathcal{O}(n^2 \cdot |\Sigma| + n \cdot m)$.*

The reason why Algorithm 2 terminates on receiving at most n counterexamples is obvious since there are n states in the periodic FDFA of L. The reason why

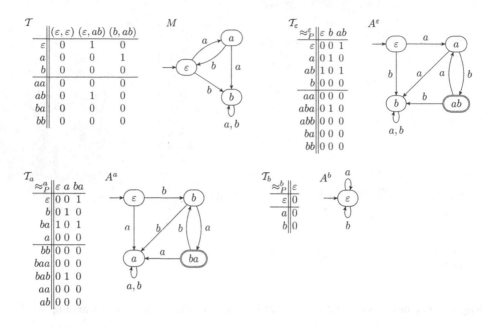

Fig. 15. The final FDFA $\mathcal{F}_6$ and its corresponding tables while learning $(ab)^\omega$

the number of membership queries is in $\mathcal{O}(n^2 \cdot |\Sigma| + n \cdot m)$ is the following: let l be the number of states in the leading DFA M and $p_1, p_2, \ldots, p_l$ be the number of states in the progress DFAs, respectively; we have $l + \sum_{i=1}^{l} p_i = n$. By Theorem 4, a DFA with k_1 states and longest counterexample of length k_2 can be learned by at most $k_1^2 \cdot |\Sigma| + k_1 \cdot k_2$ membership queries, thus we need at most $l^2 \cdot |\Sigma| + l \cdot m + \sum_{i=1} (p_i^2 \cdot |\Sigma| + p_i \cdot m) \in \mathcal{O}(n^2 \cdot |\Sigma| + n \cdot m)$ membership queries.

5.4   Learning Büchi Automata

In the previous section we presented the FDFA learning algorithm, which is our secret ingredient in learning a BA: we first learn an FDFA $\mathcal{F}$ and then transform the learned $\mathcal{F}$ to a BA. This is just one sentence introduction to the BA learning algorithm; there are however several details than need to be concretized in order to get a working algorithm.

Overview of the BA Learning Framework. In the following we begin with an introduction of the framework presented in [73] for learning BA as depicted in Fig. 16. In this section, we let the ω-regular language L be the target language and we assume that we already have a BA teacher who knows the language L and can answer membership and equivalence queries about L. In order to distinguish membership and equivalence queries posed by the FDFA learner and the BA learner, we use a superscript like FDFA and BA to mark queries from the

---

Algorithm 2. The Periodic FDFA Learner

---

1 Initialize leading table $\mathcal{T} = (U, V, T)$ with $U = \{\varepsilon\}$ and $V = \{(\varepsilon, \varepsilon)\}$;
2 $CloseTable_l(\mathcal{T}, MQ(\,\cdot\,))$ and let $M = Aut_l(\mathcal{T})$;
3 **foreach** $u \in U$ **do**
4 $\quad$ Initialize progress table $\mathcal{T}_u = (U_u, V_u, T_u)$ with $U_u = \{\varepsilon\}$ and $V_u = \{\varepsilon\}$;
5 $\quad$ $CloseTable_p(\mathcal{T}_u, MQ(\,\cdot\,))$ and let $A^u = Aut_p(\mathcal{T}_u)$;
6 Let $(a, (u, v))$ be the teacher's response on $EQ(\mathcal{F})$;
7 **while** $a =$ *"no"* **do**
8 $\quad$ Let $\tilde{u} = M(u)$;
9 $\quad$ **if** $MQ(\tilde{u}, v) \neq MQ(u, v)$ **then**
10 $\quad\quad$ $V = V \cup FindDistinguishingExperiment_l(u, v)$;
11 $\quad\quad$ $CloseTable_l(\mathcal{T}, MQ(\,\cdot\,))$ and let $M = Aut_l(\mathcal{T})$;
12 $\quad\quad$ **foreach** *newly added* $u \in U$ **do**
13 $\quad\quad\quad$ Initialize progress table $\mathcal{T}_u = (U_u, V_u, T_u)$ with $U_u = \{\varepsilon\}$ and
$\quad\quad\quad$ $V_u = \{\varepsilon\}$;
14 $\quad\quad\quad$ $CloseTable_p(\mathcal{T}_u, MQ(\,\cdot\,))$ and let $A^u = Aut_p(\mathcal{T}_u)$;
15 $\quad$ **else**
16 $\quad\quad$ $V_{\tilde{u}} = V_{\tilde{u}} \cup FindDistinguishingExperiment_p(\tilde{u}, v)$;
17 $\quad\quad$ $CloseTable_p(\mathcal{T}_{\tilde{u}}, MQ(\,\cdot\,))$ and let $A^{\tilde{u}} = Aut_p(\mathcal{T}_{\tilde{u}})$;
18 $\quad$ Let $(a, (u, v))$ be the teacher's response on $EQ(\mathcal{F})$;
19 **return** $\mathcal{F}$;

FDFA learner and the BA learner, respectively. For instance, the membership query $MQ^{FDFA}(\,\cdot\,)$ is posed by the FDFA learner while $MQ^{BA}(\,\cdot\,)$ is asked by the BA learner.

The BA learner, shown in Fig. 16 surrounded by the dashed box, has three components, namely the FDFA learner, the component transforming an FDFA $\mathcal{F}$ to a BA $B_{\mathcal{F}}$, and the counterexample analysis component. The BA learner first uses the FDFA learner to learn an FDFA $\mathcal{F}$ by means of membership and equivalence queries. This makes some problem the BA learner has to solve: on the one side, in order to answer queries posed by the FDFA learner, the BA learner needs an FDFA teacher to answer membership and equivalence queries about the target periodic FDFA of L; one the other side, there is only a BA teacher who can answer queries about the target language.

In this situation, the BA learner acts as an interface between the FDFA teacher and the FDFA learner and tries to pretend to be an FDFA teacher when he has to answer the queries from the FDFA learner. In other words, the BA learner becomes the FDFA teacher by interacting with the BA teacher. To that end, the FDFA teacher answers to a membership query $MQ^{FDFA}(u, v)$ by simply forwarding the answer to the membership query $MQ^{BA}(uv^{\omega})$ obtained from the BA teacher to the FDFA learner, which is trivial.

It is, however, more tricky for the FDFA teacher to answer an equivalence query $EQ^{FDFA}(\mathcal{F})$ posed by the FDFA learner. The FDFA teacher first needs to transform the conjectured FDFA $\mathcal{F}$ to a BA $B_{\mathcal{F}}$ and then poses the equivalence query $EQ^{BA}(B_{\mathcal{F}})$ to the BA teacher. If the BA teacher answers "yes", the BA

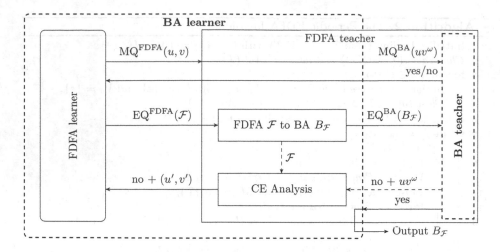

Fig. 16. Overview of the BA learning framework based on FDFA learning

learner first receives the answer and then outputs the BA $B_{\mathcal{F}}$ as he has completed the learning task. Otherwise the BA teacher returns "no" together with a counterexample uv^ω given as a decomposition (u, v). The BA learner then performs the counterexample analysis and, by acting as an FDFA teacher, he feeds the FDFA learner with a valid decomposition (u', v') which satisfies Definition 9, so that the FDFA learner can further refine the current FDFA $\mathcal{F}$.

Note that in Fig. 16 there is a dashed arrow labeled with $\mathcal{F}$ entering the counterexample analysis block: it indicates the fact that the FDFA teacher needs to use the current conjectured FDFA $\mathcal{F}$ in the analysis of the counterexample, as we will see later. We want to remark that, according to Fig. 16, the BA teacher is oblivious of the FDFA learner, since she only sees a BA learner interacting with her and similarly, the FDFA learner does not know that there is a BA teacher since it is the FDFA teacher that is answering his queries.

From the framework depicted in Fig. 16, we get the rough idea about how to build a BA learner out of an FDFA learner. Yet there are still few details we have to sort out:

– How can we transform an FDFA $\mathcal{F}$ to a BA $B_{\mathcal{F}}$?
– How can we get a valid counterexample (u', v') for the FDFA learner out of a counterexample (u, v) returned by the BA teacher?

The answers to the above questions are the missing bricks we need to build a BA learner based on an FDFA learner. In the following, we first answer the question on how to do the transformation from an FDFA to a BA and then introduce the counterexample analysis through an example.

From FDFA $\mathcal{F}$ to BA $B_{\mathcal{F}}$. Assume that we want to learn a BA which accepts the ω-regular language $L = (ab)^\omega$ over $\Sigma = \{a, b\}$. To that end, the BA learner first initializes an FDFA learner which constructs the initial conjectured FDFA

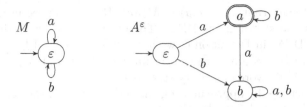

Fig. 17. An FDFA $\mathcal{F}$ such that $\text{UP}(\mathcal{F})$ does not characterize an ω-regular language

$\mathcal{F}_0$ as depicted in Fig. 9 via membership queries. On receiving the conjectured FDFA $\mathcal{F}_0$, the BA learner has to construct a BA $B_{\mathcal{F}_0}$ from $\mathcal{F}_0$ which we illustrate in the following.

To answer an equivalence query $\text{EQ}^{\text{FDFA}}(\mathcal{F})$, the BA learner needs fist to covert $\mathcal{F}$ into a BA $B_{\mathcal{F}}$ in order to exploit the BA teacher to answer the query. The first question one may ask in doing this is:

- Is it possible to construct a *precise* BA $B_{\mathcal{F}}$ for each given FDFA $\mathcal{F}$ such that $\text{UP}(\mathcal{L}(B_{\mathcal{F}})) = \text{UP}(\mathcal{F})$?

The answer is actually *no*, as the following example shows.

Example 3 (Non-regular ω-language accepted by an FDFA [73]). Consider the FDFA $\mathcal{F}$ depicted in Fig. 17 where $\text{UP}(\mathcal{F}) = \bigcup_{n=0}^{\infty} \{a, b\}^* \cdot (ab^n)^\omega$. Assume that $\text{UP}(\mathcal{F})$ characterizes an ω-regular language L. It is claimed in [11] that for every ω-regular language, there exists a periodic FDFA recognizing it and the index of each right congruence of the periodic FDFA is finite. Therefore we let $\mathcal{F}'$ be the periodic FDFA of L and we know that the right congruence $\approx_P^\varepsilon$ of $\mathcal{F}'$ is of finite index. However, we can show that the right congruence $\approx_P^\varepsilon$ of $\mathcal{F}'$ has to be of infinite index. Observe that $ab^k \not\approx_P^\varepsilon ab^j$ for any $k, j \geq 1$ and $k \neq j$, since $\varepsilon \cdot (ab^k \cdot ab^k)^\omega \in \text{UP}(\mathcal{F})$ and $\varepsilon \cdot (ab^j \cdot ab^k)^\omega \notin \text{UP}(\mathcal{F})$ according to Definition 8. It follows that $\approx_P^\varepsilon$ is of infinite index. Contradiction. Thus we conclude that $\text{UP}(\mathcal{F})$ cannot characterize an ω-regular language.

Therefore, in general, one can not construct a BA $B_{\mathcal{F}}$ from an FDFA $\mathcal{F}$ such that $\text{UP}(\mathcal{L}(B_{\mathcal{F}})) = \text{UP}(\mathcal{F})$. The authors of [73] suggested two BA constructions to approximate the set of ultimately periodic words $\text{UP}(\mathcal{F})$: the under-approximation and the over-approximation construction. In this work, we only introduce the *under-approximation* construction from [73], which produces a BA $B_{\mathcal{F}}$ that under-approximates $\text{UP}(\mathcal{F})$, i.e., $\text{UP}(\mathcal{L}(B_{\mathcal{F}})) \subseteq \text{UP}(\mathcal{F})$. This construction was originally proposed by Calbrix *et al.* in [26].

We first give the main idea behind the under-approximation method and then give its formal definition. Let $\mathcal{F}$ be the FDFA $\mathcal{F} = (M, \{A^u\})$ with $M = (Q, \bar{q}, \delta, \emptyset)$ and $A^u = (Q_u, s_u, \delta_u, F_u)$ for each $u \in Q$. Let $M_s^s = (Q, s, \delta, \{v\})$ and $(A^u)_v^s = (Q_u, s, \delta_u, \{v\})$ be the DFAs obtained from M and A^u by setting their initial state and accepting states to s and $\{v\}$, respectively. We define $N_{(u,v)} = \{ v^\omega \mid M(uv) = M(u) \wedge v \in \mathcal{L}((A^u)_v^{s_u}) \}$, which contains only the words

$v \in \mathcal{L}((A^u)_v^{s_u})$ such that $u = M(u) = M(uv)$. Recall that we use words u and v to represent the states in the DFAs. Therefore, according to the acceptance condition of FDFAs in Definition 6, we have that $\mathrm{UP}(\mathcal{F}) = \bigcup_{u \in Q, v \in F_u} \mathcal{L}(M_u^{\bar{q}}) \cdot N_{(u,v)}$ where $\mathcal{L}(M_u^{\bar{q}})$ contains the set of finite prefixes and $N_{(u,v)}$ contains the set of finite periodic words for every state pair (u, v).

We construct $B_{\mathcal{F}}$ by approximating the set $N_{(u,v)}$, i.e., the set of finite periodic words. We first define the FA $P_{(u,v)} = (Q_{(u,v)}, s_{(u,v)}, \delta_{(u,v)}, \{f_{(u,v)}\}) = M_u^u \times (A^u)_v^{s_u} \times (A^u)_v^v$ and let $\underline{N}_{(u,v)} = \mathcal{L}(P_{(u,v)})^{\omega}$. Recall that the notation $\times$ here is the intersection operation of FAs. Then we can construct the BA $(Q_{(u,v)} \cup \{f\}, s_{(u,v)}, \delta_{(u,v)} \cup \delta_f, \{f\})$ recognizing $\underline{N}_{(u,v)}$ where f is a "fresh" state and $\delta_f = \{(f, \varepsilon, s_{(u,v)}), (f_{(u,v)}, \varepsilon, f)\}$. Note that ε transitions can be taken without consuming any letters and can be removed by standard methods in automata theory, see, e.g., [56]. Intuitively, we under-approximate the set $N_{(u,v)}$ as $\underline{N}_{(u,v)}$ by only keeping $v^{\omega} \in N_{(u,v)}$ if $A^u(v) = A^u(v \cdot v)$ where $v \in \Sigma^+$.

In Definition 10 we provide the construction procedure for a BA $B_{\mathcal{F}}$ such that $\mathrm{UP}(\mathcal{L}(B_{\mathcal{F}})) = \bigcup_{u \in Q, v \in F_u} \mathcal{L}(M_u^{\bar{q}}) \cdot \underline{N}_{(u,v)} = \bigcup_{u \in Q, v \in F_u} \mathcal{L}(M_u^{\bar{q}}) \cdot (\mathcal{L}(P_{(u,v)}))^{\omega}$, as originally proposed in [26].

Definition 10 ([73]). *Let $\mathcal{F} = (M, \{A^u\})$ be an FDFA where $M = (Q, \bar{q}, \delta, \emptyset)$ and $A^u = (Q_u, s_u, \delta_u, F_u)$ for each $u \in Q$. Let $(Q_{(u,v)}, s_{(u,v)}, \delta_{(u,v)}, \{f_{(u,v)}\})$ be a BA recognizing $\underline{N}_{(u,v)}$. Then the BA $B_{\mathcal{F}}$ is defined as the tuple $B_{\mathcal{F}} = (Q_{B_{\mathcal{F}}}, \bar{q}_{B_{\mathcal{F}}}, \delta_{B_{\mathcal{F}}}, F_{B_{\mathcal{F}}})$ where*

$$- Q_{B_{\mathcal{F}}} = Q \cup \bigcup_{u \in Q, v \in F_u} Q_{(u,v)},$$

$$- \bar{q}_{B_{\mathcal{F}}} = \bar{q},$$

$$- \delta_{B_{\mathcal{F}}} = \delta \cup \bigcup_{u \in Q, v \in F_u} \delta_{(u,v)} \cup \bigcup_{u \in Q, v \in F_u} \{(u, \varepsilon, s_{(u,v)})\}, \text{ and}$$

$$- F_{B_{\mathcal{F}}} = \bigcup_{u \in Q, v \in F_u} \{f_{(u,v)}\}$$

Intuitively, we connect the leading DFA M to the BA recognizing $\underline{N}_{(u,v)}$ by linking the state u of M and the initial state $s_{(u,v)}$ of the BA with an ε-transition for every state pair (u, v) where $v \in F_u$.

We now present Lemma 2 which is used later for the counterexample analysis.

Lemma 2 (cf. [73, Lemma 4]). *Let $\mathcal{F}$ be an FDFA, and $B_{\mathcal{F}}$ be the BA constructed from $\mathcal{F}$ according to Definition 10. If (u, v^k) is accepted by $\mathcal{F}$ for every $k \geq 1$, then $uv^{\omega} \in \mathrm{UP}(\mathcal{L}(B_{\mathcal{F}}))$.*

The following theorem is the main result of our BA construction. We refer the interested reader to [72] for the proofs of Lemma 2 and Theorem 7.

Theorem 7 (cf. [73, Lemma 3]). *Let $\mathcal{F}$ be the current conjectured FDFA and $B_{\mathcal{F}}$ be the BA constructed from $\mathcal{F}$ according to Definition 10. Let n and k be the number of states in the leading DFA and the largest progress DFA of $\mathcal{F}$, respectively. Then*

- the number of states in $B_{\mathcal{F}}$ is in $\mathcal{O}(n^2 k^3)$;

$B_{\mathcal{F}_0}$ a

Fig. 18. The BA $B_{\mathcal{F}_0}$ constructed for answering the equivalence query $\mathrm{EQ}^{\mathrm{FDFA}}(\mathcal{F}_0)$, with $\mathcal{F}_0$ shown inFig. 9

- $UP(\mathcal{L}(B_{\mathcal{F}})) \subseteq UP(\mathcal{F})$;
- $UP(\mathcal{L}(B_{\mathcal{F}})) = UP(\mathcal{F})$ if $\mathcal{F}$ is the periodic FDFA accepting $UP(\mathcal{F})$.

For instance, the initial BA $B_{\mathcal{F}_0}$ constructed from the FDFA $\mathcal{F}_0$ shown in Fig. 9 is depicted in Fig. 18. The state space of $Q_{(u,v)}$ of $B_{\mathcal{F}_0}$ defined in Definition 10 is empty since F_ε of A^ε in $\mathcal{F}_0$ is empty.

The BA $B_{\mathcal{F}_0}$ is clearly not a right conjecture so the BA teacher answers "no" for the equivalence query $\mathrm{EQ}^{\mathrm{BA}}(B_{\mathcal{F}_0})$ together with a counterexample, say $(ab)^\omega \in \mathcal{L}(B_{\mathcal{F}_0}) \ominus L$, given by the decomposition (ε, ab). Since the counterexample (ε, ab) from the BA teacher is a positive counterexample for the FDFA learner, according to Definition 9, the FDFA teacher who is disguised by the BA learner just sets (u', v') to be (ε, ab) in the counterexample analysis and returns it to the FDFA learner as counterexample for the "no" answer. We remark that if the BA learner applies the counterexample analysis to the valid positive counterexample (ε, ab) for the FDFA learner, the procedure also outputs a valid positive counterexample which satisfies Definition 9. In other words, in practice the counterexample analysis on the received counterexample directly generates a valid counterexample, so the BA learner does not have to decide whether the counterexample received from the BA teacher is valid for the FDFA learner.

Since he has received a negative answer with a counterexample for the equivalence query $\mathrm{EQ}^{\mathrm{FDFA}}(\mathcal{F}_0)$, the FDFA learner refines the current FDFA $\mathcal{F}_0$ according to the received counterexample, as we have seen in Sect. 5.3, and then poses the equivalence query $\mathrm{EQ}^{\mathrm{FDFA}}(\mathcal{F}_1)$ for the new conjectured FDFA $\mathcal{F}_1$, which is shown in Fig. 10.

The BA learner then builds from $\mathcal{F}_1$ the under-approximation BA $B_{\mathcal{F}_1}$, which is depicted in Fig. 19: observe that the ω-word $(bab)^\omega \in \mathcal{L}(B_{\mathcal{F}_1})$ is accepted by $\mathcal{F}_1$ since the decomposition (ε, bab) is accepted by $\mathcal{F}_1$; the BA $\underline{N}_{(\varepsilon,ab)}$ is defined as the DFA $M_\varepsilon^\varepsilon \times (A^\varepsilon)_{ab}^\varepsilon \times (A^\varepsilon)_{ab}^{ab}$ augmented with an extra state f and it is shown in the dashed box in Fig. 19.

Again, the conjectured BA $B_{\mathcal{F}_1}$ is not the right conjecture. The BA teacher answers the equivalence query for the BA $B_{\mathcal{F}_1}$ with "no" and, say, the counterexample $(bab)^\omega \in \mathcal{L}(B_1) \ominus L$, given as the decomposition (b, abb).

The counterexample (b, abb) is however not a valid counterexample for the FDFA learner according to Definition 9 since $(bab)^\omega \notin UP(L)$ and (b, abb) is not captured by the current FDFA $\mathcal{F}_1$. Suppose that the BA learner feeds the FDFA learner with the counterexample (b, abb); it is easy to verify that he is not able to

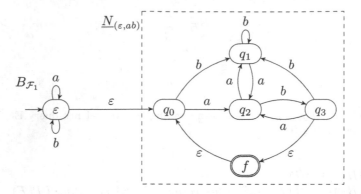

Fig. 19. The BA $B_{\mathcal{F}_1}$ constructed for answering the equivalence query $\mathrm{EQ}^{\mathrm{FDFA}}(\mathcal{F}_1)$, with $\mathcal{F}_1$ shown in Fig. 10

identify new states with the help of (b, abb), so he is going to conjecture again the FDFA $\mathcal{F}_1$. Therefore, if the FDFA learner repeatedly poses the equivalence query $\mathrm{EQ}^{\mathrm{FDFA}}(\mathcal{F}_1)$ for $\mathcal{F}_1$ and the BA teacher always answers (b, abb), the learning procedure is going to get stuck in an infinite loop. This motivates the need of the counterexample analysis, which ensures that the counterexample returned by the BA teacher can be adapted to a valid counterexample for the FDFA learner which allows him to refine the conjectured FDFA.

Counterexample Analysis for the FDFA Teacher. In order to ensure the termination of the learning procedure, the BA learner has to execute the counterexample analysis so to get a valid counterexample for the FDFA learner out of (b, abb).

To distinguish the different counterexamples from the different teachers, we define the counterexample from the BA teacher as follows.

Definition 11 (Counterexample for the FDFA teacher). *Let L be the target ω-regular language and $B_{\mathcal{F}}$ be the current conjectured BA. We say a counterexample (u, v) with $uv^\omega \in \mathcal{L}(B_{\mathcal{F}}) \ominus L$ is*

- *positive if $uv^\omega \in L$ and $uv^\omega \notin \mathcal{L}(B_{\mathcal{F}})$, and*
- *negative if $uv^\omega \notin L$ and $uv^\omega \in \mathcal{L}(B_{\mathcal{F}})$.*

This is a symmetric definition when compared with the counterexample for the FDFA learner given in Definition 9.

We call a positive counterexample uv^ω *spurious* if $uv^\omega \in \mathrm{UP}(\mathcal{F})$. A spurious positive counterexample (u, v) witnesses that $\mathrm{UP}(\mathcal{L}(B_{\mathcal{F}})) \subset \mathrm{UP}(\mathcal{F})$ holds; the reason for this is that: according to Theorem 7, we have $\mathrm{UP}(\mathcal{L}(B_{\mathcal{F}})) \subseteq \mathrm{UP}(\mathcal{F})$; by the definition of positive counterexample for the FDFA teacher, we have $uv^\omega \notin \mathrm{UP}(\mathcal{L}(B_{\mathcal{F}}))$ yet $uv^\omega \in \mathrm{UP}(\mathcal{F})$ holds.

In order to analyze the counterexample (u, v), it is useful to know how the received counterexample relates with the conjectured FDFA $\mathcal{F}$. For instance, it

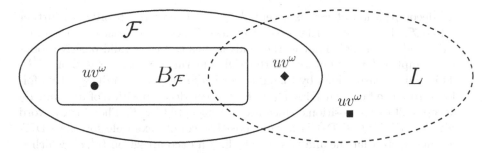

Fig. 20. The cases for the counterexample analysis

may be that $\mathcal{F}$ captures (u, v) but uv^ω is not in the target language, so (u, v) should be rejected; symmetrically, we can have that $\mathcal{F}$ rejects any decomposition of uv^ω but uv^ω is in the target language, so at least (u, v) should be captured; moreover, it may be that $\mathcal{F}$ rejects just (u, v) while capturing another decomposition (u', v') of uv^ω, but $B_{\mathcal{F}}$ does not accept (u', v'). To distinguish the above cases, which are shown in Fig. 20, we use three DFAs accepting different decompositions of uv^ω.

Let $\mathcal{F} = (M, \{A^u\})$ be the current conjectured FDFA. In order to analyze the counterexample (u, v) for the FDFA teacher, we define the following three DFAs, where \$ is a letter not in Σ.

- a DFA $D_\$$ with $\mathcal{L}(D_\$) = \{\, u'\$v' \mid u' \in \Sigma^*, v' \in \Sigma^+, u'v'^\omega = uv^\omega \,\}$,
- a DFA $\mathcal{D}_1$ with $\mathcal{L}(\mathcal{D}_1) = \{\, u'\$v' \mid u' \in \Sigma^*, v' \in \Sigma^*, v' \in \mathcal{L}(A^{M(u')}) \,\}$, and
- a DFA $\mathcal{D}_2$ with $\mathcal{L}(\mathcal{D}_2) = \{\, u'\$v' \mid u' \in \Sigma^*, v' \in \Sigma^*, v' \notin \mathcal{L}(A^{M(u')}) \,\}$.

Intuitively, $D_\$$ accepts every possible decomposition (u', v') of uv^ω; $\mathcal{D}_1$ recognizes every decomposition (u', v') which is captured by $\mathcal{F}$; and $\mathcal{D}_2$ accepts every decomposition (u', v') which is not captured by $\mathcal{F}$.

The DFA $D_\$$ can be constructed according to the procedure presented in [26, 72]; the DFA $\mathcal{D}_1$ can be obtained from $\mathcal{F}$ by simply connecting each state u of M to the initial state s_u of A^u via letter \$; finally, the construction of the DFA $\mathcal{D}_2$ is similar to the one of the DFA $\mathcal{D}_1$ except that we use the complement FDFA $\mathcal{F}^C$ of $\mathcal{F}$ instead of $\mathcal{F}$. Note that the DFAs $\mathcal{D}_1$ and $\mathcal{D}_2$ in this section are specialized for the periodic FDFA which are different from those defined for all three kinds of FDFAs in [73]. We refer the interested reader to [73] for more details on the different constructions of $\mathcal{D}_1$ and $\mathcal{D}_2$ for the recurrent and syntactic FDFAs.

The analysis for the returned counterexample has first to identify the kind of counterexample it is analyzing and then to deal with it accordingly. More concretely, the three kinds of counterexamples, shown in Fig. 20 by means of different shapes, are the following:

case U1: $uv^\omega \in \mathrm{UP}(L)$ **while** $uv^\omega \notin \mathrm{UP}(\mathcal{F})$ **(square).** The ω-word uv^ω is a positive counterexample for the FDFA teacher since $uv^\omega \notin \mathrm{UP}(\mathcal{L}(B_{\mathcal{F}}))$. On the one hand, $uv^\omega \in \mathrm{UP}(L)$ holds and all decompositions of uv^ω should be accepted by $\mathcal{F}$; on the other hand, $uv^\omega \notin \mathrm{UP}(\mathcal{F})$ holds, which indicates that no decomposition of uv^ω is accepted by $\mathcal{F}$. Therefore, in order to further refine $\mathcal{F}$, the FDFA learner needs to make $\mathcal{F}$ accept at least one decomposition (u', v') of uv^ω. That is, the analysis has to find a valid positive counterexample (u', v') out of uv^ω for the FDFA learner such that $v' \notin \mathcal{L}(A^{M(u')})$. This can be easily done by taking a word $u'\$v' \in \mathcal{L}(D_\$) \cap \mathcal{L}(\mathcal{D}_2)$. This follows from the fact that DFA $D_\$$ accepts every decomposition of uv^ω and $\mathcal{D}_2$ accepts all decompositions which are not accepted by $\mathcal{F}$. Therefore, a word $u'\$v' \in \mathcal{L}(D_\$) \cap \mathcal{L}(\mathcal{D}_2)$ is a valid positive counterexample for the FDFA learner. Note that the analysis tries to find a decomposition (u', v') which is not captured by $\mathcal{F}$ instead of a decomposition not accepted by $\mathcal{F}$. The reason is that a decomposition (u', v') not captured by $\mathcal{F}$ is also a decomposition which is not accepted by $\mathcal{F}$ according to Definition 6. We refer interested reader to [72, Appendix D.3] for more details on case U1.

case U2: $uv^\omega \notin \mathrm{UP}(L)$ **while** $uv^\omega \in \mathrm{UP}(\mathcal{F})$ **(circle).** The ω-word uv^ω is a negative counterexample for the FDFA teacher since $uv^\omega \in \mathrm{UP}(\mathcal{L}(B_\mathcal{F}))$. It follows that $\mathcal{F}$ should reject every decomposition of uv^ω since $uv^\omega \notin \mathrm{UP}(L)$. In other words, in order to further refine $\mathcal{F}$, the FDFA learner needs to make $\mathcal{F}$ not capture at least one decomposition (u', v') of uv^ω. Therefore, the analysis needs to find a valid negative counterexample (u', v') out of uv^ω for the FDFA learner that is accepted by $\mathcal{F}$. This can be done by taking a word $u'\$v' \in \mathcal{L}(D_\$) \cap \mathcal{L}(\mathcal{D}_1)$.

case U3: $uv^\omega \in \mathrm{UP}(L)$ **and** $uv^\omega \in \mathrm{UP}(\mathcal{F})$ **(diamond).** The ω-word uv^ω is a spurious positive counterexample since $uv^\omega \in \mathrm{UP}(\mathcal{F})$ but $uv^\omega \notin \mathrm{UP}(\mathcal{L}(B_\mathcal{F}))$. On the one hand, this case is quite similar to case U1 since $uv^\omega \in \mathrm{UP}(L)$ and normally we should make $\mathcal{F}$ accept uv^ω; on the other hand, however, differently from U1, $\mathcal{F}$ already accepts at least one decomposition of uv^ω in this case. Suppose that the decomposition (x, y) of uv^ω is accepted by $\mathcal{F}$; according to Lemma 2, there must exist some $k \geq 1$ such that (x, y^k) is not accepted by $\mathcal{F}$ since otherwise we would have $uv^\omega \in \mathcal{L}(B)$. Therefore, similar to case U1, it is possible for the analysis to find a valid positive counterexample (u', v') out of uv^ω for the FDFA learner such that $v' \notin \mathcal{L}(A^{M(u')})$. The word $u'\$v'$ can also be taken from $\mathcal{L}(D_\$) \cap \mathcal{L}(\mathcal{D}_2)$. We refer interested reader to [72, Appendix D.3] for more details on case U3.

We remark that from an implementation point of view, checking whether $uv^\omega \in \mathrm{UP}(L)$ can be replaced by a membership query $\mathrm{MQ}^{\mathrm{BA}}(u, v)$ while testing whether $uv^\omega \in \mathrm{UP}(\mathcal{F})$ reduces to checking whether $u\$v \in \mathcal{L}(\mathcal{D}_1)$.

Consider again the conjectured FDFA $\mathcal{F}_1$ and the counterexample (b, abb) returned by the BA teacher, which is a negative counterexample since $b \cdot (abb)^\omega \notin L$. The counterexample (b, abb) falls into case U2 since $b \cdot (abb)^\omega \notin \mathrm{UP}(L)$ while $b \cdot (abb)^\omega \in \mathrm{UP}(\mathcal{F}_1)$. In order to analyze it, the BA learner needs to construct the DFAs $D_\$$ and $\mathcal{D}_1$, which are depicted in Fig. 21. For completeness of presentation, Fig. 21 shows also the DFA $\mathcal{D}_2$, so to allow the reader to compare it with $\mathcal{D}_1$. Assume that the BA learner gets the word $\varepsilon\$bab \in \mathcal{L}(D_\$) \cap \mathcal{L}(\mathcal{D}_1)$, which gives a negative counterexample (ε, bab) for the FDFA learner.

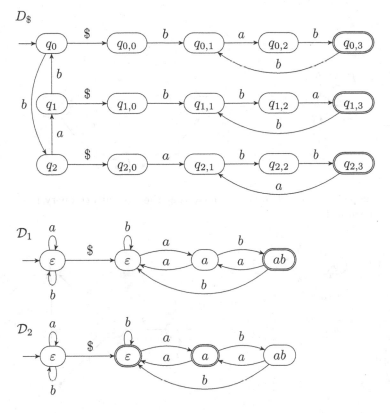

Fig. 21. The three DFAs $D_\$$, $\mathcal{D}_1$, and $\mathcal{D}_2$ for the FDFA $\mathcal{F}_1$ from Fig. 10 and the counterexample (b, abb)

As seen in Sect. 5.3, with the negative counterexample (ε, bab) at hand, the FDFA learner is able to get the refined conjecture $\mathcal{F}_2$ depicted in Fig. 11. To answer the equivalence query $\mathrm{EQ}^{\mathrm{FDFA}}(\mathcal{F}_2)$, the BA learner has again to construct a BA $B_{\mathcal{F}_2}$, depicted in Fig. 22, from $\mathcal{F}_2$; then he poses the equivalence query $\mathrm{EQ}^{\mathrm{BA}}(B_{\mathcal{F}_2})$ to the BA teacher. Note that we have $\mathrm{UP}(\mathcal{F}_2) = \mathrm{UP}(\mathcal{L}(B_{\mathcal{F}_2})) = \{a, b\}^*(ab)^\omega$ for the constructed BA $B_{\mathcal{F}_2}$. This follows from the fact that $\mathcal{F}_2$ is a periodic FDFA accepting $\{a, b\}^*(ab)^\omega$, which results in $\mathrm{UP}(\mathcal{F}_2) = \mathrm{UP}(\mathcal{L}(B_{\mathcal{F}_2}))$ according to Theorem 7.

The BA teacher answers again "no" with a counterexample, say (a, ab), which is already a negative counterexample for the FDFA learner. However, the BA learner is not aware of this fact, thus he performs a counterexample analysis on (a, ab). In order to analyze the counterexample $a \cdot (ab)^\omega$, the BA learner first builds the two DFAs $D_\$$ and $\mathcal{D}_1$ shown in Fig. 23.

Suppose that this time the BA learner takes the word $a\$ab \in \mathcal{L}(D_\$) \cap \mathcal{L}(\mathcal{D}_1)$, which means that the counterexample the FDFA learner receives is again (a, ab). After the refinement of the FDFA $\mathcal{F}_2$, the FDFA learner now asks an equivalence

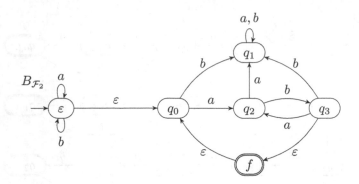

Fig. 22. The BA $B_{\mathcal{F}_2}$ constructed for answering the equivalence query $\mathrm{EQ}^{\mathrm{FDFA}}(\mathcal{F}_2)$, with $\mathcal{F}_2$ shown in Fig. 11

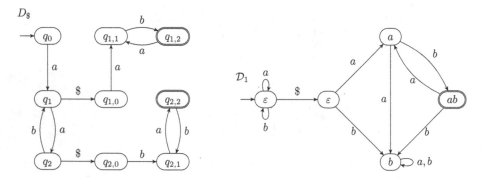

Fig. 23. The DFAs $D_\$$ and $\mathcal{D}_1$ for the FDFA $\mathcal{F}_2$ from Fig. 11 and the counterexample (a, ab)

query for the FDFA $\mathcal{F}_3$ shown in Fig. 12. On receiving the query $\mathrm{EQ}^{\mathrm{FDFA}}(\mathcal{F}_3)$, the BA $B_{\mathcal{F}_3}$ given in Fig. 24 is constructed by the BA learner to ask the BA teacher another equivalence query.

Clearly, $B_{\mathcal{F}_3}$ is not a right conjecture and the BA teacher returns "no" as well as a counterexample, say (bba, ba), which is a negative counterexample for the FDFA teacher. The BA learner builds the two DFAs $D_\$$ and $\mathcal{D}_1$ depicted in Fig. 25 in order to get a valid counterexample for the FDFA learner from $\mathcal{L}(D_\$) \cap \mathcal{L}(\mathcal{D}_1)$.

Assume that the FDFA learner receives the counterexample (bb, ab) from the FDFA teacher disguised by the BA learner. The FDFA learner is now able to get the refined FDFA $\mathcal{F}_4$ shown in Fig. 13, so he can ask $\mathrm{EQ}^{\mathrm{FDFA}}(\mathcal{F}_4)$. As usual, the BA learner constructs a BA from $\mathcal{F}_4$ in order to solve the equivalence query $\mathrm{EQ}^{\mathrm{FDFA}}(\mathcal{F}_4)$ posed by the FDFA learner.

The BA $B_{\mathcal{F}_4}$ constructed by the BA learner is shown in Fig. 26 and we can see that $B_{\mathcal{F}_4}$ exactly accepts the target language $L = (ab)^\omega$, which means that $B_{\mathcal{F}_4}$ is already a right conjecture. Therefore, the BA teacher answers positively

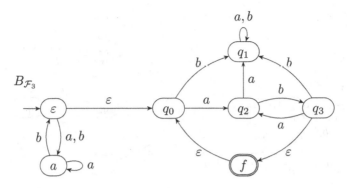

Fig. 24. The BA $B_{\mathcal{F}_3}$ constructed for answering the equivalence query $\mathrm{EQ}^{\mathrm{FDFA}}(\mathcal{F}_3)$, with $\mathcal{F}_3$ shown in Fig. 12

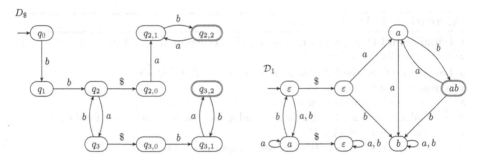

Fig. 25. The DFAs $D_\$$ and $\mathcal{D}_1$ for the FDFA $\mathcal{F}_3$ from Fig. 12 and the counterexample (bba, ba)

with "yes" to the BA learner as the result of the equivalence query $\mathrm{EQ}^{\mathrm{BA}}(B_{\mathcal{F}_4})$. The BA learner then outputs the learned BA $B_{\mathcal{F}_4}$ as he has finally completed the learning task.

We notice that the current FDFA $\mathcal{F}_4$ is still not a periodic FDFA of L yet we can build a BA such that $\mathcal{L}(B_{\mathcal{F}_4}) = L$. In practice, the BA learning algorithm very often infers a BA recognizing L before converging to a periodic FDFA of L. In the worst case, the FDFA learner inside the BA learner has to learn a periodic FDFA of L in order to get a right conjectured BA according to Theorem 7.

The BA Learner. By means of the previous example, we have introduced informally the ω-regular language learning algorithm, which is formalized in Algorithm 3 as the BA learner. We can note that the learning procedure we described in the running example follows exactly the steps of Algorithm 3. The function *constructBA* is an implementation of the under-approximation BA construction and *ceAnalysis* is the procedure for analyzing counterexamples from the BA teacher. The refinement loop of the conjecture $B_{\mathcal{F}}$ terminates once we get a positive answer from the teacher.

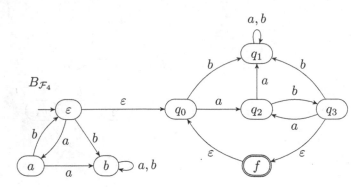

Fig. 26. The BA B_4 constructed for answering the equivalence query $\text{EQ}^{\text{FDFA}}(\mathcal{F}_4)$, with $\mathcal{F}_4$ shown in Fig. 13

Algorithm 3. The BA Learner

---
1 Initialize an FDFA learner L^ω and get the conjectured FDFA $\mathcal{F}$;
2 $B_{\mathcal{F}} = constructBA(\mathcal{F})$;
3 Let $(a, (u, v))$ be the BA teacher's response on $\text{EQ}^{\text{BA}}(B_{\mathcal{F}})$;
4 **while** $a = $ "*no*" **do**
5 $\quad (u', v') = ceAnalysis((u, v), \mathcal{F})$;
6 $\quad$ Call L^ω to refine $\mathcal{F}$ with (u', v') and get the new conjectured FDFA $\mathcal{F}$;
7 $\quad B_{\mathcal{F}} = constructBA(\mathcal{F})$;
8 $\quad$ Let $(a, (u, v))$ be the BA teacher's response on $\text{EQ}^{\text{BA}}(B_{\mathcal{F}})$;
9 **return** $B_{\mathcal{F}}$;

As discussed before, we can construct from an FDFA $\mathcal{F}$ a BA $B_{\mathcal{F}}$ such that $\text{UP}(\mathcal{F}) = \text{UP}(\mathcal{L}(B_{\mathcal{F}}))$ if $\mathcal{F}$ is a periodic FDFA of $\text{UP}(\mathcal{F})$. Thus in the worst case, the FDFA learner inside the BA learner needs to learn a periodic FDFA of target language L in order to get a right conjectured BA. The main result of this section then follows.

Theorem 8 (Correctness and Termination). *The BA learning algorithm based on the FDFA learner and the under-approximation BA construction always terminates and returns a BA recognizing the target ω-regular language L in polynomial time.*

6   Learning to Complement Büchi Automata

As we have seen in Sect. 3.3, the complementation of Büchi automata [25] is a classic problem that has been extensively studied for more than half a century; see [105] for a survey. The complementation of Büchi automata is a valuable tool in formal verification (cf. [67]), in particular when the property to be satisfied

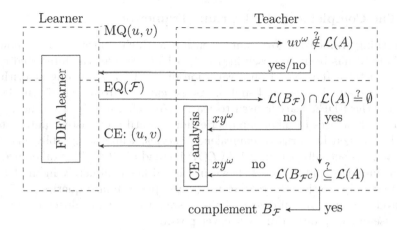

Fig. 27. The learning framework for complementing a Büchi automaton A

by a model is given by means of a Büchi automaton, in the program termination analysis (cf. Sect. 7), and when studying language inclusion problems of ω-regular languages [1,3,4]. As Proposition 4 shows, the complementation of Büchi automata is super-exponential, i.e., it can be really expensive in practice as well. While this is generally unavoidable [108], we believe that there is no inherent reason to assume that the complement language is harder than the initial language: in model checking, when the property is given as a formula ϕ, the typical approach assumes that the translation into a Büchi automaton is equally efficient for the formula and its negation, so instead of translating ϕ to A_ϕ and then complementing A_ϕ, it first negates ϕ and then translates $\neg\phi$ to $A_{\neg\phi}$ so that $\mathcal{L}(A_{\neg\phi}) = \Sigma^\omega \setminus \mathcal{L}(A_\phi)$. Would the complement language of ϕ be indeed more complex than the language of ϕ, this approach would suffer in translating the negation of the formula, since such a negation corresponds to the complement of the original property's language. Besides this, we have that complementing twice a language L gives L itself, while complementing a Büchi automaton twice would generate an automaton of incredible size: for instance, complementing twice a BA with 10 states would result in a BA accepting the same language with roughly at least $10^{7 \cdot 10^7}$ states, according to the approximation given by Proposition 4.

This begs to ask the question, whether we can disentangle the complement BA from the syntactic representation of the BA accepting the language we want to complement. By taking inspiration from the regular languages setting, where the minimal DFA accepting a given regular language can be learned by the DFA learning algorithm, in this section we show how we can learn a BA accepting the complement of a given target ω-regular language L.

6.1   The Complement BA Learning Framework

The learning framework for complementing a Büchi automaton is shown in Fig. 27 and it has been proposed in [74], to which we refer the interested reader for more details. It is based on a variation of the FDFA learning algorithm to learn $\mathcal{F}$, explained in Sects. 4 and 5. As we can see from Fig. 27, the learner is exactly the FDFA learner used to learn BAs (cf. Fig. 16). This means that the learner first uses membership queries for $\mathcal{F}$ until a consistent automaton is created and then he turns to equivalence queries, while being oblivious of the fact that he is actually learning $\Sigma^\omega \setminus \mathcal{L}(A)$ instead of $\mathcal{L}(A)$. The difference with the learning algorithm for BAs shown in Fig. 16 lies completely in the teacher: for membership queries, the teacher uses—cheap—standard queries [11,73]; the real novelty is in a careful design of the answer to the equivalence queries that makes use of cheap operations whenever possible.

These equivalence queries are *not* executed with the FDFA $\mathcal{F}$ and its complement $\mathcal{F}^C$, but with the Büchi automata $B_\mathcal{F}$ and $B_{\mathcal{F}^C}$ that under-approximate them. The teacher first checks whether $\mathcal{L}(B_\mathcal{F})$ is disjoint from $\mathcal{L}(A)$ we want to complement. This step is cheap, and if the answer is negative, then she returns to the learner an ultimately periodic word $uv^\omega \in \mathcal{L}(A)$, where at least some decomposition of uv^ω is (wrongly) accepted by $\mathcal{F}$.

In case $\mathcal{L}(B_\mathcal{F}) \cap \mathcal{L}(A) = \emptyset$, the teacher checks whether the language of $B_{\mathcal{F}^C}$ is included in the language of A. This is an interesting twist, since language inclusion is one of the traditional justifications for complementing Büchi automata, as mentioned in Sect. 3.5. But while the problem is PSPACE complete (cf. Proposition 8), it can usually be handled well by using efficient tools like RABIT [1,3,4]. In particular, RABIT makes use of a powerful set of computationally effective preprocessing and automata-exploration based heuristics that usually allow the language inclusion problem to be answered very efficiently.

Non-inclusion comes with a witness in the form of an ultimately periodic word xy^ω accepted by $B_{\mathcal{F}^C}$, but not by A. Thus, some decomposition (u, v) of xy^ω is (incorrectly) rejected by $\mathcal{F}$ and she returns it to the learner. In case $\mathcal{L}(B_{\mathcal{F}^C}) \subseteq \mathcal{L}(A)$ holds, the teacher then concludes that $\mathcal{L}(B_\mathcal{F}) = \Sigma^\omega \setminus \mathcal{L}(A)$ and terminates the algorithm with $B_\mathcal{F}$ as the complement of A. Note that the learner is not required to construct an FDFA $\mathcal{F}$ such that $\mathcal{L}(\mathcal{F}) = \Sigma^\omega \setminus \mathcal{L}(A)$; it is enough that $\mathcal{L}(B_\mathcal{F}) = \Sigma^\omega \setminus \mathcal{L}(A)$, which can save the framework to manage further membership and equivalence queries.

More details about the correctness of the proposed complementation framework, its complexity, and its experimental evaluation can be found in [74]. We want, however, to give some more detail about the use of RABIT to solve the language inclusion problem the teacher may need to answer in an equivalence query $\mathrm{EQ}(\mathcal{F})$. As said above, RABIT is equipped with a powerful set of heuristics; among others, RABIT makes use of the following ones, in an increasing order of their efficacy and amount of computation they need: (1) try simple automata-pruning algorithms, which help in reducing the size of the considered automata; (2) try delayed simulations, which is intended to prove the language inclusion by analyzing the structure of the automata; (3) if inclusion was not established in step 2 then try to find a counterexample to inclusion by the Ramsey-based method [3, 4] with a small timeout value; (4) if no counterexample was found in step 3 then try the automata minimization algorithms proposed in [33], which simplify the two automata by changing their languages while preserving their language inclusion relationship.

Since these heuristics are not complete, RABIT uses as the last resort the Ramsey-based inclusion testing algorithms already used in step 3, this time without timeout, to finally decide whether the language inclusion holds. From the experimental evaluation presented in [74] we can see that the learning-based complementation algorithm is really effective in getting the complement automaton, in particular when the automaton to be complemented is of large size. One interesting thing we noted in the experiments is that the automaton $B_{\mathcal{F}}$ used in the check $\mathcal{L}(B_{\mathcal{F}}) \cap \mathcal{L}(A) = \emptyset$ can change sensibly between an equivalence query and the following one, which makes it difficult to predict how much RABIT is able to exploit its heuristics. Anyway, in very few cases RABIT needed to use the Ramsey-based inclusion testing algorithms to finally decide whether the language inclusion holds, which usually consumes most of the running time in the corresponding experiment.

6.2   The Complement BA Learning Framework in Action

Suppose that we want to learn the complement of the NBA B depicted in Fig. 1; recall that $\mathcal{L}(B) = \Sigma^* \cdot b^\omega$. The learning algorithm works as follows: the learner first poses several membership queries and constructs the initial conjectured FDFA $\mathcal{F}_1$ shown in Fig. 28.

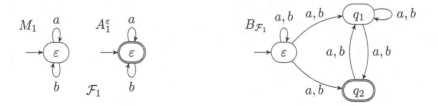

Fig. 28. Initial FDFA $\mathcal{F}_1 = (M_1, \{A_1^\varepsilon\})$ and the corresponding under-approximation Büchi automaton $B_{\mathcal{F}_1}$.

Afterwards, the learner performs the equivalence query $\mathrm{EQ}(\mathcal{F}_1)$ to verify whether $\mathcal{F}_1$ is correct. In order to answer this equivalence query, the teacher first constructs the Büchi automaton $B_{\mathcal{F}_1}$, also shown in Fig. 28, and then checks the emptiness of $\mathcal{L}(B_{\mathcal{F}_1}) \cap \mathcal{L}(B)$. This check fails: assume that the teacher gets the ω-word $b(bb)^\omega \in \mathcal{L}(B_{\mathcal{F}_1}) \cap \mathcal{L}(B)$; by means of the counterexample analysis, the teacher is able to answer negatively to the query $\mathrm{EQ}(\mathcal{F}_1)$ posed by the learner by returning the negative counterexample (ε, b), a decomposition of $b(bb)^\omega$.

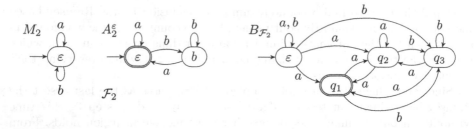

Fig. 29. Second FDFA $\mathcal{F}_2 = (M_2, \{A_2^\varepsilon\})$ and the corresponding under-approximation Büchi automaton $B_{\mathcal{F}_2}$.

Upon receiving (ε, b), the learner refines the current FDFA $\mathcal{F}_1$ to $\mathcal{F}_2$, shown in Fig. 29, by means of membership queries; then it poses the equivalence query $EQ(\mathcal{F}_2)$ for $\mathcal{F}_2$. As before, the teacher first transforms $\mathcal{F}_2$ to $B_{\mathcal{F}_2}$ and then checks for the emptiness of $\mathcal{L}(B_{\mathcal{F}_2}) \cap \mathcal{L}(B)$. It is easy to see that $\mathcal{L}(B_{\mathcal{F}_2})$ is indeed disjoint from $\mathcal{L}(B)$. Therefore, the teacher has first to compute the Büchi automaton $B_{\mathcal{F}_2^C}$ under-approximating $\mathcal{F}_2^C$, shown in Fig. 30, and then to check the language inclusion $\mathcal{L}(B_{\mathcal{F}_2^C}) \subseteq \mathcal{L}(B)$; this check fails.

Assume that the teacher finds $b(ab)^\omega \in \mathcal{L}(B_{\mathcal{F}_2^C}) \setminus \mathcal{L}(B)$; she then answers negatively to $EQ(\mathcal{F}_2)$ by means of the positive counterexample (b, ab) obtained from $b(ab)^\omega$.

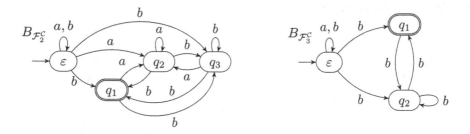

Fig. 30. Under-approximation Büchi automata $B_{\mathcal{F}_2^C}$ and $B_{\mathcal{F}_3^C}$ for $\mathcal{F}_2^C$ (depicted in Fig. 29) and $\mathcal{F}_3^C$ (shown in Fig. 31), respectively

The learner uses the received counterexample (b, ab) to further refine the current FDFA $\mathcal{F}_2$; after asking several membership queries, he generates the candidate FDFA $\mathcal{F}_3$ and then asks an equivalence query for it. As in the previous cases, the teacher starts by constructing the Büchi automaton $B_{\mathcal{F}_3}$ for $\mathcal{F}_3$, shown in Fig. 31. Since $\mathcal{L}(B_{\mathcal{F}_3}) \cap \mathcal{L}(B)$ is empty, the teacher proceeds to the second check, so she constructs the BA $B_{\mathcal{F}_3^C}$, shown in Fig. 30, and then proceeds to perform the last check, i.e., whether $\mathcal{L}(B_{\mathcal{F}_3^C}) \subseteq \mathcal{L}(B)$, which is obviously the case. Thus, the teacher terminates the learning algorithm by returning $B_{\mathcal{F}_3}$, shown in Fig. 31, as the complement of B.

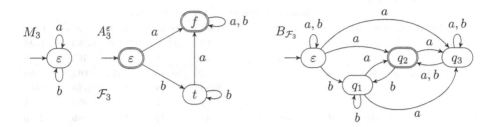

Fig. 31. Final FDFA $\mathcal{F}_3 = (M_3, \{A_3^\varepsilon\})$ and the corresponding under-approximation Büchi automaton $B_{\mathcal{F}_3}$

6.3 Experimental Evaluation

To support our claim that there is no actual super-exponential dependency between the language L we want to complement and the size of the complement A^C of the BA A such that $\mathcal{L}(A) = L$, we briefly recall the experiments we conducted in [74], where the complementation learning framework has been presented.

There we implemented our learning approach as Buechic, based on the ROLL learning library [73]; the inclusion check $\mathcal{L}(B_{\mathcal{F}^C}) \subseteq \mathcal{L}(A)$ (cf. Fig. 27) is delegated to RABIT [1,3,4]. In the experiments, we compared Buechic with two tools: GOAL [99], which is a mature and well-known tool for manipulating Büchi automata, for which we consider four different implemented complementing algorithms; and SPOT [39], which is the state-of-the-art platform for manipulating ω-automata, including Büchi automata. All tools accept as input automata represented in the Hanoi Omega-Automata (HOA) format [13]. Recall that SPOT does not provide a complementation function for generic Büchi automata directly, thus we first use SPOT to get a deterministic automaton from the given NBA, then complement the resulting deterministic automaton (for parity automata this just means adding 1 to all priorities), and finally transform the resulting complement automaton to an equivalent NBA. Since SPOT is a highly optimized tool that uses effective heuristics, it very often produces very small automata, but the heavy use of heuristics makes the comparison lopsided. Moreover, SPOT uses symbolic data structures called OBDDs which provide a more efficient way to manipulate automata compared to GOAL and Buechic.

Table 1 reports the results of the complementation on the automata from Büchi Store [100], which contains 295 NBAs with 1 to 17 states and with 0 to 123 transitions. However, since one of such automata has only one state without transitions and GOAL fails in recognizing it as a Büchi automaton, we decided to exclude it from the experiments and consider only the remaining 294 cases.

Table 1. Comparison between GOAL, SPOT, and Buechic on complementing Büchi Store. Note that the transitions in SPOT are represented denser—the same automaton attracts a lower transitions count.

Block	Experiments (States, Transitions)		GOAL				Buechic	SPOT
			Ramsey	Determinization	Rank	Slice		
1	287 NBAs (928, 2071)	$|Q|$	21610	3919	21769	4537	2428	**1629**
		$|\delta|$	964105	87033	179983	125155	35392	**13623**
		t_c	992	300	203	204	105	**6**
2	5 NBAs (55, 304)	$|Q|$	–to–	926	38172	1541	**165**	495
		$|\delta|$		21845	384378	50689	5768	**4263**
		t_c		28	42	12	474	**<1**
3	2 NBAs (20, 80)	$|Q|$	–to–	–to–	27372	11734	**96**	2210
		$|\delta|$			622071	1391424	**6260**	102180
		t_c			56	152	7	**1**

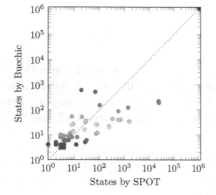 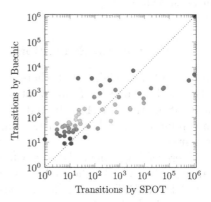

Fig. 32. Comparison between the number of states and transitions of automata generated by SPOT and Buechic on 72 automata corresponding to formulas from [92].

By inspecting the entries in Table 1 we can see that our learning based complementation method always outperforms the complementation methods offered by GOAL when we consider the number of states and transitions. When compared with SPOT, we see that the optimizations in SPOT are really effective, in both runtime and size of generated automata, for the small input automata (cf. block 1), but the transformation to parity automata starts to show its effects for larger automata (cf. blocks 2 and 3).

We have also considered 72 further Büchi automata generated from 72 formulas from [92]. In summary, Ramsey-based, Determinization-based, Rank-based, and Slice-based GOAL approaches solve 49, 58, 61, and 62 complementation tasks, respectively, within 5 min, while SPOT solves 66 tasks and Buechic solves 65 tasks. Among these, there are 64 tasks solved by both SPOT and Buechic, while the remaining cases are disjoint, which implies that our algorithm complements existing complementation approaches very well.

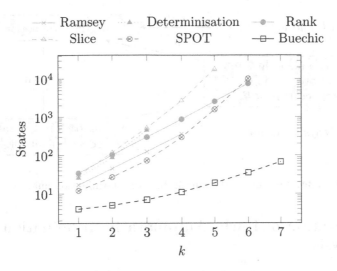

Fig. 33. States comparison of GOAL, SPOT, and Buechic on the formula pattern $\bigwedge_{i=1}^{k}(\mathsf{GF}a_i) \to \mathsf{GF}b$

In Fig. 32, relative to the 64 commonly solved tasks, the coordinate values of the y axis and x axis are the corresponding number of states (respectively, transitions) in the complement automata of Buechic and SPOT, respectively. All points below the dotted diagonal indicate that the complement automata learned by our algorithm have smaller values than the complement automata constructed by SPOT, which is the case for almost all large examples. We recall that SPOT merges transitions that share the same source state and target state as one transition, so in the right scatter plot of Fig. 32, many points are above the diagonal line. Nevertheless, we can learn from the plots that only SPOT produces those automata with more than 10^3 states or 10^4 transitions, which indicates that the reduction optimizations of SPOT do not work well on large automata and our algorithm performs much better on large automata.

In order to show how the growing trend of the number of states in the complement automata of the complementation algorithms behaves when we increase the size of the given Büchi automata in some cases, we take the generated Büchi automata for the formula pattern $\bigwedge_{i=1}^{k}(\mathsf{GF}a_i) \to \mathsf{GF}b$. The growing trend of the number of states in the complement automata for the approaches in GOAL, SPOT, and Buechic are plotted in Fig. 33. The number of states in the complement automaton constructed by GOAL and SPOT is growing exponentially with respect to the parameter k, while the number of states in the complement automaton learned by our algorithm grows linearly. The experimental results show that the performance of our algorithm can be much more stable for some automata with their growth of the states. Thus an advantage of our learning approach is that it has potentially better performance on large automata compared to classic complementation techniques.

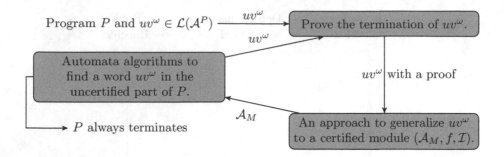

Fig. 34. The flow of the automata-based termination analysis

7 Application of Büchi Automata in Termination Analysis

In this section we present how Büchi automata and their complements are used in practice for complex verification tasks, like in program termination analysis.

Termination analysis of programs is a challenging area of formal verification, which has attracted the interest of many researchers approaching the problem from different angles; see, e.g., [14,22,36–38,47,48,52,55,64,69,70,80,84–86,95, 101,102]. In general, while analyzing the termination of a program, we need to deal with the following challenge: when a program contains loops with branching or nesting, how can we devise a termination argument that holds for any possible interleaving of the different paths through the loop body?

Due to the difficulty of solving the general problem, many researchers have focused on its simplified version that addresses only *lasso-shaped* programs, i.e., programs where the control flow consists of a stem followed by a simple loop without any branching. Proving termination for this class of programs can be done rather efficiently [15–17,23,35,54,71,83], but its extension to general programs is not easy.

7.1 Automata-Based Termination Analysis

In order to simplify our presentation, we consider only C programs without function calls and pointers; the variable updates are restricted to linear combinations. Since our goal in this section is to describe the modular termination analysis for a given program P, we assume that every sampled path can be proved to be terminating. Therefore, in the end, we can prove that P always terminates.

The approach of Heizmann *et al.* [55] proposes a modular construction of termination proofs for a general program P from termination proofs of lasso-shaped programs obtained from its concrete paths as depicted in Fig. 34. On a high level, the approach repeatedly performs the following sequence of operations: first, it samples a path $\tau = uv^\omega$ from the possible behaviours of P and attempts to prove its termination [15–17,23,35,54,71,83] by using an off-the-shelf termination checker, like LASSORANKER, part of the ULTIMATE AUTOMIZER suite [55].

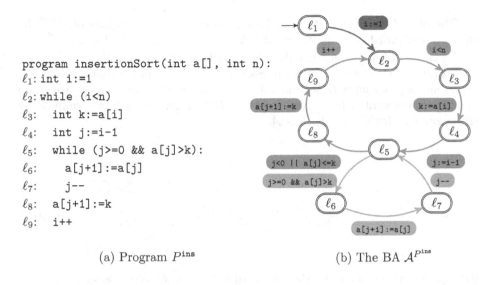

```
program insertionSort(int a[], int n):
ℓ1: int i:=1
ℓ2: while (i<n)
ℓ3:    int k:=a[i]
ℓ4:    int j:=i-1
ℓ5:    while (j>=0 && a[j]>k):
ℓ6:       a[j+1]:=a[j]
ℓ7:       j--
ℓ8:    a[j+1]:=k
ℓ9:    i++
```

(a) Program $P^{\mathtt{ins}}$ (b) The BA $\mathcal{A}^{P^{\mathtt{ins}}}$

Fig. 35. An example of program and its BA representation

The returned result of this step is possibly a termination argument of the sampled path, a non-termination argument of the sampled path, or "unknown" which indicates that the termination checker failed to decide the termination of the sampled path. Second, it generalizes τ into a (potentially infinite) set of paths $\mathcal{M}$, called a *certified module*, that all share the same termination proof with τ. Finally, it checks whether the behaviour of P contains a path τ' not covered by any certified module generated so far and, if so, the procedure is repeated. This sequence is repeated until either a non-terminating path is found, "unknown" is returned, or all behaviours of P are covered by the modules.

7.2 Automata-Based Termination Analysis: An Example

As an example of the above approach, consider the insertion sort program $P^{\mathtt{ins}}$ shown in Fig. 35(a); Fig. 35(b) shows the control flow graph (CFG) of $P^{\mathtt{ins}}$ as a Büchi automaton $\mathcal{A}^{P^{\mathtt{ins}}}$.

The alphabet of $\mathcal{A}^{P^{\mathtt{ins}}}$ is the set of all statements occurring in $P^{\mathtt{ins}}$, like assignments and guards, while the states of $\mathcal{A}^{P^{\mathtt{ins}}}$ are the locations of $P^{\mathtt{ins}}$; the initial state is the first location of the program, i.e., its entry point. The transitions connect states according to the way each location is reachable from another: for instance, we have the transition from ℓ_1 to ℓ_2 with action `i:=1` since ℓ_2 is reached after such initialization in location ℓ_1; similarly, we have a transition from ℓ_5 to ℓ_8 with action `j<0 || a[j]<=k` since ℓ_8 is reached when the guard `j>=0 && a[j]>k` of the `while` statement at location ℓ_5 is not satisfied. All states of $\mathcal{A}^{P^{\mathtt{ins}}}$ are accepting so each feasible infinite sequence of statements of the program corresponds to an infinite word in the language $\mathcal{L}(\mathcal{A}^{P^{\mathtt{ins}}})$.

The aim of the termination analysis is to cover the executions of $\mathcal{A}^{P^{\text{ins}}}$ by the accepted words of a finite set of BAs $\{\mathcal{A}_1, \ldots, \mathcal{A}_n\}$ such that $\mathcal{L}(\mathcal{A}^{P^{\text{ins}}}) \subseteq \mathcal{L}(\mathcal{A}_1) \cup \cdots \cup \mathcal{L}(\mathcal{A}_n)$ which is reduced to checking whether $\mathcal{L}(\mathcal{A}^{P^{\text{ins}}}) \cap \mathcal{L}(\mathcal{A}_1^C) \cap \cdots \cap \mathcal{L}(\mathcal{A}_n^C) = \emptyset$, as we have seen in Sect. 3.5. If we can prove that each BA $\mathcal{A}_i$ represents a program with a termination argument, then since every execution of P^{ins} is represented by a word in $\mathcal{A}^{P^{\text{ins}}}$, P^{ins} is guaranteed to terminate by the arguments for the single BAs $\mathcal{A}_i$.

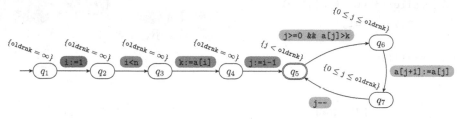

Fig. 36. A certified module for the lasso word $uv^\omega = \boxed{\texttt{i:=1}} \cdot \boxed{\texttt{i<n}} \cdot \boxed{\texttt{k:=a[i]}} \cdot \boxed{\texttt{j:=i-1}} \cdot \left(\boxed{\texttt{j>=0 \&\& a[j]>k}} \cdot \boxed{\texttt{a[j+i]:=a[j]}} \cdot \boxed{\texttt{j--}} \right)^\omega$

In order to have a termination argument, each BA $\mathcal{A}_i$ is associated with a *ranking function* f_i and a *rank certificate* $\mathcal{I}_i$ mapping each state to a *predicate* over the program variables. The triple $\mathcal{M}_i = (\mathcal{A}_i, f_i, \mathcal{I}_i)$ is called a *certified module*. The construction of the set $\{\mathcal{M}_1, \ldots, \mathcal{M}_n\}$ is progressive (see Fig. 34). First, we sample an ultimately periodic word $uv^\omega \in \mathcal{L}(\mathcal{A}^{P^{\text{ins}}})$—which is essentially a lasso-shaped program—and use an off-the-shelf tool to check if it corresponds to a terminating argument. In our example, we start with sampling the word $uv^\omega = \boxed{\texttt{i:=1}} \cdot \boxed{\texttt{i<n}} \cdot \boxed{\texttt{k:=a[i]}} \cdot \boxed{\texttt{j:=i-1}} \cdot \left(\boxed{\texttt{j>=0 \&\& a[j]>k}} \cdot \boxed{\texttt{a[j+i]:=a[j]}} \cdot \boxed{\texttt{j--}} \right)^\omega$. We can prove termination of the path corresponding to uv^ω by finding, e.g., the ranking function $f_1(\texttt{i}, \texttt{j}, \texttt{n}) = \texttt{j} + 1$, for which it holds that at each iteration of the inner loop, the value of $f_1(\texttt{i}, \texttt{j}, \texttt{n})$ decreases since $\texttt{j}$ is decreased by 1. The resulting certified module is shown in Fig. 36, where $\texttt{oldrnk}$ is a fresh variable used to keep track of the value of the ranking function at the previous visit of the accepting state.

In the following, we denote the inner loop of $\mathcal{A}^{P^{\text{ins}}}$ as $\text{INNER} = \boxed{\texttt{j>=0 \&\& a[j]>k}} \cdot \boxed{\texttt{a[j+i]:=a[j]}} \cdot \boxed{\texttt{j--}}$ and its outer loop as $\text{OUTER} = \boxed{\texttt{j<0 || a[j]<=k}} \cdot \boxed{\texttt{a[j+1]:=k}} \cdot \boxed{\texttt{i++}} \cdot \boxed{\texttt{i<n}} \cdot \boxed{\texttt{k:=a[i]}} \cdot \boxed{\texttt{j:=i-1}}$. We can observe that f_1 is also a ranking function for the set of paths obtained by generalizing uv^ω into the set of words that correspond to all paths that eventually stay in the inner loop, i.e., words from $\mathcal{L}_1 = \boxed{\texttt{i:=1}} \cdot \boxed{\texttt{i<n}} \cdot \boxed{\texttt{k:=a[i]}} \cdot \boxed{\texttt{j:=i-1}} \cdot (\text{INNER}+\text{OUTER})^* \cdot \text{INNER}^\omega$. The language $\mathcal{L}_1$ together with a ranking function f_1 and a rank certificate $\mathcal{I}_1$ can be represented by the certified module $\mathcal{M}_1 = (\mathcal{A}_1, f_1, \mathcal{I}_1)$, depicted in Fig. 37; the

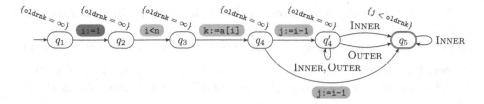

Fig. 37. The certified module $\mathcal{M}_1$ for the language $\mathcal{L}_1 =$ `i:=1` · `i<n` · `k:=a[i]` · `j:=i-1` (INNER + OUTER)* · INNER$^\omega$

transitions labelled with action INNER or OUTER are a shorthand for the corresponding sequences of transitions and states: for instance, the self-loop on q_5 with action INNER stands for the states and transitions reachable from q_5 in Fig. 36.

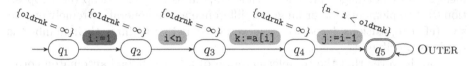

Fig. 38. A certified module for the lasso word `i:=1` · `i<n` · `k:=a[i]` · `j:=i-1` ·OUTER$^\omega$

We proceed by removing all paths covered by $\mathcal{L}_1$ from $\mathcal{A}^{P^{\mathrm{ins}}}$ to know which paths still need to be examined. The removal can be performed by executing a *BA difference algorithm*, presented in Sect. 3.4, followed by checking language emptiness (potentially finding a new counterexample uv^ω on failure). In our example, the difference corresponds to the (non-empty) language $\mathcal{L}(\mathcal{A}_{|\mathcal{A}_1}^{P^{\mathrm{ins}}}) =$ `i:=1` · `i<n` · `k:=a[i]` · `j:=i-1` ·(INNER*·OUTER)$^\omega$ represented by $\mathcal{A}_{|\mathcal{A}_1}^{P^{\mathrm{ins}}}$. Suppose the next sampling gives us $uv^\omega =$ `i:=1` · `i<n` · `k:=a[i]` · `j:=i-1` ·OUTER$^\omega$, for which, e.g., the ranking function $f_2(\mathtt{i},\mathtt{j},\mathtt{n}) = \mathtt{n} - \mathtt{i}$ is applicable; the corresponding certified module is shown in Fig. 38.

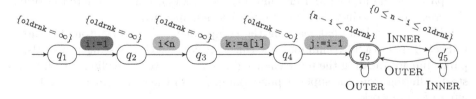

Fig. 39. The certified module $\mathcal{M}_2$ for the language $\mathcal{L}_2 =$ `i:=1` · `i<n` · `k:=a[i]` · `j:=i-1` · (INNER* · OUTER)$^\omega$

Note that f_2 is also a valid ranking function for all paths taking the outer while loop infinitely often, i.e., all paths corresponding to words from $\mathcal{L}_2 =$ `i:=1` $\cdot$ `i<n` $\cdot$ `k:=a[i]` $\cdot$ `j:=i-1` $\cdot$ $(\text{INNER}^* \cdot \text{OUTER})^\omega$. We represent these paths by the certified module $\mathcal{M}_2 = (\mathcal{A}_2, f_2, \mathcal{I}_2)$ where $\mathcal{L}(\mathcal{A}_2) = \mathcal{L}_2$, shown in Fig. 39.

After removing the words of $\mathcal{A}_2$ from $\mathcal{L}(\mathcal{A}_{|\mathcal{A}_1}^{P^{\text{ins}}})$, we, finally, obtain the BA $\mathcal{A}_{|\mathcal{A}_1,\mathcal{A}_2}^{P^{\text{ins}}}$, whose language is empty. This means that the modules $\mathcal{M}_1$ and $\mathcal{M}_2$ cover all possible paths of the program P^{ins} and, because each of them comes with a termination argument, we can conclude that all paths of P^{ins} are guaranteed to terminate.

7.3   Automata-Based Termination Analysis: Difficulties

As we have seen in the example above, the general termination analysis involves several operations based on Büchi automata, like emptiness check and complementation or language difference. While emptiness is really cheap (cf. Proposition 6), complementation or language difference are in general extremely expensive (cf. Propositions 4 and 5), so it would be better to limit their number as much as possible.

Note however that the complementation of a lasso-shaped automaton corresponding to a lasso-shaped word is really easy: it is enough to add an accepting sink state collecting all missing transitions and make the original accepting state no more accepting. While this is cheap, the net effect in the termination analysis is really limited: in this way we remove only one infinite word at a time, so there is a negligible progress in the termination analysis.

The generalizations we have seen before are useful to avoid such negligible progress, since they allow us to remove a possibly very large set of words at each iteration. This comes at the expense of the complexity of complementing the corresponding Büchi automaton, which now can suffer from the super-exponential complexity of the language difference or complementation operations.

It is easy to recognize that there is a trade-off between the size of the set of paths of the program P covered by current certified module $\mathcal{M}_i$ and the complexity of complementing $\mathcal{M}_i$ itself. There are several techniques to balance these two aspects, together with specialized algorithms for them; see [28] for more details on the different generalization techniques, their effectiveness in covering the paths of the input program, and further explanations and references about the creation of certified modules from a lasso-shaped word.

We are confident that learning the complement of Büchi automata, shown in Sect. 6, is a useful technique that can complement the existing proposals, in particular for tackling the more challenging cases where the ordinary techniques start suffering from the super-exponential grown of the complement BA. This is left to future work.

8   Conclusion

In this work, we have presented a learning algorithm for Büchi automata by means of its learning of the simple ω-regular language $(ab)^\omega$. We have also demonstrated how the learning algorithm can be used in classical automata operations such as complementation checking and in the termination analysis context. We believe that with the intuitive explanation of the different learning algorithms for both finite and ω-regular languages, it will benefit both the learning community and the model checking community.

Acknowledgement. This work has been supported by the National Natural Science Foundation of China (Grant Nos. 61532019, 61761136011), and by the CAP project GZ1023.

References

1. RABIT tool. http://languageinclusion.org/doku.php?id=tools
2. Aarts, F., Vaandrager, F.W.: Learning I/O automata. In: Gastin, P., Laroussinie, F. (eds.) CONCUR 2010. LNCS, vol. 6269, pp. 71–85. Springer, Heidelberg (2010). https://doi.org/10.1007/978-3-642-15375-4_6
3. Abdulla, P.A., et al.: Simulation subsumption in ramsey-based Büchi automata universality and inclusion testing. In: Touili, T., Cook, B., Jackson, P. (eds.) CAV 2010. LNCS, vol. 6174, pp. 132–147. Springer, Heidelberg (2010). https://doi.org/10.1007/978-3-642-14295-6_14
4. Abdulla, P.A., et al.: Advanced ramsey-based Büchi automata inclusion testing. In: Katoen, J.-P., König, B. (eds.) CONCUR 2011. LNCS, vol. 6901, pp. 187–202. Springer, Heidelberg (2011). https://doi.org/10.1007/978-3-642-23217-6_13
5. Allred, J.D., Ultes-Nitsche, U.: A simple and optimal complementation algorithm for Büchi automata. In: LICS, pp. 46–55 (2018)
6. Alpern, B., Schneider, F.B.: Recognizing safety and liveness. Distrib. Comput. **2**(3), 117–126 (1987)
7. Alur, R., Černý, P., Madhusudan, P., Nam, W.: Synthesis of interface specifications for Java classes. In: POPL, pp. 98–109 (2005)
8. Angluin, D.: Learning regular sets from queries and counterexamples. Inf. Comput. **75**(2), 87–106 (1987)
9. Angluin, D., Boker, U., Fisman, D.: Families of DFAs as acceptors of omega-regular languages. In: MFCS, pp. 11:1–11:14 (2016)
10. Angluin, D., Eisenstat, S., Fisman, D.: Learning regular languages via alternating automata. In: IJCAI, pp. 3308–3314 (2015)
11. Angluin, D., Fisman, D.: Learning regular omega languages. Theor. Comput. Sci. **650**, 57–72 (2016)
12. Arnold, A.: A syntactic congruence for rational ω-languages. Theor. Comput. Sci. **39**, 333–335 (1985)
13. Babiak, T., et al.: The hanoi omega-automata format. In: Kroening, D., Păsăreanu, C.S. (eds.) CAV 2015. LNCS, vol. 9206, pp. 479–486. Springer, Cham (2015). https://doi.org/10.1007/978-3-319-21690-4_31
14. Ben-Amram, A.M.: Size-change termination, monotonicity constraints and ranking functions. Log. Methods Comput. Sci. **6** (2010)

15. Ben-Amram, A.M., Genaim, S.: On the linear ranking problem for integer linear-constraint loops. In: POPL, pp. 51–62. ACM, New York (2013)
16. Ben-Amram, A.M., Genaim, S.: Complexity of bradley-manna-sipma lexicographic ranking functions. In: Kroening, D., Păsăreanu, C.S. (eds.) CAV 2015. LNCS, vol. 9207, pp. 304–321. Springer, Cham (2015). https://doi.org/10.1007/978-3-319-21668-3_18
17. Ben-Amram, A.M., Genaim, S.: On multiphase-linear ranking functions. In: Majumdar, R., Kunčak, V. (eds.) CAV 2017. LNCS, vol. 10427, pp. 601–620. Springer, Cham (2017). https://doi.org/10.1007/978-3-319-63390-9_32
18. Biere, A., Cimatti, A., Clarke, E.M., Zhu, Y.: Symbolic model checking without BDDs. In: TACAS, pp. 193–207 (1999)
19. Blahoudek, F., Heizmann, M., Schewe, S., Strejček, J., Tsai, M.-H.: Complementing semi-deterministic Büchi automata. In: Chechik, M., Raskin, J.-F. (eds.) TACAS 2016. LNCS, vol. 9636, pp. 770–787. Springer, Heidelberg (2016). https://doi.org/10.1007/978-3-662-49674-9_49
20. Bollig, B., Habermehl, P., Kern, C., Leucker, M.: Angluin-style learning of NFA. In: IJCAI, pp. 1004–1009 (2009)
21. Bollig, B., Katoen, J.-P., Kern, C., Leucker, M., Neider, D., Piegdon, D.R.: libalf: the automata learning framework. In: Touili, T., Cook, B., Jackson, P. (eds.) CAV 2010. LNCS, vol. 6174, pp. 360–364. Springer, Heidelberg (2010). https://doi.org/10.1007/978-3-642-14295-6_32
22. Borralleras, C., et al.: Proving termination through conditional termination. In: Legay, A., Margaria, T. (eds.) TACAS 2017. LNCS, vol. 10205, pp. 99–117. Springer, Heidelberg (2017). https://doi.org/10.1007/978-3-662-54577-5_6
23. Bradley, A.R., Manna, Z., Sipma, H.B.: Linear ranking with reachability. In: Etessami, K., Rajamani, S.K. (eds.) CAV 2005. LNCS, vol. 3576, pp. 491–504. Springer, Heidelberg (2005). https://doi.org/10.1007/11513988_48
24. Breuers, S., Löding, C., Olschewski, J.: Improved ramsey-based Büchi complementation. In: Birkedal, L. (ed.) FoSSaCS 2012. LNCS, vol. 7213, pp. 150–164. Springer, Heidelberg (2012). https://doi.org/10.1007/978-3-642-28729-9_10
25. Büchi, J.R.: On a decision method in restricted second order arithmetic. In: International Congress on Logic, Methodology and Philosophy of Science, pp. 1–11 (1962)
26. Calbrix, H., Nivat, M., Podelski, A.: Ultimately periodic words of rational ω-languages. In: Brookes, S., Main, M., Melton, A., Mislove, M., Schmidt, D. (eds.) MFPS 1993. LNCS, vol. 802, pp. 554–566. Springer, Heidelberg (1994). https://doi.org/10.1007/3-540-58027-1_27
27. Chapman, M., Chockler, H., Kesseli, P., Kroening, D., Strichman, O., Tautschnig, M.: Learning the language of error. In: ATVA, pp. 114–130 (2015)
28. Chen, Y.F., et al.: Advanced automata-based algorithms for program termination checking. In: PLDI, pp. 135–150 (2018)
29. Chen, Y.F., et al.: PAC learning-based verification and model synthesis. In: ICSE, pp. 714–724 (2016)
30. Choueka, Y.: Theories of automata on ω-tapes: a simplified approach. J. Comput. Syst. Sci. 8(2), 117–141 (1974)
31. Clarke, E.M.: Model checking – my 27-year quest to overcome the state explosion problem. In: Cervesato, I., Veith, H., Voronkov, A. (eds.) LPAR 2008. LNCS (LNAI), vol. 5330, pp. 182–182. Springer, Heidelberg (2008). https://doi.org/10.1007/978-3-540-89439-1_13
32. Clarke, E.M., Henzinger, T.A., Veith, H., Bloem, R. (eds.): Handbook of Model Checking. Springer, Cham (2018). https://doi.org/10.1007/978-3-319-10575-8

33. Clemente, L., Mayr, R.: Advanced automata minimization. In: Proceedings of POPL 2013, pp. 63–74. ACM (2013)
34. Cobleigh, J.M., Giannakopoulou, D., PǍsǍreanu, C.S.: Learning assumptions for compositional verification. In: Garavel, H., Hatcliff, J. (eds.) TACAS 2003. LNCS, vol. 2619, pp. 331–346. Springer, Heidelberg (2003). https://doi.org/10.1007/3-540-36577-X_24
35. Cook, B., Kroening, D., Rümmer, P., Wintersteiger, C.M.: Ranking function synthesis for bit-vector relations. Formal Methods Syst. Des. **43**(1), 93–120 (2013)
36. Cook, B., Podelski, A., Rybalchenko, A.: Termination proofs for systems code. In: PLDI, pp. 415–426. ACM, New York (2006)
37. Cook, B., Podelski, A., Rybalchenko, A.: Proving program termination. Commun. ACM **54**(5), 88–98 (2011)
38. Cook, B., See, A., Zuleger, F.: Ramsey vs. lexicographic termination proving. In: Piterman, N., Smolka, S.A. (eds.) TACAS 2013. LNCS, vol. 7795, pp. 47–61. Springer, Heidelberg (2013). https://doi.org/10.1007/978-3-642-36742-7_4
39. Duret-Lutz, A., Lewkowicz, A., Fauchille, A., Michaud, T., Renault, É., Xu, L.: Spot 2.0 — a framework for LTL and ω-automata manipulation. In: Artho, C., Legay, A., Peled, D. (eds.) ATVA 2016. LNCS, vol. 9938, pp. 122–129. Springer, Cham (2016). https://doi.org/10.1007/978-3-319-46520-3_8
40. Emerson, E.A., Lei, C.: Modalities for model checking: branching time strikes back. In: POPL, pp. 84–96 (1985)
41. Emerson, E.A., Lei, C.: Modalities for model checking: branching time logic strikes back. Sci. Comput. Program. **8**(3), 275–306 (1987)
42. Farzan, A., Chen, Y.-F., Clarke, E.M., Tsay, Y.-K., Wang, B.-Y.: Extending automated compositional verification to the full class of omega-regular languages. In: Ramakrishnan, C.R., Rehof, J. (eds.) TACAS 2008. LNCS, vol. 4963, pp. 2–17. Springer, Heidelberg (2008). https://doi.org/10.1007/978-3-540-78800-3_2
43. Feng, L., Kwiatkowska, M., Parker, D.: Compositional verification of probabilistic systems using learning. In: QEST, pp. 133–142 (2010)
44. Fogarty, S., Kupferman, O., Vardi, M.Y., Wilke, T.: Profile trees for Büchi word automata, with application to determinization. Inf. Comput. **245**, 136–151 (2015)
45. Fogarty, S., Kupferman, O., Wilke, T., Vardi, M.Y.: Unifying Büchi complementation constructions. Log. Methods Comput. Sci. **9**(1) (2013)
46. Friedgut, E., Kupferman, O., Vardi, M.Y.: Büchi complementation made tighter. In: Wang, F. (ed.) ATVA 2004. LNCS, vol. 3299, pp. 64–78. Springer, Heidelberg (2004). https://doi.org/10.1007/978-3-540-30476-0_10
47. Ganty, P., Genaim, S.: Proving termination starting from the end. In: Sharygina, N., Veith, H. (eds.) CAV 2013. LNCS, vol. 8044, pp. 397–412. Springer, Heidelberg (2013). https://doi.org/10.1007/978-3-642-39799-8_27
48. Giesl, J., et al.: Analyzing program termination and complexity automatically with AProVe. J. Autom. Reason. **58**, 3–31 (2017)
49. Grädel, E., Thomas, W., Wilke, T. (eds.): Automata Logics, and Infinite Games. LNCS, vol. 2500. Springer, Heidelberg (2002). https://doi.org/10.1007/3-540-36387-4
50. Grinchtein, O., Jonsson, B., Leucker, M.: Learning of event-recording automata. Theor. Comput. Sci. **411**(47), 4029–4054 (2010)
51. Gurumurthy, S., Kupferman, O., Somenzi, F., Vardi, M.Y.: On complementing nondeterministic Büchi automata. In: Geist, D., Tronci, E. (eds.) CHARME 2003. LNCS, vol. 2860, pp. 96–110. Springer, Heidelberg (2003). https://doi.org/10.1007/978-3-540-39724-3_10

52. Harris, W.R., Lal, A., Nori, A.V., Rajamani, S.K.: Alternation for termination. In: Cousot, R., Martel, M. (eds.) SAS 2010. LNCS, vol. 6337, pp. 304–319. Springer, Heidelberg (2010). https://doi.org/10.1007/978-3-642-15769-1_19

53. van Heerdt, G., Sammartino, M., Silva, A.: CALF: categorical automata learning framework. In: CSL, pp. 29:1–29:24 (2017)

54. Heizmann, M., Hoenicke, J., Leike, J., Podelski, A.: Linear ranking for linear lasso programs. In: Van Hung, D., Ogawa, M. (eds.) ATVA 2013. LNCS, vol. 8172, pp. 365–380. Springer, Cham (2013). https://doi.org/10.1007/978-3-319-02444-8_26

55. Heizmann, M., Hoenicke, J., Podelski, A.: Termination analysis by learning terminating programs. In: Biere, A., Bloem, R. (eds.) CAV 2014. LNCS, vol. 8559, pp. 797–813. Springer, Cham (2014). https://doi.org/10.1007/978-3-319-08867-9_53

56. Hopcroft, J.E., Motwani, R., Ullman, J.D.: Introduction to Automata Theory, Languages, and Computation. Addison-Wesley Longman Publishing Co., Inc., Boston (2006)

57. Howar, F., Steffen, B., Jonsson, B., Cassel, S.: Inferring canonical register automata. In: Kuncak, V., Rybalchenko, A. (eds.) VMCAI 2012. LNCS, vol. 7148, pp. 251–266. Springer, Heidelberg (2012). https://doi.org/10.1007/978-3-642-27940-9_17

58. Isberner, M., Howar, F., Steffen, B.: Learning register automata: from languages to program structures. Mach. Learn. 96(1–2), 65–98 (2014)

59. Isberner, M., Howar, F., Steffen, B.: The TTT algorithm: a redundancy-free approach to active automata learning. In: Bonakdarpour, B., Smolka, S.A. (eds.) RV 2014. LNCS, vol. 8734, pp. 307–322. Springer, Cham (2014). https://doi.org/10.1007/978-3-319-11164-3_26

60. Isberner, M., Howar, F., Steffen, B.: The open-source LearnLib. In: Kroening, D., Păsăreanu, C.S. (eds.) CAV 2015. LNCS, vol. 9206, pp. 487–495. Springer, Cham (2015). https://doi.org/10.1007/978-3-319-21690-4_32

61. Kähler, D., Wilke, T.: Complementation, disambiguation, and determinization of Büchi automata unified. In: Aceto, L., Damgård, I., Goldberg, L.A., Halldórsson, M.M., Ingólfsdóttir, A., Walukiewicz, I. (eds.) ICALP 2008. LNCS, vol. 5125, pp. 724–735. Springer, Heidelberg (2008). https://doi.org/10.1007/978-3-540-70575-8_59

62. Kaminski, M.: A classification of ω-regular languages. Theor. Comput. Sci. 36, 217–229 (1985)

63. Kearns, M.J., Vazirani, U.V.: An Introduction to Computational Learning Theory. MIT Press, Cambridge (1994)

64. Kroening, D., Sharygina, N., Tsitovich, A., Wintersteiger, C.M.: Termination analysis with compositional transition invariants. In: Touili, T., Cook, B., Jackson, P. (eds.) CAV 2010. LNCS, vol. 6174, pp. 89–103. Springer, Heidelberg (2010). https://doi.org/10.1007/978-3-642-14295-6_9

65. Kupferman, O., Vardi, M.Y.: Weak alternating automata are not that weak. ACM Trans. Comput. Logic 2(3), 408–429 (2001)

66. Kurshan, R.P.: Complementing deterministic Büchi automata in polynomial time. J. Comput. Syst. Sci. 35(1), 59–71 (1987)

67. Kurshan, R.P.: Computer-Aided Verification of Coordinating Processes: The Automata-theoretic Approach. Princeton University Press, Princeton (1994)

68. Landweber, L.H.: Decision problems for ω-automata. Math. Syst. Theory 3(4), 376–384 (1969)

69. Le, T.C., Qin, S., Chin, W.: Termination and non-termination specification inference. In: PLDI, pp. 489–498. ACM, New York (2015)

70. Lee, W., Wang, B.-Y., Yi, K.: Termination analysis with algorithmic learning. In: Madhusudan, P., Seshia, S.A. (eds.) CAV 2012. LNCS, vol. 7358, pp. 88–104. Springer, Heidelberg (2012). https://doi.org/10.1007/978-3-642-31424-7_12
71. Leike, J., Heizmann, M.: Ranking templates for linear loops. Log. Methods Comput. Sci. **11**(1) (2015)
72. Li, Y., Chen, Y., Zhang, L., Liu, D.: A novel learning algorithm for Büchi automata based on family of DFAs and classification trees. CoRR abs/1610.07380 (2016). http://arxiv.org/abs/1610.07380
73. Li, Y., Chen, Y.-F., Zhang, L., Liu, D.: A novel learning algorithm for Büchi automata based on family of DFAs and classification trees. In: Legay, A., Margaria, T. (eds.) TACAS 2017. LNCS, vol. 10205, pp. 208–226. Springer, Heidelberg (2017). https://doi.org/10.1007/978-3-662-54577-5_12
74. Li, Y., Turrini, A., Zhang, L., Schewe, S.: Learning to complement Büchi automata. In: VMCAI, vol. 10747, pp. 313–335 (2018)
75. Lin, S.W., André, E., Liu, Y., Sun, J., Dong, J.S.: Learning assumptions for compositional verification of timed systems. IEEE Trans. Softw. Eng. **40**(2), 137–153 (2014)
76. Maler, O., Pnueli, A.: On the learnability of infinitary regular sets. Inf. Comput. **118**(2), 316–326 (1995)
77. Maler, O., Staiger, L.: On syntactic congruences for omega-languages. In: STACS, pp. 586–594 (1993)
78. McMillan, K.L.: Symbolic Model Checking. Kluwer (1993)
79. Moerman, J., Sammartino, M., Silva, A., Klin, B., Szynwelski, M.: Learning nominal automata. In: POPL, pp. 613–625 (2017)
80. Padon, O., Hoenicke, J., Losa, G., Podelski, A., Sagiv, M., Shoham, S.: Reducing liveness to safety in first-order logic. ACM Program. Lang. **2**(POPL), 26:1–26:33 (2018)
81. Peled, D., Vardi, M.Y., Yannakakis, M.: Black box checking. J. Automata Lang. Comb. **7**(2), 225–246 (2002)
82. Piterman, N.: From nondeterministic Büchi and streett automata to deterministic parity automata. In: LICS, pp. 255–264 (2006)
83. Podelski, A., Rybalchenko, A.: A complete method for the synthesis of linear ranking functions. In: Steffen, B., Levi, G. (eds.) VMCAI 2004. LNCS, vol. 2937, pp. 239–251. Springer, Heidelberg (2004). https://doi.org/10.1007/978-3-540-24622-0_20
84. Podelski, A., Rybalchenko, A.: Transition invariants. In: LICS, pp. 32–41. IEEE Computer Society, Washington, DC (2004)
85. Podelski, A., Rybalchenko, A., Wies, T.: Heap assumptions on demand. In: Gupta, A., Malik, S. (eds.) CAV 2008. LNCS, vol. 5123, pp. 314–327. Springer, Heidelberg (2008). https://doi.org/10.1007/978-3-540-70545-1_31
86. Popeea, C., Rybalchenko, A.: Compositional termination proofs for multithreaded programs. In: Flanagan, C., König, B. (eds.) TACAS 2012. LNCS, vol. 7214, pp. 237–251. Springer, Heidelberg (2012). https://doi.org/10.1007/978-3-642-28756-5_17
87. Rivest, R.L., Schapire, R.E.: Inference of finite automata using homing sequences. In: STOC, pp. 411–420 (1989)
88. de Ruiter, J., Poll, E.: Protocol state fuzzing of TLS implementations. In: USENIX, pp. 193–206 (2015)
89. Safra, S.: On the complexity of omega-automata. In: FOCS, pp. 319–327 (1988)
90. Schewe, S.: Büchi complementation made tight. In: STACS. LIPIcs, vol. 3, pp. 661–672 (2009)

91. Schewe, S.: Tighter bounds for the determinisation of Büchi automata. In: de Alfaro, L. (ed.) FoSSaCS 2009. LNCS, vol. 5504, pp. 167–181. Springer, Heidelberg (2009). https://doi.org/10.1007/978-3-642-00596-1_13
92. Sickert, S., Esparza, J., Jaax, S., Křetínský, J.: Limit-deterministic Büchi automata for linear temporal logic. In: Chaudhuri, S., Farzan, A. (eds.) CAV 2016. LNCS, vol. 9780, pp. 312–332. Springer, Cham (2016). https://doi.org/10.1007/978-3-319-41540-6_17
93. Sistla, A.P., Vardi, M.Y., Wolper, P.: The complementation problem for Büchi automata with appplications to temporal logic. Theor. Comput. Sci. 49, 217–237 (1987)
94. Staiger, L.: Research in the theory of omega-languages. Elektronische Informationsverarbeitung und Kybernetik 23(8/9), 415–439 (1987)
95. Ströder, T., et al.: Automatically proving termination and memory safety for programs with pointer arithmetic. J. Autom. Reason. 58, 33–65 (2017)
96. Thomas, W.: Automata on infinite objects. In: Handbook of Theoretical Computer Science, vol. B: Formal Models and Sematics, chap. 4, pp. 133–192 (1990)
97. Thomas, W.: Languages, automata, and logic. In: Rozenberg, G., Salomaa, A. (eds.) Handbook of Formal Languages, pp. 389–455. Springer, Heidelberg (1997). https://doi.org/10.1007/978-3-642-59126-6_7
98. Tsai, M., Fogarty, S., Vardi, M.Y., Tsay, Y.: State of Büchi complementation. Log. Methods Comput. Sci. 10(4) (2014)
99. Tsai, M.-H., Tsay, Y.-K., Hwang, Y.-S.: GOAL for games, omega-automata, and logics. In: Sharygina, N., Veith, H. (eds.) CAV 2013. LNCS, vol. 8044, pp. 883–889. Springer, Heidelberg (2013). https://doi.org/10.1007/978-3-642-39799-8_62
100. Tsay, Y.-K., Tsai, M.-H., Chang, J.-S., Chang, Y.-W.: Büchi store: an open repository of Büchi automata. In: Abdulla, P.A., Leino, K.R.M. (eds.) TACAS 2011. LNCS, vol. 6605, pp. 262–266. Springer, Heidelberg (2011). https://doi.org/10.1007/978-3-642-19835-9_23
101. Urban, C., Gurfinkel, A., Kahsai, T.: Synthesizing ranking functions from bits and pieces. In: Chechik, M., Raskin, J.-F. (eds.) TACAS 2016. LNCS, vol. 9636, pp. 54–70. Springer, Heidelberg (2016). https://doi.org/10.1007/978-3-662-49674-9_4
102. Urban, C., Miné, A.: An abstract domain to infer ordinal-valued ranking functions. In: Shao, Z. (ed.) ESOP 2014. LNCS, vol. 8410, pp. 412–431. Springer, Heidelberg (2014). https://doi.org/10.1007/978-3-642-54833-8_22
103. Vaandrager, F.: Model learning. Commun. ACM 60(2), 86–95 (2017)
104. Vardi, M.Y.: An automata-theoretic approach to linear temporal logic. In: Moller, F., Birtwistle, G. (eds.) Logics for Concurrency. LNCS, vol. 1043, pp. 238–266. Springer, Heidelberg (1996). https://doi.org/10.1007/3-540-60915-6_6
105. Vardi, M.Y.: The Büchi complementation saga. In: Thomas, W., Weil, P. (eds.) STACS 2007. LNCS, vol. 4393, pp. 12–22. Springer, Heidelberg (2007). https://doi.org/10.1007/978-3-540-70918-3_2
106. Vardi, M.Y., Wilke, T.: Automata: from logics to algorithms. In: Logic and Automata: History and Perspectives [in Honor of Wolfgang Thomas], pp. 629–736 (2008)
107. Wang, F., Wu, J.-H., Huang, C.-H., Chang, K.-H.: Evolving a test oracle in black-box testing. In: Giannakopoulou, D., Orejas, F. (eds.) FASE 2011. LNCS, vol. 6603, pp. 310–325. Springer, Heidelberg (2011). https://doi.org/10.1007/978-3-642-19811-3_22
108. Yan, Q.: Lower bounds for complementation of ω-automata via the full automata technique. Log. Methods Comput. Sci. 4(1:5) (2008)

Securing Emergent IoT Applications

Prabhakaran Kasinathan[1,2](✉) [iD] and Jorge Cuellar[1,2]

[1] Siemens AG, CT, IT Security, Munich, Germany
{prabhakaran.kasinathan,jorge.cuellar}@siemens.com
[2] University of Passau, Passau, Germany

Abstract. Attacks on IoT, Cyber-Physical-Systems (CPS), and other computing systems are evolving rapidly. As a result, IoT devices used in critical infrastructures such as energy, health-care, and water supply systems are vulnerable to attacks. A successful attack on such safety-critical infrastructures may have life-threatening consequences. On the other hand, existing security mechanisms are not enough to protect constrained IoT devices. Therefore, we need better security mechanisms and tools to manage and protect IoT devices from malicious use.

In emerging paradigms like Internet-of-Things (IoT) platforms, Industry 4.0, collaborative portals, and many others, we deal with a multi-tenant architecture. In a multi-tenant architecture, the owners want to secure their own integrity, confidentiality, and functionality goals without being concerned about the goals of other entities. In this paper, we present a framework to negotiate, compromise, and inter-operate between different services or platforms to fulfill a *purpose*. Furthermore, to ensure correct and safe operation of IoT systems, we must assure that the integrity of the underlying systems and processes is properly executed as intended i.e., the processes cannot be changed in an unauthorized way.

In this paper, we present our Petri Net based workflow specification and enforcement framework to realize *workflow-aware access control* and to protect the *process integrity* of IoT applications. The Petri Net models are amenable to formal verification. The resulting workflows have other properties such as the ability to recover from error conditions. In addition, we present a method to achieve distributed access control and accountability integrated with our framework. We allow practitioner-friendly tools to collect requirements and goals to design secure IoT systems and processes. Finally, we present a guide to implement our framework with existing development environments and validate the methodology using concrete use case scenarios.

1 Introduction

The EU Research Cluster on IoT (IERC) [68] defines Internet of Things (IoT) as "an infrastructure with self-configuring capabilities based on standard and interoperable communication protocols where physical and virtual *things* have identities, physical attributes, and virtual personalities and use intelligent interfaces, and are seamlessly integrated into the information network".

© Springer Nature Switzerland AG 2019
J. P. Bowen et al. (Eds.): SETSS 2018, LNCS 11430, pp. 99–147, 2019.
https://doi.org/10.1007/978-3-030-17601-3_3

Constrained IoT devices are categorized by their ability to process and store data, energy consumption, and communication capabilities (see [12]). *Class 0* devices are really constrained sensor-like motes with less than 10 KB of RAM and 100 KB of flash memory. *Class 1* devices are quite constrained, and cannot use standard Internet Protocol stack; however, class 1 devices support protocols designed for constrained devices. *Class 2* devices are less constrained, can support some security functionalities specifically designed for constrained devices. Finally, the devices with capabilities beyond class 2 support most of the traditional Internet and security protocols like HTTP and TLS; however, they can still be constrained by limited energy supply. Generally, IoT devices use both long and short-range communication technologies such as Zigbee, Bluetooth, LTE, etc. combined with constrained communication protocols such as Constrained Application Protocol (CoAP) for Internet connectivity. Constrained IoT devices are cheap, compact, easy to deploy, and consume less energy. Recently, organizations use data collected from IoT devices to get insights, predict, and to optimize their services with the help of Artificial Intelligence (AI) technologies. This approach is used in various applications such as smart manufacturing, industrial control systems, financial services, retail, intelligent logistics, transportation, medical and healthcare applications, smart grid, intelligent traffic, environmental monitoring, smart home, assisted living, agriculture, and many more.

Constrained IoT devices are vulnerable to attacks because existing state-of-the-art security mechanisms do not fit within the constrained devices and often they can be accessed physically by an attacker. For example, modern remote attestation technique is difficult to achieve in constrained IoT devices because of the lack of space and processing power [13,61]. Implementing secure key generation and key storage in constrained IoT devices are hard (see guidelines from Trusted Computing Group [71]) because these devices lack sufficient entropy to generate random numbers and are prone to side-channel attacks. Several attacks on industrial IoT devices are presented in [61]. Due to the vulnerabilities, hackers frequently target IoT devices to escalate attacks on valuable assets. The 21st century has seen a sudden rise of insecure IoT devices in an unexpected scale which require immediate attention i.e., we must secure those emergent IoT devices. Now, since IoT devices are used in critical infrastructures, it is evident that we need better security mechanisms and tools to protect them. Researchers in academia and industry are working together to secure emergent IoT devices, protocols, and applications. Furthermore, IoT devices collect personal information or data that can be used to infer private activities or habits without proper consent. As a consequence, the European Union's privacy regulation GDPR (see [22]) has enforced strict regulations for handling private information of users.

In emergent IoT applications, the multi-tenant architecture is more prominent. In such applications, different entities provide and consume services from one another and each entities might want to enforce their own integrity, confidentiality or functionality goals on other entities consuming his service. The main problem with multi-tenant systems and architecture is the "trust problem": in order to achieve his goals, each party requires that the others behave in a particular way. Ideally, the party would like to specify a "contract" that declares his assumptions about the behavior of other entities as well as the guarantees that he offers to them about his actions. But how can he trust other parties to behave according to the contract? How can he be sure that they do not "cheat"? In this paper, we investigate a way to automatically enforce a contract.

This is the purpose of a "smart contract": it declares what happens if some of the parties misbehave and what will happen in case of other error or unexpected conditions. Each party imposes his rules on entities while they interact with his services. In the case of electronic money, this is easier to enforce: the party that cheats lose money. In the case where money is not available directly, it may be difficult to penalize a party that is not complying with the stipulated rules. In general, those sequences of interactions defined by "smart contracts" may be seen as a set of allowed actions, or in other words, a workflow. Clearly, there is a need to negotiate, compromise, and inter-operate the tasks to be completed by the different entities within such a system.

To enforce such tasks to be executed in a particular order we need a workflow specification and enforcement method. It is important to notice that securing the assumption-commitment semantics of a smart contract is also the key for its verification. The smart contracts are given as a refinement of Petri Nets, which are subject to verification, see [59].

More specifically, we use the Petri Net based Workflow Specification and Enforcement method presented in [39,40] to write such smart contracts which guarantee the integrity of processes. The method also supports dynamic workflows that adapt to error conditions by allowing services to create on the fly sub-workflows. Furthermore, the framework provides accountability and transparency without assuming a central authority.

1.1 Security and Privacy Challenges in IoT

Security and Privacy challenges in IoT and Industrial Internet of Things (IIoT) are discussed in [61,66,76] where the authors discuss technical, financial and legal issues involved in IoT and existing solutions. In this paper, we discuss the technical aspects of security and privacy challenges in IoT/IIoT. The OWASP (Open Web Application Security Project) presented the Top 10 IoT vulnerabilities and attack surfaces (see [47]), we discuss the topics relevant to this paper here:

– *Authentication and Authorization*: the goal of an authentication system is to verify that entities are correctly identified [11]. After authenticating an entity, the security mechanism of verifying whether the entity is allowed to perform certain actions is known as authorization. Existing state-of-the-art authentication and authorization mechanisms do not fit in constrained IoT devices; academic and industrial researchers are working towards addressing them (see IETF ACE working group [32]). Since IoT devices are cheap, they do not have interactive interfaces to implement traditional authentication mechanisms such as a display to present security info to the user, or a keypad to enter passwords. Sometimes, even when proper security mechanisms are in place, users do not use them properly. For example, the default password for many IoT devices is not changed by their users because of its complexity i.e., the user needs to connect the device to the local network and login into it via a web interface using default credentials to change it. For instance, hackers have used this vulnerability to mount denial-of-service attacks on popular websites by sending remote commands to billions of IoT devices - see Mirai botnet attack [4]. On the other hand, most IoT devices implement single-factor authentication such as the username and password, and authorization does not consider the context of activities involved like tasks in a workflow.

- *Confidentiality and privacy*: IoT devices can collect sensitive information, including personal data. Therefore, the data subjects want their information to be confidential. Constrained IoT devices cannot use standard encryption mechanisms, such as Transport Layer Security (TLS). Light-weight protocols, such as Datagram Transport Layer Security (DTLS) over CoAP (See [24]) have been designed to support the confidentiality and integrity of transported data. One of the challenges is that for instance, class 1 devices cannot properly support DTLS, and therefore, packet losses will result in retransmission of messages, affecting the performance of battery powered devices. Compromised devices holding private data will expose information about the private life of the data subjects. This demands the need for privacy-preserving (enhancing) and confidentiality mechanisms integrated with the IoT device communication [76].

- *Integrity*: there are at least three aspects of integrity. First, we have data integrity – the assurance that the data transferred from one entity to another has not been altered or tampered with. Second, we have the integrity of data stored in memory – this includes, firmware, key material, data, or programs stored in memory – is not altered. Third, we have *process integrity*. A business/technical process specified must be executed as it is specified i.e., no one is able to change, add additional steps or skip steps defined in the process. This property is called "process integrity", and it is discussed in detail below. Security mechanisms such as Message Authenticate Code (MAC) exist to ensure data integrity, and hardware or software attestation techniques exist to ensure the integrity of firmware or application code. But achieving process integrity is difficult, and no solutions exist to enforce it. One of the main goals of this paper is to specify a process and ensure that it is properly enforced on the entities executing it.

- *Interoperability*: IoT devices are heterogeneous in terms of processing power, memory capacity, and communication technologies. Some IoT devices may or may not operate with each other because of non-interoperable standards. Different organizations collaborate to create interoperable standards such as the Alliance for the Internet of Things Innovation (AIOTI) (see [3]). Also, the research community such as ACE (see [32]) is working towards standardizing security protocols to make IoT devices interoperable and secure. In particular, we need interoperable security mechanisms that can be implemented on the majority of IoT devices.

- *Self-Configuration and Multi-Tenancy*: is evident that IoT devices are getting powerful, cheaper, (see Moore's law [63]) and energy-efficient day-by-day. Installing and configuring such advanced IoT devices with existing IoT applications should not require too much human involvement. The IoT devices should have self-configuring features i.e., backward compatibility, resilient to connection loses and device failures, etc. In such error cases, the IoT system must re-adapt to the changes and work normally. Multi-tenancy refers to the fact that devices or services belong to different owners with different or competing goals. Those parties prefer to cooperate by exchanging information with each other such that both parties will profit from information or activities exchanged. IoT devices need to support such kind of multi-tenant features without losing the security requirements of parties involved.

Protecting the Process Integrity of IoT Applications. A *process* is a set of interrelated activities or tasks that must be carried out to accomplish a goal [11]. A business/technical process is also called a workflow, but we use the two words as synonymous. Different owners/stakeholders of devices or services will probably try optimizing their own results and to secure their own integrity, confidentiality or functionality goals, without really being concerned about the goals of other entities. We call this property as Multi-Tenancy. We need a method to protect the integrity of business processes of each owner/stakeholder without compromising the integrity of the process of other involved entities.

A workflow can be defined as a pattern of activities or tasks to be completed in a particular partial order by the involved entities, following predefined rules, in order to accomplish a specific goal or subgoal. A workflow must be executed as it is specified i.e., ensuring *process-integrity*. During the execution of the workflow, the participants may exchange with each other documents, information, see [77]. Confidentiality is not as important as the availability and integrity of the cybersecurity processes, which is mission-critical. Achieving process integrity of different owners/stakeholders collaborating with each other is the main focus of the paper.

We describe a small case study to gather the requirements, study the challenges, and to formulate the goals of our work. Let us consider the following use case scenario (UC1): a manufacturing company requires continuous monitoring and maintenance of equipment in its factory. For example, IoT devices are used to monitor temperature, smoke, and fire, etc. IoT devices can also be used as actuators to control access to doors, equipment, and emergency exits. The provenance of IoT devices, quality, and maintenance of the manufacturing plant are strictly enforced by predefined processes (workflows) defined by the manufacturing owner. The integrity of such processes must be enforced to ensure quality products being produced in the plant. Usually, a manufacturing plant consists of different equipment or systems from different manufacturers, each will have their own maintenance processes. If the production stops because of an equipment malfunction or a supply chain problem or a worker who failed to follow the predefined rules, etc., then the problem must be identified and addressed as soon as possible. To ensure the integrity of the processes strict access control methods must be used. With this use case, we will formulate the requirements, challenges, and goals of our work.

1.2 Goals of Our Framework

We want our framework to have a *workflow-driven access control* in contrast to the commonly used mandatory (MAC), discretionary (DAC), or role-based access control (RBAC), which have been well-studied in the literature, see [62]. Thus, the goals of our framework are:

- To provide a generic, interoperable, and distributed workflow-aware access control method that restricts the entities to execute tasks in a predefined order defined in the workflow. By doing this, we can guarantee the process integrity of that particular workflow.
- Our Petri Net based workflow specification and enforcement method should be interoperable i.e., it should support existing authorization standards such as OAuth.
- Our method should support dynamic workflows that adapt to error conditions i.e., allowing services to interact with each other and create on the fly sub-workflows without changing the objective of the main workflow.
- Our framework should be extendable and support the integration of practitioner-friendly tools.
- Our framework should support distributed accountability i.e., when necessary, we can prove the actions of entities executing the workflow.

In this paper, we extend our Petri Net based workflow specification and enforcement framework presented in [39, 40] to present a comprehensive access control security framework for the Internet of Things (IoT); however, this approach can be applied to any generic computing system. The main contributions of this paper are: first, we summarize our Petri Net extensions such as timeout transitions contracts and open Petri Net places; second, we extend our framework to support requirement elicitation methods with practitioner-friendly tools, distributed accountability, and generation of Petri Net based smart contracts for Blockchain; third, we use our framework to solve three use case scenarios; finally, we present a high-level guide to implement our framework with existing systems.

To summarize, we present a method:

- To specify processes as workflows that can be created in a stepwise manner using standard software engineering processes and tools. Such workflows specified as Petri Nets are amenable to formal verification.
- To constrain an entity using an application/services to obey a prescribed workflow with fine-grained authorization constraints based on *least privilege* and *need to access* principle.
- That allows entities participating in a workflow to have a choice, for example, to accept (or reject) "contracts" or conditions.

- That allows services and entities executing a workflow to handle error conditions by supporting the creation of dynamic workflows, and that provides accountability without assuming a central authority.
- To exchange authorization tokens in a secure and privacy-enhanced way. Note: this method can also be used to transfer other tokens (such as money, information, etc.) not just authorization tokens.
- To support distributed accountability while executing the workflow i.e., actions executed by entities executing the workflow is recorded in an immutable database.
- To support the generation of Petri Net based smart contracts to be deployed in a Blockchain.

The Rest of the Paper is Organized as Follows: Section 2 describes security and privacy requirements of IoT and motivates the need for advanced security mechanisms such as workflow-aware access control methods for emergent IoT applications; Sect. 3 describes the evolution and background of Petri Nets; Sect. 4 describes the existing background work published in the literature; Sect. 5 presents the contributions of our work; Sect. 6 describes three different use case scenarios where we apply our method and solve them; Sect. 7 describes a high-level summary of our method and a guide to implement our method with existing systems; finally, we present limitations of our approach in Sect. 8 and conclusion in Sect. 9.

2 Security and Privacy Requirements for IoT Applications

The technical challenges of securing emerging IoT applications were described in Sect. 1.1. Now, we discuss the relevant security and privacy *requirements* for securing the emergent IoT applications. In particular, we refer to the maintenance of manufacturing plant use case scenario UC1 to formulate the following requirements.

2.1 Requirements Elicitation

The requirements engineering process can be divided into four tasks namely the elicitation, negotiation, specification/documentation, and verification/validation of requirements [55]. When we want to solve a problem, first, we need to gather more information about the problem i.e., elicitation of the requirements, needs, and constraints about the system. Often, information about the problem (or system) is distributed among many stakeholders i.e., the knowledge is not available from one source (user or customer). Therefore, the identification of the relevant sources during the elicitation task is crucial. Modern tools such as Unified Modeling Language (UML) or Systems Modeling Language (SysML) allow us to collect requirements, use cases, draw activity diagrams, and finally to validate requirements of a complete system. In particular, SysML provides tight integration of both software and hardware components. Thus, requirement elicitation is important to understand the problem and to gather requirements. For example, in UC1, we need to understand which processes are critical and the actors involved in the manufacturing plant. A detailed interview with managers and workers handling the production equipment and IoT devices will give the required information to define a workflow.

2.2 Distributed Authorization

Distributed authorization mechanisms are important to support a growing number of IoT devices. Authorization in distributed systems is complex to achieve [25] as the resources are spread across a network of devices under different domains, multi-tenant systems, and they might know each other or not. As described earlier in the introduction, this is a trust problem. A smart lock installed in a smart home opens or closes the door based on the access control (AC) policies defined by the owner. The owner may use his smartphone to present his credentials to the smart lock. The smart lock may use OAuth based mechanism to verify authorization tokens and update its AC policies periodically. From the perspective of an IoT device (i.e., smart lock), whenever a request from a Client (i.e., in this case, the owner's smartphone) arrives, the IoT device evaluates the authorization token attached with the request and sends an appropriate response. This standard approach (for instance, IETF ACE [32]) ensures interoperability. In our work, we introduce changes only to the clients and to the authorization service, but not to the IoT devices. For example, in UC1 there could be several scenarios where we need distributed authorization. For example, scenario 1: a worker wants to update some software in an IoT device; for this purpose, the administrator authorizes the worker. Scenario 2: an IoT device needs to authenticate, present authorization credentials to a secured server to write some data; for this purpose, the IoT device needs to get an authorization token from an authorization server. The role of the client and resource server from the context of OAuth ACE protocol changes depending on the use case but clearly we need distributed authorization. More information about this topic is presented in Sect. 4.1.

2.3 Device Commissioning and Secure Software Updates

Often, IoT devices are deployed in large scale. To protect that infrastructure, it is important to deploy devices with unique authentication credentials. Secure device commissioning i.e., key-provisioning, device hardening, etc. helps to protect the device from attacks, and also perform secure software updates. Software updates are often required to fix the software bugs or vulnerabilities in any computer software. In particular, firmware updates can patch vulnerable IoT devices, but an update from an untrusted source can install a Trojan or malware into the device. Various commercial software update solutions exist, but they are not interoperable and may not work with constrained devices. The IETF working group - 'software updates for IoT' [72] is working towards creating an interoperable and secure software update solution for IoT devices (class 1 or above) with approximately 100 KB of flash memory. Commissioning a large number of IoT devices is still a challenge, we need automated tools, protocols for secure device commissioning (see Enrollment over Secure Transport (EST) is used as a certificate provisioning protocol over HTTPS [67]. For example, in UC1, secure device commissioning is crucial to ensure that deployed manufacturing equipment and IoT devices are malware free, credentials provisioned are safe, etc. After deploying the equipment or IoT device, it is important to have the ability to provide updates i.e., for introducing new features, roll back to the previous stable state, or apply security-patches for the existing software, etc.

2.4   Attack Escalation Resilience

Compromising one IoT device means that the attacker can escalate the attack on other IoT devices or systems connected to the same network. Attack escalation is a serious problem, and we need resilience mechanisms. Authorization coupled with the context of task execution workflow stops the attack escalation problem. In this work, we describe a workflow-aware access control method which prevents attack escalation to an extent. On the other hand, when multicast security is used i.e., a group key is used for controlling a set of IoT devices. The IETF RFC [26] specifies requirements and security considerations for generic group key management protocols. The IETF draft [74] specifies a secure group communication for IoT devices that use the Constrained Application Protocol (CoAP). In this work, we do not focus on multicast security. For example, in UC1, let us assume that one of the IoT devices is physically accessible at the perimeter of the manufacturing plant and the IoT device is compromised by an attacker (how it is compromised is out of scope). For instance, the attacker may plan to escalate the attack by accessing other devices via the network. Therefore, we need proper security mechanisms to restrict the attacker from compromising other devices or equipment via a weak compromised device. Let us assume that there exists a workflow for initializing software update or updating the configuration of devices inside the manufacturing plant, then the attacker cannot perform his attack unless he was able to execute that workflow and reach the state which allows him to perform a software update. Note: at the first place, we should have proper access control and authorization mechanisms for initializing and executing the workflow.

2.5   Fine-Grained Access Control

In common Access Control (AC) methods such as role-based access control (RBAC) see [62], access control and authorization is given to an entity based on a Role. A role like *admin* is very powerful and has (almost all) permissions such as to change, add, and delete features of a system. If such an entity (with admin role) is compromised, then the attacker can do a lot of damage. Therefore, we want to limit the set of permissions (fine-grained) given to an entity based on a workflow i.e., an entity can complete/execute a legitimate set of actions/tasks in a particular order defined in the workflow. This motivates the need for a fine-grained access control model such as the *workflow-aware access control*. Such access control methods can protect the assets to an extent even if an entity is compromised i.e., the entity should be executing the workflow in order to access a particular service. For example, in UC1, it is a bad idea to give access to all equipment and IoT devices to one single administrator account, because if that admin credential is stolen or misused, then the attacker is able to access entire system associated with the credential.

To achieve this, we need a *least privilege* principle for task authorizations within each workflow. The least privilege principle is a security concept where every computer module (such as a process, user, or program, depending on the subject) may be able to access only the information and resources that are necessary for its legitimate purpose. As a particular case, the principle "Need to Know" is a confidentiality policy which states that no subject should be able to read objects unless reading them is necessary for that subject to perform its functions [11]. What we need is a similar policy, but regarding integrity. We call this principle "Need to Access": it states that no subject should be able to *write or change* objects unless it is necessary to complete the required task of a process or workflow at that particular state. By enforcing the need to access principle, an entity can get privileges to execute a task only at the required step of the workflow. This provides workflow-driven (workflow-aware) access control.

The workflow-aware access control needs an error-free workflow (free from deadlocks) and a device to execute it. A powerful computing device like a smart-phone is used to execute the workflow, not a constrained IoT device. Any generic application logic or process that we want to enforce is represented as one or more workflows. We elaborate further the requirements of the workflow-aware access control below.

Verification of Workflows. Formal methods refer to mathematically rigorous techniques and tools for specification, design, verification of software and hardware systems. Formal verification is the act of proving or disproving the correctness of a system with respect to a certain formal specification or property [82]. A verified system may satisfy safety and liveness properties such as no deadlocks, mutual exclusion is satisfied, each request will have a response, freedom from starvation, etc. Therefore, we need a modeling language with which we can verify some properties such as deadlocks in a workflow. A survey of formal verification of business process modeling is presented in [49].

Adapt and Recover from Error Situations. An error-resilient IoT application should be capable of recovering from unforeseen error situations to an extent. Therefore, it is important to allow human interaction to solve a problem that cannot be fixed by the system itself. A workflow may allow the owner of the services to create on the fly sub-workflows without changing the main workflow to recover from error conditions. This requirement is necessary to build a usable security in an IoT application.

2.6   Distributed Accountability

Accountability is a fact or condition where an entity is accountable for actions committed directly or indirectly. To enforce accountability in a system, we must record (e.g., log) all important actions/interactions of an entity with the system, including solicitation and execution. Logging is a standard feature in many computing systems, it records system activities, process executions, user interactions, etc. with relevant information such as timestamps and user identifier. Thus, logging helps to achieve accountability. An accountability system needs more than just logging i.e, it should satisfy integrity requirements of logs generated and stored by all processes. For example, the logs cannot be tampered or destroyed in case of an attack i.e., mirroring logs on different servers or backup solutions is necessary. Such accountability information is commonly used to perform various analysis such as auditing and forensic security analysis. Auditing is an independent analysis of accounting records i.e., in a computer system, it can be a program trace, log information, etc. Forensic security analysis is performed to investigate a computer attack i.e., to find bugs in software processes, irregularities, and frauds committed by people, malware, etc. For example, in UC1, in case of an attack or system/equipment failure, the production plant auditors must have the capability to find the root cause of the incident. For this purpose, we need proper accountability mechanisms by default. An accountability system records every major decision (e.g., change logs, etc.) taken by the administrators or workers.

3   Evolution of Petri Nets

In this section, we introduce Petri Nets and evolution over the decades since their inception on the year 1966. In traditional Petri Nets (PN) (see [54]), there are places, tokens, and transitions.

A place in a traditional Petri Net can hold one or more tokens (*markings*) of the same type. A transition may have one or more input and output places. A transition fires if its input places have sufficient tokens and as a result, it produces tokens in output places. We recall the classical definition of a Petri Net (P/T net) from [60, 78]:

A Petri Net is a triple (P, T, F), where

- P is a finite set of places,
- T is a finite set of transitions $(P \cap T = \oslash)$
- $F \subseteq (P \times T) \cup (T \times P)$ is a finite set of arcs (the flow relation)

A transition t has input and output places. A place p is input or output for transition t based on the directed arc from p to t or from t to p. A place can contain zero or more tokens. A token is represented by a black dot •. The global state of a Petri Net, also called a marking, is the distribution of tokens over places. Formally, a state or marking M is a function $M : P \rightarrow N$ that assigns to every place p the number of tokens M (p) that reside in p. We use the notation

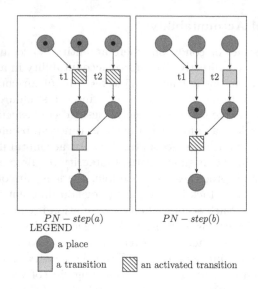

$PN - step(a)$
LEGEND

$PN - step(b)$

⬤ a place

▢ a transition   ▨ an activated transition

Fig. 1. PN-Step(a) shows the initial state of a Petri Net and PN-Step(b) shows the state of the Petri Net after transitions *t1* and *t2* have fired.

$\bullet t$ to denote the set of input places for a transition t; similarly, $t\bullet$, $\bullet p$ and $p\bullet$. Figure 1 shows a simple Petri Net in two steps: first, in step(a) transitions t1 and t2 are activated because $\bullet t1$ and $\bullet t2$ have sufficient tokens; second, in step(b) t1 and t2 fire to produce tokens in output places of $t1\bullet$ and $t2\bullet$.

Several extensions of Petri Nets such as Time Petri Nets and Colored Petri Nets have enabled us to model different constraints such as time and types of tokens, and so on. Thus, Petri Nets were widely used in various application areas to verify network protocols, supply chain, etc. For a deeper understanding of Petri Nets, we recommend the book of Reisig [60] to the readers. We briefly present the most important extensions of Petri Net relevant for our work below.

Time Petri Nets (TPN) is used to model and simulate real systems as it is often important to describe the temporal behavior of the system, i.e., we need a way to model duration and delays (time) of transition firing (see [46]). The classical Petri Net is not capable of handling this.

Colored Petri Nets (CPN) is an extension of Petri Nets where different types of tokens can exist in the same place (see [34,35]). In a colored Petri Net, each token is represented by specific colors (types). CPN have the same kind of concurrency properties as Place/Transition Nets. Different tools such as CPN-Tools [37] are available to model and validate concurrent systems.

High-level Petri Nets simplify the process of creating complex workflows by breaking them into smaller partial workflows. At a high-level, it provides an overall description of the process without considering all details. As we navigate to a lower level, it provides in-depth description that particular component. The extension of Petri Net with *color*, *time* and *hierarchy* allows us to model complex industrial systems with several layers of hierarchy without losing the details (see [2,36]).

Workflow Nets (WF-net) are used to model a typical business process workflow using Petri Nets. Research advancements in the area of workflow nets contributed to our research. Most of the research discusses about mapping workflow concepts such as task execution, synchronization (split and join) actions, etc. into Petri Nets (see [1,78]). Workflow Nets showed that Petri Nets can be used to design and model complex workflows. In addition, Petri Net tools can be used to verify traditional Petri Net properties such as liveness, etc. in Workflow Nets.

Open Petri Nets provide interfaces that enable two or more workflows to exchange information in the form of tokens. Open Petri Nets provide entry and exit points via Open Petri Net places to exchange information between workflows (see [27]). One of the goals of this work is to support multi-tenancy, i.e., to support activities, tasks from different organizations. *Composition* is a common approach in software engineering i.e., to assemble small systems into larger ones. Reisig in [60] describes the composition of nets using *interfaces* that can be used for asynchronous and directed communication between Petri Nets.

Petri Nets and its applications are well studied in the literature. Petri Nets enable us to create verified workflows with properties like guaranteed termination, separation-of-duties, reachability, liveness (deadlock-free), and coverability [1,19,51]. In this section, we presented the important extensions of Petri Net that help us to specify and verify workflows. By enforcing verified workflows with fine-grained access control, we achieve workflow-aware access control.

4 Background Work

In this section, we present relevant background and existing work on the three topics we focus in this paper.

4.1 Authorization for Constrained IoT Devices

Authorization mechanisms are important to restrict or allow an entity to access a resource in an IoT device. One of the important goals of our workflow-aware access control is to use appropriate authorization tokens within the workflow. Therefore, we present the state-of-the-art authorization methods for IoT in this section.

The OAuth 2.0 was developed for the web to create and transfer authorization tokens to an authenticated entity that wants to access a resource from the server. For instance, a browser is typically the client and a resource in OAuth 2.0 can be a restricted web-page (that needs special access rights) hosted on a server. The IETF working group (WG) Authentication and Authorization for constrained devices (ACE) [32] is specifying a framework for authentication and authorization in IoT environments called "ACE-OAuth" [65].

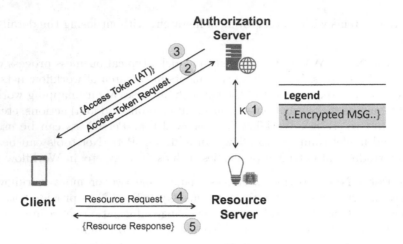

Fig. 2. An example ACE-OAuth scenario and actors involved. The numbers explain the sequence of an authorization process and resource request between three actors. Notations: K is a shared secret and {encrypted message}.

ACE-OAuth is based on OAuth 2.0 and CoAP. The motivation of ACE-OAuth is to create an authorization solution suitable for IoT devices. To describe the ACE-OAuth actors, let us consider an example use case. John owns a smartwatch (a typical IoT consumer device), and with that he wants to track, store his steps, heartbeat, etc. John wants complete control over his data i.e., deleting information stored on the device or in the cloud. John uses his smartphone to access or modify information stored on his smartwatch. For special access i.e., deleting information or changing the owner information on his smartwatch, John needs an access token from the cloud service provided by the smartwatch manufacturer. Thus, we can map the use case actors with the ACE-OAuth actors: the smartphone is a client (C), the smartwatch is the resource server (RS), the cloud service is the authorization server (AS), and John is the resource owner (RO). Below, we describe the simple ACE-OAuth messages exchanges to create the access token required by the client to access a resource on a resource server.

In Fig. 2, we show three important actors of ACE scenario. ACE-OAuth uses the term *Resource Server (RS)* to represent an IoT Device with several resources, i.e., typically sensors such as temperature, heartbeat recognizing sensor, gyroscope, etc. A smart lock, smart bulb, or a building automation device is a typical example of a resource server. The term *Client (C)* is used to represent the device that the resource owner (RO) uses to access the resource on an IoT device. Sometimes, simple client functionalities are embedded into the IoT device itself. For example, a user can access or modify certain functions on his smartwatch via the on-board display. Typically, an *authorization server (AS)* creates an access token and transfers it to the client. Now, we describe a particular ACE scenario as shown in Fig. 2: to access a resource on a Resource Server (RS), a Client (C) should request an access-token (AT) from AS, either directly or using its Client

Authorization Server (CAS). For the sake of simplicity, we do not consider introspective calls between the resource server and the authorization server or client authorization server.

Based on the above described scenario, a simple ACE OAuth message flow as shown in Fig. 2 can be described as follows:

- A C may perform a resource-request to RS without a valid access-token, then RS will reject, and it may provide AS information to the C in the response. Such that, the C may go to the AS to get a valid access-token. The Resource Owner (RO) may define access control policies on the Authorization Server (AS) describing who can access the resources on a RS.
- (1) A common secret (k) is shared between the AS and RS while device commissioning. We assume that RS stays offline after deployment and cannot perform introspective calls to AS to verify the access token presented by the C.
- (2) The C performs an Access-Request to AS to ask for an access token (AT) that allows accessing the required resource (R) on RS. The AS checks if C can access the resource (R) on RS or not, based on permissions assigned by the RO.
- (3) If C has sufficient permissions, then AS generates an Access-Token (AT) plus a proof-of-possession (PoP) key bounded to the access-token and the secret (k). AS sends both the AT and the PoP key to C via a secure encrypted channel.
- (4) After receiving AT and PoP key, C performs a resource-request to RS by ACE-OAuth token construction method defined in one of the ACE profiles. For example, the client may use privacy enhanced token construction method as described below.
- (5) The RS can reconstruct the PoP key from the AT and verifies the received AT. If it is valid, RS encrypts the response with the PoP key.

In the ACE working group, several other proposals with different profiles exist to solve specific problems. One of the proposed profile is Privacy-Enhanced Authorization token (PAT) profile. Note: at the time of writing this paper PAT profile was expired.

Privacy-Enhanced Authorization tokens (PAT) is a profile specified for ACE-OAuth [16] with a special focus on creating privacy-enhanced unlinkable authorization tokens. The PAT profile for ACE-OAuth provides unlinkability features even when a client performs non-encrypted authorization requests (i.e., sending request without network or transport layer encryption such as DTLS). PAT was designed such that the Resource Server (RS) is able to verify the access tokens without performing the introspective call to the Authorization server (AS) to verify and validate the client authorization token.

History based Capability systems for IoT (HCAP) proposes a history-based capability system for enforcing permission sequencing constraints in a distributed authorization environment [70]. The authors formally establish the security guarantees of HCAP, and empirically evaluate its performance. In their work, permission sequencing constraints are encoded as a Security Automaton and embedded in a capability.

4.2   Modeling Workflows for Access Control Systems

In the literature, we can find extensive work on the specification and enforcement of workflows; in particular, Bertino et al. [10] studied how to model and enforce workflow authorization constraints such as separation-of-duties in workflows, but using a centralized workflow management system. Workflow based access control is also well-known (Knorr [41] calls them "Dynamic access control"), but this requires a centralized WF enforcement engine. Basin et al. [9] model the business process activities as workflows with a special focus on optimizing the authorizations permissions.

Petri Nets [54] provide a graphical modeling tool used to describe processes performing an orchestrated activity, or in other words, a workflow [1,78]. Petri Nets have the advantage that many properties such as liveness (deadlock-freeness), reachability are easy to verify [19,51,58]. Atluri et al. [5,6] studied how to model workflows using Petri Nets, but did not describe the implementation details. Huang et al. [28] presented a web-enabled workflow management system, and Compagna et al. [15] presented an automatic enforcement of security policies based on workflow-driven web application, but both work presented a centralized architecture. Heckel [27] showed how open Petri Nets are suitable for modeling workflows spanning different enterprises. No existing work discusses about how to handle error conditions during workflow execution, support or integrate practitioner-friendly design and specification tools, enforcing cross-organizational agreements or commitments (i.e., process integrity) and to enforce them to achieve workflow-aware access control with a special focus on modern IoT systems.

Wolter et al. [79] showed a model-driven transformation approach from modeled security goals in the context of business process models into concrete security implementation. Their work focuses on service-oriented architecture. The security annotated business processes are transformed into platform specific security access control or policy languages such as XACML; in particular, they considered security goals such as confidentiality, authentication, and data integrity. Basin et al. [44] presented SecureUML, an UML based modeling language for model-driven security, their approach is based on role-based access control with additional support for specifying authorization constraints. Similarly, Jürjens [38] presented UMLsec (an extension of UML) for secure software development.

Mortensen [50] presented a method for automatic implementation of systems based on Colored Petri Nets (CP-nets or CPN) models. The paper does not describe the algorithms and data structures used to implement the code generation tool, but rather the context of the tool. The paper shows that the method introduced reduces the development time and cost compared with prevailing system development methods where system implementation is accomplished manually by evaluating it on a real-world access control system. We refer to the concepts presented in this work for generating smart contract code from our Petri Net workflows.

Linhares et al. in [43] presented an empirical evaluation of OMG SysML's to model an industrial automation unit using the open source modeling tool Modelio [48] but not in the context of modeling workflows for access control.

4.3 Distributed Accountability and Smart Contracts

To achieve accountability in a system, we need to record all system activities and store them in a database with data properties such as availability, integrity, persistence, and consistency. Distributed database management systems (DDBS) provide data consistency, reliability, and availability (see [53]). In addition, with strong access control systems integrated with a DDBS, we could enforce who can access (read and write) the database. Just integrating access control is not enough to provide accountability in a system i.e., a person with access to the database may insert/update/delete malicious data into the database. Such that the person with access to the DDBS could tamper the data without being noticed by other entities.

The Blockchain technology provides availability, data integrity, non-repudiation (if public-key signatures are used), and persistence properties i.e., once a data block is added by a user and becomes a valid block of the Blockchain, it is impossible to update/delete it without being noticed by others participating in the Blockchain. There are two main types of Blockchain: permissioned and permissionless. A permissioned Blockchain includes an access control layer that can enforce who can read, publish, or approve transactions in a block chain (see IBM Hyperledger [29]). A classic example of permissionless Blockchain is bitcoin [52] i.e., anyone can participate (publish and verify transactions) in the Blockchain. To approve a transaction or a block consisting of many transactions different consensus methods exist such as proof-of-work, but it is not the focus of the paper.

Smart Contracts, introduced in [69], have become popular with the advancements in Blockchain technology. Smart contracts are often written to ensure fairness between participating entities even when one entity may attempt to cheat the other entity in arbitrary ways (see [17]). Smart contracts (SC) deployed in a Blockchain can be seen as arbitrary code expressing one or more business logic, and they are automatically triggered if some preconditions defined in the SC match. A smart contract is executed, the results are verified by the nodes participating in the Blockchain. In [14] and [7] an example of an IoT application using Smart Contracts and Blockchains is presented. The Bitcoin blockchain has a simple stack language to express the rules and conditions for a successful transaction and how new coins are produced and consumed. Ethereum, which has popularized the use of smart contracts, uses a Turing complete language to specify them. In [45], the authors have studied the security of running smart contracts based on Ethereum, and presented some problems in Ethereum's smart contract language solidity; they also show some ways to enhance the operational semantics of Ethereum to make smart contracts less vulnerable.

5   Contributions

In this paper, we present a security framework that addresses the following security requirements of constrained IoT environment described in Sect. 2: distributed authorization, requirements elicitation, fine-grained access control, secure software updates, attack escalation resilience, and distributed accountability.

We present a security framework to design, specify, verify, and enforce IoT processes or workflows using Petri Nets. Our framework adapts to error conditions during workflow execution, supports the integration of practitioner-friendly design and specification tools, and enforces cross-organizational agreements or commitments (i.e., the process integrity) as workflows. Thereby, we achieve workflow-aware access control for multi-tenant IoT systems.

We presented our *Petri Net based Workflow Specification and Enforcement* framework earlier in [39,40]. In this paper, besides summarizing the basic ideas, we extend our framework to support the generation of blockchain-based smart contracts from Petri Nets and to achieve distributed accountability. Furthermore, we demonstrate the applicability of the method by solving three use cases. We also present a high-level guide to implement the framework with practitioner-friendly tool and development systems.

5.1   Petri Nets for Workflow Specification

We use Petri Nets and its extensions for specifying workflows. Existing solutions and methods for modeling workflows are described in Sect. 4.2. Petri Nets were chosen to specify workflows for the following advantages and properties. Petri Nets (PN)provide the formal semantics for designing workflows such that PN workflows are amenable to verification of certain properties such as being deadlock free. The expressiveness of Petri Nets and the state-transition model of Petri Nets support all primitives needed to model a workflow process precisely. Extensions of Petri Nets enable us to specify and model complex workflows by solving different workflow issues including concurrent task execution and separation-of-duties between different processes interacting with each other. Petri Nets are a graphical language and as a result, it is simple to design workflows using graphical tools. Also, other practitioner-friendly tools that collect requirements and create activity diagrams can be integrated to generate Petri Net workflows. Petri Nets workflows are technology or platform-independent, therefore, it can be used to implement and integrate platform or technology dependent multi-tenant processes. Overall, it satisfies all requirements that we need to achieve the integrity of the process. Thus, we use Petri nets to enforcing workflow-aware access control (Fig. 3).

In addition to the classical and existing Petri Net extensions, we introduce additional concepts in our Petri Net model:

- Permissions, endorsements, money (crypto coins), signature, or any information that is required for the workflow execution can be represented as *tokens*

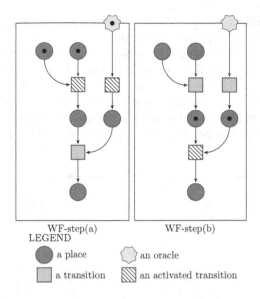

WF-step(a)   WF-step(b)
LEGEND
⬤ a place   ✦ an oracle
▢ a transition   ▨ an activated transition

Fig. 3. WF-step(a) shows the initial state of a Petri Net workflow specification with an *Oracle*. WF-step(b) shows the state of the workflow after the first two activated transitions have fired.

within the Petri Net. Thanks to CPN, different types of tokens can be used in the same Petri Net to model workflows where entities exchange different information between them. In particular, OAuth tokens are used to enforce access control in a stepwise manner as specified in the workflow.

– An *Oracle* is a type of place, represented in star shape that can receive tokens (as described earlier) from an external source. In classical Petri Nets, places are represented as circles and always receive tokens from a transition. An oracle is drawn on the boundary of a Petri Net to represent that it receives information from an external source. Note: the term oracle is used in different computer science fields including cryptography, blockchain, and smart contracts, etc. Our concept of an Oracle is similar to the Oracles introduced in Ethereum blockchain, i.e., it is used to receive external information into a blockchain smart contract. The difference is: an Oracle in our method need not be a contract that is accessed by other contracts to pull information as described in [8,83]. If blockchain is implemented in an IoT application as a back end distributed database, then an external service can push some information into the blockchain. The published information in the blockchain can be accessed by the Oracle via a predefined URL. Note: it is critical to enforce strict access control that restricts who can publish such information in the blockchain.

Our PN workflows are designed to solve use cases that include interaction with real world IoT devices and actors. In such cases, a workflow should handle error conditions or unexpected situations to an extent. We introduce *dynamic*

Workflows to handle such special situation with authorized user decisions and so on. Note: such dynamic workflows must also be verified together with the main workflow (at least during its creation) i.e., without changing the goal or purpose of the main workflow. Protecting the integrity of the processes and allowing dynamic workflows may be competing goals, but, it must be assured that only "authorized" entity can create dynamic workflow and any misuse must be penalized. Therefore, we also need a system to provide accountability of actions performed by the participants executing the workflow.

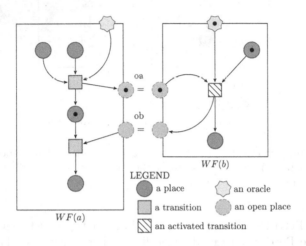

Fig. 4. Two different workflows WF (a) and (b) exchange information using Open Petri Net places (*oa* and *ob*)

Thanks to Open Petri Nets (see [27]), we apply this concept to create an entry and exit points i.e., Open Petri Net places to exchange information between Petri Net workflows. Exchanging information in the form of tokens simplifies the integrating of two or more PN workflows. Open Petri Nets enable to satisfy one of our goal i.e., interaction between different stakeholders' processes. For instance, Fig. 4 shows two different workflows WF (a) and WF (b) exchanging tokens via the open place (*oa* and *ob*). An open place exists on the boundary of the workflow, and the equivalence (=) sign identifies the entry and exit places between two workflows. The open place (*oa*) is an exit place for WF (a) and entry place for WF (b). The main difference between an oracle and an open place is: an oracle can receive information from external sources whereas, the open places are mainly used to exchange tokens between workflows. Open Petri net places are particularly useful when creating a dynamic workflow to exchange information with the main workflow.

We showed how workflows can be specified using Petri Nets, but we need a mechanism to enforce them on entities executing it. For this purpose, we use small *smart contracts* written in the transitions of Petri Net. A brief introduction of Smart Contracts is presented in the previous Sect. 4.3. For our requirements

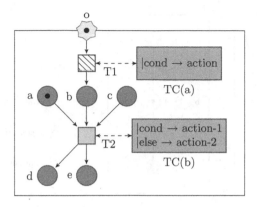

Fig. 5. Petri Net with transition contracts *t1* and *t2*.

both Bitcoin and Ethereum languages are not suitable. Bitcoin's stack language is not flexible therefore, we cannot express workflow conditions on it. Ethereum's solidity language could be vulnerable (see [45]), and we cannot verify such contracts. Therefore, a smart contract language that is flexible to specify conditions and at the same time verifiable is required. To clarify, a complete Petri Net workflow can be seen as a big smart contract comparable to a blockchain based smart contract. The conditions that are written in the transitions of Petri Nets workflows are called *transition contract*.

5.2 Transition Contracts

To implement a workflow-driven access control system in Petri Nets, the transitions should be able to verify conditions and evaluate information encoded in the tokens. The conditions written on a single transition using a simple smart contract language is called a *transition contract*. We use a simple guarded command (a conditionally executed statement) language (similar to [18]) to write transition contracts.

Figure 5 shows a simple Petri Net where two transitions (*T1 and T2*) have a pointer to the transition contracts (*TC (a) and TC (b)*) respectively. Note: smart contracts do not always have to run on blockchain, they can also be implemented between two or more parties without blockchain technology.

The properties (or rules) for each transition can be seen as small smart contracts that restrict the choices of the participants of the workflow for this step, or they impose additional conditions. The combination of a few transition contracts allows us to create *multi-step smart contracts*: say, the first transition creates a token based on some conditions (which may verify authentication or authorization status of participants), and then the second transition produces an OAuth token that can only be used in a subsequent transition in a particular way. The allowed actions, permissions of workflow participants are determined by the Petri Net and the next transition contracts. We use the combination

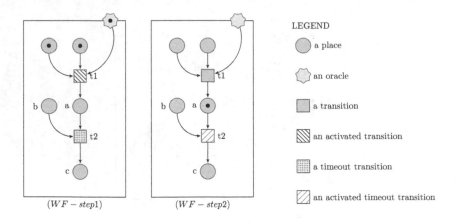

Fig. 6. Timeout transitions in Petri Net workflows

of Petri Nets and transition contracts to specify, enforce sequences of atomic transitions (transactions), and properties that must be satisfied in a workflow.

A transition performs three steps before firing:

– First, it takes tokens from the input places (could be a normal place, open place, or an oracle).
– Next, it verifies the validity, properties of input tokens.
– Finally, it evaluates the conditions described (as guarded commands) in the transition contract and produces the output tokens in output places (could be a normal place, open place, or an oracle).

An output produced by the transition contract can be a token representing information or a workflow for one or more entities. When our workflow-aware access control method is used, compromising one device may not compromise other devices. To explain, let us consider a workflow that is defined by a company for updating Firmware on its IoT devices. Assume that the devices could be triggered to update its Firmware Over-the-Air (OTA) whenever a new Firmware is available. Assume that an attacker compromises one device (how he compromises is not relevant here) and updates a malicious firmware on it. The attacker broadcast the new (malicious) firmware to other legitimate devices such that he could take control over other devices too. This attack is mitigated because the corresponding firmware update workflow as specified by the company must be initiated and a legitimate service person needs to do several steps (for example, provide authorization credentials) before the devices may get into the state where it will accept firmware via the broadcasts channel.

By default, the Petri Net transitions fire when the input places have enough tokens. In many real-world use cases, it is important to have the notion of time required for a task completion. Some tasks in the real-world might require just 10 min, and others might need some hours. If a transition is waiting for a token to arrive in one of its input places, probably it does not want to wait indefinitely.

Timeout Transitions are required to stop transitions from waiting indefinitely. Sometimes, a user or an entity may fail to complete a task in a workflow that is expected to be completed within a certain time. That transition may wait forever to get a token in one of its input places. To solve this, we introduce timeout transitions i.e., after a predefined time expires, the timeout transition executes set of predefined timeout conditions (in contrast to the regular conditions) and fires a timeout token in its output place. These timeout tokens may contain or invoke the dynamic workflows. It is important to specify when the timeout timer should start and stop in the timeout transition. If all the input tokens are available before the timeout occurs, then conditions of regular transition contract is executed to produce tokens. Therefore, every timeout transition has two instructions: first, a timeout instruction (timeout contract) is enforced when timeout occurs and some of the input tokens are not available; second, a regular instruction (transition contract) is enforced when all the input tokens are available before timeout.

The example workflow is shown in Fig. 6 explains a simple use case of a timeout transition. Consider that the task *t2* must be completed within some time (x minutes) after the task *t1* is completed. When task t1 is completed, then transition t1 produces a token in place (a). A token in place (a) triggers the timer to start in transition t2. Now, the timeout transition t2 executes one of the three possible cases:

- Case 1: the timer expires after x minutes (timeout) and place (b) has no token then, the timeout transition contract is executed. A timeout transition contract is similar to a traditional contract but is used only to defined what happens after a timeout.
- Case 2: the timer has not expired and place (b) has a token then, the regular transition contract is executed.
- Case 3: place (b) has already a token before task t1 is completed then, the transition t2 waits until task t1 is completed. When both the input tokens (a and b) are available, the regular transition contract is executed.

5.3 Systems Modeling Language (SysML) - Activity Diagram

We investigated how a practitioner (a software developer or engineer) could use our method with existing and familiar tools. It could be complex to design and model a multi-organizational, human interactive process that includes different software and hardware components using Petri Net tools only. Therefore, an existing practitioner-friendly tool is used to model a high-level activity diagram of complex processes and systems. Later, this activity diagram is translated into Petri Net workflows.

Software developers, engineers, and similar practitioners are familiar with UML, since, SysML is an extension to UML, it is easy to understand and learn SysML's notations. The generally accepted method is to refine the specification in a stepwise manner using software engineering tools such as the object management group (OMG) system modeling language's (SysML) activity diagram presented in [73]. The Object Management Group's OMG SysML [73] is a general-purpose graphical modeling language that supports the specification, design, analysis, and verification of systems that may include different software and hardware components, people, tasks, and other entities. SysML supports the practice of model-based systems engineering (MBSE) and is an extension of Unified Modeling Language (UML) version 2.

SysML is used to develop system solutions to solve technologically challenging problems. One of the challenges is interconnectivity among systems. Therefore, systems can no longer be treated as stand-alone, but behave as part of a larger ecosystem including humans. Such complex systems are known as the system of systems (SoS) [23].

SysML can represent different aspects of systems, components, and other entities [23] such as:

- Structural composition, interconnection, and classification.
- Function-based, message-based, and state-based behavior.
- Constraints on the physical and performance properties.
- Allocations between behavior, structure, and constraints.
- Requirements and their relationship to other requirements, design elements, and test cases.

SysML uses nine diagrams including the *Activity diagram* to represent the relationships between entities in a complex SoS. In particular, the SysML Activity diagram (modified from UML) represents the business/technical process in a defined order i.e., a sequence of actions to be executed based on the availability of their inputs, outputs, and control. Moreover, SysML's activity diagram describes how the actions transform the inputs to outputs. As this is a standardized approach, it is easy for practitioners to use SysML Activity to describe complex systems and processes (both technical and business).

Furthermore, SysML activities are based on token-flow semantics related to Petri-Nets [59]. Thus, SysML provides a semantic foundation for modeling system requirements, and the SysML's activity diagram can be transformed intuitively into a Petri Nets model. The Petri Net tokens hold the values of inputs, outputs, and controls that flow from one action to another. Therefore, it is easy to transfer the SysML activity diagram into Petri Net workflows. For our purposes, we use only the SysML's activity diagram to model the process or workflow.

We use the open source modeling tool known as "Modelio" [48] to draw SysML activity diagrams. Modelio implements all SysML features according to the OMG's specification, and it can also be used to model BPMN and UML diagrams. An example screenshot of the Modelio tool is presented in Fig. 10.

The requirements and SysML activity diagrams lack mathematical semantics to check for inconsistencies, but the SysML activity diagrams can be converted into Petri Nets (for example, colored) and then can be verified using model checking tools [33, 57].

5.4   Petri Net Execution Engine

We use the open source Python library called "Snakes" [56] to implement basic Petri Net functions. We extended the Petri Net library to represent different types of tokens, places, and conditions. Furthermore, we present future requirements to extend the standard Petri Net Markup Language (PNML) exchange format. Similarly, there are several Petri Net libraries available for other programming languages such as Java, C, etc.

We implemented and evaluated the core part of the above simple use case scenario application using Snakes and other Python library. For doing this, we have extended the Snakes library to realize additional functions and modules that can recognize our new types of tokens, places, and conditions (guarded expressions). The Snakes library is extended to support features such as oracles, open places, timeout transitions, and different types of tokens. The Petri Net workflow evaluates transitions with conditions – for example, validates security tokens from an oracle –, and if necessary, produce tokens in a specific format that will be required for subsequent transitions. The prototype implementation was developed with Ubuntu operating system and Python libraries for implementing REST services, and Petri Net functions. In our current implementation, the transition contracts are expressed with limited features of Snakes library's arc notations, expressions. Note: extreme caution must be taken to avoid side effects – by calling native Python functions to evaluate input tokens and produce required tokens. Further implementation work is required to realize a smart phone application with an integrated Petri Net execution engine.

We need additional XML tags to represent workflow and its rules i.e., expressions and conditions written in a Transition, token types, open Petri Net places, and how they could interact or interface with dynamic or sub-workflows. We implemented a part of building automation use case presented in Sect. 5.6. Our future work is to extend the standard PNML with additional tags for exchanging Petri Net workflows between different entities and users of any platform.

5.5   Petri Net Based Smart Generation Framework

In our next investigation, we looked at various problems in traditional Blockchain based Smart Contracts. We noticed that we could use our method to create *safe and understandable* Smart Contracts (SC). In this section, we introduce a framework that can create Blockchain based smart contracts from Petri Net workflows.

Blockchain-based applications use open source blockchain implementations such as IBM's Hyperledger Fabric [30], and Ethereum [21]. The corresponding business logic is written using Smart Contracts (SC) in their respective languages i.e., Chaincode [31], and Solidity [20]. Solidity is a Turing-complete computer programming language specifically designed to write Smart Contracts (i.e., to write the business logic). Chaincode is (used synonymous with Smart Contracts) also used to write smart contracts for IBM's Hyperledger Fabric. But, Chaincode can be written using popular Turing complete languages such as GO, Java, etc.

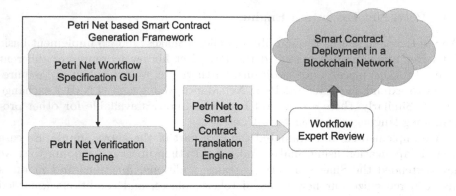

Fig. 7. Components of Blockchain based Smart Contract generation framework

Turing complete languages are known to have problems such as undecidability [17].

With Petri Net workflows (which can be seen as high level Smart Contracts), it is possible to check the properties such as deadlock, etc. Therefore, if a Petri Net is verified (properties are checked), then translating the verified Petri Net into a solidity code is also safe. We present the software prototype architecture below.

The requirements of a smart contract (SC) should be as follows:

- A SC should be easy to understand and write.
- A SC should be amenable to verification of process integrity i.e., it should only allow what it is specified to do.
- If necessary, the SC should support human interaction for example, to approve or reject conditions specified in a SC. Also, the smart contracts should allow recovering from error conditions by allowing dynamic workflows.

The Smart Contract can be a standalone contract, or a part of a big contract consisting of many small SCs. Our proposed Blockchain based SC generation framework consists of three main modules: Petri Net workflow specification GUI, Petri Net verification engine and the Petri Net translation engine into Smart Contract translation engine. Figure 7 shows the main components of the proposed Framework.

In this paper, we provide a brief overview of our proposed framework. In our forthcoming paper, we will describe the specifics of implementation, user interfaces, etc. in detail.

Petri Net Workflow Specification GUI provides the user with a simplified GUI interface to the practitioners. The GUI interface consists of places, transitions, and arcs to connect places and transitions. PNML is the standard and recognized format for exchanging Petri Nets.

Petri Net verification engine simulates and evaluates whether the Petri Net satisfies the properties such as no deadlocks, etc. We propose to use any standard Petri Net tool or library to implement this functionality.

Petri Net to Smart Contract Translation Engine works by mapping places and transitions from the specified Petri Net into blockchain based smart contracts. We are currently working on a prototype that can translate a PN workflow into an Ethereum's based Solidity code - details will be discussed in our forthcoming paper. Nevertheless, the translation engine can be extended to translate the Petri Net smart contracts into other types of blockchain executable smart contact code (executable byte-code = compiled smart contract) such as IBM's Hyperledger fabric's chain code.

Once the Petri Net is translated into a Smart Contract (SC), a workflow expert reviews the generated SC code and published it in the blockchain.

5.6 Distributed Accountability and Access Control

Our framework uses a distributed blockchain network for achieve accountability and transparency. A private blockchain is used to set access control restrictions i.e., who can participate in the blockchain. For instance, the user publishes the status of every task when he/she is executing the workflow – i.e., the state of the Petri Net workflow – in the private blockchain. The stakeholders will verify and approve the transactions in the blockchain, and this provides transparency and accountability in an immutable database without assuming a trusted centralized entity.

Distributed access control is achieved by enforcing token validation on the handhelds. Usually, a PN workflow is executed by one or more entities with the help of a handheld or more powerful device capable of executing a Petri Net workflow. We use a trusted application installed on entity's handheld enforcing the validity of the tokens generated and received. Sometimes, the handhelds may also delegate some tasks to a cloud service, for example, to check the blockchain for updates, or, to pull information tokens from an oracle, etc.

Distributed access control is generally used in web technologies. Typically, a browser is a *client* accessing a service hosted on (cloud based) web servers. For instance, in an IoT scenario, the authorization server (AS) evaluates (or delegates evaluation of) the client credentials – the user submits the credentials to AS via a handheld device – and if those client credentials are valid, then the AS presents the client with an authorization token to access the IoT device (or its services).

Our method introduces *Workflow aware access control*, and it is enforced by restricting the users to perform tasks as specified (in an order) in the workflow. Each user uses a handheld device to execute the workflow. The user executing the workflow needs to authenticate to the App (i.e., to prove that the user can execute the workflow). The handheld uses an App that binds a *secret* with a workflow – note: we assume that the client is not able to extract this secret from the handheld or the workflow. The IETF draft "Privacy Enhanced Tokens" a profile for OAuth 2.0 for constrained devices [16] provides an example of how these proof-of-possession tokens can be generated using the secret. Some actions or tasks that the user needs to perform are enforced on the resource servers. The resource server can verify the tokens without having to communicate with the authorization server.

Publishing and distributing the Workflow or Smart contracts through a contract store (i.e., a distributed database) similar to existing smartphone app store or browser add-on/extensions store. The users can download preferred Petri Net workflows and contracts from the Petri Net smart contract store – we use a single contract store based on one distributed database technology. The contract store enforcing a strict process that analyses and validates the contract before publishing it. The distributed database similar to a blockchain can be used to store the Petri Net workflows based smart contracts. We propose to use a single blockchain for publishing contracts. If necessary, access to these contracts may also be restricted by using a permissioned blockchain. For example, IBM's Hyperledger can be deployed as a permissioned blockchain where entities require permissions to access and publish information in the blockchain.

Verification of Petri Net Workflow: we use the term verification in terms of verifying the properties of the workflow by simulation, model checking, theorem proving, etc. Verification of Petri Nets must not be confused with validity checking (=validation) of validity tokens as described in Sect. 5.6.

The author of the Petri Net workflow is responsible for verifying the correctness of the workflow's application or the process itself. The Petri Net (PN) engine assists the authors while creating the Workflow in terms of simulating and verifying Petri Net properties. The PN engine simulates the workflow after saving and provides a comprehensive report to the author about potential problems such as deadlocks, etc. via a notification panel. This feature minimizes the errors while creating the workflow and provides a detailed analysis when the workflow is completed.

Workflow expert: the author requests to publish the PN workflow through a process. The objective of the workflow expert is to have "/Quality Control/". A trusted entity (a workflow expert) checks whether the workflow is designed properly and represents the process defined. Additionally, the workflow expert may use automated tools to check whether the contract follows standard guidelines or not.

Even when the properties of the Petri Nets satisfy, the workflow could perform unnecessary steps not related to the goal of the process. So far, the best process to solve this human problem is to use the *four-eyes* principle [80, 81]. The four-eyes principle means that a certain activity, i.e., a decision, transaction, etc., must be approved by at least two people with expertise. Therefore, before publishing the contract, a workflow expert analyses the process or activity requirements, and verifies whether the designed workflow does the same as described.

Enforcing AC, validating tokens and conditions by delegation is a validity checking process that includes checking the validity of an access token, vali-

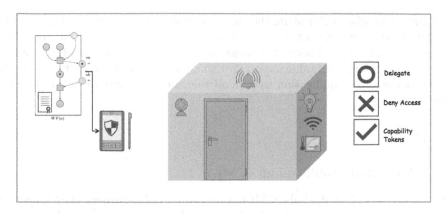

Fig. 8. Building automation - Petri Net workflow enforcement - access denied or granted based on the workflow specification.

dating the signature, integrity checks, etc. By enforcing proper validity checking we enforce access control. Some IoT applications perform this process by delegating validation tasks to trusted (more powerful) devices. We call those devices *handhelds*. Handhelds are more powerful in terms of connectivity, power supply and processing capacity than constrained IoT devices.

Consider a simple use case where a building owner delegates installation or maintenance work to a contracting company. The RFC 7744 [64], provides a summary of authorization problems that emerge during the device life-cycle (commissioning, maintenance, re-commissioning, decommissioning). In addition to the authorization problems, the building owners may wish to ensure that only products with a certain provenance or quality are installed, and that the process complies to standard operating procedures. The building owner may also wish that the contractor obeys other conditions written on a contract. This use case is described in detail in Sect. 6.

The workflow (WF) is created and signed by the building owner. Next, the WF is provided to the contractor. The contractor uses his handheld device as shown in Fig. 8 to execute the WF. The workflow contains a secret material with which the authorization tokens are constructed, please refer to [16] for more details on token construction. We assume that the secret cannot be extracted by the contractor. The building automation devices use the standard ACE-OAuth [32] protocol to validate the token that it receives, and if the tokens are valid, then access to resource is granted otherwise not. If the IoT device receives a request that it is unable to process, it may also delegate this request to an authorization server or other trusted entity. All these three types of response are shown in Fig. 8. The IoT devices can evaluate the validity of the proof-of-possession tokens (i.e., whether this token is constructed based on the shared secret or not) and can respond appropriately to the client device.

Enforcing Accountability using Blockchain is possible with our method. When some tasks of a workflow are executed, all information related to that task including who is executing the task, when it started, when it stopped, and what were the outcomes of the tasks must be logged for future reference. It is important that only authorized persons can write into the log, and no one can tamper with the logging information. For this purpose, we propose to enable the workflow execution application to append relevant logging information into the blockchain.

6   Use Cases

6.1   Connected Mobility Lab (CML)

The Connected Mobility Lab (CML) is a public funded project that integrates the services from different stakeholders – such as mobility, financial, and IT services – to provide a comprehensive mobility solution by seamlessly exchanging data and analytics (see [42]). The CML has core services such as IT security, accounting, data management, and identity management that integrate data and processes from different mobility providers. The CML mobile application (CML App) assists users (i.e., travelers) to experience the CML mobility solution with an intuitive user interface. A complete overview of CML is shown in Fig. 9.

The users of CML can be private persons or employees of a company that has a service agreement with the CML. A user may want to use different mobility services to complete one single journey. In CML, different mobility service providers have different specifications and implement "equivalent" tasks differently. For example, validating a ticket or a payment is done differently by each mobility service provider. It is important to guarantee the process integrity of such processes defined by each service provider therefore, we need a workflow-driven access control and a high-level workflow specification language to express those processes.

Consider a simple use case: a user might use a car sharing service from his home to the main train station, then park the car in one of the available parking lots and take a train to reach the final destination. During the trip, the user must obey the rules and conditions specified by that particular mobility provider. The CML mobility service enforces a global workflow specified using our method.

Now, let us consider a more complex business mobility use case scenario: two companies A and B decide to use the mobility services offered by CML to enforce some public funded project-specific travel restrictions on its employees. The use case requirements are:

- Every business travel must be approved by the respective managers of participating companies, and in special cases, the public funding project manager approval is also required.
- Special conditions whenever necessary could be inserted by authorized persons (i.e., the Managers)
- Travelers/Users using CML should be able to recover from error conditions, for instance, if a train or flight is canceled then rebooking should be possible.
- Reimbursement of travel cost after a successful trip should be automated.

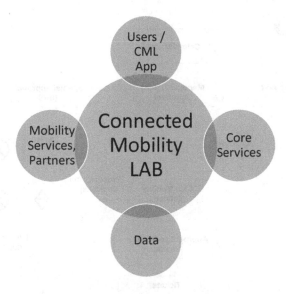

Fig. 9. The Connected Mobility Lab (CML) offers a comprehensive mobility service by integrating different mobility service provides, partners using its core services and CML App.

– Actions executed by the users/travelers must be recorded in a distributed immutable database for accountability.

As the first step, the requirement engineering experts perform the elicitation process i.e., to collect information from the involved stakeholders. The business mobility process and conditions are defined after consulting with participating companies (A and B) and the public funding project manager. The collected use case requirements are used to create the OMG SysML's activity diagram. The open-source modeling tool "Modelio", for example, can be used to create a SysML activity diagram. Figure 10 shows the SysML activity diagram of the above mentioned CML business mobility use case. An employee (e) is able to make a travel request which can be approved or rejected by his manager (mA). In case of a special request, the public funded project manager (mP) must also approve. The CML calendar service provides information about the meeting such as location, time, etc. If the trip is approved, then the employee (i.e., the traveler) may choose the transportation type (for example, public transport, car sharing, and so on) and get the tickets from the CML App. Finally, when the trip comes to an end, the reimbursement process is initiated. Later, the workflow expert transforms the SysML activity diagram into a Petri Net workflow specification as shown in Fig. 11. Finally, the Petri Net workflow is executed by the employee using the CML App.

Let us assume the following:

– The CML App has access to CML core services including the CML calendar service.

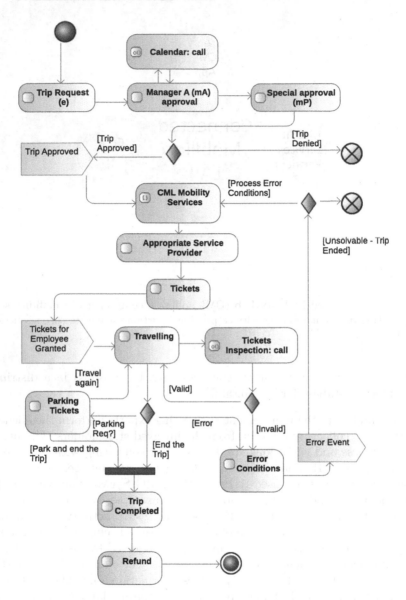

Fig. 10. SysML activity diagram of the CML business mobility use case

– The WF (a), (b) and (c) as shown in Fig. 11 are the resulting Petri Net workflow created by the workflow experts and are available in the central CML repository or the Contract Store. These PN workflows can be accessed by CML App i.e., the users are able to download the required workflows and execute them in the CML App. The sub-workflow (c) is a dynamic workflow and can be invoked to manage unexpected (error) situations. Notice that

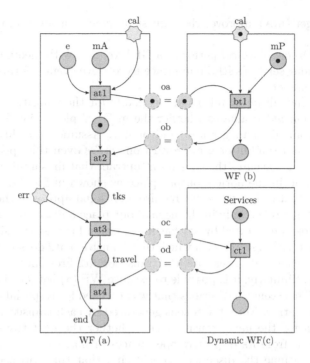

Fig. 11. Petri Net workflows of the business mobility use case

all three workflows are pre-defined, the workflow experts have created one
sub-workflow to manage all unexpected (or error) situations.
- The CML services (such as mobility, parking, etc.) provide tickets, parking
lot information, visiting passes for authorized requests similar to an OAuth
resource request.

We use the following notations in Fig. 11: employee as e, manager of company
A, B, and public funded project as mA, mB, and mP respectively, and CML
calendar service as cal. The Petri Net places and transitions are marked with
corresponding identifiers such as $at1$ for WF (a) transition 1 and $bt1$ for WF
(b) transition respectively. Below, we describe step by step process the business
mobility use case involving three workflows (a), (b) and (c) as shown in Fig. 11.
Assume that the employee (e) from company A wants to attend a business
meeting organized by the manager (mB) in company B.

- The project manager of company B (mB) creates a meeting with an identifier
(mID) in the CML calendar. This identifier is required by the employee (e)
of company A to initiate the travel request using the CML App.
- The employee (e) of Company A makes a travel request using the meeting
identifier mID in his CML App.
- When a travel request is raised, the CML App executes the WF (a) as shown
in Fig. 11 i.e., it sends an approval request to his manager (mA).

- The manager (mA) approves the request by placing a token in the place *mA* in Fig. 11.
- Next, the Oracle place *cal* performs a GET request with meeting mID to the CML calendar service's REST interface to retrieve event information such as location, time, etc.
- Assuming that all input tokens are available for the transition (at1) of WF (a), transition *at1* evaluates whether the mID, employee email address, and approval from his manager are valid or not. Assume that this is a special trip that requires additional approval from *mP*. Given this special case, the transition (at1) executes the transition contract that fires a token in the open place (*oa*) and in the normal output place as shown in Fig. 11.
- Alternatively, if this trip doesn't require additional approval, then transition at1 generates a token only in the normal out place and not in the open place (oa). The token generated by at1 has information for next transition at2 e.g., oAuth token with a secret with which that transition at2 doesn't need a token from open place (ob). Therefore, the transition at2 fires only with its normal input place. Similarly, it is possible to execute WF (a) without invoking WFs (b and c). This scenario describes that was no need for a special approval and there was no error. Note: the tokens generated by each transition contain the information for the next transition i.e., whether the next transition should expect tokens from its respective open places or not.
- Note: we continue the discussion considering that this trip needs a special approval from *mP* as described earlier.
- The CML workflow enforcement engine processes the token from the WF (a) open place (oa) and downloads the workflow WF (b) from CML repository to be executed in special cases. The project manager (mP) approves or rejects the trip request. As a result, WF (b) transition contract (bt1) evaluates and fires output tokens in the open place (ob).
- The token in place (ob) provides a secret (similar to an OAuth access-token) required by the transition at2 to get the tickets from CML mobility services.
- In case of unforeseen circumstances (delay or cancellation of chosen mobility service), the traveler can request an alternative transportation option via CML App. The oracle place (err) monitors the information of selected train from the mobility service provider. The transition (at3) evaluates the error token, if the traveler wants to end the trip, then it places a token in place (end) and places a cancellation/new tickets request in open place (oc).
- If the traveler requests alternative tickets, then transition (at3) places this request in the open place (oc). This token is processed by a dynamically generated WF (c) of the mobility service provider. If the error conditions cannot be solved in an automated fashion, then a human intervention is invoked. Thus, new tickets are delivered via the open place (od). Note: Fig. 11 shows the workflow only until this stage, the rest of the workflow steps can be executed with more transitions and places.
- Thanks to the transition contracts in Petri Net based workflows, fine-grained access – such as, temporary access valid during the meeting period – can be granted to enter company B (for example, access to meeting rooms), reim-

bursements can be automated i.e., after a successful trip a waiting time is introduced using timeout transition, if the trip is not successful then a default process is initiated.

- In the end, the organizer of the meeting mB can confirm the attendees through his CML mobile App, therefore the payment transition is activated such that payment to mobility providers, reimbursements to the employees can be handled appropriately.

A private blockchain can be used in the CML for accountability. Every Petri Net transitions' input and output tokens are recorded as transactions on the blockchain. This feature provides data immutability and opportunity for future auditing in case of any fraud without a centralized trusted entity. There are several advantages for companies to enforce such business mobility conditions on its employees. The companies could restrict its employees from using transportation service for private purposes. Further, the employees can only use the cost-effective transportation available. By automating this process, the overhead for the employees and its managers is reduced. The companies can satisfy regional policies such as reducing the carbon footprint.

6.2 Building Automation

Modern buildings use building automation systems to control lighting, heating, ventilation, and physical safety systems within the building. These building automation systems consist of embedded devices equipped with sensors and actuators, and can collaborate autonomously. For example, the lighting system can adjust the light intensity and color of a room based on the ambient light available in the room; the security system can alert the nearest emergency responders or fire-stations in case of an emergency. In such a scenario, often it is required to perform software-updates, quality-control inspection, fix security patches and upgrade the firmware on the devices. Usually, the building owner delegates the installation or maintenance work to a contracting company. The RFC 7744 [64], provides a summary of authorization problems that emerge during the device life-cycle (commissioning, maintenance, recommissioning, decommissioning). In addition to the authorization problems, the building owners may wish to ensure that only products with a certain provenance or quality are installed, and that the process complies to standard operating procedures.

The building owner also wants that the contractor to obey the conditions agreed in the contract, for instance, the building owner:

- Wants to track the status of the work in progress remotely.
- Wants to configure the installed devices with custom-rules such that the newly installed devices are interoperable with existing systems and devices.
- Automatically enforce the contract conditions agreed with the contractor. For instance, a penalty if the contractor breaks any agreed condition, or a complete payment if agreed conditions were satisfied.
- Wants to control authorization permissions given to the contractors enforcing fine-grained access control i.e., the least privilege principle.

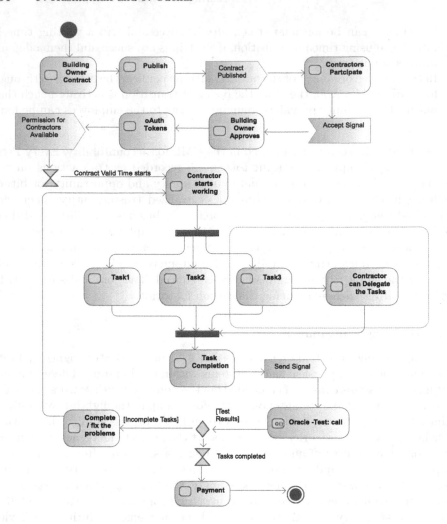

Fig. 12. SysML activity diagram of building automation

First, the requirements elicitation process is conducted to gather the requirements; second, as a result, a SysML activity diagram is created as shown in Fig. 12.

Finally, the building owner with the help of workflow experts has created the Petri Net workflow (*BA*) as shown in Fig. 13. The workflow is published in a private blockchain i.e., in a decentralized contract store as described in Sect. 5.6 after performing strict evaluation. The workflow mobile application certified by the building is downloaded and used by the contractor to execute the workflow. We refer to the similar example described earlier in Fig. 8, where the person executing the workflow gets (security access) tokens for accessing services which are otherwise restricted.

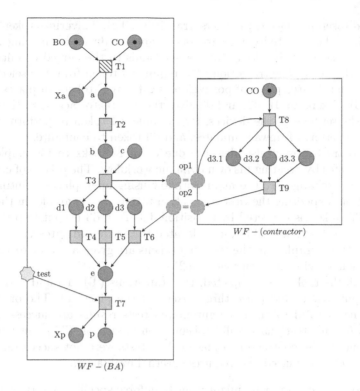

Fig. 13. Open PN workflow of building automation

Below, we explain the steps involved in the workflow:

- Once the contract is published, the contractors can evaluate the contract, the workflow, and the requirements to decide whether to participate in the workflow or not. The interested contractor places his decision as a token using the mobile application. The contractor signs the token using his private key, this signed-token is placed in the place (CO).
- Next, let us assume that the building owner selects one of the contractors based on provenance and credibility of the contractor. The building owner uses the mobile application to approve the selected contractor to begin the work. This event creates a token signed by the building owner in the place (BO). The token contains information about the chosen contractor and enables a transition (T1).
- The transition (T1) verifies the tokens in the input places (BO and CO), verify the signature of the token using pre-configured certificates. If both tokens are valid, then T1's transition contract creates an OAuth-token in place (a). This token in place (a) permits the contractor to access the devices for maintenance purposes as defined in the next steps of the workflow. As expected, only one contractor can be selected i.e., the T1 places the input tokens of contractors not chosen in the output place (Xa).

– A valid token in place (a) triggers Transition (T2). T2 verifies token in place (a). Now, the selected contractor once again confirms by placing a signed token in place (c). By doing this he/she binds to the agreed conditions and begins the work. The transition (T3) requires a token from the selected contractor and creates proof-of-possession OAuth ACE tokens in places (d1, d2, and d3). Tokens in d1, d2, and d3 gives the contractor access to three different tasks/services in the devices, for example, d1 token to perform tests, d2 token to perform firmware updates, and d3 token to configure.

– The Contractor may also delegate one or more tasks to his employees or subordinates by creating his own dynamic workflow. The tokens of completed tasks are exchanged to the main workflow using open places pointing to the transitions expecting the task completion tokens. For example, in the Fig. 13 task d3's token is expected by transition T6. Task d3 is split into three subtasks (d3.1, d3.2, and d3.3) and delegated to the subordinates via open place (op1). After completion, the resulting tokens are given as input tokens to the transition T6 via the open place (op2).

– Once all the tasks are completed, the transitions (T4, T5 and T6) evaluate the input tokens and place three tokens in the place (e). The oracle place (test) has a valid token if the automated tests results are successful. If the places (e, and test) have valid tokens then transition (T7) can trigger the payment for the contractor in place (p). If tests were not successful, a token in place (Xp) is placed and requires external evaluation.

The contracting company might want to enforce specific conditions by creating dynamic workflows on their employees (to handle special or error conditions). The open places introduced in the main contract must not change the main objective of the workflow. To enable this feature, the building owner may allow some transitions (for example, T3 and T6 in Fig. 13) to allow open places from authorized participants. Figure 13 shows the owner of the task (the contractor) can create dynamic workflows for other entities to complete a task or resource that he owns. In this way, we have realized a distributed workflow management system. This use case shows how we can execute and enforce a workflow in a distributed setting.

6.3   Car Sharing

Car sharing services such as DriveNow and Car2Go are popular for short-term car rental. For instance, DriveNow and Car2Go have their own workflow to rent a car, finish the rental, and for payment. A customer must first register to the service with his/her driving license, proof of address, payment method (credit card or bank account details), and personal identity. The customer is provided with either a card, login credentials, or other means of authentication credentials to access the service. Most car sharing services provide a web-service and mobile application.

Our aim was to apply our framework and methods to solve a real use case. Therefore, as an example, we chose the car hire process of DriveNow and applied

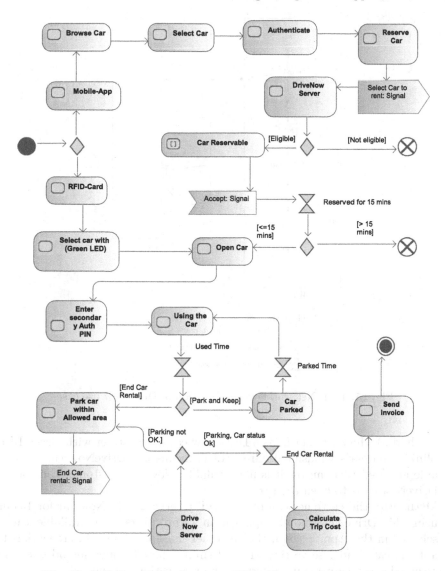

Fig. 14. SysML activity diagram of DriveNow car sharing platform

our methods to solve it. Note: the rental process described in this use case is only based on our experience, and this process can be updated (or outdated) anytime by the service provider and might not be valid anymore. A SysML activity diagram describing the rental process of DriveNow is shown in Fig. 14.

We translate the SysML activity diagram of DriveNow car hire process into our Petri Network workflows as shown in Fig. 15.

The customer chooses one of the two available methods to rent a car: (a) using the DriveNow card; (b) using the DriveNow mobile application (App).

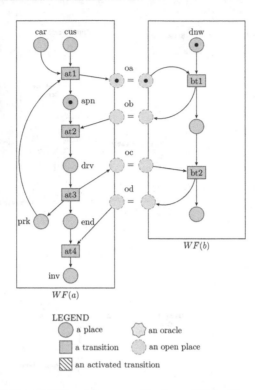

Fig. 15. Petri Net workflow specification of DriveNow use case

- Method(a): the customer finds a DriveNow car in the street with Green LED blinking on car's windshield. Green LED means the DriveNow car is available and Red LED means it is not available. Now, the customer can use his DriveNow card to open the car.
- Method(b): the customer can plan ahead, reserve a DriveNow car for 15 min using his DriveNow mobile application (App). First, an available car is selected in the App. Second, the customer must use his login credentials to authenticate and reserve the car for 15 min. The customer should open the reserved car within 15 min otherwise the reservation is canceled.
- Step1: Assume that the customer used one of the two available methods (a or b) as described above to get inside the car. This action is depicted as placing a token at place *cus* by the customer in Fig. 15. The Transition (at1) process this token in place (cus), availability of the car (with inbuilt car information) in place (car) and opens the door.
- Step2: The customer must enter his secondary authentication PIN in place (apn) using the car's touch interface in the dashboard. The transition (at2) checks the PIN entered via the information available from DriveNow server. If the PIN is valid, transition at2 places the token in place (drv). Now, the customer can start and use the car.

- Dashboard information for the driver: if the car leaves the DriveNow business area of city it belongs to, then a warning notification appears on the dashboard i.e., it is not possible to end the rental outside the business area – *park and keep* option is allowed, but with probably different charges. DriveNow is also offering rental packages for hours and days and with this contract business area restriction does not apply.
- Step3: the customer can park and keep the car or end the car rental via the App or car's dashboard. This decision is recorded and processed by the transition (at3).
  - Step3.1: if the customer parks and keeps the car using *park and keep* option, then he can re-enter the car using his App or DriveNow card using the same steps described in step1 to continue.
  - Step3.2: Note: this step is not available within the described car sharing service. We included this to show that our method can handle error conditions. Assume an error condition such as breakdown or malfunction, the transition at3 allows the customer to report it via the App and that can be processed by DriveNow to allow new business logic that can help the customer to reach his destination via other methods, etc.
- Step4: the customer can end car rental if the car is in the business area (geofenced area). If the conditions are valid, then transition (at4) allows to end the rental and places a token in place (inv). The trip invoice is calculated and sent to his email based on his usage. If automatic payment is enabled, then the amount is billed to his credit card.

Figure 15 shows the Petri Net workflow of DriveNow use case. The interaction between the customer and a DriveNow car is described on WF (a), and WF (b) describes the DriveNow (DN) server processing the car sharing requests (i.e., in the form of tokens) from WF (a) via open Petri Net places. As you can see, when using a particular service the customer must download an application provided by that particular service provider. If our method is applied, a common workflow application can be used to rent cars from different service providers - only the car hire process and their specific workflows must be modeled and provided to our workflow application.

7   A High-Level Summary and Implementation Guide

So far, we presented our method and solved some specific use cases using our framework. Now, we want to summarize the ideas, present a simple guide for solving any generic use case, and a high-level guide to implementation.

First, a use case that one wants to implement must be identified. Next, the process including technical and business details is discussed and finalized with relevant stakeholders. Once the process is defined, an engineer uses a SysML activity diagram using tools such as Modelio to describe the process. Later, this activity diagram can be exported to a Petri Net workflow. Next, a Petri Net simulator is used to check properties of the exported Petri Net Workflow such as deadlocks, etc. Then a Petri Net library such as Snakes can be used for implementing Petri Net functionalities into the existing software application. After this, a workflow expert should check if the Petri Net workflow and the transition contract conditions represent the process defined. Now, this verified PN workflow is published in a distributed database with appropriate access control such that only authorized persons can access the PN workflow. Now, an entity that needs to execute the process should download the corresponding PN workflow and the workflow execution application. With our framework, we provide workflow-aware access control by enforcing the process integrity. Additionally, for blockchain based solutions, we presented a framework to translate verified Petri Net workflow into Blockchain based smart contracts.

To explain a simple implementation guide, consider a simple use case that includes one or more stakeholders. All stakeholders provide their services as Representational State Transfer (REST) based web services. The workflows are created by practitioners (for example, engineers) and are verified by workflow experts, and finally, approved by the stakeholders. The approved workflow is available within a centralized (or a distributed) repository. A participant can download the application (Trusted App) in his handheld and the required workflow from the repository, and then he may start executing the workflow. The APP provides the communication interface with the core services – standard security protocols are used to protect the communication channel. How participants authenticate with the back end is out of scope. A secret material is used to verify the validity tokens and to create tokens to represent the entity that is executing the workflow, how this secret material is delivered to the App is out of scope. The enforcement of the Petri Net tokens is implemented in the App. We suggest using the ACE-OAuth based protocol to create such tokens. These proof-of-possession tokens are used by the client to prove to the resource server that the client is the valid entity to access the resources. The workflows are executed i.e., transitions and tokens are precisely processed in the Trusted Execution Environment (TEE) of the handheld. We assume that the participants are not able to extract or modify any secrets from the workflow. The Snakes Python library is used in the App to execute the Petri Nets workflows. Weber et al. [75] introduced Petri Net Markup Language (PNML) which is based on XML, and in this work, we propose to use PNML to express Petri Net workflows.

8   Limitations of Our Approach

8.1   Error Free Petri Net Workflow vs Design Flaw in the Process

A Petri Net simulator cannot detect a design problem or a flaw in the process itself. For example, assume that a Petri Net workflow is developed to protect some assets in the building. For instance, if the process does not include closing the secure door after accessing the assets, so this is a major design flaw and cannot be detected by the Petri Net. Therefore, designing workflows using Petri Nets does not guarantee error freeness.

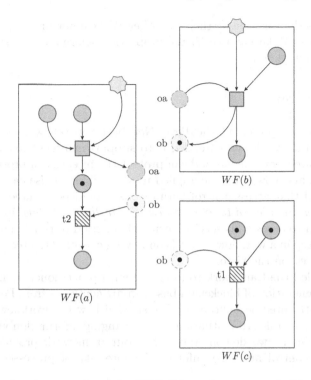

Fig. 16. The token in open place *ob* of WF (b) can be consumed either by *t2* of WF (a) or *t1* of WF (c). This prevents either WFs (a or c) to proceed forward.

The four-eyes principle is used to verify any process designed using another expert in the same field. This approach could find significant obvious problems in the process itself. The process can be improved without errors when it is reviewed by several experts. Once the process is designed without obvious design flaws, then it can be evaluated with Petri Nets simulators for properties such as deadlocks, etc.

8.2   Open Petri Nets and Deadlocks by Merging Different Processes

Consider three small individual processes a, b, and c designed and verified for Petri Nets properties. We can use open Petri Nets to create interfaces between those three different processes a, b and c. This enables us to create a main workflow consisting of two or three sub-workflows.

It is possible to have deadlocks when merging two or more sub-workflows without proper validation. For example, when we combine only two of them (a and b) or (b or c) then there may not be any deadlock but, when all three workflows (a, b, and c) are combined then there could be a deadlock. Figure 16 shows such an example with three WFs a, b, and c where the WF(b) is in a state after producing a token in its open place *ob*, then the token in *ob* can be either consumed by WF(a) via transition *t2* or WF(c) via transition *t1*. If one

WF consumes the token in *ob* then the other WF cannot proceed. Therefore, it is important to validate and verify the properties before merging sub-workflows with the main workflow.

9 Conclusion

In this paper, we presented the Petri Net based workflow specification and enforcement framework and extended it to support emergent IoT applications. We demonstrated how the method can protect the integrity of processes defined as Petri Nets, and how it can be applied to solve different use cases.

We showed that access control permissions should be granted to entities in the form: '*You are allowed to execute this task in this workflow*' instead of 'You are authorized to access this service during this period of time'. The permission to execute a step in a workflow depends on having executed the required previous steps (i.e., based on the history).

We extended the framework to integrate with practitioner-friendly tools, to support the generation of blockchain based smart contracts from Petri Nets, and to achieve distributed accountability. We showed how the workflow specified in Petri Nets may handle error situations by exchanging information via open Petri Net places. Finally, we demonstrated that our framework provides workflow-aware access control and also enforces the integrity of processes specified as Petri Nets.

Acknowledgements. We thank Professor Jonathan P. Bowen for his suggestions and reviewing this article.

References

1. van der Aalst, W.M.P.: Verification of workflow nets. In: Azéma, P., Balbo, G. (eds.) ICATPN 1997. LNCS, vol. 1248, pp. 407–426. Springer, Heidelberg (1997). https://doi.org/10.1007/3-540-63139-9_48
2. van der Aalst, W.M.P.: Putting high-level Petri nets to work in industry. Comput. Ind. **25**(1), 45–54 (1994). https://doi.org/10.1016/0166-3615(94)90031-0
3. AIOTI: The Alliance for the Internet of Things Innovation (2018). https://aioti.eu/. Accessed Dec 2018
4. Antonakakis, M., et al.: Understanding the Mirai Botnet. In: 26th USENIX Security Symposium, pp. 1092–1110 (2017). https://www.usenix.org/conference/usenixsecurity17/technical-sessions/presentation/antonakakis
5. Atluri, V., Huang, W.-K.: An authorization model for workflows. In: Bertino, E., Kurth, H., Martella, G., Montolivo, E. (eds.) ESORICS 1996. LNCS, vol. 1146, pp. 44–64. Springer, Heidelberg (1996). https://doi.org/10.1007/3-540-61770-1_27
6. Atluri, V., Huang, W.: A Petri net based safety analysis of workflow authorization models. J. Comput. Secur. **8**(2/3), 209–240 (2000). http://content.iospress.com/articles/journal-of-computer-security/jcs113
7. Bahga, A., Madisetti, V.K.: Blockchain platform for industrial internet of things. J. Softw. Eng. Appl. **9**, 533–546 (2016). https://doi.org/10.4236/jsea.2016.910036

8. Bartoletti, M., Pompianu, L.: An empirical analysis of smart contracts: platforms, applications, and design patterns. In: Brenner, M., et al. (eds.) FC 2017. LNCS, vol. 10323, pp. 494–509. Springer, Cham (2017). https://doi.org/10.1007/978-3-319-70278-0_31

9. Basin, D., Burri, S.J., Karjoth, G.: Optimal workflow-aware authorizations. In: ACM Symposium on Access Control Models and Technologies (SACMAT 2012), pp. 93–102 (2012). https://doi.org/10.1145/2295136.2295154

10. Bertino, E., Ferrari, E., Atluri, V.: The specification and enforcement of authorization constraints in workflow management systems. ACM Trans. Inf. Syst. Secur. 2(1), 65–104 (1999). https://doi.org/10.1145/300830.300837

11. Bishop, M.: Computer Security: Art and Science. Addison-Wesley, Boston (2002). https://doi.org/10.1093/toxsci/kft059. https://books.google.de/books?id=b4gcs wEACAAJ

12. Bormann, C., Ersue, M., Keranen, A.: Terminology for constrained-node networks. Technical report, IETF, May 2014. https://doi.org/10.17487/rfc7228

13. Castelluccia, C., Francillon, A., Perito, D., Soriente, C.: On the difficulty of software-based attestation of embedded devices. In: Proceedings of the 16th ACM conference on Computer and communications security - CCS 2009, p. 400. ACM Press, New York (2009). https://doi.org/10.1145/1653662.1653711

14. Christidis, K., Devetsikiotis, M.: Blockchains and smart contracts for the internet of things. IEEE Access 4, 2292–2303 (2016). https://doi.org/10.1109/ACCESS. 2016.2566339. http://ieeexplore.ieee.org/document/7467408/

15. Compagna, L., dos Santos, D.R., Ponta, S.E., Ranise, S.: Aegis: automatic enforcement of security policies in workflow-driven web applications. In: Proceedings of ACM on Conference on Data and Application Security and Privacy - CODASPY 2017, pp. 321–328 (2017). https://doi.org/10.1145/3029806.3029813

16. Cuellar, J., Kasinathan, P., Calvo, D.: Privacy-enhanced-tokens (PAT) profile for ACE. Technical report, IETF (2018). https://datatracker.ietf.org/doc/draft-cuellar-ace-pat-priv-enhanced-authz-tokens/

17. Delmolino, K., Arnett, M., Kosba, A.E., Miller, A., Shi, E.: Step by step towards creating a safe smart contract: lessons and insights from a cryptocurrency lab. IACR Cryptology ePrint Archive 2015, 460 (2015). https://doi.org/10.1007/978-3-662-53357-4_6. https://eprint.iacr.org/2015/460.pdf

18. Dijkstra, E.W.: Guarded commands, nondeterminacy and formal derivation of programs. Commun. ACM 18(8), 453–457 (1975). https://doi.org/10.1145/360933. 360975

19. Esparza, J.: Decidability and complexity of Petri net problems—an introduction. In: Reisig, W., Rozenberg, G. (eds.) ACPN 1996. LNCS, vol. 1491, pp. 374–428. Springer, Heidelberg (1998). https://doi.org/10.1007/3-540-65306-6_20

20. Ethereum: Solidity—Solidity (2018). https://solidity.readthedocs.io/en/develop/. Accessed Aug 2018

21. Ethereum: What Are Smart Contracts - EthereumWiki (2018). http://www. ethereumwiki.com/ethereum-wiki/smart-contracts/. Accessed Mar 2018

22. European Union (EU): EU GDPR Information Portal (2018). https://www.eugdpr. org/. Accessed July 2018

23. Friedenthal, S., Moore, A., Steiner, R.: A Practical Guide to SysML, 3rd edn. Morgan Kaufmann, San Francisco (2008). https://doi.org/10.1016/B978-0-12-374379-4.X0001-X

24. Gerdes, S., Bergmann, O., Bormann, C., Selander, G., Seitz, L.: Datagram Transport Layer Security (DTLS) Profile for Authentication and Authorization for Constrained Environments (ACE) (2018). https://tools.ietf.org/html/draft-ietf-ace-dtls-authorize-03. Accessed Mar 2018

25. Hardt, D.: The OAuth 2.0 Authorization Framework (2012). https://tools.ietf.org/html/rfc6749. Accessed Dec 2017

26. Harney, H., Muckenhirn, C.: Group Key Management Protocol (GKMP) Specification, July 1997. https://doi.org/10.17487/rfc2093

27. Heckel, R.: Open Petri nets as semantic model for workflow integration. In: Ehrig, H., Reisig, W., Rozenberg, G., Weber, H. (eds.) Petri Net Technology for Communication-Based Systems. LNCS, vol. 2472, pp. 281–294. Springer, Heidelberg (2003). https://doi.org/10.1007/978-3-540-40022-6_14

28. Huang, W.K., Atluri, V.: SecureFlow: a secure web-enabled workflow management system. In: Proceedings of the Fourth ACM Workshop on Role-Based Access Control - RBAC 1999, pp. 83–94 (1999). https://doi.org/10.1145/319171.319179

29. IBM: Energy-Blockchain Labs and IBM Create Carbon Credit Management Platform Using Hyperledger Fabric on the IBM Cloud, pp. 2–3. IBM Press Release (2017). https://www-03.ibm.com/press/us/en/pressrelease/51839.wss

30. IBM: Hyperledger Fabric – Hyperledger (2018). https://www.hyperledger.org/projects/fabric. Accessed Aug 2018

31. IBM: Hyperledger-Smart Contract Language – Chaincode (2018). https://hyperledger-fabric.readthedocs.io/en/release-1.2/blockchain.html. Accessed Aug 2018

32. IETF ACE Working Group: Authentication and Authorization for Constrained Environments (ACE) (2017). https://datatracker.ietf.org/doc/draft-ietf-ace-oauth-authz/. Accessed Dec 2017

33. Jamal, M., Zafar, N.A.: Transformation of activity diagram into coloured Petri nets using weighted directed graph. In: 2016 International Conference on Frontiers of Information Technology (FIT), pp. 181–186. IEEE, December 2016. https://doi.org/10.1109/FIT.2016.041. http://ieeexplore.ieee.org/document/7866750/

34. Jensen, K.: Coloured Petri nets. In: Brauer, W., Reisig, W., Rozenberg, G. (eds.) Petri Nets: Central Models and Their Properties. LNCS, vol. 254, pp. 248–299. Springer, Heidelberg (1987). https://doi.org/10.1007/BFb0046842

35. Jensen, K.: Coloured Petri nets: a high level language for system design and analysis. In: Rozenberg, G. (ed.) ICATPN 1989. LNCS, vol. 483, pp. 342–416. Springer, Heidelberg (1991). https://doi.org/10.1007/3-540-53863-1_31

36. Jensen, K.: Coloured Petri Nets - Basic Concepts, Analysis Methods and Practical Use. Monographs in Theoretical Computer Science. An EATCS Series, vol. 1, 2nd edn. Springer, Heidelberg (1996). https://doi.org/10.1007/978-3-662-03241-1

37. Jensen, K., Kristensen, L.M., Wells, L.: Coloured Petri nets and CPN tools for modelling and validation of concurrent systems. STTT 9(3–4), 213–254 (2007). https://doi.org/10.1007/s10009-007-0038-x

38. Jürjens, J.: UMLsec: extending UML for secure systems development. In: Jézéquel, J.-M., Hussmann, H., Cook, S. (eds.) UML 2002. LNCS, vol. 2460, pp. 412–425. Springer, Heidelberg (2002). https://doi.org/10.1007/3-540-45800-X_32

39. Kasinathan, P., Cuéllar, J.: Securing the integrity of workflows in IoT. In: Proceedings of the 2018 International Conference on Embedded Wireless Systems and Networks, EWSN 2018, Madrid, Spain, 14–16 February 2018, pp. 252–257 (2018). http://dl.acm.org/citation.cfm?id=3234908

40. Kasinathan, P., Cuellar, J.: Workflow-aware security of integrated mobility services. In: Lopez, J., Zhou, J., Soriano, M. (eds.) ESORICS 2018. LNCS, vol. 11099, pp. 3–19. Springer, Cham (2018). https://doi.org/10.1007/978-3-319-98989-1_1

41. Knorr, K.: Dynamic access control through Petri net workflows. In: 16th Annual Computer Security Applications Conference (ACSAC 2000), New Orleans, Louisiana, USA, 11–15 December 2000, pp. 159–167 (2000). https://doi.org/10.1109/ACSAC.2000.898869

42. Krebs, B., BMW: connected mobility lab – center digitization.bayern (2017). https://zentrum-digitalisierung.bayern/connected-mobility-lab/. Accessed Oct 2018

43. Linhares, M.V., da Silva, A.J., de Oliveira, R.S.: Empirical evaluation of SysML through the modeling of an industrial automation unit. In: 2006 IEEE Conference on Emerging Technologies and Factory Automation, pp. 145–152. IEEE, September 2006. https://doi.org/10.1109/ETFA.2006.355190. http://ieeexplore.ieee.org/document/4178305/

44. Lodderstedt, T., Basin, D., Doser, J.: SecureUML: a UML-based modeling language for model-driven security. In: Jézéquel, J.-M., Hussmann, H., Cook, S. (eds.) UML 2002. LNCS, vol. 2460, pp. 426–441. Springer, Heidelberg (2002). https://doi.org/10.1007/3-540-45800-X_33

45. Luu, L., Chu, D.H., Olickel, H., Saxena, P., Hobor, A.: Making smart contracts smarter. In: Proceedings of the 2016 ACM SIGSAC Conference on Computer and Communications Security - CCS 2016, pp. 254–269. ACM Press, New York (2016). https://doi.org/10.1145/2976749.2978309

46. Merlin, P.M., Farber, D.J.: Recoverability of communication protocols-implications of a theoretical study. IEEE Trans. Commun. (1976). https://doi.org/10.1109/TCOM.1976.1093424

47. Miessler, D., Smith, C., Haddix, J.: OWASP Internet of Things Top Ten Project (2014). Accessed Dec 2017

48. Modelio – Open Source Tool: Modelio – the open source modeling tool. https://www.modelio.org/. Accessed Aug 2018

49. Morimoto, S.: A survey of formal verification for business process modeling. In: Bubak, M., van Albada, G.D., Dongarra, J., Sloot, P.M.A. (eds.) ICCS 2008. LNCS, vol. 5102, pp. 514–522. Springer, Heidelberg (2008). https://doi.org/10.1007/978-3-540-69387-1_58

50. Mortensen, K.H.: Automatic code generation method based on coloured Petri net models applied on an access control system. In: Nielsen, M., Simpson, D. (eds.) ICATPN 2000. LNCS, vol. 1825, pp. 367–386. Springer, Heidelberg (2000). https://doi.org/10.1007/3-540-44988-4_21

51. Murata, T.: Petri nets: properties, analysis and applications. Proc. IEEE **77**(4), 541–580 (1989). https://doi.org/10.1109/5.24143. http://ieeexplore.ieee.org/document/24143/

52. Nakamoto, S.: Bitcoin: a peer-to-peer electronic cash system (2008). https://bitcoin.org/bitcoin.pdf. Accessed Oct 2018

53. Özsu, M.T., Valduriez, P.: Principles of Distributed Database Systems, 3rd edn. Springer, New York (2011). https://doi.org/10.1007/978-1-4419-8834-8

54. Petri, C.A.: Communication with automata (1966). http://edoc.sub.uni-hamburg.de/informatik/volltexte/2010/155/

55. Pohl, K.: Requirements Engineering: An Overview. RWTH, Fachgruppe Informatik, Aachen (1996). ftp://ftp8.de.freebsd.org/pub/packages/CREWS/CREWS-96-02.pdf

56. Pommereau, F.: SNAKES: a flexible high-level Petri nets library (tool paper). In: Devillers, R., Valmari, A. (eds.) PETRI NETS 2015. LNCS, vol. 9115, pp. 254–265. Springer, Cham (2015). https://doi.org/10.1007/978-3-319-19488-2_13

57. Rahim, M., Boukala-Ioualalen, M., Hammad, A.: Petri nets based approach for modular verification of SysML requirements on activity diagrams. In: Proceedings of the International Workshop on Petri Nets and Software Engineering (PNSE), Tunis, Tunisia, 23–24 June 2014, pp. 233–248 (2014). http://ceur-ws.org/Vol-1160/paper14.pdf

58. Reisig, W.: Petri Nets: An Introduction. EATCS Monographs on Theoretical Computer Science, vol. 4. Springer, Heidelberg (1985). https://doi.org/10.1007/978-3-642-69968-9

59. Reisig, W.: A Primer in Petri Net Design. Springer Compass International. Springer, Heidelberg (1992). https://doi.org/10.1007/978-3-642-75329-9

60. Reisig, W.: Understanding Petri Nets – Modeling Techniques, Analysis Methods, Case Studies. Springer, Heidelberg (2013). https://doi.org/10.1007/978-3-642-33278-4

61. Sadeghi, A.R., Wachsmann, C., Waidner, M.: Security and privacy challenges in industrial internet of things. In: Proceedings of the 52nd Annual Design Automation Conference on - DAC 2015, pp. 1–6. ACM Press, New York (2015). https://doi.org/10.1145/2744769.2747942

62. Sandhu, R.S., Samarati, P.: Access control: principles and practice. IEEE Commun. Mag. **32**(9), 40–48 (1994). https://doi.org/10.1109/35.312842. http://ieeexplore.ieee.org/document/312842/

63. Schaller, R.: Moore's law: past, present and future. IEEE Spectr. **34**(6), 52–59 (1997). https://doi.org/10.1109/6.591665

64. Seitz, L., Gerdes, S., Selander, G., Mani, M., Kumar, S.: Use cases for authentication and authorization in constrained environments (2016). ISSN 2070-1721. https://tools.ietf.org/html/rfc7744

65. Seitz, L., Selander, G., Wahlstroem, E., Erdtman, S., Tschofenig, H.: Authentication and authorization for constrained environments (ACE) using the OAuth 2.0 framework (ACE-OAuth). Technical report, IETF (2018)

66. Sicari, S., Rizzardi, A., Grieco, L., Coen-Porisini, A.: Security, privacy and trust in internet of things: the road ahead. Comput. Netw. **76**, 146–164 (2015). https://doi.org/10.1016/J.COMNET.2014.11.008. https://www.sciencedirect.com/science/article/pii/S1389128614003971

67. van der Stok, P., Kampanakis, P., Kumar, S., Richardson, M., Furuhed, M., Raza, S.: EST over secure CoAP (EST-coaps). Technical report, IETF (2018). https://datatracker.ietf.org/doc/draft-ietf-ace-coap-est/

68. Sundmaeker, H., Guillemin, P., Friess, P., Woelfflé, S. (eds.): Vision and Challenges for Realising the Internet of Things. Publications Office of the European Union, Luxembourg (2010). https://doi.org/10.2759/26127

69. Szabo, N.: Smart contracts: building blocks for digital markets, 1996. EXTROPY: The Journal of Transhumanist Thought (2001). http://www.fon.hum.uva.nl/rob/Courses/InformationInSpeech/CDROM/Literature/LOTwinterschool2006/szabo.best.vwh.net/smart_contracts_2.html

70. Tandon, L., Fong, P.W.L., Safavi-Naini, R.: HCAP: a history-based capability system for IoT devices. In: Proceedings of the 23nd ACM on Symposium on Access Control Models and Technologies, SACMAT 2018, Indianapolis, IN, USA, 13–15 June 2018, pp. 247–258 (2018). https://doi.org/10.1145/3205977.3205978

71. TCG WG: TCG guidance for securing resource-constrained devices. Technical report, Trusted Computing Group (TCG) (2017). https://trustedcomputinggroup. org/wp-content/uploads/TCG-Guidance-for-Securing-Resource-Constrained-Dev ices-v1r22.pdf

72. Thaler, D., Waltermire, D., Housley, R.: Software Updates for Internet of Things (suit) (2018). https://datatracker.ietf.org/wg/suit/about/. Accessed Oct 2018

73. The Official OMG SysML site: What Is OMG SysML? (2012). http://www. omgsysml.org/. Accessed Apr 2018

74. Tiloca, M., Selander, G., Palombini, F., Park, J.: Secure group communication for CoAP (2018). https://datatracker.ietf.org/doc/draft-tiloca-core-multicast-oscoap/. Accessed Oct 2018

75. Weber, M., Kindler, E.: The Petri net markup language. In: Ehrig, H., Reisig, W., Rozenberg, G., Weber, H. (eds.) Petri Net Technology for Communication-Based Systems. LNCS, vol. 2472, pp. 124–144. Springer, Heidelberg (2003). https://doi. org/10.1007/978-3-540-40022-6_7

76. Weber, R.H.: Internet of things – new security and privacy challenges. Comput. Law Secur. Rev. **26**(1), 23–30 (2010). https://doi.org/10.1016/J.CLSR.2009.11. 008. https://www.sciencedirect.com/science/article/pii/S0267364909001939

77. WfMC: Workflow Management Coalition (2009). http://www.wfmc.org/. Accessed July 2017

78. Van der Aalst, W.M.P.: The application of Petri nets to workflow management. J. Circuits Syst. Comput. **08**(01), 21–66 (1998). https://doi.org/10. 1142/S0218126698000004. http://www.worldscientific.com/doi/abs/10.1142/S0218 126698000043

79. Wolter, C., Menzel, M., Schaad, A., Miseldine, P., Meinel, C.: Model-driven business process security requirement specification. J. Syst. Arch. **55**(4), 211–223 (2009). https://doi.org/10.1016/J.SYSARC.2008.10.002. https://www.sci encedirect.com/science/article/pii/S1383762108001471

80. Wolter, C., Schaad, A.: Modeling of task-based authorization constraints in BPMN. In: Alonso, G., Dadam, P., Rosemann, M. (eds.) BPM 2007. LNCS, vol. 4714, pp. 64–79. Springer, Heidelberg (2007). https://doi.org/10.1007/978-3-540-75183-0_5

81. Wolter, C., Schaad, A., Meinel, C.: Task-based entailment constraints for basic workflow patterns. In: Proceedings of the 13th ACM Symposium on Access Control Models and Technologies - SACMAT 2008, p. 51. ACM Press, New York (2008). https://doi.org/10.1145/1377836.1377844

82. Woodcock, J., Larsen, P.G., Bicarregui, J., Fitzgerald, J.: Formal methods: practice and experience. ACM Comput. Surv. **41**(4), 1–36 (2009). https://doi.org/10.1145/ 1592434.1592436

83. Zhang, F., Cecchetti, E., Croman, K., Juels, A., Shi, E.: Town Crier: an authenticated data feed for smart contracts. In: Proceedings of the 2016 ACM SIGSAC Conference on Computer and Communications Security, CCS 2016, pp. 270–282. ACM, New York (2016). https://doi.org/10.1145/2976749.2978326

Programming Z3

Nikolaj Bjørner[1]([⊠]), Leonardo de Moura[1], Lev Nachmanson[1],
and Christoph M. Wintersteiger[2][iD]

[1] Microsoft Research, Redmond, USA
nbjorner@microsoft.com
[2] Microsoft Research, Cambridge, UK

Abstract. This tutorial provides a programmer's introduction to the
Satisfiability Modulo Theories Solver Z3. It describes how to use Z3
through scripts, provided in the Python scripting language, and it
describes several of the algorithms underlying the decision procedures
within Z3. It aims to broadly cover almost all available features of Z3
and the essence of the underlying algorithms.

1 Introduction

Satisfiability Modulo Theories (SMT) problem is a decision problem for logical
formulas with respect to combinations of background theories such as arithmetic, bit-vectors, arrays, and uninterpreted functions. Z3 is an efficient SMT
solver with specialized algorithms for solving background theories. SMT solving
enjoys a synergetic relationship with software analysis, verification and symbolic
execution tools. This is in many respects thanks to the emphasis on supporting domains commonly found in programs and specifications. There are several
scenarios where part of a query posed by these tools can be cast in terms of
formulas in a supported logic. It is then useful for the tool writer to have an
idea of what are available supported logics, and have an idea of how formulas
are solved. But interacting with SMT solvers is not always limited to posing a
query as a single formula. It may require a sequence of interactions to obtain
a usable answer and the need emerges for the tool writer for having an idea of
what methods and knobs are available. In summary, this tutorial aims to answer
the following types of questions through examples and a touch of theory:

- What are the available features in Z3, and what are they designed to be used
  for?
- What are the underlying algorithms used in Z3?
- How can I program applications on top of Z3?

Figure 1 shows an overall systems diagram of Z3, as of version 4.8. The top
left summarizes the interfaces to Z3. One can interact with Z3 over SMT-LIB2
scripts supplied as a text file or pipe to Z3, or using API calls from a high-level
programming language that are proxies for calls over a C-based API. We focus

© Springer Nature Switzerland AG 2019
J. P. Bowen et al. (Eds.): SETSS 2018, LNCS 11430, pp. 148–201, 2019.
https://doi.org/10.1007/978-3-030-17601-3_4

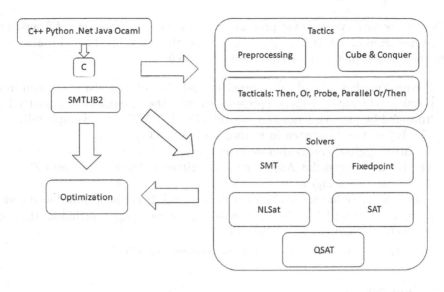

Fig. 1. Overall system architecture of Z3

on using the Python front-end as a means of interfacing with Z3, and start out describing the abstract syntax of terms and formulas accepted by Z3 in Sect. 2. Formulas draw from symbols whose meaning are defined by a set of *Theories*, Sect. 3. *Solvers*, Sects. 4, 5 and 6, provide services for deciding satisfiability of formula. *Tactics*, Sect. 7, provide means for pre-processing simplification and creating sub-goals. Z3 also provides some services that are not purely satisfiability queries. *Optimization*, Sect. 8, services allow users to solve satisfiability modulo objective functions to maximize or minimize values. There are also specialized procedures for enumerating *consequences* (backbone literals) described in Sect. 4.6.6.

1.1   Resources

The main point of reference for Z3 is the GitHub repository
  https://github.com/z3prover/z3
There is an interactive tutorial using the SMT-LIB2 front-end on
  https://rise4fun.com/Z3/tutorial/guide
Examples from this tutorial that are executable can be found on
  https://github.com/Z3Prover/doc/tree/master/programmingz3/code

There are several systems that program with Z3. They use a variety of front-ends, some use OCaml, others C++, and others use the SMT-LIB2 text interfaces. A few instances that use the Python front-end include

- Dennis Yurichev assembled a significant number of case studies drawn from puzzles and code analysis and presents many of the examples using the Python front-end https://yurichev.com/writings/SAT_SMT_by_example.pdf.
- The Ivy system is written in Python and uses Z3
    https://github.com/Microsoft/ivy.
- The binary analysis kit Angr system is written in Python and uses Z3
    https://docs.angr.io/.
- There was an online interactive Python tutorial. It is discontinued as it ended up being a target for hacks. A snapshot of the web pages, including the non-interactive examples can be found at
    http://www.cs.tau.ac.il/~msagiv/courses/asv/z3py

1.2 Sources

The material in this tutorial is assembled from several sources. Some of the running examples originate from slides that have circulated in the SAT and SMT community. The first SAT example is shamelessly lifted from Armin Biere's SAT tutorials and other examples appear in slides by Natarajan Shankar.

2 Logical Interfaces to Z3

Z3 takes as input simple-sorted formulas that may contain symbols with pre-defined meanings defined by a *theory*. This section provides an introduction to logical formulas that can be used as input to Z3.

As a basis, propositional formulas are built from atomic variables and logical connectives. An example propositional logical formula accepted by Z3 is:

```
from z3 import *
Tie, Shirt = Bools('Tie Shirt')
s = Solver()
s.add(Or(Tie, Shirt),
      Or(Not(Tie), Shirt),
      Or(Not(Tie), Not(Shirt)))
print(s.check())
print(s.model())
```

The example introduces two Boolean variables `Tie` and `Shirt`. It then creates a `Solver` object and adds three assertions.

$$(Tie \lor Shirt) \land (\neg Tie \lor Shirt) \land (\neg Tie \lor \neg Shirt)$$

The call to s.check() produces a verdict sat; there is a satisfying assignment for the formulas. A satisfying model, where Tie is false and Shirt is true, can be extracted using s.model(). For convenience the Python front-end to Z3 contains some shorthand functions. The function solve sets up a solver, adds assertions, checks satisfiability, and prints a model if one is available.

Propositional logic is an important, but smaller subset of formulas handled by Z3. It can reason about formulas that combine symbols from several theories, such as the theories for arrays and arithmetic:

```
Z = IntSort()
f = Function('f', Z, Z)
x, y, z = Ints('x y z')
A = Array('A', Z, Z)
fml = Implies(x + 2 == y, f(Store(A, x, 3)[y - 2]) == f(y - x + 1))
solve(Not(fml))
```

The formula fml is valid. It is true for all values of integers x, y, z, array A, and no matter what the graph of the function f is. Note that we are using array[index] as shorthand for Select(array, index). We can manually verify the validity of the formula using the following argument: The integer constants x and y are created using the function Ints that creates a list of integer constants. Under the assumption that x + 2 = y, the right side of the implication simplifies to

```
f(Store(A, x, 3)[x]) == f(3)
```

as we have replaced occurrences of y by x - 2. There are no restrictions on what f is, so the equality with f on both sides will only follow if the arguments to f are the same. Thus, we are left to establish

```
Store(A, x, 3)[x] == 3
```

The left side is a term in the theory of arrays, which captures applicative maps. Store updates the array A at position x with the value 3. Then ...[x] retrieves the contents of the array at index x, which in this case is 3. Dually, the *negation* of fml is unsatisfiable and the call to Z3 produces unsat.

Formulas accepted by Z3 generally follow the formats described in the SMT-LIB2 standard [3]. This standard (currently at version 2.6) defines a textual language for first-order multi-sorted logic and a set of *logics* that are defined by a selection of background theories. For example, the logic of *quantifier-free linear integer arithmetic*, known in SMT-LIB2 as QF_LIA, is a fragment of first-order logic, where formulas are *quantifier free*, variables range over integers, interpreted constants are integers, the allowed functions are +, −, integer multiplication, division, remainder, modulus with a constant, and the allowed relations are, besides equality that is part of every theory, also $<$, $<=$, $>=$, $>$. As an example, we provide an SMT-LIB and a Python variant of the same arbitrary formula:

```
(set-logic QF_LIA)
(declare-const x Int)
(declare-const y Int)
```

```
(assert (> (+ (mod x 4) (* 3 (div y 2))) (- x y)))
(check-sat)
```

Python version:

```
solve((x % 4) + 3 * (y / 2) > x - y)
```

It is also possible to extract an SMT-LIB2 representation of a solver state.

```
from z3 import *
x, y = Ints('x y')
s = Solver()
s.add((x % 4) + 3 * (y / 2) > x - y)
print(s.sexpr())
```

produces the output

```
(declare-fun y () Int)
(declare-fun x () Int)
(assert (> (+ (mod x 4) (* 3 (div y 2))) (- x y)))
```

2.1 Sorts

Generally, SMT-LIB2 formulas use a finite set of simple sorts. It includes the built-in sort `Bool`, and supported theories define their own sorts, noteworthy `Int`, `Real`, bit-vectors `(_ BitVec n)` for every positive bit-width n, arrays `(Array Index Elem)` for every sort *Index* and *Elem*, `String` and sequences `(Seq S)` for every sort *S*. It is also possible to declare new sorts. Their domains may never be empty. Thus, the formula

```
S = DeclareSort('S')
s = Const('s', S)
solve(ForAll(s, s != s))
```

is unsatisfiable.

2.2 Signatures

Formulas may include a mixture of interpreted and free functions and constants. For example, the integer constants 0 and 28 are interpreted, while constants x, y used in the previous example are free. Constants are treated as nullary functions. Functions that take arguments can be declared, such as `f = Function('f', Z, Z)` creates the function declaration that takes one integer argument and its range is an integer. Functions with Boolean range can be used to create formulas.

2.3 Terms and Formulas

Formulas that are used in assertions or added to solvers are terms of Boolean sort. Otherwise, terms of Boolean and non-Boolean sort may be mixed in any combination where sorts match up. For example

```
B = BoolSort()
f = Function('f', B, Z)
g = Function('g', Z, B)
a = Bool('a')
solve(g(1+f(a)))
```

could produce a solution of the form

```
[a = False, f = [else -> 0], g = [else -> True]]
```

The model assigns a to False, the graph of f maps all arguments to 0, and the graph of g maps all values to True. Standard built-in logical connectives are And, Or, Not, Implies, Xor. Bi-implication is a special case of equality, so from Python, when saying a == b for Boolean a and b it is treated as a logical formula for the bi-implication of a and b.

A set of utilities are available to traverse expressions once they are created. Every function application has a function *declaration* and a set of *arguments* accessed as children.

```
x = Int('x')
y = Int('y')
n = x + y >= 3
print("num args: ", n.num_args())
print("children: ", n.children())
print("1st child:", n.arg(0))
print("2nd child:", n.arg(1))
print("operator: ", n.decl())
print("op name:  ", n.decl().name())
```

2.4 Quantifiers and Lambda Binding

Universal and existential quantifiers bind variables to the scope of the quantified formula. For example

```
solve([y == x + 1, ForAll([y], Implies(y <= 0, x < y))])
```

has no solution because no matter what value we assigned to x, there is a value for y that is non-positive and smaller than that value. The bound occurrence of y is unrelated to the free occurrence where y is restricted to be x + 1. The equality constraint y == x + 1 should also not be mistaken for an assignment to y. It is *not* the case that bound occurrences of y are a synonym for x + 1. Notice that the slightly different formula

```
solve([y == x + 1, ForAll([y], Implies(y <= 0, x > y))])
```

has a solution where x is 1 and the free occurrence of y is 2.

Z3 supports also λ-binding with rudimentary reasoning support based on a model-constructing instantiation engine. λs may be convenient when expressing properties of arrays and Z3 uses array sorts for representing the sorts of lambda expressions. Thus, the result of memset is an array from integers to integers, that produces the value y in the range from lo to hi and otherwise behaves as m outside the range. Z3 reasons about quantifier free formulas that contains memset by instantiating the body of the λ.

```
m, m1 = Array('m', Z, Z), Array('m1', Z, Z)
def memset(lo, hi, y, m):
    return Lambda([x], If(And(lo <= x, x <= hi), y, Select(m, x)))
solve([m1 == memset(1, 700, z, m), Select(m1, 6) != z])
```

Lambda binding is convenient for creating closures. Recall that meaning of Lambda([x,y], e), where e is an expression with free occurrences of x and y is as a function that takes two arguments and substitutes their values for x and y in e. Z3 uses Lambda lifting, in conjunction with Reynold's defunctionalization, to reduce reasoning about closures to universally quantified definitions. Z3 treats arrays as general function spaces. All first-order definable functions may be arrays. Some second-order theorems can be established by synthesizing λ terms by instantiation. Thus,

```
Q = Array('Q', Z, B)
prove(Implies(ForAll(Q, Implies(Select(Q, x), Select(Q, y))),
              x == y))
```

is provable. Z3 synthesizes an instantiation corresponding to Lambda(z, z == x) for Q.

3   Theories

We will here summarize the main theories supported in Z3. In a few cases we will give a brief taste of decision procedures used for these theories. Readers who wish to gain a more in-depth understanding of how these decision procedures are implemented may follow some of the citations.

3.1   EUF: Equality and Uninterpreted Functions

The logic of *equality and uninterpreted function*, EUF, is a basic ingredient for first-order predicate logic. Before there are theories, there are constants, functions and predicate symbols, and the built-in relation of equality. In the following example, f is a unary function, x a constant. The first invocation of solve is feasible with a model where x is interpreted as an element in S and f is an identify function. The second invocation of *solve* is infeasible; there are no models where f maps x to anything but itself given the two previous equalities.

```
S = DeclareSort('S')
f = Function('f', S, S)
x = Const('x', S)
solve(f(f(x)) == x, f(f(f(x))) == x)
solve(f(f(x)) == x, f(f(f(x))) == x, f(x) != x)
```

Decision procedures for quantifier-free EUF formulas are usually based on *union-find* [57] to maintain equivalence classes of terms that are equated. Pictorially, a sequence of equality assertions $a = b, b = c, b = s$ produce one equivalence class that captures the transitivity of equality.

$$a = b, b = c, d = e, b = s, d = t : \quad \boxed{a, b, c, s} \quad \boxed{d, e, t}$$

It is possible to check for satisfiability of disequalities by checking whether the equivalence classes associated with two disequal terms are the same or not. Thus, adding $a \neq d$ does not produce a contradiction, and it can be checked by comparing a's class representative with d's representative.

$$a = b, b = c, d = e, b = s, d = t, a \neq d : \quad \boxed{a, b, c, s} \quad \boxed{d, e, t}$$

On the other hand, when asserting $c \neq s$, we can deduce a conflict as the two terms asserted to be disequal belong to the same class. Class membership with union-find data-structures is amortized nearly constant time.

$$a = b, b = c, d = e, b = s, d = t, c \neq s : \quad \boxed{a, b, c, s} \quad \boxed{d, e, t}$$

Union-find alone is insufficient when function symbols are used, as with the following example,

$$a = b, \ b = c, \ d = e, \ b = s, \ d = t, f(a, g(d)) \neq f(b, g(e))$$

In this case decision procedures require reasoning with the congruence rule

$$x_1 = y_1 \cdots x_n = y_n \ \Rightarrow \ f(x_1, \ldots, x_n) = f(y_1, \ldots, y_n)$$

As a preparation for solving our example, let us introduce constants that can be used as shorthands for sub-terms. Thus, introduce constants v_1, v_2, v_3, v_4 as representatives for the four compound sub-terms.
$a = b, b = c, d = e, b = s, d = t, v_3 \neq v_4 \ v_1 := g(e), v_2 := g(d), v_3 := f(a, v_2), v_4 := f(b, v_1)$

Having only the equality information available we obtain the equivalence classes:

Working bottom-up, the congruence rule dictates that the classes for v_1 and v_2 should be merged. Thus,

$$e = d \ \Rightarrow \ g(e) = g(d)$$

implies the following coarser set of equivalences.

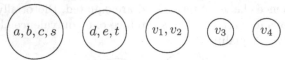

At this point, the congruence rule can be applied a second time,

$$a = b, v_2 = v_1 \Rightarrow f(a, v_2) = f(b, v_1)$$

producing the equivalence classes

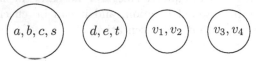

The classes for v_3 and v_4 are now merged. As our original formula required these to be distinct, congruence closure reasoning determines that the formula is unsatisfiable.

3.1.1 Congruence Closure

We have implicitly used the notion of *congruence closure* [20] to check satisfiability of equalities. Let us more formally define this notion. Let $\mathcal{T}$ be a set of terms and $\mathcal{E}$ set of equalities over $\mathcal{T}$. A *congruence closure* over $\mathcal{T}$ modulo $\mathcal{E}$ is the finest partition cc of $\mathcal{T}$, such that:

- if $(s = t) \in \mathcal{E}$, then s, t are in the same partition in cc.
- for $s := f(s_1, \ldots, s_k), t := f(t_1, \ldots, t_k) \in \mathcal{T}$,
  - if s_i, t_i are in same partition of cc for each $i = 1, \ldots k$,
  - then s, t are in the same partition under cc.

Definition 1. $cc : \mathcal{T} \to 2^{\mathcal{T}}$, maps term to its equivalence class.

3.1.2 EUF Models

A satisfiable version of the running example is:

$a = b, b = c, d = e, b = s, d = t, f(a, g(d)) \neq f(g(e), b)$

It induces the following definitions and equalities: $a = b, b = c, d = e, b = s, d = t, v_3 \neq v_4$

$v_1 := g(e), v_2 := g(d), v_3 := f(a, v_2), v_4 := f(v_1, b)$ and we can associate a distinct value with each equivalence class.

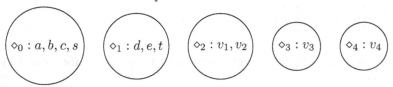

When presenting the formula to Z3 as

```
S = DeclareSort('S')
a, b, c, d, e, s, t = Consts('a b c d e s t', S)
f = Function('f', S, S, S)
g = Function('g', S, S)
solve([a == b, b == c, d == e, b == s,
        d == t, f(a, g(d)) != f(g(e), b)])
```

it produces a model, that may look as follows:

```
[s = S!val!0, b = S!val!0, a = S!val!0,
 c = S!val!0, d = S!val!1, e = S!val!1, t = S!val!1,
 f = [(S!val!2, S!val!0) -> S!val!4, else -> S!val!3],
 g = [else -> S!val!2]]
```

In the model the value $S!val!0$ is a fresh constant that is distinct from $S!val!1$. The graph for f maps the arguments $(S!val!2, S!val!0)$ to $S!val!4$. All other arguments are mapped by the else clause to $S!val!3$. The else clause is used as the default interpretation of arguments that are not listed in the interpretation. The interpretation of S is a finite set

$$\{S!val!0, S!val!1, S!val!2, S!val!3, S!val!4\}.$$

3.2 Arithmetic

Arithmetical constraints are nearly ubiquitous in software models. Even though mainstream software operates with finite precision arithmetic, that is modeled precisely using bit-vectors, arithmetic over unbounded integers can often be used in a sound way to model software. Furthermore, arithmetic over the reals has been used for diverse areas such as models of cyber-physical systems or for axiomatic economics.

3.2.1 Solving LRA: Linear Real Arithmetic

We provide an outline of Z3's main procedure for solving formulas over linear real arithmetic [21]. It maintains a (dual) Simplex tableau that encodes equalities of the form $Ax = 0$. Feasibility of the equalities depends on bounds, $lo_j \leq x_j \leq hi_j$, currently associated with the variables. For the following formula

```
x, y = Reals('x y')
solve([x >= 0, Or(x + y <= 2, x + 2*y >= 6),
                Or(x + y >= 2, x + 2*y > 4)])
```

Z3 introduces auxiliary variables s_1, s_2 and represents the formula as

$$s_1 \equiv x + y, \; s_2 \equiv x + 2y,$$
$$x \geq 0, \; (s_1 \leq 2 \vee s_2 \geq 6), \; (s_1 \geq 2 \vee s_2 > 4)$$

Only bounds (e.g., $s_1 \leq 2$) are asserted during search.

The first two equalities form the tableau. Thus, the definitions $s_1 \equiv x+y, s_2 \equiv x + 2y$ produce the equalities

$$s_1 = x + y, \; s_2 = x + 2y$$

They are equivalent to the normal form:

$$s_1 - x - y = 0, \quad s_2 - x - 2y = 0$$

where s_1, s_2 are basic (dependent) and x, y are non-basic. In dual Simplex tableaux, values of a non-basic variable x_j can be chosen between lo_j and hi_j. The value of a basic variable is a function of non-basic variable values. It is the unique value that satisfies the unique row where the basic variable occurs. Pivoting swaps basic and non-basic variables and is used to get values of basic variables within bounds. For example, assume we start with a set of initial values $x = y = s_1 = s_2 = 0$ and bounds $x \geq 0, s_1 \leq 2, s_1 \geq 2$. Then s_1 has to be 2 and it is made non-basic. Instead y becomes basic:

$$y + x - s_1 = 0, \quad s_2 + x - 2s_1 = 0$$

The new tableau updates the assignment of variables to $x = 0, s_1 = 2, s_2 = 4, y = 2$. The resulting assignment is a model for the original formula.

3.2.2 Solving Arithmetical Fragments

The solvers available to reason about arithmetical constraints are wildly different depending on what fragments of arithmetic is used. We summarize the main fragments, available decision procedures, and examples in Table 1 where x, y range over reals and a, b range over integers.

There are many more fragments of arithmetic that benefit from specialized solvers. We later discuss some of the fragments where integer variables are restricted to the values $\{0, 1\}$ when describing Pseudo-Boolean constraints. Other fragments that are *not* currently handled in Z3 in any special way include fragments listed in Table 2.

Table 1. Arithmetic theories

Logic	Description	Solver	Example
LRA	Linear Real Arithmetic	Dual simplex [21]	$x + \frac{1}{2}y \leq 3$
LIA	Linear Integer Arithmetic	Cuts + Branch	$a + 3b \leq 3$
LIRA	Mixed Real/Integer	[7,11,13,19,21]	$x + a \geq 4$
IDL	Integer Difference Logic	Floyd-Warshall	$a - b \leq 4$
RDL	Real Difference Logic	Bellman-Ford	$x - y \leq 4$
UTVPI	Unit two-variable/inequality	Bellman-Ford	$x + y \leq 4$
NRA	Polynomial Real Arithmetic	Model based CAD [34]	$x^2 + y^2 < 1$
NIA	Non-linear Integer Arithmetic	CAD + Branch [33] Linearization [14]	$a^2 = 2$

Table 2. Fragments of arithmetic

Description	Example
Horn Linear Real Arithmetic at most one variable is positive	$3y + z - \frac{1}{2}x \leq 1$
Two-variable per inequality [15]	$3x + 2y \geq 1$
Min-Horn [17]	$x \geq \min(2y + 1, z)$
Bi-linear arithmetic	$3xx' + 2yy' \geq 2$
Transcendental functions	$e^{-x} \geq y$
Modular linear arithmetic	$a + 3b + 2 \equiv 0 \mod 5$

A user of Z3 may appreciate that a domain can be modeled using a fragment of the theory of arithmetic that is already supported, or belongs to a class where no special support is available. On a practical side, it is worth noting that Z3 uses infinite precision arithmetic by default. Thus, integers and rationals are represented without rounding. The benefit is that the representation ensures soundness of the results, but operations by decision procedures may end up producing large numerals taking most of the execution time. Thus, users who produce linear arithmetic constraints with large coefficients or long decimal expansions may face performance barriers.

3.3 Arrays

The declaration

```
A = Array('A', IntSort(), IntSort())
```

introduces a constant A of the array sort mapping integers to integers. We can solve constraints over arrays, such as

```
solve(A[x] == x, Store(A, x, y) == A)
```

which produces a solution where x necessarily equals y.

Z3 treats arrays as function spaces, thus a function f(x, y) can be converted to an array using a λ

```
Lambda([x, y], f(x, y))
```

If f has sort $A \times B \rightarrow C$, then Lambda([x, y], f(x, y)) has sort Array(A, B, C). A set of built-in functions are available for arrays. We summarize them together with their representation using Lambda bindings.

```
a[i]          # select array 'a' at index 'i'
              # Select(a, i)

Store(a, i, v)  # update array 'a' with value 'v' at index 'i'
              # = Lambda(j, If(i == j, v, a[j]))
```

```
K(D, v)            # constant Array(D, R), where R is sort of 'v'.
                   # = Lambda(j, v)


Map(f, a)          # map function 'f' on values of 'a'
                   # = Lambda(j, f(a[j]))


Ext(a, b)          # Extensionality
                   # Implies(a[Ext(a, b)] == b[Ext(a, b)], a == b)
```

3.3.1   Deciding Arrays by Reduction to EUF

Formulas using the combinators Store, K, Map, Ext are checked for satisfiability by *expanding* the respective λ definitions on sub-terms. We illustrate how occurrences of Store produce constraints over EUF. In the following, assume we are given a solver s with ground assertions using arrays.

For each occurrence in s of Store(a, i, v) and b[j], add the following assertions:

```
- s.add(Store(a, i, v)[j] == If(i == j, v, a[j]))
- s.add(Store(a, i, v)[i] == v)
```

The theory of arrays is *extensional*. That is, two arrays are equal if they behave the same on all selected indices. When Z3 produces models for quantifier free formulas in the theory of extensional arrays it ensures that two arrays are equal in a model whenever they behave the same on all indices. Extensionality is enforced on array terms a, b in s by instantiating the axiom of extensionality.

```
- s.add(Implies(ForAll(i, a[i] == b[i]), a == b))
```

Since the universal quantifier occurs in a negative polarity we can introduce a Skolem function Ext that depends on a and b and represent the extensionality requirement as:

```
- s.add(Implies(a[Ext(a, b)] == b[Ext(a, b)], a == b))
```

We can convince ourselves that asserting these additional constraints force models of a solver s to satisfy the array axioms. Suppose we are given a model M satisfying all the additional asserted equalities. These equalities enforce the axioms for Store on all indices that occur in s. They also enforce extensionality between arrays: Two arrays are equal if and only if they evaluate to the same value on all indices in s.

3.4   Bit-Vectors

Let us play with some bit-fiddling. The resource

https://graphics.stanford.edu/~seander/bithacks.html,

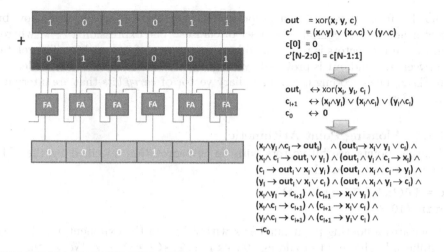

Fig. 2. Bit-vector addition circuit

lists a substantial repertoire of bit-vector operations that can be used as alternatives to potentially more expensive operations. Note that modern compilers already contain a vast set of optimizations that automatically perform these conversions and Z3 can be used to check and synthesize such optimizations [38]. For example, to test whether a bit-vector is a power of two we can use a combination of bit-wise operations and subtraction:

```
def is_power_of_two(x):
    return And(x != 0, 0 == (x & (x - 1)))
x = BitVec('x', 4)
prove(is_power_of_two(x) == Or([x == 2**i for i in range(4)]))
```

The absolute value of a variable can be obtained using addition and xor with a sign bit.

```
v = BitVec('v',32)
mask = v >> 31
prove(If(v > 0, v, -v) == (v + mask) ^ mask)
```

Notice that the Python variable `mask` corresponds to the expression `v >> 31`, the right arithmetic (signed) shift of v. Notice also, that in classical first-order logic, all operations are *total*. In particular, for bit-vector arithmetic -v is fully specified, in contrast to, say C, which specifies that -v is *undefined* when v is a signed integer with the value -2^{31}.

3.4.1   Solving Bit-Vectors

Z3 mostly uses a bit-blasting approach to deciding bit-vectors. By bit-blasting we refer to a reduction of bit-vector constraints to propositional logic by treating each bit in a bit-vector as a propositional variable. Let us illustrate how bit-vector addition is compiled to a set of clauses. The expression v + w, where v and w are bit-vectors is represented by a vector out of output bits. The relation between v, w and out is provided by clauses the encode a ripple-carry adder seen in Fig. 2. The encoding uses an auxiliary vector of *carry bits* that are internal to the adder.

3.4.2 Floating Point Arithmetic

Floating points are bit-vectors with an interpretation specified by the IEEE floating point standard.

```
x = FP('x', FPSort(3, 4))
print(10 + x)
```

It declares a floating point number x with 3 bits in the exponent and 4 for the significand. The result of adding 10 to x is 1.25*(2**3) + x. We see that 10 is represented as a floating point number with exponent 3, that is the bit-vector 011. The significand is 1010.

3.5   Algebraic Datatypes

The theory of first-order algebraic data-types captures the theory of finite trees. It is characterized by the properties that:

– All trees are finite (occurs check).
– All trees are generated from the constructors (no junk).
– Two trees are equal if and only if they are constructed exactly the same way (no confusion).

A basic example of a binary tree data-type is given in Fig. 3.
It may produce the solution

```
[t = Node(Empty, 0, Empty)]
```

Similarly, one can prove that a tree cannot be a part of itself.

```
prove(t != Tree.Node(t, 0, t))
```

```
Tree = Datatype('Tree')
Tree.declare('Empty')
Tree.declare('Node', ('left', Tree), ('data', Z), ('right', Tree))
Tree = Tree.create()
t = Const('t', Tree)
solve(t != Tree.Empty)
```

Fig. 3. Binary tree datatypes

3.6 Sequences and Strings

The theory of strings and sequences extend on the theory of the free monoid with a few additional functions that are useful for strings and sequences. A length operation is built-in for strings and sequences, and there are operations for converting strings to natural numbers and back.

If the lengths of a prefix and suffix of a string add up to the length of the string, the string itself must be the concatenation of the prefix and suffix:

```
s, t, u = Strings('s t u')
prove(Implies(And(PrefixOf(s, t), SuffixOf(u, t),
                  Length(t) == Length(s) + Length(u)),
           t == Concat(s, u)))
```

One can concatenate single elements to a sequence as units:

```
s, t = Consts('s t', SeqSort(IntSort()))
solve(Concat(s, Unit(IntVal(2))) == Concat(Unit(IntVal(1)), t))
prove(Concat(s, Unit(IntVal(2))) != Concat(Unit(IntVal(1)), s))
```

There are two solvers available in Z3 for strings. They can be exchanged by setting the parameter

- s.set("smt.string.solver","seq") with contributions by Thai Trinh, or
- s.set("smt.string.solver","z3str3") by Murphy Berzish.

4 Interfacing with Solvers

Solvers maintain a set of formulas and supports satisfiability checking, and scope management: Formulas that are added under one scope can be retracted when the scope is popped. In this section we describe the interface to solvers. Section 5 provides a set of use cases and Sect. 6 describes the underlying solver implementations available in Z3.

4.1 Incrementality

Solvers can be used to check satisfiability of assertions in an incremental way. An initial set of assertions can be checked for satisfiability followed by additional assertions and checks. Assertions can be retracted using scopes that are pushed and popped. Under the hood, Z3 uses a one-shot solver during the first check. If further calls are made into the solver, the default behavior is to switch to an *incremental* solver. The incremental solver uses the SMT core, see Sect. 6.1.1, by default. For use-cases that don't require all features by the SMT core, it may be beneficiary to use specialized solvers, such as solvers for finite domains (bit-vectors, enumeration types, bounded integers, and Booleans) as specified using the QF_FD logic.

4.2 Scopes

The operations push and pop create, respectively revert, local scopes. Assertions that are added within a push are retracted on a matching pop. Thus, the following session results in the verdicts sat, unsat, and sat.

```
p, q, r = Bools('p q r')
s = Solver()
s.add(Implies(p, q))
s.add(Not(q))
print(s.check())
s.push()
s.add(p)
print(s.check())
s.pop()
print(s.check())
```

4.3 Assumptions

Alternative to scopes, it is possible to check satisfiability under the assumption of a set of literals. Thus, the session

```
s.add(Implies(p, q))
s.add(Not(q))
print(s.check(p))
```

also produces the verdict unsat as the conjunction of $p \rightarrow q$, $\neg q$, p is unsat. The method assert_and_track(q, p) has the same effect of adding Implies(p, q), and it adds p as an implicit assumption. Our running example becomes

```
p, q = Bools('p q')
s = Solver()
s.add(Not(q))
s.assert_and_track(q, p)
print(s.check())
```

4.4 Cores

We can extract a subset of assumptions used to derive unsatisfiability. Such subsets of assumptions are known as *unsatisfiable cores*, or simply as a *core*. In the following example, the unsatisfiable core has the single element p. The unrelated assumption v does not appear in the core.

```
p, q, r, v = Bools('p q r v')
s = Solver()
s.add(Not(q))
s.assert_and_track(q, p)
s.assert_and_track(r, v)
```

```
print(s.check())
print(s.unsat_core())
```

Note that we invoke s.check() prior to extracting a core. Cores are only available after the last call to s.check() produced unsat.

By default solvers do not return minimal cores. A core is *minimal* if there is no proper subset that is also a core. The default behavior can be changed when the solver corresponds to either the SMT Core or SAT Core (if the underlying solver is created from a sequence of pre-processing tactics, core minimization is not guaranteed to take effect). To force core minimization users can rely on setting the following parameters:

```
def set_core_minimize(s):
    s.set("sat.core.minimize","true")  # For Bit-vector theories
    s.set("smt.core.minimize","true")  # For general SMT
```

4.5   Models

When s.check() returns sat Z3 can provide a model that assigns values to the free constants and functions in the assertions. The current model is accessed using s.model() and it offers access to an interpretation of the active assertions in s. Consider the example:

```
f = Function('f', Z, Z)
x, y = Ints('x y')
s.add(f(x) > y, f(f(y)) == y)
print(s.check())
print(s.model())
```

A possible model for s is:

```
[y = 0, x = 2, f = [0 -> 3, 3 -> 0, else -> 1]]
```

You can access models. They have a set of entries. Each entry maps a constant or function declaration (constants are treated as nullary functions) to an interpretation. It maps constants to a constant expression and it maps functions to a *function interpretation*. The stub

```
m = s.model()
for d in m:
    print(d, m[d])
```

iterates over the assignments in a model and produces the output

```
y 0
x 2
f [0 -> 3, 3 -> 0, else -> 1]
```

Function interpretations comprise a set of entries that specify how the function behaves on selected argument combinations, and a *else_ value* that covers arguments not listed in the entries.

```
num_entries = m[f].num_entries()
for i in range(num_entries):
    print(m[f].entry(i))
print("else", m[f].else_value())
```

It produces the output

```
[0, 3]
[3, 0]
else 1
```

The easiest way to access a model is to use the `eval` method that lets you evaluate arbitrary expressions over a model. It reduces expressions to a constant that is consistent with the way the model interprets the constants and functions. For our model from above

```
print(m.eval(x), m.eval(f(3)), m.eval(f(4)))
```

produces the output 2, 0, 1.

4.6   Other Methods

4.6.1   Statistics

You can gain a sneak peak at what the solver did by extracting statistics. The call

```
print(s.statistics())
```

displays values of internal counters maintained by the decision procedures. They are mostly valuable when coupled with a detailed understanding of how the decision procedures work, but may be used as an introductory view into the characteristics of a search.

4.6.2   Proofs

Proof objects, that follow a natural deduction style, are available from the Solver interface [42]. You have to enable proof production at top level in order to retrieve proofs.

```
s.set("produce-proofs", True)
s.add(φ)
assert unsat == s.check()
print(s.proof())
```

The granularity of proof objects is on a best-effort basis. Proofs for the SMT Core, are relatively fined-grained, while proofs for procedures that perform quantifier elimination, for instance QSAT described in Sect. 6.4, are exposed as big opaque steps.

4.6.3   Retrieving Solver State

You can retrieve the current set of assertions in a solver using s.assertions(), the set of unit literals using s.units() and literals that are non-units using s.non_units(). The solver state can be printed to SMT-LIB2 format using s.sexpr().

4.6.4   Cloning Solver State

The method s.translate(ctx) clones the solver state into a new solver based on the context that is passed in. It is useful for creating separate non-interfering states of a solver.

4.6.5   Loading Formulas

The methods s.from_file and s.from_string adds constraints to a solver state from a file or string. Files are by default assumed to be in the SMT2 format. If a file name ends with dimacs they are assumed to be in the DIMACS propositional format.

4.6.6   Consequences

Product configuration systems use constraints to describe the space of all legal configurations. As parameters get fixed, fewer and fewer configuration options are available. For instance, once the model of a car has been fixed, some options for wheel sizes become unavailable. It is furthermore possible that only one option is available for some configurations, once some parameters are fixed. Z3 can be used to answer queries of the form: Given a configuration space of values V, when fixing values $V_0 \subseteq V$, what is the largest subset $V_0 \subseteq V_1 \subseteq V$ of values that become fixed? Furthermore, for some value v_1 that is fixed, provide an explanation, in terms of the values that were fixed in V_0, for why v_1 got fixed. The functionality is available through the consequences method.

```
a, b, c, d = Bools('a b c d')

s = Solver()
s.add(Implies(a, b), Implies(c, d))   # background formula
print(s.consequences([a, c],          # assumptions
                      [b, c, d]))      # what is implied?
```

produces the result:

```
(sat, [Implies(c, c), Implies(a, b), Implies(c, d)])
```

In terms for SAT terminology, consequence finding produces the set of all *backbone* literals. It is useful for finding fixed parameters [29] in product configuration settings.

Z3 relies on a procedure that integrates tightly with the CDCL, *Conflict Driven Clause Learning* [56], algorithm, and it contains two implementations

```
s = SolverFor("QF_FD")
s.add(F)
s.set("sat.restart.max", 100)
def cube_and_conquer(s):
    for cube in s.cube():
        if len(cube) == 0:
            return unknown
        if is_true(cube[0]):
            return sat
        is_sat = s.check(cube):
        if is_sat == unknown:
            s1 = s.translate(s.ctx)
            s1.add(cube)
            is_sat = cube_and_conquer(s1)
        if is_sat != unsat:
            return is_sat
    return unsat
```

Fig. 4. Basic cube and conquer

of the procedure, one in the SAT core, another in the SMT core. Section 6.1.1 expands on CDCL and integrations with theories (Fig. 4).

4.6.7 Cubes

You can ask Z3 to suggest a case split or a sequence of case splits through the cubing method. It can be used for partitioning the search space into sub-problems that can be solved in parallel, or alternatively simplify the problem for CDCL engines.

When the underlying solver is based on the SAT Core, see Sect. 6.2, it uses a lookahead solver to select cubes [25]. By default, the cuber produces two branches, corresponding to a case split on a single literal. The SAT Core based cuber can be configured to produce cubes that represent several branches. An empty cube indicates a failure, such as the solver does not support cubing (only the SMT and SAT cores support cubing, and generic solvers based on tactics do not), or a timeout or resource bound was encountered during cubing. A cube comprising of the Boolean constant **true** indicates that the state of the solver is satisfiable. Finally, it is possible for the s.cube() method to return an empty set of cubes. This happens when the state of s is unsatisfiable. Each branch is represented as a conjunction of literals. The cut-off for branches is configured using

- sat.lookahead.cube.cutoff

Table 3. Lookahead parameters

sat.lookahead		Used when cube.cutoff is	Description
cube.depth	1	depth	A fixed maximal size of cubes is returned
cube.freevars	0.8	freevars	The depth of cubes is governed by the ratio of non-unit literals in a branch compared to non-unit variables in the root
cube.fraction	0.4	adaptive_freevars adaptive_psat	Adaptive fraction to create lookahead cubes
cube.psat. clause_base	2	psat	Base of exponent used for clause weight

We summarize some of the configuration parameters that depend on the value of cutoff in Table 3.

Heuristics used to control which literal is selected in cubes can be configured using the parameter:

– sat.lookahead.reward

5 Using Solvers

We now describe a collection of algorithms. They are developed on top of the interfaces described in the previous section.

5.1 Blocking Evaluations

Models can be used to refine the state of a solver. For example, we may wish to invoke the solver in a loop where new calls to the solver blocks solutions that evaluate the constants to the exact same assignment.

```
def block_model(s):
    m = s.model()
    s.add(Or([ f() != m[f] for f in m.decls() if f.arity() == 0]))
```

5.2 Maximizing Satisfying Assignments

Another use of models is to use them as a guide to a notion of optimal model. A *maximal satisfying solution*, in short *mss*, for a set of formulas ps is a subset of ps that is consistent with respect to the solver state s and cannot be extended to a bigger subset of ps without becoming inconsistent relative to s. We provide a procedure, from [40], for finding a maximal satisfying subset in Fig. 5. It extends a set mss greedily by adding as many satisfied predicates from ps in each round

```
def tt(s, f):
    return is_true(s.model().eval(f))

def get_mss(s, ps):
    if sat != s.check():
        return []
    mss = { q for q in ps if tt(s, q) }
    return get_mss(s, mss, ps)

def get_mss(s, mss, ps):
    ps = ps - mss
    backbones = set([])
    while len(ps) > 0:
        p = ps.pop()
        if sat == s.check(mss | backbones | { p }):
            mss = mss | { p } | { q for q in ps if tt(s, q) }
            ps  = ps - mss
        else:
            backbones = backbones | { Not(p) }
    return mss
```

Fig. 5. An algorithm for computing maximal satisfying subsets

as possible. If it finds some predicate p that it cannot add, it notes that it is a backbone with respect to the current mss. As a friendly hint, it includes the negation of p when querying the solver in future rounds.

Exercise 5a: Suppose ps is a list corresponding to digits in a binary number and ps is ordered by most significant digit down. The goal is to find an mss with the largest value as a binary number. Modify get_mss to produce such a number.

5.3 All Cores and Correction Sets

The Marco procedure [37] combines models and cores in a process that enumerates all unsatisfiable cores and all maximal satisfying subsets of a set of formulas ps with respect to solver s. It maintains a map solver that tells us which subsets of ps are not yet known to be a superset of a core or a subset of an mss.

Efficiently enumerating cores and correction sets is an active area of research. Many significant improvements have been developed over the above basic implementation [1, 2, 40, 49, 53].

5.4 Bounded Model Checking

Figure 7 illustrates a bounded model checking procedure [4] that takes a transition system as input and checks if a goal is reachable. Transition systems are described as

```
def ff(s, p):
    return is_false(s.model().eval(p))

def marco(s, ps):
    map = Solver()
    set_core_minimize(s)
    while map.check() == sat:
        seed = {p for p in ps if not ff(map, p)}
        if s.check(seed) == sat:
            mss = get_mss(s, seed, ps)
            map.add(Or(ps - mss))
            yield "MSS", mss
        else:
            mus = s.unsat_core()
            map.add(Not(And(mus)))
            yield "MUS", mus
```

Fig. 6. The MARCO algorithm for computing cores and maximal satisfying assignments

$$\langle Init,\ Trans,\ Goal, \mathcal{V}, \mathcal{Y} \rangle$$

where $Init$ is a predicate over $\mathcal{V}$, that describes the initial states, $Trans$ is a transition relation over $\mathcal{V} \times \mathcal{Y} \times \mathcal{V}'$. The set of reachable states is the set inductively defined as valuations s of $\mathcal{V}$, such that either $s \models Init$ or there is a reachable s_0 and values v for $\mathcal{Y}$, such that $s_0, v, s \models Trans$. A goal is reachable if there is some reachable state where $s \models Goal$ (Fig. 6).

In Python we provide the initial condition as `init`, using variables `xs`, the transition `trans` that uses variables `xs`, `xns`, `fvs`, and `goal` using variables `xs`. Bounded model checking unfolds the transition relation `trans` until it can establish that the goal is reachable. Bounded model checking diverges if `goal` is unreachable. The function `substitute(e, subst)` takes an expression `e` and a list of pairs `subst` of the form `[(x1, y1), (x2, y2),..]` and replaces variables `x1, x2,..` by `y1, y2,..` in `e`.

Example 1. Let us check whether there is some k, such that $\underbrace{3 + 3 + \ldots + 3}_{k} = 10$ when numbers are represented using 4 bits. The corresponding transition system uses a state variable `x0` which is named `x1` in the next state. Initially `x0 == 0` and in each step the variable is incremented by 3. The goal state is `x0 == 10`.

```
x0, x1 = Consts('x0 x1', BitVecSort(4))
bmc(x0 == 0, x1 == x0 + 3, x0 == 10, [], [x0], [x1])
```

Bounded model checking is good for establishing reachability, but does not produce certificates for non-reachability (or safety). The IC3 [9] algorithm is

```
index = 0
def fresh(s):
    global index
    index += 1
    return Const("!f%d" % index, s)

def zipp(xs, ys):
    return [p for p in zip(xs, ys)]

def bmc(init, trans, goal, fvs, xs, xns):
    s = Solver()
    s.add(init)
    count = 0
    while True:
        print("iteration ", count)
        count += 1
        p = fresh(BoolSort())
        s.add(Implies(p, goal))
        if sat == s.check(p):
            print (s.model())
            return
        s.add(trans)
        ys = [fresh(x.sort()) for x in xs]
        nfvs = [fresh(x.sort()) for x in fvs]
        trans = substitute(trans,
                            zipp(xns + xs + fvs, ys + xns + nfvs))
        goal = substitute(goal, zipp(xs, xns))
        xs, xns, fvs = xns, ys, nfvs
```

Fig. 7. Bounded model checking of a transition system

complete for both reachability and non-reachability. You can find a simplistic implementation of IC3 using the Python API online

https://github.com/Z3Prover/z3/blob/master/examples/python/mini_ic3.py

5.5 Propositional Interpolation

It is possible to compute interpolants using models and cores [12]. A procedure that computes an interpolant I for formulas A, B, where $A \wedge B$ is unsatisfiable proceeds by initializing $I = true$ and saturating a state $\lceil A, B, I \rceil$ with respect to the rules:

$$\lceil A, B, I \rceil \quad \Longrightarrow \quad \lceil A, B, I \wedge \neg L \rceil \qquad \text{if } B \vdash \neg L, \ A \wedge I \nvdash \neg L$$

$$I \qquad \qquad \text{if } A \vdash \neg I$$

The partial interpolant I produced by pogo satisfies $B \vdash I$. It terminates when $A \vdash \neg I$. The condition $A \wedge I \nvdash \neg L$ ensures that the algorithm makes progress and suggests using an implicant $L' \supseteq L$ of $A \wedge I$ in each iteration. Such an implicant can be obtained from a model for $A \wedge I$ (Fig. 8).

```
def mk_lit(m, x):
    if is_true(m.eval(x)):
        return x
    else:
        return Not(x)

def pogo(A, B, xs):
    while sat == A.check():
        m = A.model()
        L = [mk_lit(m, x) for x in xs]
        if unsat == B.check(L):
            notL = Not(And(B.unsat_core()))
            yield notL
            A.add(notL)
        else:
            print("expecting unsat")
            break
```

Fig. 8. Propositional interpolation

Example 2. The (reverse) interpolant between $A : x_1 = a_1 \neq a_2 \neq x_2$ and $B : x_1 = b_1 \neq b_2 = x_2$ using vocabulary x_1, x_2 is $x_1 \neq x_2$. It is implied by B and inconsistent with A.

```
A = SolverFor("QF_FD")
B = SolverFor("QF_FD")
a1, a2, b1, b2, x1, x2 = Bools('a1 a2 b1 b2 x1 x2')
A.add(a1 == x1, a2 != a1, a2 != x2)
B.add(b1 == x1, b2 != b1, b2 == x2)
print(list(pogo(A, B, [x1, x2])))
```

5.6 Monadic Decomposition

Suppose we are given a formula $\varphi[x, y]$ using variables x and y. When is it possible to rewrite it as a Boolean combination of formulas $\psi_1(x), \ldots, \psi_k(x)$ and $\theta_1(y), \ldots, \theta_n(y)$? We say that the formulas ψ_j and θ_j are *monadic*; they only depend on one variable. An application of monadic decomposition is to convert *extended* symbolic finite transducers into *regular* symbolic finite transducers. The regular versions are amenable to analysis and optimization. A procedure for monadic decomposition was developed in [58], and we here recall the Python prototype (Fig. 9).

```
from z3 import *
def nu_ab(R, x, y, a, b):
    x_ = [ Const("x_%d" %i, x[i].sort()) for i in range(len(x))]
    y_ = [ Const("y_%d" %i, y[i].sort()) for i in range(len(y))]
    return Or(Exists(y_, R(x+y_) != R(a+y_)), Exists(x_, R(x_+y) != R(x_+b)))

def isUnsat(fml):
    s = Solver(); s.add(fml); return unsat == s.check()

def lastSat(s, m, fmls):
    if len(fmls) == 0: return m
    s.push(); s.add(fmls[0])
    if s.check() == sat: m = lastSat(s, s.model(), fmls[1:])
    s.pop(); return m

def mondec(R, variables):
    print(variables)
    phi = R(variables);
    if len(variables)==1: return phi
    l = int(len(variables)/2)
    x, y = variables[0:l], variables[l:]
    def dec(nu, pi):
        if isUnsat(And(pi, phi)):
            return BoolVal(False)
        if isUnsat(And(pi, Not(phi))):
            return BoolVal(True)
        fmls = [BoolVal(True), phi, pi]
        #try to extend nu
        m = lastSat(nu, None, fmls)
        #nu must be consistent
        assert(m != None)
        a = [ m.evaluate(z, True) for z in x ]
        b = [ m.evaluate(z, True) for z in y ]
        psi_ab = And(R(a+y), R(x+b))
        phi_a = mondec(lambda z: R(a+z), y)
        phi_b = mondec(lambda z: R(z+b), x)
        nu.push()
        #exclude: x~a and y~b
        nu.add(nu_ab(R, x, y, a, b))
        t = dec(nu, And(pi, psi_ab))
        f = dec(nu, And(pi, Not(psi_ab)))
        nu.pop()
        return If(And(phi_a, phi_b), t, f)
    #nu is initially true
    return dec(Solver(), BoolVal(True))
```

Fig. 9. Monadic decomposition

Example 3. A formula that has a monadic decomposition is the bit-vector assertion for x, y being bit-vectors of bit-width $2k$.

$$y > 0 \wedge (y\&(y-1)) = 0 \wedge (x\&(y\%((1 \ll k) - 1))) \neq 0$$

We can compute the monadic decomposition

```
def test_mondec(k):
    R = lambda v:And(v[1] > 0, (v[1] & (v[1] - 1)) == 0,
                     (v[0] & (v[1] % ((1 << k) - 1))) != 0)
    bvs = BitVecSort(2*k)                          #use 2k-bit bitvectors
    x, y = Consts('x y', bvs)
    res = mondec(R, [x, y])
    assert(isUnsat(res != R([x, y])))              #check correctness
    print("mondec1(", R([x, y]), ") =", res)
test_mondec(2)
```

6 Solver Implementations

There are five main solvers embedded in Z3. The SMT Solver is a general purpose solver that covers a wide range of supported theories. It is supplemented with specialized solvers for SAT formulas, polynomial arithmetic, Horn clauses and quantified formulas over theories that admit quantifier-elimination.

6.1 SMT Core

The SMT Solver is a general purpose solver that covers a wide range of supported theories. It is built around a CDCL(T) architecture where theory solvers interact with a SAT + EUF blackboard. Theory solvers, on the right in Fig. 10, communicate with a core that exchanges equalities between variables and assignments to atomic predicates. The core is responsible for case splitting, which is handled by a CDCL SAT solver, and for letting each theory learn constraints and equalities that are relevant in the current branch.

To force using the SMT solver a user can create a *simple solver* using the function SimpleSolver.

The SMT solver integrates two strategies for quantifier instantiation. By default, both strategies are enabled. To disable them, one has to disable automatic configuration mode and then disable the instantiation strategy:

```
s.set("smt.auto_config", False)    # disable automatic SMT core
                                   # configuration
s.set("smt.mbqi", False)           # disable model based
                                   # quantifier instantiation
s.set("smt.ematching", False)      # disable ematching based
                                   # quantifier instantiation
```

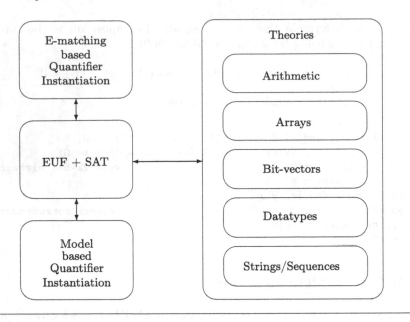

Fig. 10. Architecture of Z3's SMT core solver.

6.1.1 CDCL(T): SAT + Theories

The architecture of mainstream SMT solvers, including Z3's SMT core, uses a SAT solver to enumerate combinations of truth assignments to atoms. The truth assignments satisfy a propositional abstraction of the formula. Theory solvers are used to check if assignment admit a model modulo the theories. The resulting architecture is known as DPLL(T) [52], but we refer to this as CDCL(T) because it really relies on SAT solvers that incorporate *Conflict Driven Clause Learning* [56], which goes beyond the algorithm associated with DPLL [18]. Importantly, CDCL supplies facilities for learning new clauses during search. The learned clauses block future case splits from exploring the same failed branches. Take the following example

```
s.add(x >= 0, y == x + 1, Or(y > 2, y < 1))
```

by introducing the names:

```
p1, p2, p3, p4 = Bools('p1 p2 p3 p4')
#                    = x >= 0, y == x + 1, y > 2, y < 1
```

we obtain a propositional formula

```
And(p1, p2, Or(p3, p4))
```

It is satisfiable and a possible truth assignment is

```
p1, p2, p3, p4 = True, True, False, True
```

It requires satisfiability of the following conjunction:

```
def simple_cdclT(clauses):
    prop   = Solver()
    theory = Solver()
    abs = {}
    prop.add(abstract_clauses(abs, clauses))
    theory.add([p == abs[p] for p in abs])
    while True:
        is_sat = prop.check()
        if sat == is_sat:
            m = prop.model()
            lits = [mk_lit(m, abs[p]) for p in abs]
            if unsat == theory.check(lits):
                prop.add(Not(And(theory.unsat_core())))
            else:
                print(theory.model())
                return
        else:
            print(is_sat)
            return
```

Fig. 11. Simple CDCL(T)

x >= 0, y == x + 1, Not(y > 2), y < 1

It is already the case that

x >= 0, y == x + 1, y < 1

is unsat. To avoid this assignment we require also satisfying the blocking clause

Or(Not(p1), Not(p2), Not(p4))

The new truth assignment

p1, p2, p3, p4 = True, True, True, False

produces

x >= 0, y == x + 1, y > 2, Not(y < 1)

which is satisfiable. The example illustrates the steps used in a CDCL(T) integration where the Theory Solver processes the final result of a SAT Solver. We can simulate this procedure using Z3's API. Figure 11 shows a CDCL(T) solver that leverages a propositional solver **prop** to check a propositional abstraction and a theory solver **theory** whose role is to check conjunctions of literals produced by **prop**. Figure 12 lists auxiliary routines required to create the abstraction.

We call it a *simple* CDCL(T) solver as it does not expose important features to drive performance. Importantly, efficient CDCL(T) solvers integrate *theory*

```
index = 0
def abstract_atom(abs, atom):
    global index
    if atom in abs:
        return abs[atom]
    p = Bool("p%d" % index)
    index += 1
    abs[atom] = p
    return p

def abstract_lit(abs, lit):
    if is_not(lit):
        return Not(abstract_atom(abs, lit.arg(0)))
    return abstract_atom(abs, lit)

def abstract_clause(abs, clause):
    return Or([abstract_lit(abs, lit) for lit in clause])

def abstract_clauses(abs, clauses):
    return [abstract_clause(abs, clause) for clause in clauses]

def mk_lit(m, p):
    if is_true(m.eval(p)):
        return p
    else:
        return Not(p)
```

Fig. 12. Auxiliary routines for lazy CDCL(T)

propagation that let theories interact with the SAT solver to propagate assignments to atoms. Instead of adding blocking clauses by the time the SAT solver is done the theory solver interacts tightly with the SAT solver during back-jumping.

Exercise 6a

Dual Propagation and Implicants: The propositional assignment produced by prop is not necessarily minimal. It may assign truth assignments to literals that are irrelevant to truth of the set of clauses. To extract a smaller assignment, one trick is to encode the *negation* of the clauses in a separate *dual* solver. A truth assignment for the *primal* solver is an unsatisfiable core for the *dual* solver. The exercise is to augment `simple_cdclT` with a dual solver to reduce assignments sent to the theory solver.

6.1.2 Theories + Theories

In practice we need to solve a combination of theories. The formulas we used in the initial example

```
x + 2 == y, f(Store(A, x, 3)[y - 2]) != f(y - x + 1)
```

integrate several theory solvers. For modularity, it is desirable to maintain separate solvers per theory. To achieve this objective the main questions that an integration needs to address are:

  Determine when the union of two theories $T_1 \cup T_2$ is consistent.
- Given solvers for T_1 and T_2, how can we build a solver for $T_1 \cup T_2$.

We can address this objective when there is an *effective* theory T_0 over the shared signature of T_1, T_2, that when embedable into T_1, T_2 implies $T_1 \cup T_2$ is consistent. Sufficient conditions for this setting were identified by Nelson and Oppen [50]:

Theorem 1. The union of two consistent, disjoint, stably infinite theories is consistent.

Let us define the ingredients of this theorem.

Disjoint Theories. Two theories are disjoint if they do not share function/constant and predicate symbols. $=$ is the only exception. For example,

- The theories of arithmetic and arrays are disjoint.
    - Arithmetic symbols: `0, -1, 1, -2, 2, +, -, *, >, <, ==, >=`.
    - Array symbols: `Select, Store`

The process of *purification* can be used as a formal tool to bring formulas into signature-disjoint form. It introduces fresh symbols for shared sub-terms. A purified version of our running example is:

```
Functions:   f(v1) != f(v2)
Arrays:      v1 == v3[v4], v3 == Store(x, y, v5)
Arithmetic:  x + 2 == y, v2 == y - x + 1, v4 == y - 2, v5 == 2
```

In reality, purification is a no-op: the fresh variables correspond directly to nodes in the abstract syntax trees for expressions.

Stably Infinite Theories. A theory is stably infinite if every satisfiable quantifier-free formula is satisfiable in an infinite model.

- EUF and arithmetic are stably infinite.
- Bit-vectors are not.

Nelson-Oppen Combination. Let T_1 and T_2 be consistent, stably infinite theories over disjoint (countable) signatures. Assume satisfiability of conjunction of literals can be decided in $O(T_1(n))$ and $O(T_2(n))$ time respectively. Then

1. The combined theory T is consistent and stably infinite.
2. Satisfiability of quantifier free conjunction of literals can be decided in $O(2^{n^2} \times (T_1(n) + T_2(n)))$.
3. If T_1 and T_2 are *convex*, then so is T and satisfiability in T can be decided in $O(n^3 \times (T_1(n) + T_2(n)))$.

Convexity. A theory T is *convex* if for every finite sets S of literals, and every disjunction $a_1 = b_1 \vee \ldots \vee a_n = b_n$:

$$S \models a_1 = b_1 \vee \ldots \vee a_n = b_n \text{ iff } S \models a_i = b_i \text{ for some } 1 \leq i \leq n.$$

Many theories are convex and therefore admit efficient theory combinations

- Linear Real Arithmetic is convex.
- Horn equational theories are convex.
  - Horn equations are formulas of the form $a_1 \neq b_1 \vee \ldots a_n \neq b_n \vee a = b$.

Finally note that every convex theory with non trivial models is stably infinite. But, far from every theory is convex. Notably,

- Integer arithmetic
  - $1 \leq a \leq 2, b = 1, c = 2$ implies $a = b \vee a = c$.
- Real non-linear arithmetic
  - $a^2 = 1, b = 1, c = -1$ implies $a = b \vee a = c$.
- The theory of arrays
  - `Store(a, i, v)[j]` == v implies i == j or a[j] == v.

A Reduction Approach to Theory Combination[35,43]. Theory Combination in Z3 is essentially by reduction to a set of core theories comprising of Arithmetic, EUF and SAT. Bit-vectors and finite domains translate to propositional SAT. Other theories are *reduced* to core theories. We provided an example of this reduction in Sect. 3.3.

6.1.3   E-Matching Based Quantifier Instantiation

E-matching [46] based quantifier instantiation uses ground terms to find candidate instantiations of quantifiers. Take the example

```
a, b, c, x = Ints('a b c x')
f = Function('f', Z, Z)
g = Function('g', Z, Z, Z)
prove(Implies(And(ForAll(x, f(g(x, c)) == a), b == c, g(c, b) == c),
              f(b) == a))
```

The smallest sub-term that properly contains x is `g(x, c)`. This *pattern* contains all the bound variables of the universal quantifier. Under the ground equality b == c and instantiation of x by c, it equals `g(c, b)`. This triggers an instantiation by the following tautology

```
Implies(ForAll(x, f(g(x, c)) == a), f(g(c, c)) == a))
```

Chasing the equalities `f(g(c, c))` == a, `g(c, b)` == c, b == c we derive `f(b)` == a, which proves the implication.

The example illustrated that E-matching takes as starting point a *pattern* term p, that captures the variables bound by a quantifier. It derives an substitution θ, such that $p\theta$ equals some *useful* term t, modulo some *useful* equalities. A useful source of *useful* terms are the current ground terms $\mathcal{T}$ maintained during search, and the current asserted equalities during search may be used as the *useful* equalities. The *congruence closure* structure cc introduced in Sect. 3.1.1 contains relevant information to track ground equalities. For each ground term it represents an equivalence class of terms that are congruent in the current context. Now, given a pattern p we can compute a set of substitutions modulo the current congruence closure by invoking

$$\bigcup_{t \in \mathcal{T}} match(p, t, \emptyset)$$

where E-matching is defined by recursion on the pattern p:

$$
\begin{aligned}
match(x, t, S) &= \{\theta[x \mapsto t] \mid \theta \in S,\, x \notin \theta\} \\
&\quad \cup \{\theta \mid \theta \in S,\, x \in \theta,\, \theta(x) \in cc(t)\} \\
match(c, t, S) &= \emptyset \qquad \text{if } c \notin cc(t) \\
match(c, t, S) &= S \qquad \text{if } c \in cc(t) \\
match(f(\boldsymbol{p}), t, S) &= \textstyle\bigcup_{f(t)\,\in cc(t)} match(\boldsymbol{p}_n, \boldsymbol{t}_n, \ldots, match(\boldsymbol{p}_1, \boldsymbol{t}_1, S))
\end{aligned}
$$

It is not always possible to capture all quantified variables in a single pattern. For this purpose E-matching is applied to a sequence of patterns, known as a *multi-pattern*, that collectively contains all bound variables.

The secret sauce to efficiency is to find instantiations

- with as little overhead as possible,
- across large sets of terms, and
- incrementally.

Z3 uses code-trees [54] to address scale bottlenecks for search involving thousands of patterns and terms.

6.1.4   Model-Based Quantifier Instantiation

E-matching provides a highly syntactic restriction on instantiations. An alternative to E-matching is based on using a current model of the quantifier-free part of the search state. It is used to evaluate the universal quantifiers that have to be satisfied in order for the current model to extend to a full model of the conjunction of all asserted constraints. We call this method *Model-Based Quantifier Instantiation* [8, 22, 47, 59]. Take the following example:

```
from z3 import *
Z = IntSort()
f = Function('f', Z, Z)
g = Function('g', Z, Z)
a, n, x = Ints('a n x')
solve(ForAll(x, Implies(And(0 <= x, x <= n), f(x + a) == g(x))),
      a > 10, f(a) >= 2, g(3) <= -10)
```

It may produce a model of the form

```
s.add(ψ)
while True:
   if unsat == s.check():
      return unsat
   M = s.model()
   checker = Solver()
   checker.add(¬φ^M[x])
   if unsat == checker.check():
      return sat
   M = checker.model()
   find t, such that x ∉ t, t^M = x^M.
   s.add(φ[t])
```

Fig. 13. Model-Based Quantifier Instantiation algorithm. Notice that this proto-algorithm code is not directly executable.

```
[a = 11,
 n = 0,
 f = [else -> 2],
 g = [3 -> -10, else -> f(Var(0) + 11)]]
```

The interpretation of g maps 3 to -10, and all other values x are mapped to however $f(11 + x)$ is interpreted (which happens to be the constant 2).

The method that allowed finding this satisfying assignment is based on a model evaluation loop. At a high level it can be described as the following procedure, which checks satisfiability of

$$\psi \wedge \forall x . \varphi[x]$$

where ψ is quantifier free and for sake of illustration we have a single quantified formula with quantifier free body φ. The Model-Based Quantifier Instantiation, MBQI, procedure is described in Fig. 13:

We use the notation t^M to say that t is partially evaluated using interpretation M, for example:

- Let $M := [y \mapsto 3, f(x) \mapsto$ *if* $x = 1$ *then* 3 *else* 5], and
- $t := y + f(y) + f(z)$, then
- $t^M = 3 + 5 +$ *if* $z = 1$ *then* 3 *else* 5

For our example formula assume we have a model of the quantifier-free constraints as follows

```
[a = 11, n = 0, f = [else -> 2], g = [else -> -10]]
```

The negated body of the quantifier, instantiated to the model is

```
And(0 <= x, x <= 0, [else -> 2](x + 11) != [else -> -10](x))
```

It is satisfied with the instantiation x = 0, which is congruent to n under the current model. We therefore instantiate the quantifier with x = n and add the constraint

```
Implies(And(0 <= n, n <= n), f(n + a) == g(n))
```

But notice a syntactic property of the quantifier body. It can be read as a definition for the graph of g over the range 0 <= x, x <= n. This format is an instance of *guarded definitions* [28]. Hence, we record this reading when creating the next model for g. In the next round, a, n, and f are instantiated as before, and g(3) evaluates to −10 as before, but elsewhere follows the graph of f(x + a), and thus the model for g is given by [3 -> -10, else -> f(11 + Var(0))].

Model-Based Quantifier Instantiation is quite powerful when search space for instantiation terms is finite. It covers many decidable logical fragments, including EPR (Effectively Propositional Reasoning), UFBV (uninterpreted functions and bit-vectors), the Array property fragment [10] and extensions [22]. We will here only give a taste with an example from UFBV [59]:

```
Char = BitVecSort(8)
f  = Function('f', Char, Char)
f1 = Function('f1', Char, Char)
a, x = Consts('a x', Char)
solve(UGE(a, 0), f1 (a + 1) == 0,
    ForAll(x, Or(x == a + 1, f1(x) == f(x))))
```

The following model is a possible solution:

```
[a = 0, f = [else -> 1], f1 = [1 -> 0, else -> f(Var(0))]]
```

UFBV is the quantified logic of uninterpreted functions of bit-vectors. All sorts and variables have to be over bit-vectors, and standard bit-vector operations are allowed. It follows that the problem is finite domain and therefore decidable. It isn't easy, however. The quantifier-free fragment is not only NP hard, it is NEXPTIME hard; it can be encoded into EPR [55]. The quantified fragment is another complexity jump. Related to UFBV, decision procedures for quantified bit-vector formulas were developed by John and Chakraborty in [31,32], and by Niemetz et al. in [51].

Recall that EPR is a fragment of first-order logic where formulas have the quantifier prefix $\exists \boldsymbol{x} \forall \boldsymbol{y}$, thus a block of existential quantified variables followed by a block of universally quantified variables. The formula inside the quantifier prefix is a Boolean combination of equalities, disequalities between bound variables and free constants as well as predicate symbols applied to bound variables or free constants. Noteworthy, EPR formulas do not contain functions. It is easy to see that EPR is decidable by first replacing the existentially quantified variables by fresh constants and then instantiate the universally quantified variables by all combinations of the free constant. If the resulting ground formula is satisfiable, we obtain a finite model of the quantified formula by bounding the size of the universe by the free constants. The formula $\exists x \forall y.(p(x, y) \lor q(a, y) \lor y = a)$, where a is a free constant, is in EPR.

6.2 SAT Core

The SAT Core is an optimized self-contained SAT solver that solves propositional formulas. It takes advantage of the fact that it operates over propositional theories and performs advanced in-processing steps. The SAT solver also acts as a blackboard for select Boolean predicates that express cardinality and arithmetical (pseudo-Boolean) constraints over literals.

Generally, theories that are finite domain, are solved using the SAT solver. Z3 identifies quantifier-free finite domain theories using a designated logic QF_FD. It supports propositional logic, bit-vector theories, pseudo-Boolean constraints, and enumeration data-types. For example, the following scenario introduces an enumeration type for color, and bit-vectors u, v. It requires that at least 2 out of three predicates u + v <= 3, v <= 20, u <= 10 are satisfied.

```
from z3 import *
s = SolverFor("QF_FD")
Color, (red, green, blue) = EnumSort('Color', ['red','green','blue'])
clr = Const('clr', Color)
u, v = BitVecs('u v', 32)
s.add(u >= v,
      If(v > u + 1, clr != red, clr != green),
      clr == green,
      AtLeast(u + v <= 3, v <= 20, u <= 10, 2))
print(s.check())
print(s.model())
```

is satisfiable, and a possible model is:

```
[v = 4, u = 2147483647, clr = green]
```

Figure 14 shows the overall architecture of Z3's SAT solver.

There are four main components. Central to the SAT solver is an engine that performs case splits, lemma learning and backtracking search. It is the main CDCL engine and is structured similar to mainstream CDCL solvers. It can draw on auxiliary functionality.

6.2.1 In-processing

In-processing provides a means for the SAT solver to simplify the current set of clauses using *global* inferences. In-processing is performed on a periodic basis. It integrates several of the techniques that have been developed in the SAT solving literature in the past decade, known as Blocked Clause Elimination, Asymmetric Literal Addition, Asymmetric Covered Clause Elimination, Subsumption, Asymmetric Branching [24].

6.2.2 Co-processing

A set of co-processors are available to support alternative means of search. The SAT Core solver can also be a co-processor of itself.

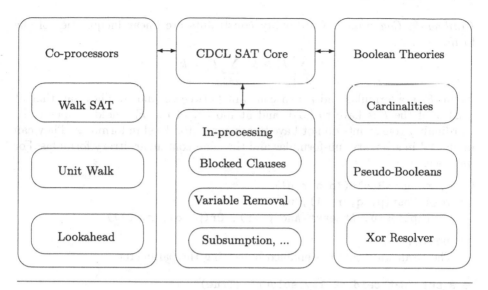

Fig. 14. Architecture of Z3's SAT Solver

- `s.set("sat.local_search_threads", 3)` spawns 3 concurrent threads that use walk-sat to find a satisfying assignment while the main CDCL solver attempts to find either a satisfying assignment or produce an empty clause.
- `s.set("sat.threads", 3)` spawns 2 concurrent threads, in additional to the main thread, to find a proof of the empty clause or a satisfying assignment. The threads share learned unit literals and learned clauses.
- `s.set("sat.unit_walk_threads", 1)` spawns 1 concurrent thread that uses a local search heuristic that integrates unit propagation.
- `s.set("sat.lookahead_simplify", True)` enables the lookahead solver as a simplifier during in-processing. It enables slightly more powerful techniques for learning new units and binary clauses.

The lookahead solver is used to find case splits through the Cube features, described in Sect. 4.6.7.

6.2.3 Boolean Theories

Three classes of Boolean functions are supported using specialized Boolean theory handlers. They are optional, as many problems can already be solved using the SAT core where the functions have been clausified. The cardinality and Pseudo-Boolean theory handlers are suitable for constraints where the encoding into clauses causes a significant overhead. The Xor solver is unlikely to be worth using, but is available for evaluation.

Cardinality Constraints. Cardinality constraints are linear inequalities of the form

$$\sum_{i=1}^{n} F_i \geq k, \ \sum_{i=1}^{n} F_i \leq k$$

where F_i are formulas and k is a constant between 1 and n. They say that at least k of the F_i;s have to hold, and at most k of the F_i's hold, respectively. Cardinality constraints do not have to appear at top-level in formulas. They can be nested in arbitrary sub-formulas and they can contain arbitrary formulas. For instance,

```
p, q, r, u = Bools('p q r u')
solve(AtMost(p, q, r, 1), u,
      Implies(u, AtLeast(And(p, r), Or(p, q), r, 2)))
```

has no solution.

The cardinality solver is enabled by setting the parameter

```
- s.set("sat.cardinality.solver", True)
```

If the parameter is false, cardinality constraints are compiled to clauses. A few alternative encoding methods are made available, and they can be controlled using the parameter `sat.cardinality.encoding`.

Pseudo-Boolean Constraints. Pseudo-Boolean constraints generalize cardinality constraints by allowing coefficients in the linear inequalities. They are of the form

$$\sum_{i=1}^{n} a_i F_i \geq k, \ \sum_{i=1}^{n} a_i F_i \leq k$$

where a_i are positive natural numbers. A value of a_i above k is legal, but can be safely truncated to k without changing the meaning of the formulas.

The constraints

$$p + 2q + 2r \leq 2 \wedge p + 2u + 3r \geq 4 \wedge u$$

can be written as

```
solve(PbLe([(p,1),(q,2),(r,2)], 3),
      PbGe([(p,1),(u,2),(r,3)], 4),
      u)
```

and have a solution

```
[q = False, u = True, r = True]
```

The pseudo-Boolean solver is enabled by setting the parameter

```
- s.set("sat.pb.solver", "solver")
```

Other available options for compiling Pseudo-Boolean constraints are `circuit`, `sorting`, and `totalizer`. They compile Pseudo-Booleans into clauses.

6.3 Horn Clause Solver

The Horn Solver contains specialized solvers for *Constrained Horn Clauses* [5,23,26,27,39]. As a default it uses the SPACER Horn clause solver by Arie Gurfinkel to solve Horn clauses over arithmetic [36]. A Constrained Horn Clause is a disjunction of literals over a set of uninterpreted predicates and interpreted functions and interpreted predicates (such as arithmetical operations + and relations <=). The uninterpreted predicates, may occur negatively without restrictions, but only occur positively in at most one place.

The solver also contains a Datalog engine that can be used to solve Datalog queries (with stratified negation) over finite domains and "header spaces" that are large finite domains, but can be encoded succinctly using ternary bit-vectors. The **Fixedpoint** context contains facilities for building Horn clauses, and generally a set of stratified Datalog rules, and for querying the resulting set of rules and facts. Additional information on the Fixedpoint engine can be found on https://rise4fun.com/z3/tutorial/fixedpoints.

We provide a very simple illustration of Horn clause usage here. McCarthy's 91 function illustrates nested recursion in a couple of lines, but otherwise makes no sense: It computes a function that can be described directly as

```
If(x > 101, 91, x - 10).
```

We will pretend this is a partial and interesting specification and prove this automatically using Horn clauses.

```python
def mc(x):
    if x > 100:
        return x - 10
    else:
        return mc(mc(x + 11))


def contract(x):
    assert(x > 101 or mc(x) == 91)
    assert(x < 101 or mc(x) == x - 10)
```

Rewriting the functional program into logical form can be achieved by introducing a binary relation between the input and output of mc, and then representing the functional program as a logic program, that is, a set of Horn clauses. The assertions are also Constrained Horn Clauses: they contain the uninterpreted predicate mc negatively, but have no positive occurrences of mc.

```python
s = SolverFor("HORN")
mc = Function('mc', Z, Z, B)
x, y, z = Ints('x y z')
s.add(ForAll(x, Implies(x > 100, mc(x, x - 10))))
s.add(ForAll([x, y, z],
            Implies(And(x <= 100, mc(x + 11, y), mc(y, z)),
                    mc(x, z))))
s.add(ForAll([x, y], Implies(And(x <= 101, mc(x, y)), y == 91)))
s.add(ForAll([x, y], Implies(And(x >= 101, mc(x, y)), x == y + 10)))
print(s.check())
```

```
s = SolverFor("LIA") # Quantified Linear Integer Arithmetic
x, y, u, v = Ints('x y u v')
a = 5
b = 7
s.add(ForAll(u, Implies(u >= v,
                        Exists([x, y], And(x >= 0, y >= 0, u == a*x + b*y)))))
print(s.check())
print(s.model())
```

Fig. 15. Given a supply of 5 and 7 cent stamps. Is there a lower bound, after which all denominations of stamps can be produced? Thus, find v, such that every u larger or equal to v can be written as a non-negative combination of 5 and 7.

```
s = SolverFor("LRA") # Quantified Linear Real Arithmetic
x, y, z = Reals('x y z')
s.add(x < y, ForAll(z, Or(z <= x, y <= z)))
print(s.check())
```

Fig. 16. The set of reals is dense

Z3 finds a solution for mc that is a sufficient invariant to establish the assertions.

We get a better view of the invariant for mc by evaluating it on symbolic inputs x and y.

```
print(s.model().eval(mc(x, y)))
```

produces the invariant

```
And(Or(Not(y >= 92), Not(x + -1*y <= 9)),
    Not(x + -1*y >= 11),
    Not(y <= 90))
```

6.4   QSAT

The QSAT Solver is a decision procedure for satisfiability of select theories that admit quantifier elimination. It can be used to check satisfiability of quantified formulas over Linear Integer (Fig. 15), Linear Real (Fig. 16), Non-linear (polynomial) Real arithmetic (Fig. 17), Booleans, and Algebraic Data-types (Fig. 18). It is described in [6]. It is invoked whenever a solver is created for one of the supported quantified logics, or a solver is created from the qsat tactic.

Figure 18 encodes a simple game introduced in [16]. There is no SMT-LIB2 logic for quantified algebraic data-types so we directly instantiate the solver that performs QSAT through a tactic. Section 7 provides a brief introduction to tactics in Z3.

```
s = SolverFor("NRA") # Quantified Non-linear Real Arithmetic
x, y, z = Reals('x y z')
s.add(x < y)
s.add(y * y < x)
s.add(ForAll(z, z * x != y))
print(s.check())
```

Fig. 17. Quantified non-linear real polynomial arithmetic

```
from z3 import *
s = Tactic('qsat').solver()
Nat = Datatype('Nat')
Nat.declare('Z')
Nat.declare('S', ('pred', Nat))
Nat = Nat.create()
Z = Nat.Z
S = Nat.S
def move(x, y):
    return Or(x == S(y), x == S(S(y)))
def win(x, n):
    if n == 0:
        return False
    y = FreshConst(Nat)
    return Exists(y, And(move(x, y), Not(win(y, n - 1))))

s.add(win(S(S(S(S(Z)))), 4))
print(s.check())
```

Fig. 18. Checking for winning positions in a game of successors

The solver builds on an abstraction refinement loop, originally developed for quantifier elimination in [41]. The goal of the procedure is, given a quantifier-free f, find a quantifier free G, such that $G \equiv \exists v . F$. It assumes a tool, *project*, that eliminates v from a conjunction M into a satisfiable strengthening. That is, project$(v, M) \Rightarrow \exists v . M$. The procedure, uses the steps:

– **Initialize**: $G \leftarrow \bot$
– **Repeatedly**: find conjunctions M that imply $F \wedge \neg G$
– **Update**: $G \leftarrow G \vee$ project(v, M).

An algorithm that realizes this approach is formulated in Fig. 19.

QESTO [30] generalizes this procedure to nested QBF (Quantified Boolean Formulas), and the implementation in Z3 generalizes QESTO to SMT. The approach is based on playing a quantifier game. Let us illustrate the game for Boolean formulas. Assume we are given:

```
def qe(∃v . F):
    e, a = Solver(), Solver()
    e.add(F)
    a.add(¬F)
    G = False
    while sat == e.check():
        M₀ = e.model()
        M₁ = [ lit for lit in literals(F) if is_true(M₀.eval(lit)) ]
        # assume F is in negation normal form
        assert unsat == a.check(M₁)
        M₂ = a.unsat_core()
        π = project(M₂, v)
        G = G ∨ π
        e.add(¬π)
    return G
```

Fig. 19. Quantifier elimination by core extraction and projection. Notice that this proto-algorithm code is not directly executable

$$G = \forall u_1, u_2 \, \exists e_1, e_2 \; . \; F$$

$$F = (u_1 \wedge u_2 \rightarrow e_1) \wedge (u_1 \wedge \neg u_2 \rightarrow e_2) \wedge (e_1 \wedge e_2 \rightarrow \neg u_1)$$

Then the game proceeds as follows:

- $\forall$: starts. $u_1, u_2, \overline{e}_1, \overline{e}_2 \models \neg F$.
- $\exists$: strikes back. $u_1, u_2, e_1, \overline{e}_2 \models F$.
- $\forall$: has to backtrack. It doesn't matter what u_1 is assigned to. It is already the case that $u_2, e_1, \overline{e}_2 \models F$.
- $\forall$: learns $\neg u_2$.
- $\forall$: $\overline{u}_2, u_1, \overline{e}_1, \overline{e}_2 \models \neg F$.
- $\exists$: counters - $\overline{u}_2, u_1, \overline{e}_1, e_2 \models F$.
- $\forall$: has lost!. It is already the case that $\overline{u}_2, \overline{e}_1, e_2 \models F$.

To summarize the approach:

- There are two players
    - $\forall$ - tries to satisfy $\neg F$
    - $\exists$ - tries to satisfy F
- Players control their variables. For example, take $\exists x_1 \forall x_2 \exists x_3 \forall x_4 \ldots F$ at round 2:
    - value of x_1 is already fixed,
    - $\forall$ fixes value of x_2,
    - $\forall$ fixes value of x_4, but can change again at round 4,
    - $\forall$ can guess values of x_3 to satisfy $\neg F$.

– Some player loses at round $i + 2$:
  • Create succinct *no-good* to strengthen F resp. $\neg F$ depending on who lost.
  • Backjump to round i (or below).

The main ingredients to the approach is thus *projection* and *strategies*.

– Projections are added to *learn* from mistakes. Thus, a player avoids repeating same losing moves.
– Strategies *prune* moves from the opponent.

We will here just illustrate an example of projection. Z3 uses *model based projection* [36,44] to find a satisfiable quantifier-free formula that implies the existentially quantified formula that encodes the losing state.

Example 4. Suppose we would want to compute a quantifier-free formula that implies $\exists x . (2y \leq x \wedge y - z \leq x \wedge x \leq z)$. Note that the formula is equivalent to a quantifier free formula:
$$\exists x . (2y \leq x \wedge y - z \leq x \wedge x \leq z) \equiv (y - z \leq 2y \leq z) \vee (2y \leq y - z \leq z)$$
but the size of the equivalent formula is quadratic in the size of the original formula. Suppose we have a satisfying assignment for the formula inside of the existential quantifier. Say $M = [x \mapsto 3, y \mapsto 1, z \mapsto 6]$. Then $2y^M = 2$ and $(y - z)^M = -5$, and therefore $2y > y - z$ under M. The greatest lower bound for x is therefore $2y$ and we can select this branch as our choice for elimination of x. The result of projection is then $y - z \leq 2y \leq z$.

6.5 NLSat

The solver created when invoking `SolverFor('QF_NRA')` relies on a self-contained engine that is specialized for solving non-linear arithmetic formulas [34]. It is a decision procedure for quantifier-free formulas over the reals using polynomial arithmetic.

```
s = SolverFor("QF_NRA")
x, y = Reals('x y')
s.add(x**3 + x*y + 1 == 0, x*y > 1, x**2 < 1.1)
print(s.check())
```

The NLSat solver is automatically configured if the formula is syntactically in the `QF_NRA` fragment. So one can directly use it without specifying the specialized solver:

```
set_option(precision=30)
print "Solving, and displaying result with 30 decimal places"
solve(x**2 + y**2 == 3, x**3 == 2)
```

7   Tactics

In contrast to solvers that ultimately check the satisfiability of a set of assertions, tactics transform assertions to sets of assertions, in a way that a proof-tree is comprised of nodes representing goals, and children representing subgoals. Many useful pre-processing steps can be formulated as tactics. They take one goal and create a subgoal.

7.1   Tactic Basics

You can access the set of tactics

```
print(tactics())
```

and for additional information obtain a description of optional parameters:

```
for name in tactics():
    t = Tactic(name)
    print(name, t.help(), t.param_descrs())
```

We will here give a single example of a tactic application. It transforms a goal to a simplified subgoal obtained by eliminating a quantifier that is trivially reducible and by combining repeated formulas into one.

```
x, y = Reals('x y')
g   = Goal()
g.add(2 < x, Exists(y, And(y > 0, x == y + 2)))
print(g)

t1 = Tactic('qe-light')
t2 = Tactic('simplify')
t  = Then(t1, t2)
print(t(g))
```

Additional information on tactics is available from [45], https://rise4fun.com/ Z3/tutorial/strategies and http://www.cs.tau.ac.il/~msagiv/courses/asv/z3py/ strategies-examples.htm.

7.2   Solvers from Tactics

Given a tactic t, the method t.solver() extracts a solver object that applies the tactic to the current assertions and reports sat or unsat if it is able to reduce subgoals to a definite answer.

7.3   Tactics from Solvers

There is no method that corresponds to producing a tactic from a solver. Instead Z3 exposes a set of built-in tactics for the main solvers. These are accessed through the names sat, smt, qsat (and nlqsat for quantified non-linear real arithmetic, e.g., the logic NRA), qffd for QF_FD and nlsat for QF_NRA.

7.4   Parallel Z3

The parameter `set_param("parallel.enable", True)` enables Z3's parallel mode. Selected tactics, including `qfbv`, that uses the SAT solver for sub-goals the option, when enabled, will cause Z3 to use a cube-and-conquer approach to solve subgoals. The tactics `psat`, `psmt` and `pqffd` provide direct access to the parallel mode, but you have to make sure that `"parallel.enable"` is true to force them to use parallel mode. You can control how the cube-and-conquer procedure spends time in simplification and cubing through other parameters under the `parallel` name-space.

The main option to toggle is `parallel.threads.max`. It caps the maximal number of threads. By default, the maximal number of threads used by the parallel solver is bound by the number of processes.

8   Optimization

Depending on applications, learning that a formula is satisfiable or not, may not be sufficient. Sometimes, it is useful to retrieve models that are *optimal* with respect to some objective function. Z3 supports a small repertoire of objective functions and invokes a specialized optimization module when objective functions are supplied. The main approach for specifying an optimization objective is through functions that specify whether to find solutions that *maximize* or *minimize* values of an arithmetical (in the case of Z3, the term has to a *linear* arithmetic term) or bit-vector term t. Thus, when specifying the objective $maximize(t)$ the solver is instructed to find solutions to the variables in t that maximizes the value of t. An alternative way to specify objectives is through *soft constraints*. These are assertions, optionally annotated with weights. The objective is to satisfy as many soft constraints as possible in a solution. When weights are used, the objective is to find a solution with the least penalty, given by the sum of weights, for unsatisfied constraints. From the Python API, one uses the `Optimize` context to specify optimization problems. The `Optimize` context relies on the built-in solvers for solving optimization queries. The architecture of the optimization context is provided in Fig. 20.

The `Optimize` context provides three main extensions to satisfiability checking:

```
o = Optimize()

x, y = Ints('x y')
o.maximize(x + 2*y)              # maximizes LIA objective

u, v = BitVecs('u v', 32)
o.minimize(u + v)                # minimizes BV objective

o.add_soft(x > 4, 4)             # soft constraint with
                                 # optional weight
```

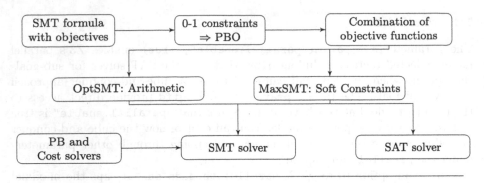

Fig. 20. Optimization engines in Z3

Using soft assertions is equivalent to posing an 0-1 optimization problem. Thus, the following formulations are equivalent and Z3 detects the second variant and turns it into a set of weighted soft assertions.

```
a, b = Bools('a b')
o.add_soft(a, 3)
o.add_soft(b, 4)
```

is equivalent to

```
o.minimize(If(a, 0, 3) + If(b, 0, 4))
```

8.1   Multiple Objectives

It is possible to add multiple objectives. There are three ways to combine objective functions.

$\text{Box}(x, y)$	$v_x := \max\{x \mid \varphi(x, y)\}$
	$v_y := \max\{y \mid \varphi(x, y)\}$
$\text{Lex}(x, y)$	$v_x := \max\{x \mid \varphi(x, y)\}$
	$v_y := \max\{y \mid \varphi(v_x, y)\}$
$\text{Pareto}(x, y)$	$\left\{(v_x, v_y) \mid \begin{array}{l} \varphi(v_x, v_y), \ \forall x, y. \\ \varphi(x, y) \to x \le v_x \lor y \le v_y \end{array}\right\}$

For instance, Pareto objectives can be specified as follows:

```
x, y = Ints('x y')
opt = Optimize()
opt.set(priority='pareto')
opt.add(x + y == 10, x >= 0, y >= 0)
mx = opt.maximize(x)
my = opt.maximize(y)
while opt.check() == sat:
    print (mx.value(), my.value())
```

8.2   MaxSAT

The conventional definition of MaxSAT is to minimize the number of violated *soft* assertions. There are several algorithms for MaxSAT, and developing new algorithms is a very active area of research. We will here describe MaxRes from [48]. It is also Z3's default solver for MaxSAT/MaxSMT problems. As an illustration assume we are given an *unweighted* (all soft constraints have weight 1) MaxSAT problem $F, F_1, \ldots, F_5$, where the first four soft constraints cannot be satisfied in conjunction with the hard constraint F. Thus, we have the case:

$$A : F, \underbrace{F_1, F_2, F_3, F_4}_{core}, F_5$$

The system is transformed to a weakened MaxSAT problem as follows:

$$A' : F, \ F_2 \vee F_1, F_3 \vee (F_2 \wedge F_1), F_4 \vee (F_3 \wedge (F_2 \wedge F_1)), F_5$$

The procedure is formalized in Fig. 21. We claim that by solving A', we can find an optimal solution to A. For this purpose, consider the *cost* of a model with respect to a MaxSAT problem. The cost, written $cost(M, A)$ is the number of soft constraints in A that are *false* under M. More precisely,

Lemma 1. *For every model M of F, $cost(M, A) = 1 + cost(M, A')$*

Proof (*of Lemma 1*). To be able to refer to the soft constraints in the transformed systems A' we will give names to the new soft constraints, such that F_1' is a name for $F_2 \vee F_1$, F_2' names $F_3 \vee (F_2 \wedge F_1)$, F_3' is the name for $F_4 \vee (F_3 \wedge (F_2 \wedge F_1))$ and F_4' is the new name of F_5.

Consider the soft constraints in the core. Since it is a core, at least one has to be false under M. Let j be the first index among where $M(F_j)$ is false. Then M evaluates all other soft constraints the same, e.g., $\forall i < j : M(F_i') = M(F_i)$, and $\forall i > j : M(F_{i-1}') = M(F_i)$.   □

Thus, eventually, it is possible to satisfy all soft constraints (weakening could potentially create 0 soft constraints), and a solution to the weakened system is an optimal solution.

Weighted assertions can be handled by a reduction to unweighted MaxSAT. For example,

```
a, b, c = Bools('a b c')
o = Optimize()
o.add(a == c)
o.add(Not(And(a, b)))
o.add_soft(a, 2)
o.add_soft(b, 3)
o.add_soft(c, 1)
print(o.check())
print(o.model())
```

```
def add_def(s, fml):
    name = Bool("%s" % fml)
    s.add(name == fml)
    return name

def relax_core(s, core, Fs):
    prefix = BoolVal(True)
    Fs -= { f for f in core }
    for i in range(len(core)-1):
        prefix = add_def(s, And(core[i], prefix))
        Fs |= { add_def(s, Or(prefix, core[i+1])) }

def maxsat(s, Fs):
    cost = 0
    Fs0 = Fs.copy()
    while unsat == s.check(Fs):
        cost += 1
        relax_core(s, s.unsat_core(), Fs)
    return cost, { f for f in Fs0 if tt(s, f) }
```

Fig. 21. Core based MaxSAT using MaxRes

Efficient implementations of MaxSAT flatten weights on demand. Given a core of soft constraints it is split into two parts: In one part all soft constraints have the same coefficient as the weight of the soft constraint with the minimal weight. The other part comprises of the remaining soft constraints. For our example, a, b is a core and the weight of a is 2, while the weight of b is 3. The weight of b can therefore be split into two parts, one where it has weight 2, and the other where it has weight 1. Applying the transformation for the core we obtain the simpler MaxSAT problem:

```
a, b, c = Bools('a b c')
o = Optimize()
o.add(a == c)
o.add(Not(And(a, b)))
o.add_soft(Or(a, b), 2)
o.add_soft(b, 1)
o.add_soft(c, 1)
print(o.check())
print(o.model())
```

9   Summary

This tutorial has presented an overview of main functionality exposed by Z3. By presenting some of the underlying algorithms in an example driven way we have attempted to give a taste of the underlying decision procedures and proof engines. By presenting examples of programming queries on top of Z3 we have attempted to provide an introduction to turning SMT solving into a service for logic queries that go beyond checking for satisfiability of a single formula. Tuning extended queries on top of the basic services provided by SAT and SMT solvers is a very active area of research with new application scenarios and new discoveries.

References

1. Alviano, M.: Model enumeration in propositional circumscription via unsatisfiable core analysis. TPLP **17**(5–6), 708–725 (2017)
2. Bacchus, F., Katsirelos, G.: Finding a collection of MUSes incrementally. In: Quimper, C.-G. (ed.) CPAIOR 2016. LNCS, vol. 9676, pp. 35–44. Springer, Cham (2016). https://doi.org/10.1007/978-3-319-33954-2_3
3. Barrett, C., Fontaine, P., Tinelli, C.: The Satisfiability Modulo Theories Library (SMT-LIB). www.SMT-LIB.org (2016)
4. Biere, A.: Bounded model checking. In: Biere, A., Heule, M., van Maaren, H., Walsh, T. (eds.) Handbook of Satisfiability, Frontiers in Artificial Intelligence and Applications, vol. 185, pp. 457–481. IOS Press (2009). https://doi.org/10.3233/978-1-58603-929-5-457
5. Bjørner, N., Gurfinkel, A., McMillan, K., Rybalchenko, A.: Horn clause solvers for program verification. In: Beklemishev, L.D., Blass, A., Dershowitz, N., Finkbeiner, B., Schulte, W. (eds.) Fields of Logic and Computation II. LNCS, vol. 9300, pp. 24–51. Springer, Cham (2015). https://doi.org/10.1007/978-3-319-23534-9_2
6. Bjørner, N., Janota, M.: Playing with alternating quantifier satisfaction. In: LPAR Short Presentation Papers (2015)
7. Bjørner, N., Nachmanson, L.: Theorem recycling for theorem proving. In: Kovács, L., Voronkov, A. (eds.) Vampire 2017, Proceedings of the 4th Vampire Workshop. EPiC Series in Computing, vol. 53, pp. 1–8. EasyChair (2018). https://doi.org/10.29007/r58f, https://easychair.org/publications/paper/qGfG
8. Bonacina, M.P., Lynch, C., de Moura, L.M.: On deciding satisfiability by theorem proving with speculative inferences. J. Autom. Reason. **47**(2), 161–189 (2011)
9. Bradley, A.R., Manna, Z.: Checking safety by inductive generalization of counterexamples to induction. In: Formal Methods in Computer-Aided Design, 7th International Conference, FMCAD 2007, Austin, Texas, USA, 11–14 November 2007, Proceedings, pp. 173–180 (2007). https://doi.org/10.1109/FAMCAD.2007.15
10. Bradley, A.R., Manna, Z., Sipma, H.B.: What's decidable about arrays? In: Verification, Model Checking, and Abstract Interpretation, 7th International Conference, VMCAI 2006, Charleston, SC, USA, 8–10 January 2006, Proceedings, pp. 427–442 (2006). https://doi.org/10.1007/11609773_28
11. Bromberger, M., Weidenbach, C.: New techniques for linear arithmetic: cubes and equalities. Form. Methods Syst. Des. **51**(3), 433–461 (2017). https://doi.org/10.1007/s10703-017-0278-7
12. Chockler, H., Ivrii, A., Matsliah, A.: Computing interpolants without proofs. In: Biere, A., Nahir, A., Vos, T. (eds.) HVC 2012. LNCS, vol. 7857, pp. 72–85. Springer, Heidelberg (2013). https://doi.org/10.1007/978-3-642-39611-3_12
13. Christ, J., Hoenicke, J.: Cutting the mix. In: Kroening, D., Păsăreanu, C.S. (eds.) CAV 2015. LNCS, vol. 9207, pp. 37–52. Springer, Cham (2015). https://doi.org/10.1007/978-3-319-21668-3_3

14. Cimatti, A., Griggio, A., Irfan, A., Roveri, M., Sebastiani, R.: Experimenting on solving nonlinear integer arithmetic with incremental linearization. In: Beyersdorff, O., Wintersteiger, C.M. (eds.) SAT 2018. LNCS, vol. 10929, pp. 383–398. Springer, Cham (2018). https://doi.org/10.1007/978-3-319-94144-8_23

15. Cohen, E., Megiddo, N.: Improved algorithms for linear inequalities with two variables per inequality. SIAM J. Comput. **23**(6), 1313–1347 (1994). https://doi.org/10.1137/S0097539791256325

16. Colmerauer, A., Dao, T.-B.-H.: Expressiveness of full first order constraints in the algebra of finite or infinite trees. In: Dechter, R. (ed.) CP 2000. LNCS, vol. 1894, pp. 172–186. Springer, Heidelberg (2000). https://doi.org/10.1007/3-540-45349-0_14

17. Costan, A., Gaubert, S., Goubault, E., Martel, M., Putot, S.: A policy iteration algorithm for computing fixed points in static analysis of programs. In: Etessami, K., Rajamani, S.K. (eds.) CAV 2005. LNCS, vol. 3576, pp. 462–475. Springer, Heidelberg (2005). https://doi.org/10.1007/11513988_46

18. Davis, M., Logemann, G., Loveland, D.: A machine program for theorem proving. Commun. ACM **5**, 394–397 (1962)

19. Dillig, I., Dillig, T., Aiken, A.: Cuts from proofs: a complete and practical technique for solving linear inequalities over integers. In: Bouajjani, A., Maler, O. (eds.) CAV 2009. LNCS, vol. 5643, pp. 233–247. Springer, Heidelberg (2009). https://doi.org/10.1007/978-3-642-02658-4_20

20. Downey, P.J., Sethi, R., Tarjan, R.E.: Variations on the common subexpression problem. J. ACM **27**(4), 758–771 (1980). https://doi.org/10.1145/322217.322228

21. Dutertre, B., de Moura, L.: A fast linear-arithmetic solver for DPLL(T). In: Ball, T., Jones, R.B. (eds.) CAV 2006. LNCS, vol. 4144, pp. 81–94. Springer, Heidelberg (2006). https://doi.org/10.1007/11817963_11

22. Ge, Y., de Moura, L.: Complete instantiation for quantified formulas in satisfiabiliby modulo theories. In: Bouajjani, A., Maler, O. (eds.) CAV 2009. LNCS, vol. 5643, pp. 306–320. Springer, Heidelberg (2009). https://doi.org/10.1007/978-3-642-02658-4_25

23. Grebenshchikov, S., Lopes, N.P., Popeea, C., Rybalchenko, A.: Synthesizing software verifiers from proof rules. In: ACM SIGPLAN Conference on Programming Language Design and Implementation, PLDI 2012, Beijing, China, 11–16 June 2012, pp. 405–416 (2012). https://doi.org/10.1145/2254064.2254112

24. Heule, M., Järvisalo, M., Lonsing, F., Seidl, M., Biere, A.: Clause elimination for SAT and QSAT. J. Artif. Intell. Res. **53**, 127–168 (2015). https://doi.org/10.1613/jair.4694

25. Heule, M.J.H., Kullmann, O., Wieringa, S., Biere, A.: Cube and conquer: guiding CDCL SAT solvers by lookaheads. In: Eder, K., Lourenço, J., Shehory, O. (eds.) HVC 2011. LNCS, vol. 7261, pp. 50–65. Springer, Heidelberg (2012). https://doi.org/10.1007/978-3-642-34188-5_8

26. Hoder, K., Bjørner, N.: Generalized property directed reachability. In: Cimatti, A., Sebastiani, R. (eds.) SAT 2012. LNCS, vol. 7317, pp. 157–171. Springer, Heidelberg (2012). https://doi.org/10.1007/978-3-642-31612-8_13

27. Hoder, K., Bjørner, N., de Moura, L.: μz– an efficient engine for fixed points with constraints. In: Gopalakrishnan, G., Qadeer, S. (eds.) CAV 2011. LNCS, vol. 6806, pp. 457–462. Springer, Heidelberg (2011). https://doi.org/10.1007/978-3-642-22110-1_36

28. Ihlemann, C., Jacobs, S., Sofronie-Stokkermans, V.: On local reasoning in verification. In: Ramakrishnan, C.R., Rehof, J. (eds.) TACAS 2008. LNCS, vol. 4963, pp. 265–281. Springer, Heidelberg (2008). https://doi.org/10.1007/978-3-540-78800-3_19

29. Janota, M., Lynce, I., Marques-Silva, J.: Algorithms for computing backbones of propositional formulae. AI Commun. **28**(2), 161–177 (2015). https://doi.org/10.3233/AIC-140640

30. Janota, M., Marques-Silva, J.: Solving QBF by clause selection. In: Proceedings of the Twenty-Fourth International Joint Conference on Artificial Intelligence, IJCAI 2015, Buenos Aires, Argentina, 25–31 July 2015, pp. 325–331 (2015). http://ijcai.org/Abstract/15/052

31. John, A.K., Chakraborty, S.: A quantifier elimination algorithm for linear modular equations and disequations. In: Gopalakrishnan, G., Qadeer, S. (eds.) CAV 2011. LNCS, vol. 6806, pp. 486–503. Springer, Heidelberg (2011). https://doi.org/10.1007/978-3-642-22110-1_39

32. John, A.K., Chakraborty, S.: A layered algorithm for quantifier elimination from linear modular constraints. Form. Methods Syst. Des. **49**(3), 272–323 (2016). https://doi.org/10.1007/s10703-016-0260-9

33. Jovanović, D.: Solving nonlinear integer arithmetic with MCSAT. In: Bouajjani, A., Monniaux, D. (eds.) VMCAI 2017. LNCS, vol. 10145, pp. 330–346. Springer, Cham (2017). https://doi.org/10.1007/978-3-319-52234-0_18

34. Jovanović, D., de Moura, L.: Solving non-linear arithmetic. In: Gramlich, B., Miller, D., Sattler, U. (eds.) IJCAR 2012. LNCS (LNAI), vol. 7364, pp. 339–354. Springer, Heidelberg (2012). https://doi.org/10.1007/978-3-642-31365-3_27

35. Kapur, D., Zarba, C.: A reduction approach to decision procedures. Technical report, University of New Mexico (2006). https://www.cs.unm.edu/~kapur/mypapers/reduction.pdf

36. Komuravelli, A., Gurfinkel, A., Chaki, S.: SMT-based model checking for recursive programs. In: Biere, A., Bloem, R. (eds.) CAV 2014. LNCS, vol. 8559, pp. 17–34. Springer, Cham (2014). https://doi.org/10.1007/978-3-319-08867-9_2

37. Liffiton, M.H., Previti, A., Malik, A., Marques-Silva, J.: Fast, flexible mus enumeration. Constraints **21**(2), 223–250 (2016)

38. Lopes, N.P., Menendez, D., Nagarakatte, S., Regehr, J.: Practical verification of peephole optimizations with alive. Commun. ACM **61**(2), 84–91 (2018). https://doi.org/10.1145/3166064

39. McMillan, K.L.: Lazy annotation revisited. In: Computer Aided Verification - 26th International Conference, CAV 2014, Held as Part of the Vienna Summer of Logic, VSL 2014, Vienna, Austria, 18–22 July 2014, Proceedings, pp. 243–259 (2014). https://doi.org/10.1007/978-3-319-08867-9_16

40. Mencía, C., Previti, A., Marques-Silva, J.: Literal-based MCS extraction. In: Proceedings of the Twenty-Fourth International Joint Conference on Artificial Intelligence, IJCAI 2015, Buenos Aires, Argentina, 25–31 July 2015, pp. 1973–1979 (2015). http://ijcai.org/Abstract/15/280

41. Monniaux, D.: A quantifier elimination algorithm for linear real arithmetic. In: Cervesato, I., Veith, H., Voronkov, A. (eds.) LPAR 2008. LNCS (LNAI), vol. 5330, pp. 243–257. Springer, Heidelberg (2008). https://doi.org/10.1007/978-3-540-89439-1_18

42. de Moura, L.M., Bjørner, N.: Proofs and refutations, and Z3. In: Rudnicki, P., Sutcliffe, G., Konev, B., Schmidt, R.A., Schulz, S. (eds.) Proceedings of the LPAR 2008 Workshops, Knowledge Exchange: Automated Provers and Proof Assistants, and the 7th International Workshop on the Implementation of Logics, Doha, Qatar, 22 November 2008, CEUR Workshop Proceedings, vol. 418. CEUR-WS.org (2008). http://ceur-ws.org/Vol-418/paper10.pdf

43. de Moura, L.M., Bjørner, N.: Generalized, efficient array decision procedures. In: Proceedings of 9th International Conference on Formal Methods in Computer-Aided Design, FMCAD 2009, 15–18 November 2009, Austin, Texas, USA, pp. 45–52 (2009). https://doi.org/10.1109/FMCAD.2009.5351142

44. de Moura, L., Jovanović, D.: A model-constructing satisfiability calculus. In: Giacobazzi, R., Berdine, J., Mastroeni, I. (eds.) VMCAI 2013. LNCS, vol. 7737, pp. 1–12. Springer, Heidelberg (2013). https://doi.org/10.1007/978-3-642-35873-9_1

45. de Moura, L., Passmore, G.O.: The strategy challenge in SMT solving. In: Bonacina, M.P., Stickel, M.E. (eds.) Automated Reasoning and Mathematics. LNCS (LNAI), vol. 7788, pp. 15–44. Springer, Heidelberg (2013). https://doi.org/10.1007/978-3-642-36675-8_2

46. de Moura, L., Bjørner, N.: Efficient E-Matching for SMT solvers. In: Pfenning, F. (ed.) CADE 2007. LNCS (LNAI), vol. 4603, pp. 183–198. Springer, Heidelberg (2007). https://doi.org/10.1007/978-3-540-73595-3_13

47. de Moura, L., Bjørner, N.: Bugs, moles and skeletons: symbolic reasoning for software development. In: Giesl, J., Hähnle, R. (eds.) IJCAR 2010. LNCS (LNAI), vol. 6173, pp. 400–411. Springer, Heidelberg (2010). https://doi.org/10.1007/978-3-642-14203-1_34

48. Narodytska, N., Bacchus, F.: Maximum satisfiability using core-guided MaxSAT resolution. In: Brodley, C.E., Stone, P. (eds.) AAAI 2014, 27–31 July 2014, Quebec City, Quebec, Canada, pp. 2717–2723. AAAI Press (2014)

49. Narodytska, N., Bjørner, N., Marinescu, M., Sagiv, M.: Core-guided minimal correction set and core enumeration. In: Lang, J. (ed.) Proceedings of the Twenty-Seventh International Joint Conference on Artificial Intelligence, IJCAI 2018, 13–19 July 2018, Stockholm, Sweden, pp. 1353–1361. ijcai.org (2018). https://doi.org/10.24963/ijcai.2018/188

50. Nelson, G., Oppen, D.C.: Simplification by cooperating decision procedures. ACM Trans. Program. Lang. Syst. 1(2), 245–257 (1979). https://doi.org/10.1145/357073.357079

51. Niemetz, A., Preiner, M., Reynolds, A., Barrett, C., Tinelli, C.: Solving quantified bit-vectors using invertibility conditions. In: Chockler, H., Weissenbacher, G. (eds.) CAV 2018. LNCS, vol. 10982, pp. 236–255. Springer, Cham (2018). https://doi.org/10.1007/978-3-319-96142-2_16

52. Nieuwenhuis, R., Oliveras, A., Tinelli, C.: Solving SAT and SAT modulo theories: from an abstract Davis-Putnam-Logemann-Loveland procedure to DPLL(T). J. ACM 53(6), 937–977 (2006)

53. Previti, A., Mencía, C., Järvisalo, M., Marques-Silva, J.: Improving MCS enumeration via caching. In: Gaspers, S., Walsh, T. (eds.) SAT 2017. LNCS, vol. 10491, pp. 184–194. Springer, Cham (2017). https://doi.org/10.1007/978-3-319-66263-3_12

54. Ramakrishnan, I.V., Sekar, R.C., Voronkov, A.: Term indexing. In: Robinson, J.A., Voronkov, A. (eds.) Handbook of Automated Reasoning (in 2 volumes), pp. 1853–1964. Elsevier and MIT Press (2001)

55. Seidl, M., Lonsing, F., Biere, A.: qbf2epr: a tool for generating EPR formulas from QBF. In: Third Workshop on Practical Aspects of Automated Reasoning, PAAR-2012, Manchester, UK, 30 June–1 July 2012, pp. 139–148 (2012). http://www.easychair.org/publications/paper/145184
56. Silva, J.P.M., Sakallah, K.A.: GRASP: a search algorithm for propositional satisfiability. IEEE Trans. Comput. **48**(5), 506–521 (1999)
57. Tarjan, R.E.: Efficiency of a good but not linear set union algorithm. J. ACM **22**(2), 215–225 (1975). https://doi.org/10.1145/321879.321884
58. Veanes, M., Bjørner, N., Nachmanson, L., Bereg, S.: Monadic decomposition. J. ACM **64**(2), 14:1–14:28 (2017). https://doi.org/10.1145/3040488
59. Wintersteiger, C.M., Hamadi, Y., de Moura, L.M.: Efficiently solving quantified bit-vector formulas. Form. Methods Syst. Des. **42**(1), 3–23 (2013)

The Impact of Alan Turing: Formal Methods and Beyond

Jonathan P. Bowen[1,2]([⊠]) [iD]

[1] Faculty of Computer and Information Science,
Centre for Research and Innovation in Software Engineering (RISE),
Southwest University, Chongqing 400715, China
[2] School of Engineering, London South Bank University,
Borough Road, London SE1 1AA, UK
jonathan.bowen@lsbu.ac.uk
http://www.jpbowen.com

Abstract. In this paper, we discuss the influence and reputation of Alan Turing since his death in 1954, specifically in the field of formal methods, especially for program proving, but also in a much wider context. Although he received some recognition during his lifetime, this image was tarnished by the controversy at the time of his death. While he was known and appreciated in scientific circles, he did not enter the public's consciousness for several decades. A turning point was the definitive biography produced by Andrew Hodges in 1983 but, even then, the tide did not turn very rapidly. More recent events, such as the celebrations of his birth centenary in 2012 and the official British royal pardon in 2013, have raised Turing's fame and popularity among the informed general public in the United Kingdom and elsewhere. Cultural works in the arts featuring Turing have enhanced his profile still further. Thus, the paper discusses not only Turing's scientific impact, especially for formal methods, but in addition his historical, cultural, and even political significance. Turing's academic 'family tree' in terms of heritage and legacy is also covered.

1 Background

Alan Turing (1912–1954) has a rightful claim to the title of "Founder of Computer Science" [30]. He has also been called the "Father of Computer Science" [65]. Before World War II, Turing laid the theoretical groundwork for a universal machine that models a computer in its most general form. During the War, Turing was instrumental in developing and influencing actual computing devices that have been said to have shortened the War by up to two years by decoding encrypted enemy messages that were generally believed to be unbreakable [57]. Unlike some theorists he was willing to be involved with practical aspects and was as happy to wield a soldering iron as he was to wrestle with a mathematical problem, normally from a unique angle.

J. P. Bowen et al. (Eds.): SETSS 2018, LNCS 11430, pp. 202–235, 2019.
https://doi.org/10.1007/978-3-030-17601-3_5

With hindsight, Turing's 1936 seminal paper on computable numbers [154] foretold the capabilities of the modern computer. The War then brought about a radical, but perhaps fortuitous, change of direction in Turing's career, as his unique mathematical abilities were recognized during his time at Cambridge and he was invited to join Bletchley Park, the secret centre of the United Kingdom's efforts, to break German codes [116]. Decryption by hand was too laborious and time-consuming to succeed in the acutely limited time available. Turing recognized that machines, together with great human ingenuity, could tackle the problem far more quickly and reliably.

Despite his success in decryption, Turing was a victim of the times in which he happened to live. Homosexuality was illegal, remaining so in the United Kingdom until 1967. A mere fifteen years after Turing's arrest and prosecution, the atmosphere had become very different. But in the somewhat stifling and rigid Britain of the early 1950s, which was also the period of McCarthyism in America, a maverick and rather naïve person such as Turing was living in a dangerous world, unprotected by any public reputation. First and foremost, the secrecy surrounding his wartime work meant that public knowledge of his national importance was severely limited. Secondly, his ground-breaking 1936 paper would have seemed abstruse and not very relevant in a still largely pre-computer age to most scientists. Lastly, his later work on early artificial intelligence and morphogenesis made little practical impact in his lifetime, even among his closest colleagues.

1.1 Polymath

Alan Turing's interests were wide-ranging. This leads to the question of his field. Was Alan Turing a:

mathematician? He was certainly educated as a mathematician at Cambridge University and many of his papers were highly mathematical.
philosopher? His early ideas culminating in his 1952 paper on Artificial Intelligence (machine intelligence, as he called it) and the concept of the Turing test are admired by many philosophers.
computer scientist? His 1936 paper introducing the Turing machine, a simple generic model for an abstract computing device, is considered foundational for the discipline by many computer scientists. That said, the field was not formally recognized as an academic discipline until the 1960s [27].
codebreaker? His wartime work during World War II (1939–1945) on breaking the German Enigma code using the bombe machine is what he is best known for by many members of the general public.
biologist/chemist? His 1952 paper on morphogenesis has "chemical" in the title and is foundational for mathematical biology, a very active field currently with the concept of Turing patterns [43] in biological organisms and even elsewhere in nature.

The polymathic Turing is claimed by all these fields to a greater or lesser extent. He is known to have influenced people in many different fields, even in digital art

using mathematical techniques inspired by his ideas on morphogenesis [29, 39].
He is known to have been considering quantum effects towards the end of his
life and perhaps physicists would claim him as well had he lived longer.

1.2 Genius

The term 'genius' is difficult to define precisely, but Alan Turing is generally
acknowledged to be one. The 2010 book *Genius of Britain* accompanied a Channel 4 television series in the UK on scientists that changed the world [163] and
Turing appears prominently in a chapter on *The Expediency of War.*

The mathematician Peter Hilton (1923–2010), a colleague of Alan Turing at
Bletchley Park, wrote of Turing [90]:

> ...the experience of sharing the intellectual life of a genius is entirely
> different; one realizes that one is in the presence of an intelligence, a sensi-
> tivity of such profundity and originality that one is filled with wonder and
> excitement.

Andrew Robinson has posited that it normally takes around a decade to become
a genius [136]. In Turing's case, his first work of real genius was his 1936 paper
[154], introducing what has become known as a Turing machine, an abstract
version of a computer, at the age of 24. A decade earlier in the late 1920s, he was
at Sherborne School, where at the age of 15 he handwrote a paper on Albert
Einstein's Theory of Relativity, demonstrating an understanding of Einstein's
ideas [153].

In a Lent Term 1927 Sherborne School report for Turing [145], at the age of
14, he was top of the form in mathematics with the comment:

> Very good. He has considerable powers of reasoning and should do well if
> he can quicken up a little and improve his style.

Under Natural Science, it states "Chemistry. Good." But Turing's housemaster
comments:

> He is frankly not one who fits comfortably for himself into the ordinary
> life of the place – on the whole I think he is tidier.

At the bottom of the one-page report is a summary comment from Nowell Smith,
in his last year as Headmaster of Sherborne:

> He should do very well when he finds his métier: but meantime he would
> do much better if he would try to do his best as a member of this school
> – he should have more esprit de corps.

The following year in Michaelmas Term 1928, his young mathematics teacher,
Donald Eperson, only eight years older than Turing, comments [25]:

He thinks very rapidly & is apt to be "brilliant", but unsound in some of his work. He is seldom defeated by a problem, but his methods are often crude, cumbersome & untidy. But thoroughness & polish will no doubt come in time.

The new Headmaster, Charles L.F. Boughey, comments more optimistically than his predecessor that "This report is full of promise." With hindsight, these comments are particularly apposite and some are farsighted, especially with respect to his powers of reasoning, finding his métier, increasing speed at mathematics, his brilliance, and promise, all indicative of Turing's embryonic genius.

2 Scientific Impact

Turing received an OBE (Officer of the Order of the British Empire) honour from the United Kingdom government for his codebreaking work at Bletchley Park in World War II and was made a Fellow of the Royal Society, the UK's foremost scientific society, in 1951 [125]. However, the real recognition of his contribution came long after his death with the development of computer science [27] and as the truth of his crucial wartime role at Bletchley Park was gradually revealed. It is notable that Turing's three most cited papers by far (by an order of magnitude compared to others, with more than 10,000 citations each in subsequent publications according to Google Scholar [78]) were published in 1936 [154], 1950 [157], and 1952 [159]. Each of these was foundational in the fields of theoretical computer science, artificial intelligence, and mathematical biology respectively. Without Turing's premature death in 1954, soon after two of his three most influential publications, it is highly likely that he would have gone on to produce further inspirational ideas.

A lasting scientific memorial to Turing is the Association for Computing Machinery (ACM) *A.M. Turing Award* [4], presented to one and sometimes up to three leading computer scientists each year since 1966 by the world's foremost computing association [42]. This is the highest scientific honour available to a computer scientist, widely considered as the equivalent to the Nobel Prize in the field. Many of the award winners have worked in areas for which Alan Turing was foundational, such as artificial intelligence and formal methods (the application of mathematics to software engineering).

33 Turing Award winners attended the *ACM A.M. Turing Centenary Celebration* on 15–16 June 2012 in San Francisco, USA, to honour Turing's anniversary [2]. A.M. Turing Award winners are listed chronologically on the ACM website [5] and some who have worked in areas related to Turing's interests are recorded in sections below. Although Turing died before the existence of computer science's highest annual award, it is likely that most computer scientists would agree that he would have been very deserving of it [165].

2.1 Theoretical Computer Science

In theoretical computer science, the idea of a 'Turing machine' [66], a mathematical model of computation in the form of an abstract machine with an infinite memory tape that can be read and written by the machine, has continued to be important in discussing what is and is not computable [83]. In addition, the related 'halting problem' on determining whether or not a given program terminates, building on the concept of the Turing machine, is a fundamental issue of reasoning about programs and a canonical problem in computer science [40,146]. It is a decision problem that has proved to be undecidable in the general case. Certainly Christopher Strachey (1916–1975), who knew Turing since they were both at King's College, Cambridge, and was an expert programmer of both the Pilot ACE and Manchester Mark 1 computers, knew this as part of programming folklore even in the 1950s. He recounted how Turing gave him a verbal proof in a railway carriage in 1953 [128]. Strachey went on to found the Programming Research Group (PRG) at Oxford University, which became leading site for formal methods research.

The halting problem relates to program loops that may or may not continue forever. When proving programs correct, the concepts of partial and total correctness are important. The former only proves the program correct if it terminates whereas the latter also proves that the program does terminate, which requires additional effort for programs that include looping constructs. Hoare logic, devised by C.A.R. Hoare (born 1934, the 1980 A.M. Turing Award winner, who took over at the head of the PRG at Oxford after Christopher Strachey's death), building on the ideas of Robert Floyd (1936–2001, the 1978 A.M. Turing Award winner) [75], provides a mathematical framework using an axiomatic approach that allows reasoning about the correctness of programs [93]. Turing himself published a very early proof of program correctness in 1949 (arguably the first) and this work was rediscovered and appreciated much later after his death [122]. Even computing developments since Turing's death such as quantum computing [18] still rely on the concept of the Turing machine [67]. Turing machines have also influenced philosophy and the general concept of computability [59].

2.2 Artificial Intelligence

As well as theoretical computer science, Alan Turing can be considered a founding father for the field of Artificial Intelligence (AI) with his 1950 paper [157], although he himself used the term 'machine intelligence' and 'AI' was coined two years after Turing's death, in 1956 by John McCarthy of Stanford University (1927–2011, the 1971 A.M. Turing Award winner) [84]. McCarthy emphasised the use of mathematical logic [115], leading to the Lisp functional programming language and the Prolog logic programming language, where programming is brought to the level of mathematical functions and relations, which surely would have been appreciated by Turing.

Marvin Minsky of MIT (1927–2016, the 1969 A.M. Turing Award winner) was also a leading light in the AI community and was influenced by Turing [89]. He discovered a four-symbol seven-state universal Turing machine in 1962. Donald Michie (1923–2007) [147], who himself worked at Bletchley Park contemporaneously with Alan Turing and Max Newman (1897–1984), Turing's mentor at Cambridge in the 1930s [79]). He worked in the 'Testery' (a section named after the founder, Major Ralph Tester) and discussed early ideas of problem solving using searching techniques with Turing at Bletchey Park, in the form of early AI [55]. Michie later established himself as a leading AI researcher at the University of Edinburgh, where the field remains a speciality to this day. He developed an early example of machine learning, based on the game of noughts and crosses (aka Tic-Tac-Toe), in the early 1960s and also founded the Turing Institute in Glasgow, which was active during 1983–94 as an applied AI research laboratory.

During the 1980s, there was a perceived threat from Japan due to significant funding in AI and the 'Fifth Generation' of computing [74]. This helped to prompt the funding of the UK Alvey Programme for Advanced Information Technology that supported collaborative projects between academia and industry. AI continues to be of wide interest, with attempts to perform the Turing test successfully [12] and interest in the idea of 'superintelligence' where machines can outperform humans in their general intelligence [24].

Developments in deep learning, based on machine learning using learning data representations rather than task-specific algorithms (e.g., learning to play games in general rather than just a specific game like chess for example) using approaches such as neural networks are now proving to be increasingly possible in practice [63]. Deep learning is an area that most likely would be of interest to Turing and to which he could have contributed his ideas.

2.3 Mathematical Biology

Turing's 1952 paper on morphogenesis [159] was foundational in the field of mathematical biology; it demonstrated that relatively simple mathematics can generate seemingly complex biological patterns and shapes through chemical reactions. In fact, according to Google Scholar [78], this is Turing's most cited paper, with over 600 citations annually in recent years. The approach has become increasingly important in the understanding of biological processes. It is interesting to note that Turing's original paper cited only two references, whereas nowadays it is normal to include far more citations, including foundational papers, such as those produced by Turing. This was not uncommon for innovative papers in the past; for example, Albert Einstein included no citations in his 1905 paper on relativity.

2.4 General Computer Science

The Hungarian-American mathematician John von Neumann (1903–1957) was another great foundational figure of modern computing. The term 'von Neumann architecture' is used to describe the standard architecture of a computer, as described by him in 1945. This is often compared with a Turing machine, but the two serve very different purposes. A Turing machine is a theoretical model to aid in reasoning about computation, whereas the von Neumann architecture is a more practical description of the configuration of a standard electronic digital computer. Von Neumann knew of and acknowledged Turing's pioneering work. A colleague of von Neumann at Los Alamos, Stan Frankel, noted [134]:

> I know that in or about 1943 or '44 von Neumann was well aware of the fundamental importance of Turing's paper of 1936 ... Von Neumann introduced me to that paper and at his urging I studied it with care. Many people have acclaimed von Neumann as the "father of the computer" (in a modern sense of the term) but I am sure that he would never have made that mistake himself. He might well be called the midwife, perhaps, but he firmly emphasized to me, and to others I am sure, that the fundamental conception is owing to Turing – in so far as not anticipated by Babbage, Lovelace, and others.

So, the main contender to Turing's impact with respect to the foundations of computing acknowledged the leading role of Turing and the scientific debt due to him.

Turing was a mathematician and philosopher at a time when computer science did not exist as a separate discipline [27]. As well as being foundational for a new discipline, Turing has also been highly influential in mathematics and philosophy. Perhaps a leading example is the provocative 1989 book *The Emperor's New Mind* by the Oxford mathematician and philosopher of science Roger Penrose born 1931) [130]. The first two chapters on 'Can a computer have a mind?' and 'Algorithms and Turing machines' are largely based around Turing's 1936 and 1950 papers [154,157]. The book goes on to cover the philosophical 'mind-body problem', attempting to explain how mental states, events, and processes are related to physical manifestations of these. Penrose's subsequent 1994 book *Shadows of the Mind* [131] later argues that human consciousness is not algorithmic and thus cannot be modelled by a Turing machine. He posits that quantum effects may be a critical part of consciousness and that the human mind has qualities that no Turing machine can possess. With Turing's interest in quantum mechanics, he could well have contributed to Penrose's debate.

Subsequent models of computation have all been related to Turing machines in some way. John Conway's 'Game of Life' introduced in 1970 is an example of a two-dimensional space forming a cellular automaton with very simple rules that has the potential to produce complex patterns and undertake computation, with the power of a universal Turing machine. It can even be used to model a Turing machine visually [29,135]. Stephen Wolfram has studied cellular automata extensively, as covered in his 2002 book *A New Kind of Science* [169]. This includes much material on Turing machines in particular, as well as other ideas conceived by Turing.

The two-volume set *The Legacy of Turing* of 1996 covers aspects of artificial intelligence and computer science in Volume I, together with philosophy and cognitive science in Volume II, with an extensive set of contributors [119]. In 2004, some of Turing's most important scientific contributions, with annotations, were compiled and annotated by Jack Copeland in *The Essential Turing* [54]. An archive of Turing-related material by the same editor is also available online [60].

The centenary of Turing's birth in 2012 led to a number of special issues and articles in scientific journals themed around the achievements of Turing. The leading scientific journal in the world, *Nature*, featured Turing on the front cover during 2012 for a special issue entitled *Alan Turing at 100* [123]. One of the foremost professional magazines in computing, the *Communications of the ACM*, also had a special article on Turing in 2012 and featured a slate sculpture by Stephen Kettle of Turing at Bletchley Park [108] on the front cover [50]. The year of 2012 was obviously a highpoint for interest in Turing, scientific and otherwise, but still his importance to computer science, mathematics and philosophy remains undiminished.

2.5 Formal Methods and Program Proving

The application of mathematics to the specification and development of computer-based systems, especially software, but also hardware, has been dubbed 'formal methods' [36] since around the late 1970s. The term has been borrowed from the field of mathematical logic (e.g., see the 1962 book on logic by Evert Willem Beth entitled *Formal Methods* [20]). Beth used the term even earlier in his 1955 book *Semantic Entailment and Formal Derivability* [19].

Much earlier in 1910, Paul Carus wrote in conclusion on the Saxon term 'kenlore', describing the process of cognition, in the context of epistemology [47]:

> From this norm which dominates the world and which is reconstructed in our mind we derive those principles of all our purely *formal methods*, our principles of logic and logical necessity, of universality, of our fundamental conditions for mathematical thought and geometrical constructions, and here accordingly lies the corner stone of kenlore.

The term was also used by Bertrand Russell in the context of logic in 1912 [142].

Alan Turing wrote what can be considered the first 'formal methods' paper in the context of program proving in 1949, in a short (three-page) paper entitled *Checking a Large Routine* for a *Conference on High Speed Automatic Calculating Machines* at Cambridge [156]. This has subsequently been examined in detail in 1984 [122]. Although it contains minor errors in the detail, not atypical for Turing, the overall idea presented was correct. The following are some short extracts from Turing's 1949 paper [156] with some relevant words emphasised;

- "In order to assist the checker, the programmer should make *assertions* about the various states that the machine can reach."
- "The checker has to *verify* that the ... initial condition and the stopped condition agree with the claims that are made for the routine as a whole."
- "He has also to *verify* that each of the assertions ... is correct."
- "Finally the checker has to *verify* that the process comes to an end."

None of these comments would be out of place in a formal methods paper of today, except that the "checker" would most likely now be computer-based software (perhaps with human guidance) rather than a human alone. The paper also states:

The following convention is used:
(i) a dashed letter indicates the value at the end of the process represented by the box;
(ii) an undashed letter represents the initial value of a quantity.

This could be describing an operation schema box in the modern-day Z notation [28]. Further work on Turing's 1949 paper and its impact has been undertaken more recently by Cliff Jones [104–106].

The Dutch mathematician and early computer scientist Aad van Wijngaarden (1916–1987), a pioneer of programming language grammars (after whom the term 'Wijngaarden grammar' was coined for his two-level approach to grammars) was at the 1949 Cambridge meeting where Turing presented his pioneering paper on program proving [156], but it had no great influence on his research at the time [105]. Only by the 1960s is there evidence of influence [104]. Peter Naur (1928–2016, the 2005 ACM A.M. Turing Award winner), best known for BNF notation (Backus-Naur Form) with John Backus (1924–2007) for the formal description of programming language syntax, considered proofs of algorithms in 1966 [124].

Robert W. (Bob) Floyd (1936–2001) and others rediscovered ideas for program proving similar to those of Turing in the 1960s [75]. C.A.R. (Tony) Hoare developed these further with his axiomatic approach based on assertions [93]. Had Turing lived longer, perhaps formal methods (in particular, program proving) would have developed more rapidly, rather than being rediscovered more than a decade later. As with most of Turing's research interests, he was well ahead of his time compared with others because of his novel approach to problems, working from first principles.

Turing's 1949 paper was essentially ignored during the 1950s. However, by the 1960s, Turing's ideas on program proving were being rediscovered independently. Figure 1 shows some key publications in formal methods with respect to proving programs correct from Turing's 1949 paper onwards during the second half of the 20th century [122].

Publications in the 1960s relating to formal methods were mainly foundational research papers. Later key publications were mostly works leading on from these papers in the form of tutorial-style books. In the 1970s, structured programming became prominent, as extolled by Ole-Johan Dahl (1931–2002), Edsger W. Dijkstra (1930–2002), and Tony Hoare [61] (all ACM A.M. Turing Award winners in 2001, 1972, and 1980 respectively). *The Science of Programming* book [81] by David Gries (born 1939) builds on Dijkstra's book *A Discipline of Programming* [68], which concentrates on abstraction, suggesting that a program and its proof of correctness should be developed in tandem. The 1986 book *Systematic Software Development Using VDM* by Cliff Jones (born 1944) provides an approach to refinement from a formal specification towards a program in the context of VDM (Vienna Development Method), an early formal method.

The paper *Laws of Programming* presents some general algebraic laws for imperative programming languages [94]. The work of Carroll Morgan (born 1952)

1949: Alan Turing, *Checking a Large Routine* [156].
1966: Peter Naur, *Proof of Algorithms by General Snapshots* [124].
1967: Robert Floyd, *Assigning Meaning to Programs* [75].
1969: Tony Hoare, *An Axiomatic Basis for Computer Programming* [93].
1972: Ole-Johan Dahl et al., *Structured Programming* [61].
1976: Edsger Dijkstra, *A Discipline of Programming* [68].
1981: David Gries, *The Science of Programming* [81].
1986: Cliff Jones, *Systematic Software Development Using VDM* [103].
1987: Tony Hoare et al., *Laws of Programming* [94].
1990: Carroll Morgan, *Programming from Specifications* [121].
1996: Jean-Raymond Abrial, *The B-Book* [1].
1998: Tony Hoare & He Jifeng, *Unifying Theories of Programming* [95].

Fig. 1. Some key 20th-century publications on program proving.

on *Programming from Specifications* [121] explicitly depends on [68, 75, 93], as stated in the book's preface. Jean-Raymond Abrial (born 1938), progenitor of the Z notation [28], later produced *The B-Book: Assigning Programs to Meanings* [1] on the B-Method to derive a program from a formal specification in a rigorous manner with tool support.

The book on *Unifying Theories of Programming* (UTP) [95] by Hoare and the Chinese computer scientist He Jifeng (born 1943) aims to provide a coherent formal basis for the specification, design, and implementation of programs, using denotational, algebraic, and operational styles of semantics in a unified framework. It has spawned an international research community with its own regular UTP conference that is still active after 20 years of the existence of UTP. The bibliography in the book cites all the previous publications listed in Fig. 1, including the 1949 Turing paper [156].

Turing made significant contributions to mathematics, philosophy, computer science, and even mathematical biology. His multifarious interests extended to what is now known as formal methods, especially with respect to proving programs correct. Developments have continued in proving computer systems at various levels of abstraction [91], yet there are still significant issues, such as scaling to handle large systems.

Despite their benefits, not all have been convinced that formal methods are worthwhile in practice [35]. However, formal methods communities continue [31, 38], especially for application in high-integrity systems where safety or security is important [37]. The state of the art moves on [22] and increasingly complex systems can be tackled using formal methods [92]. Most comprehensive books on software engineering include a section on formal methods [152].

3   Academic Legacy and Heritage

3.1   Family Scientific Heritage

The Turing family itself, apart from Alan Turing, has been undistinguished scientifically, although there is a Turing Baronetcy, created in 1638. The 12th Baronet, Sir John Dermot Turing (born 1961), a solicitor, is a nephew of Alan Turing and has written a 2015 biography about him [161]. However, Alan Turing's mother was Ethel Sara Turing (née Stoney, 1881–1976), who herself wrote a biography of her son, originally published in 1959 and republished for Turing's centenary in 2012 [162]. Her father was Edward Waller Stoney (1844–1931), chief engineer of the Madras Railways in India.

The Anglo-Irish Stoney family included George Johnstone Stoney FRS (1826–1911), an Irish physicist most famous for suggesting the term 'electron' (initially 'electrine') [161], highly apt with respect to Turing's early pioneering work on electronic computers. His brother was Bindon Blood Stoney FRS (1828–1909), an engineer and astronomer. His children included George Gerald Stoney FRS (1863–1942), a mechanical engineer, Edith Anne Stoney (1869–1938), a medical physicist, and Florence Ada Stoney OBE (1870–1932), a radiologist. The Stoney family genes meant that Turing's family heritage included both scientists and engineers, an excellent grounding for Turing's combination of theoretical and practical genius.

3.2   Academic Background

Academically, after studying mathematics at King's College, Cambridge, as an undergraduate, Turing was then supervised by the mathematician and logician Alonzo Church (1903–1995) for his PhD studies at Princeton University in the United States, which he completed in 1938 [155] (see Fig. 2) with less than two years of study [133]. Alan Turing himself only supervised two PhD students, both at the University of Cambridge, according to the Mathematics Genealogy Project [118]. His most famous student was the mathematician and logician Robin Gandy (1919–1995), who subsequently moved to the University of Oxford.

Dana Scott (born 1932, the joint 1976 A.M. Turing Award winner with Michael O. Rabin) was a later PhD student of Alonzo Church at Princeton who was also based at Oxford from 1972 to 1981. He worked with Christopher Strachey (1916–1975), a former colleague of Turing at the University of Manchester, on the denotational semantics of programming languages, which became dubbed the Scott-Strachey approach [148]. One of Dana Scott's students at Oxford was the philosopher Jack Copeland (born 1950), subsequently a leading Turing scholar [54,56,58–60], based at the University of Canterbury in New Zealand. He was also a colleague of Robin Gandy at Oxford as indicated by the additional horizontal arrow link in Fig. 2.

As well as Robin Gandy, Turing co-supervised Beatrice Worsley (1921–1972) at Cambridge, with the mathematician and physicist Douglas Hartree (1897–1958) in the EDSAC group of Maurice Wilkes (1913–2010, the 1967 ACM A.M.

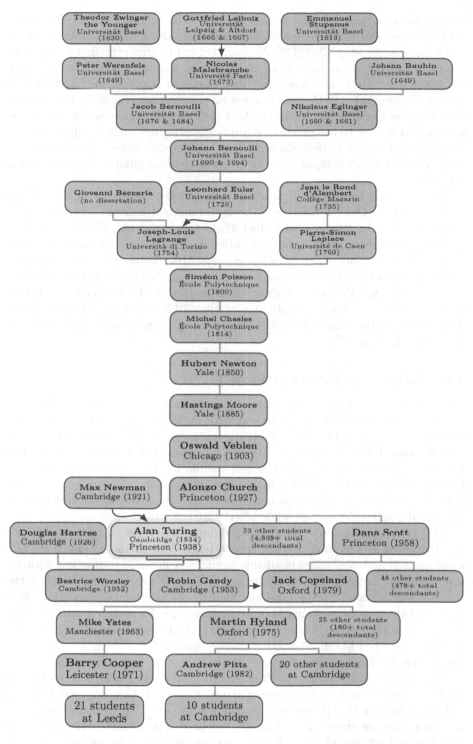

Fig. 2. Academic supervisor tree for Alan Turing [118].

Turing Award winner). This was arguably the first computer science doctorate, entitled *Serial Programming for Real and Idealised Digital Calculating Machines* and submitted in May 1952 [170]. Worsley helped to write the first program to run on the EDSAC computer at Cambridge. She was subsequently a very early computer science academic based in Canada before her premature death in 1972 at only 50 years old [44]. Douglas Hartree was himself supervised by the eminent New Zealand physicist Ernest Rutherford (1871–1937, discoverer of the proton and known as the father of nuclear physics), who in turn was supervised by Joseph Thomson (1856–1940, discoverer of the electron), both at Cambridge and both Nobel prize winners, so Beatrice Worseley had an outstanding supervision pedigree.

Robin Gandy supervised 27 students, three at the University of Manchester and the rest at Oxford. Of these, the mathematical logician and theoretical computer scientist Martin Hyland had 21 doctoral students, all at Cambridge, including the theoretical computer scientist Andrew Pitts, also based at Cambridge. Another student, at Manchester, was Mike Yates, who himself supervised the mathematician and computability theorist Barry Cooper (1943–2015) at Leicester, later Professor of Pure Mathematics at the University of Leeds. Barry Cooper was a major instigator of the 2012 centenary celebrations for Alan Turing in the United Kingdom, including at Manchester [51], resulting in a later publication [52].

3.3   Mathematics Genealogy Project

The ancestry for Alan Turing's line of supervisors can be traced back on the Mathematics Genealogy Project website [118]. Turing's supervisor Alonzo Church was supervised by the mathematician, geometer, and topologist, Oswald Veblen (1880–1960), at Chicago. It has been claimed that Veblen, rather than Church or Turing for example, was responsible for the start of computing at Princeton University [71]. Veblen taught mathematics at Princeton between 1905 and 1932. He was one of the two original faculty members in the Institute for Advanced Study (IAS), along with Albert Einstein (1879–1955).

In 1930, Veblen invited John von Neumann (1903–1957), then aged 27, to join Princeton as a lecturer in quantum statistics. Von Neumann joined the IAS itself in 1933 and was of course highly influential in early computing with his von Neumann architecture for a computer, a more practical model than the theoretically oriented Turing machine. Sharing an interest in topology, Veblen was also helpful in encouraging Max Newman to visit Princeton as early as 1928 [166]. This in turn led to Newman encouraging Turing, while both at Cambridge, to study for his PhD at Princeton under Church. So, Veblen was indirectly responsible for Turing's presence at Princeton, as well as von Neumann.

Newman spent six months at Princeton in 1937 when Turing was working on his PhD there. However, later during World War II, Veblen opposed Newman visiting Princeton due to wartime considerations [126]. This was fortuitous for Britain's wartime effort since although Newman was initially reticent, due to his German background on his father's side (despite being of Jewish origin), he joined Bletchley Park in 1942, where Turing was already based. There he led the 'Newmanry', which worked on breaking the German Lorenz cipher, for which the Colossus computers were developed [53].

3.4 Historic Academic Lineage

Turing's academic pedigree can be traced back more historically, as covered in this subsection for the interested reader.

Veblen was supervised by the mathematician Eliakim 'Hastings' Moore (1862–1932) at the University of Chicago. Moore was supervised by the astronomer and mathematician Hubert Anson Newton (1830–1896), at Yale University. Newton, also at Yale, studied under the French mathematician Michel Floréal Chasles (1793–1880).

Then the line moves from the United States to France with Michel Chasles who studied under the mathematician, engineer, and physicist, Siméon Denis Poisson (1781–1840) at the École Polytechnique in Paris. Poisson is known for Poisson's equation, a partial differential equation that is useful in mechanical engineering and theoretical physics, and the Poisson distribution in probability theory and statistics, among other contributions to mathematics. Poisson studied under the Italian-Frenchman Joseph-Louis Lagrange (1736–1813) and Pierre-Simon Laplace (1749–1827) at the École Polytechnique, both very eminent mathematicians, and both also with an interest in astronomy. Lagrange is known for the reformulation of classical (Newtonian) mechanics, Lagrangian mechanics, using Lagrange equations, among other mathematical contributions. Laplace is especially known for the Laplace transform, used in the transformation of integrals.

Laplace's adviser was Jean-Baptiste le Rond d'Alembert (1717–1783), the polymathic French mathematician, mechanician, philosopher, music theorist, and physicist. According to the Mathematics Genealogy Project, d'Alembert's adviser is unknown so the lineage cannot be traced back further. Lagrange's advisor was the Italian physicist Giovanni Battista (Giambattista) Beccaria (1716–1781) in Turin. Beccaria's adviser is unknown, and no dissertation is known. However, Laplace also worked with and was highly influenced by the Swiss astronomer, engineer, logician, mathematician, and physicist, Leonhard Euler (1707–1783), largely through correspondence by letter. Laplace wrote: "Read Euler, read Euler, he is the master of us all" [69].

Euler undertook his doctorate with the Swiss mathematician Johann Bernoulli (1667–1748) as his advisor at Basel. Johann Bernoulli undertook two dissertations, one under Jacob Bernoulli (1655–1705) and another under Nikolaus Eglinger (1645–1711), both at Basel. Jacob Bernoulli studied under the Swiss theologian Peter Werenfels (1627–1703) and the French priest and rationalist philosopher Nicolas Malebranche (1638–1715) for two dissertations, both at Basel. Peter Werenfels studied under the preacher and theology professor, Theorode Zwinger the Younger (1597–1654) at Basel. Nicolas Malebranche met the renowned German polymath, mathematician and philosopher, Gottfried Wilhelm Leibniz (1646–1716) in Paris and they corresponded after this. They discussed the laws of motion extensively. Leibniz conceived differential and integral calculus, independently of Isaac Newton (1642–1726/27). Leibniz's notation for calculus has become the accepted notation by mathematicians.

Nikolaus Eglinger studied under the Swiss physician Emmanuel Stupanus (1587–1664, aka Stuppan) and the Swiss botanist and physician Johann Bauhin (1541–1613) for two dissertations, both at Basel. Bauhin himself also studied under Stupenus at Basel.

Thus, Turing's academic lineage goes back to Euler and Leibniz, two of the most renowned mathematicians in history, and beyond, as well as Lagrange, Laplace, and two members of the Bernoulli family. Turing's supervisor lineage, both historically and for those after him, is illustrated in Fig. 2.

3.5 Turing's Mentor

Although not officially his supervisor, Max Newman was a great mentor for Turing [79], both early on at Cambridge and later at Manchester, as well as at Bletchley Park during World War II. Newman's 1935 lectures on the foundations and mathematics at Cambridge inspired Turing to write his 1936 paper introducing the concept of Turing machines [154], which Newman recognized as a novel and important piece of work. Without Newman, it could well have not been published and Turing's genius might not have been recognized so quickly. Newman himself never studied for a doctorate.

Newman was a 'Wrangler' (gaining a first-class undergraduate degree in mathematics) at St John's College, Cambridge, in 1921. He wrote a thesis on using 'symbolic machines' to make physical predictions, a precursor to his interest in computing later in his career [126]. Newman spent 1922–3 at the University of Vienna [79], but returned to Cambridge in 1923 with a Fellowship at St John's College. He became a lecturer in mathematics for Cambridge University in 1927 and his 1935 lectures were attended by the young Turing. Later it was Newman who encouraged Turing to join Manchester University after World War II, working on early computers there.

4   Turing Eponyms

Alan Turing's name is associated with a number of different concepts and ideas related to his work. Many of these are notable enough to have their own individual entries on Wikipedia [167].

'Turing machine' and 'Turing test' are well-known Turing terms resulting from the ideas in Turing's 1936 and 1950 papers [154,157], with many specialized versions of both [167]. Increasingly in use is the term 'Turing pattern', often used in the plural, to describe the complex patterns generated by mathematics based on that presented in his 1952 paper on morphogenesis [159] (e.g., see [43]).

The previously mentioned 'Turing Institute' (1983–94) was an AI laboratory in Glasgow, Scotland, established by Donald Michie, a wartime colleague

of Turing. The newer and unrelated 'Alan Turing Institute' is a national governmental data sciences institute in the United Kingdom, founded in 2015, located
in London, and overseen by a group of leading UK universities.

There are a number of roads, streets, and buildings named after Turing in
the UK and elsewhere, especially in locations associated with him. Examples
include Alan Turing Buildings in Guildford and Manchester, Alan Turing Roads
in Guildford and Loughborough, and Alan Turing Way in Manchester. There
are a Turing Drive in Bracknell, Turing Gate near Bletchley Park, and Turing
Roads in Biggleswade and Teddington, west London, the latter very near the
National Physical Laboratory where Turing worked after World War II.

The BCS (British Computer Society), the professional IT association in the
UK, holds an annual Turing Lecture jointly with the IET (Institution of Engineering and Technology). Finally, and most internationally, as mentioned earlier
in this paper, Turing is honoured by the annual 'ACM A.M. Turing Award', the
world's highest award in computer science, and a fitting tribute to Turing for
providing the foundations of the discipline.

More recently, a 2017 law in England and Wales that pardons gay people
for what were historically offences has been dubbed the 'Alan Turing law', also
just 'Turing law' or 'Turing's law' [14,120]. This will be discussed in more detail
later in the paper. Further Turing terms are presented in [30] and many more
eponyms can be found on Wikipedia citewik18 for the interested reader.

5   Historical Impact

Turing is considered an important figure in the overall history of science. For
example, the 1991 book *A History of Knowledge* attempts to cover the entire
range of human invention and creativity, and yet devotes a section to Alan Turing
and Turing machines even in such an all-encompassing book [164]. *The Oxford
Companion to the History of Modern Science* (2003) naturally includes an entry
for 'Computer Science' [27], but also a separate entry for 'Artificial Intelligence',
and both cover Turing's foundational role [85]. In addition, there is a specific
entry for Turing himself, which notes presciently that "Turing's status as a cult
hero will undoubtedly increase".

Any book covering the history of computing would be incomplete without an
explanation of Turing's role in it. The 1979 book *The Mighty Micro* on the impact
of the computer revolution by the British computer scientist and psychologist
Christopher Evans (1931–1979) has many entries in the index for Alan Turing
and the Turing test but interestingly not specifically for the Turing machine
[73]. There is a concentration on whether machines can think, with Evans' psy-
chological background, including reference to Turing's 1950 paper on machine
intelligence [157]. Simon Lavington's 1980 book on *Early British Computers* naturally has multiple entries on Turing. It includes a chapter on the development
of Turing's ACE computer and a photograph of the eventually constructed Pilot
ACE on the back cover [110].

The detailed biography *Alan Turing: The Enigma* by Andrew Hodges dating
from 1983 and reissued in 2012 for Turing's centenary has played a significant

part in increasing Turing's visibility over the years since it originally appeared, when the secrecy surrounding the wartime Bletchley Park had only relatively recently started to be lifted in the 1970s [96]. It remains the definitive account of Turing's life, from both professional and personal viewpoints, with which other biographies of Turing have difficulty in competing [149]. Hodges also produced an early website on Turing associated with his book in the early 1990s [98], linked with the online *Virtual Museum of Computing*, and still in existence today [32].

Figure 3 shows a graph of mentions of Alan Turing in books digitized on Google Books, using the online Ngram Viewer facility, which has a database of phrases mentioned in books by year (apart from the most recent decade). Since the late 1970s, after the significance of Bletchley Park began to be revealed, there has been a steady rise in mentions of Alan Turing in books over the years. There was a very significant peak in 1983, the original year of publication of Andrew Hodges biography of Turing [96]. It will be interesting to see the peak that is likely around the 2012 centenary of Turing when this is available.

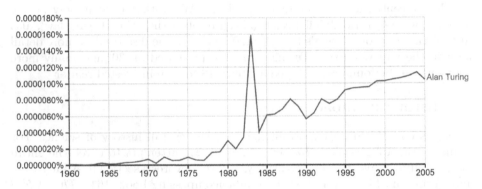

Fig. 3. Graph of mentions of 'Alan Turing' in books (1960–2005). (Ngram Viewer, Google Books: http://books.google.com/ngrams.)

The practically oriented and wide-ranging book *Bit by Bit* on the history of computers by the American author Stan Augarten in 1984 has a significant section on Alan Turing and Turing machines [8]. *The Silicon Idol*, also published in 1984, covered the microprocessor revolution and its social impact [143]. Despite its relatively modern focus on the recent period before its publication, Alan Turing features a number of times in sections on thinking machines and the origins of computing.

The 1991 book *The Dream Machine* was associated with a BBC television series in the United Kingdom covering the computer age, including multiple references to Alan Turing [129]. In 1997, *Darwin Among the Machines* covered the emergence of thinking machines, in which Turing played a key early part [70]. All of Turing's most significant achievements are included in the book. *The Code Book* by Simon Singh in 1999 surveyed the history of secret messages from the days of Ancient Egypt to the use of quantum cryptography [144]. Turing is mentioned extensively along the way, mainly with respect to the breaking of the Enigma code using the Bombe machines.

In 1999, *Time* magazine published *The Great Minds of the Century* (Time 100) [151], covering the 20th century, including Alan Turing among its selection, labelled as a 'computer scientist' [80]. The mathematician Kurt Gödel, whose ideas influenced Turing (introduced to him through Max Newman's lectures in Cambridge), and the philosopher Ludwig Wittgenstein, whose lectures Turing attended at Cambridge, were also listed, together with John von Neumann, who acknowledged and appreciated Turing's contribution to computing ideas. The only more recent computer scientist (trained as a physicist) to be included was Tim Berners-Lee (born 1955), inventor of the World Wide Web.

Turing's impact is also felt in all the institutions for which he worked. The National Physical Laboratory (NPL), where the Pilot ACE computer was produced based on Turing's ACE designs, continued pioneering work, most notably with computer communications and the development of packet-switching in the 1960s, led by Donald W. Davies (1924–2000), a colleague of Turing [171]. King's College, Cambridge, where Turing studied as a student and was later a Fellow, holds an extensive archive of Turing-related material, some of which is available online in the *Turing Digital Archive* [109]. The 2007 Alan Turing Building at the University of Manchester houses the School of Mathematics there.

Some accounts of Turing and his contemporaries, with regard to building early computers, appeared for the 2012 centenary of Turing's birth in a collection of contributions edited by the British historian of computing Simon Lavington [111]. The collection includes a section covering the legacy of Turing in the context of early British computers [112].

The 2012 *Alan Turing Year* [51], led by the mathematician and computability theorist Barry Cooper (1943–2015), with the help of others, coordinated a significant number of celebratory events, especially at institutions associated with Turing and during the month of June. Many of the authors in the volume were associated with three of these meetings on successive weekends in June 2012: *ACE 2012 (Alan Turing's 100th Birthday Party)* was held at King's College, Cambridge, Turing's college; *Turing's Worlds* took place at Rewley House, Oxford, in association with the British Society for the History of Mathematics (BSHM); and the *Turing Educational Day* (TED) was held at Bletchley Park. A major event at the University of Manchester with over 70 leading experts led to an associated book, *Alan Turing: His Work and Impact*, providing in-depth coverage of Turing's scientific influence [52].

More recent accounts of the history of computers [45] and computer science [62] continue to devote significant space to Turing's ideas. Even though computer science can be considered to have started with Charles Babbage, there was a significant reawakening of ideas in modern computing through the work of Turing that continues to be important today, especially at the theoretical level.

The London Science Museum has the original Pilot ACE computer, developed at the National Physical Laboratory (NPL) from Turing's more ambitious ACE design, on permanent display in the Information Age gallery [21]. This gallery

Fig. 4. An exhibit on Alan Turing and Claude Shannon, in the Information Age gallery [21] at the Science Museum, London. (Photograph by Jonathan Bowen).

includes a showcase (see Fig. 4) featuring both Alan Turing and Claude Shannon (1916–2001), considered by many to be the "father of information theory". The showcase includes the following apt quotation:

> "The idea behind digital computers may be explained by saying that these machines are intended to carry out any operations which could be done by a human computer." – Alan Turing (see Fig. 4)

Turing and Shannon met during World War II at Bell Labs in New York [77] and discussed ideas such as machine intelligence. Turing also features in the recently updated mathematics gallery at the museum, especially with respect to his work on breaking the German Enigma code at Bletchley Park during World War II [141]. Turing himself visited the Science Museum in 1951 and was fascinated by an electromechanical cybernetic 'tortoise' (a small autonomous robot) on display that could detect and respond to its surroundings [88, 102].

During 2012–13 for the Turing centenary celebrations, a special exhibition, *Codebreaker – Alan Turing's Life and Legacy* [140], was held at the Science Museum, featuring the Pilot ACE, Enigma machines, and other Turing-related items, including the 'tortoise' that he viewed in 1951 [87]. The Pilot ACE was used in calculations concerning the fatal flaw in the rectangular windows of the early Comet passenger jet aircraft of the 1950s. The exhibition covered such historical impact and overall was a fitting celebration of Turing's life and achievements.

Fig. 5. Slate sculpture of Alan Turing with an Enigma machine at Bletchley Park, by Stephen Kettle [29,108]. (Photograph by Jonathan Bowen).

6 Popular and Cultural Impact

Turing's life, cut short as it was at the age of 41, has attracted works from the arts, including the 1986 play *Breaking the Code* by Hugh Whitemore, the 1995 novel *Enigma* by Robert Harris, *A Man from the Future* in 2014 by the Pet Shop Boys, and scultures in Manchester and at Bletchley Park (see Fig. 5), to name but a few examples [30].

Alan Turing's life was dramatized in the 2014 film *The Imitation Game*, especially with respect to his codebreaking work during World War II [99]. Since then, the 2015 biographical film *Steve Jobs* directed by Danny Boyle featured Turing in background pictures [49]. The bitten apple used by Steve Jobs as his Apple company logo has been linked with Turing, even if erroneously [76,100]. The film alludes to this in a passage in which Steve Jobs admits that it is not so, but wishes that it were true [138].

6.1 Memorabilia

Items associated with Alan Turing have become increasingly valuable, especially his papers and notes. Google helped Bletchley Park acquire preprints of papers by Turing owned by Max Newman, some annotated by Turing, for a significant sum in 2011 and these are now on display there [117]. In 2015, a 56-page notebook by Alan Turing, subsequently owned by his student and close friend Robin

Gandy, sold at auction in New York for more than a million dollars [86]. This is the only known extensive handwritten manuscript by Turing, which he authored at Bletchley Park in 1942.

In May 2017, a filing cabinet at the University of Manchester was found to contain around 150 documents relating to Turing, dating from 1949 until his death in 1954 [15]. They provide some insight into his personal views as well as his professional life at Manchester. One briefly documents a debate on whether machines can think, opened by Max Newman following by Turing, with Richard Braithwaite and Douglas Hartree also contributing [114]. R.B. Braithwaite (1900–1990), a Fellow at King's College, Cambridge, was a philosopher with an interest in science and religion.

A similar debate was recorded by the BBC on 10 January 1952 for broadcast twice on the radio later that month [160]. This was opened and led by Braithwaite. Instead of Hartree, Sir Geoffrey Jefferson (1886–1961), a neurologist and pioneering neurosurgeon based at the University of Manchester, contributed to this discussion. Although the original recording has been lost, a transcript has survived [160]. Turing's ideas on whether machines can think raised much debate in the early 1950s, although not all were convinced. For example, see an article by Maurice Wilkes [168], who was not completely enamoured of Turing and his ideas.

Turing also delivered a 1951 BBC radio broadcast on thinking machines, in a series with other scientists [101,102], entitled *Can Digital Computers Think?*. Turing's original typewritten transcript still exists [158]. The broadcast was heard by Christopher Strachey, who was prompted to write to Turing on the subject [7]. Despite the fact that Turing was broadcast on the radio, it is unfortunate that there is no known audio or film recording of him, or even a colour photograph, in existence.

In November 2017, a handwritten and autographed two-page letter by Alan Turing was sold for UK £75,000 at Bonhams in London [23]. The letter was written by Turing from his home in Wilmslow around 1950 (although the letter is undated) to his former mathematics teacher at Sherborne School, Donald Eperson (1904–2001) [127], who had by then become vicar at the church in the village of Charminster, Dorset, in southern England not far from Sherborne. They shared an interest in the puzzles and logic of Charles Lutwidge Dodgson (1832–1898), aka Lewis Carroll, author of the 'Alice in Wonderland' books. Eperson studied mathematics as an undergraduate at Christ Church, Oxford, the same college were Dodgson studied and had also been a Fellow.

Turing is known to have read Lewis Carroll's 1886 book *The Game of Logic* [46] at school. Eperson wrote a book in 1948 on Lewis Carroll puzzles [72] and Turing was writing for two copies of a new edition, enclosing a cheque for 7 shillings (35 UK pence). In the letter, Turing states that he has joined Manchester University and is working on "the use of electronic computers". He mentions that there is the possibility of exhibiting a computer at the Festival of Britain (held in London during 1951). He opines [23]:

It is most entertaining work: one can make these machines do almost anything one wants, at any rate anything which one could explain rules for working out.

He goes on to mention a recent visit with his PhD student Robin Gandy to Cerne in Dorset, not far from Eperson, regretting that he did not know that Eperson was in Dorset at the time. Gandy's parents lived in Dorset, a likely reason for the visit. Overall, the letter gives the impression that Turing is enjoying his new life based at Manchester University.

In summary, Turing's memory has entered the cultural consciousness of the British public and the wider public around the world through the many faceted aspects of his life and work, bringing together a number of communities in a united respect for him. Artefacts such as manuscripts associated with Turing are increasingly valuable as a result, but are very limited in number. Although interest may have peaked especially for his 2012 centenary, it is likely to continue to increase over time.

7   Political Impact

The British wartime leader Winston Churchill (1874–1965) recognized the role of Alan Turing and others at Bletchley Park in winning World War II as the "the geese who laid the golden eggs and never cackled" [113]. However, the secrecy around Bletchley Park meant that Turing only received an OBE award, whereas in other circumstances a knighthood could have been expected. Turing's subsequent arrest for "gross indecency" in 1952 only lowered his esteem in political eyes after the War. It was not until much later after the decriminalisation of homosexuality in 1967 and the lifting of secrecy around Bletchley Park in the 1970s that it became possible for Turing to be truly politically acceptable and appreciated.

By 1998, at the unveiling of the blue plaque marking the birthplace of Turing in Maida Vale, west London (see Fig. 6), during an oration by Turing's biographer Andrew Hodges, Chris Smith, one of the first openly gay UK Members of Parliament, was able to send the following message [97]:

Alan Turing did more for his country and for the future of science than almost anyone. He was dishonourably persecuted during his life; today let us wipe that national shame clean by honouring him properly.

In a wider context, the 2006 book rebutting religion, *The God Delusion*, by the Oxford biologist and declared atheist Richard Dawkins includes mention of Turing in the context of his homosexuality and persecution due to religious legacy [64]. Dawkins notes:

As the pivotal intellect in the breaking of the German Enigma codes, Turing arguably made a greater contribution to defeating the Nazis than Eisenhower or Churchill. ... he should have been knighted and feted as a saviour of his nation. Instead this gentle, stammering, eccentric genius was destroyed, for a 'crime', committed in private, which harmed nobody.

Fig. 6. The mathematician and Turing biographer, Andrew Hodges, unveiling the English Heritage blue plaque at Turing's birthplace, now the Colonnade Hotel, London, on 23 June 1998, exactly 86 years after Turing's birth. (Photograph by Jonathan Bowen).

The UK computer scientist John Graham-Cumming led a campaign for a governmental apology for Turing's treatment at the hands of British justice. The campaign received the backing of a wide range of people, including the scientist Richard Dawkins, the writer Ian McEwan, and the gay rights campaigner Peter Tatchell. In 2009, after a petition on the prime ministerial website, Gordon Brown, then Prime Minister of the UK, delivered an official apology from the British Government for the treatment of Alan Turing in his final years [9]. Brown wrote in *The Daily Telegraph* UK newspaper [41]:

> While Turing was dealt with under the law of the time and we can't put the clock back, his treatment was of course utterly unfair and I am pleased to have the chance to say how deeply sorry I and we all are for what happened to him. ... This recognition of Alan's status as one of Britain's most famous victims of homophobia is another step towards equality, and long overdue.

In 2011, an e-petition on a UK government website requested an official pardon. The request was rejected in 2012, Turing's centenary year, by Lord McNally, the Justice Secretary, who stated that Turing was "properly convicted" [10]. However, on 24 December 2013, after much campaigning, Queen Elizabeth

II issued an official posthumous royal pardon for Alan Turing, in recognition for his wartime contributions [150]:

> NOW KNOW YE that we, in consideration of circumstances humbly repre-
> sented to us, are graciously pleased to grant our grace and mercy unto the
> said Alan Mathison Turing and grant him our free pardon posthumously
> in respect of the said convictions; AND to pardon and remit unto him the
> sentence imposed upon him as aforesaid; AND for so doing this shall be a
> sufficient Warrant.

It was granted under the Royal Prerogative of Mercy, on request from the UK Justice Minister at the time, Chris Grayling, who stated [11]:

> Turing deserves to be remembered and recognised for his fantastic con-
> tribution to the war effort and his legacy to science. A pardon from the
> Queen is a fitting tribute to an exceptional man.

A general pardon for convicted homosexuals in the UK was delayed, no doubt due to the fear of compensation costs. However, in 2016, new law in England and Wales, through amendment of the *Policing and Crime Act*, was initiated, widely called the 'Alan Turing law' [13]. This received Royal Assent for approval as law on 31 January 2017 [14]. The new Justice Minister stated [120]:

> This is a truly momentous day. We can never undo the hurt caused, but we
> have apologised and taken action to right these wrongs. I am immensely
> proud that 'Turing's Law' has become a reality under this government.

Similar changes in Scottish law were announced later in 2017 [6]. It is to be hoped for the future that this could have a wider impact to laws in other countries around the world.

8   Conclusion

Andrew Hodges' 1983 biography of Turing was updated with a new edition for the 2012 centenary [96] and has inspired a number of works, including a play, film, and music [30]. A more recent edited book in 2017, *The Turing Guide*, provides an accessible and comprehensive guide to Turing's work [58]. This book has been of interest for a number of fields including computer science [107], philosophy [132], physics [48], and even digital humanities [82]. Whereas the Hodges book is a single-author biography that covers Turing's work, [58] is an edited volume with 33 contributing authors covering the many aspects of Turing's work and research interests, complementing the biographical work [139].

Sadly, Turing lived too early for the change in the UK law to decriminalize homosexuality in 1967, but as Sir Dermot Turing, Alan Turing's nephew, notes in the conclusion of his own 2015 book on Turing [161]:

Alan Turing's life was not, except perhaps towards the end, governed by his sexuality. The dominant passion in his life was his ideas; it is those for which he should be remembered.

So, on a brighter note, Turing was selected as one of 43 top scientists of all time in the 2012 book *The Scientists* edited by Andrew Robinson [137], fortuitously published during the year of Turing's centenary. John von Neumann was also selected, but with an entry of half the length of that of Turing. Naturally the celebrated theoretical physicist Albert Einstein, who died in 1955, a year after Turing but following a much longer life, was also included in the book. It is interesting to speculate on the relative stature of Einstein and Turing, who overlapped in Princeton during the late 1930s and may have even met there, for example through Max Newman. Of course, Einstein has had a head start and is probably the most well-known scientist in the world, but as this paper has illustrated, Turing has been rapidly rising in the public's consciousness not only in the UK but worldwide. Alan Turing's place in the historical pantheon of scientists is now assured.

In the field of formal methods, although there is apparently no direct link from Turing's early interest in program proving, with hindsight it can be seen that Turing's ideas are highly relevant to this domain. Had Turing lived longer as the interests of other researchers caught up with those of Turing in the 1960s, it is quite possible that he could have been involved in the early formation of the formal methods community [31, 38].

In 2019, the BBC held a public vote for the greatest person of the 20th century under a BBC Two programme series named *ICONS* [16]. This included seven categories presented week by week, namely leaders, explorers, scientists, entertainers, activists, sports, and artists/writers. As well as Turing, the shortlisted scientists for selection were the Polish physicist and chemist Marie Curie (1867–1934), Albert Einstein, and the Chinese pharmaceutical chemist and 2015 Nobel Laureate Tu Youyou (屠呦呦, born 1930), known for a breakthrough in the treatment of malaria. Turing won the scientist category and went on to the final, against the finalists in the other categories, namely Muhammad Ali, David Bowie, Martin Luther King Jr, Nelson Mandela, Pablo Picasso, and Ernest Shackleton. The naturalist and broadcaster Chris Packham gave an impassioned and rousing speech supporting Alan Turing in the live final on 6 February 2019, which Turing duly won. Packham has Asperger's syndrome, so is able to empathise with Turing on both a scientific and personal level. He said that Turing was "a genius, a savour, but he was also autistic and gay" [17]. He continued:

The scientists are the only ones that are going to save us and they are armed with Alan Turing's legacy. [applause] I've got an idea. Get your phones out of your pocket, and turn them on, and hold them up, just so that they can sparkle. In each of your hands, you hold a little bit of Alan Turing. He's with us when we wake up, he's with us when we go to bed at night, and he's with us when we talk to our loved ones. He's

Fig. 7. Posters displayed during the SETSS 2018 Spring School at Southwest University, Chongqing, including a young Turing, publicizing the ACM TURC 2018 Turing Celebration Conference in Shanghai, China, 19–20 May 2018 [3]. (Photograph by Jonathan Bowen).

beautiful, isn't he, glistening in our darkest hour. You see, Alan Turing's legacy hasn't passed, he's not a relic of the 20th century, his gift to us is our future. Thank you.

9   Postscript

In 1994, a formal methods meeting, the Z User Meeting, was held in Cambridge [34], 45 years to the week after the 1949 Cambridge meeting organized by Maurice Wilkes at which Turing presented his pioneering program proving paper [156]. The 1949 meeting was mentioned in the opening remarks of the 1994 Z User Meeting (ZUM) proceedings [26] and Wilkes, who led the Computer Laboratory in Cambridge until 1980, gave the after-dinner speech for the ZUM'94 conference. It could have been even more appropriate if Alan Turing, who would have been 82 years old in 1994 had he lived (almost exactly a year older than Wilkes), could have delivered the speech. Sadly of course he died aged 41, half the age that he would have been in 1994. We can only imagine, if he had lived a further 41 years, how he could have contributed to the development of formal methods in particular and computer science in general – and most likely beyond, as we have seen in this paper that he did in any case, scientifically, culturally, and politically.

Acknowledgments. Parts of this paper are based on an earlier version of a book chapter [33]. Thank you especially to Troy Astarte, and also to Andrew Robinson and Tula Giannini, for comments on earlier drafts. The author is grateful to Southwest University and Museophile Limited for financial support in attending the SETSS 2018 Spring School (see Fig. 7).

References

1. Abrial, J.-R.: The B-Book: Assigning Programs to Meanings. Cambridge University Press, Cambridge (1996)
2. ACM: ACM A.M. Turing centenary celebration. Association for Computing Machinery (2012). http://turing100.acm.org
3. ACM: ACM Turing Celebration Conference – China (ACM TURC 2018, ACM 中国图灵大会). Association for Computing Machinery (2018). http://china.acm. org/TURC/2018/
4. ACM: A.M. Turing Award. Association for Computing Machinery. http:// amturing.acm.org
5. ACM: Chronological listing of A.M. Turing Award winners by year. Association for Computing Machinery. http://amturing.acm.org/byyear.cfm
6. Adams, L: Gay men to receive 'Turing Law' pardons. BBC News, BBC Scotland, 31 August 2017. http://www.bbc.com/news/uk-scotland-41108768
7. Alton, J., Weiskittel, H., Latham-Jackson, J.: Catalogue of the papers and correspondence of Christopher Strachey, 1930–1983. Department of Special Collections, Bodleian Library, University of Oxford, UK (2016). http://www.bodley.ox.ac.uk/ dept/scwmss/wmss/online/modern/strachey-c/strachey-c.html
8. Augarten, S.: Bit by Bit: An Illustrated History of Computers, pp. 142–148. Ticknor & Fields (1984)
9. BBC: PM apology after Turing petition, BBC News, 11 September 2009. http:// news.bbc.co.uk/1/hi/technology/8249792.stm
10. BBC: Government rejects pardon request for Alan Turing. BBC News, 8 March 2012. http://www.bbc.co.uk/news/technology-16919012
11. BBC: Royal pardon for codebreaker Alan Turing. BBC News, 24 December 2013. http://www.bbc.co.uk/news/technology-25495315
12. BBC: Computer AI passes Turing test in 'world first'. BBC News, 9 June 2014. http://www.bbc.co.uk/news/technology-27762088
13. BBC: 'Alan Turing law': Thousands of gay men to be pardoned. BBC News, 20 October 2016. http://www.bbc.co.uk/news/uk-37711518
14. BBC: Thousands of gay men pardoned for past convictions. BBC News, 31 January 2017. http://www.bbc.co.uk/news/uk-38814338
15. BBC: Turing letters found in old filing cabinet. BBC News, 19 August 2017. http://www.bbc.co.uk/news/technology-41082391
16. BBC: ICONS. BBC Two (2019). http://www.bbc.co.uk/programmes/b0by86tp
17. BBC: Chris Packham on Alan Turing. ICONS, BBC Two, 6 February 2019. http://www.bbc.co.uk/programmes/p0704h04
18. Berma, P., Doolen, G.D., Mainieri, R., Tsifrinovich, V.I.: Turing machines. In: Introduction to Quantum Computers, chap. 2, pp. 8–12. World Scientific (1998)
19. Beth, E.W.: Semantic Entailment and Formal Derivability. Noord-Hollandsche (1955)
20. Beth, E.W.: Formal Methods. Gordon & Breach, New York (1962)

21. Blyth, T. (ed.): Information Age: Six Networks that Changed the World. Scala Arts & Heritage Publishers (2014)
22. Boca, P.P., Bowen, J.P., Siddiqi, J.I.: Formal Methods: State of the Art and New Directions. Springer, London (2010). https://doi.org/10.1007/978-1-84882-736-3
23. Bonhams: Lot 103 - Turing (Alan). Fine Books, Atlases, Manuscripts and Photographs. Bonhams, London, 15 November 2017
24. Bostrom, N.: Superintelligence: Paths, Dangers, Strategies. Oxford University Press, Oxford (2014)
25. Boughey, C.L.F., et al.: Upper School, Form V a (Group III), Name Turing, Age 16. School report. Sherborne School, UK (Michaelmas Term (1928)
26. Bowen, J.P.: Introductory and opening remarks. In: Bowen, J.P., Hall, J.A. (eds.) [34], pp. v–vii (1994)
27. Bowen, J.P.: Computer science. In: Heilbron, J.L. (ed.) [85], pp. 171–174 (2003)
28. Bowen, J.P.: The Z notation: whence the cause and whither the course? In: Liu, Z., Zhang, Z. (eds.) SETSS 2014. LNCS, vol. 9506, pp. 103–151. Springer, Cham (2016). https://doi.org/10.1007/978-3-319-29628-9_3
29. Bowen, J.P.: Alan Turing: virtuosity and visualisation. In: Bowen, J.P., Diprose, G., Lambert, N. (eds.) EVA London 2016: Electronic Visualisation and the Arts, pp. 197–205. BCS, Electronic Workshops in Computing (eWiC) (2016). https://doi.org/10.14236/EVA2016.40
30. Bowen, J.P.: Alan Turing: founder of computer science. In: Bowen, J.P., Liu, Z., Zhang, Z. (eds.) SETSS 2016. LNCS, vol. 10215, pp. 1–15. Springer, Cham (2017). https://doi.org/10.1007/978-3-319-56841-6_1
31. Bowen, J.P.: Provably correct systems: community, connections, and citations. In: Hinchey, M.G., et al. (eds.) [91], pp. 313–328 (2017)
32. Bowen, J.P., et al.: The development of science museum websites: case studies. In: Hin, L.T.W., Subramaniam, R. (eds.) E-learning and Virtual Science Centers, chap. XVIII, pp. 366–392. Idea Group Publishing (2005)
33. Bowen, J.P., Copeland, B.J.: Turing's legacy. In: Copeland, J., et al. [58], chap. 42, pp. 463–474 (2017)
34. Bowen, J.P., Hall, J.A. (eds.): Z User Workshop, Cambridge 1994. Workshops in Computing. Springer, London (1994). https://doi.org/10.1007/978-1-4471-3452-7
35. Bowen, J.P., Hinchey, M.G., Glass, R.L.: Formal methods: point-counterpoint. Computer 29(4), 18–19 (1996)
36. Bowen, J.P., Hinchey, M.G.: Formal methods. In: Gonzalez, T., et al. (eds.) [152], part VIII, Programming Languages, chap. 71, pp. 71-1–71-25 (2014)
37. Bowen, J.P., Hinchey, M.G., Janicke, H., Ward, M., Zedan, H.: Formality, agility, security, and evolution in software engineering. In: Software Technology: 10 Years of Innovation in IEEE Computer, chap. 16, pp. 282–292. Wiley/IEEE Computer Society Press (2018)
38. Bowen, J.P., Reeves, S.: From a community of practice to a body of knowledge: a case study of the formal methods community. In: Butler, M., Schulte, W. (eds.) FM 2011. LNCS, vol. 6664, pp. 308–322. Springer, Heidelberg (2011). https://doi.org/10.1007/978-3-642-21437-0_24
39. Bowen, J.P., Trickett, T., Green, J.B.A., Lomas, A.: Turing's genius – defining an apt microcosm. In: Bowen, J.P., Weinel, J., Diprose, G., Lambert, N. (eds.) EVA London 2018: Electronic Visualisation and the Arts, pp. 155–162. BCS, Electronic Workshops in Computing (eWiC) (2018). https://doi.org/10.14236/EVA2018.31

40. Brattka, V.: Computability and analysis, a historical approach. In: Beckmann, A., Bienvenu, L., Jonoska, N. (eds.) CiE 2016. LNCS, vol. 9709, pp. 45–57. Springer, Cham (2016). https://doi.org/10.1007/978-3-319-40189-8_5

41. Brown, G.: I'm proud to say sorry to a real war hero. The Telegraph, 10 September 2009

42. Bullynck, M., Daylight, E.G., De Mol, L.: Why did computer science make a hero out of Turing? Commun. ACM **58**(3), 37–39 (2015). https://doi.org/10.1145/2658985

43. Campagna, R., Cuomo, S., Giannino, F., Severino, G., Toraldo, G.: A semi-automatic numerical algorithm for Turing patterns formation in a reaction-diffusion model. IEEE Access **6**, 4720–4724 (2017). https://doi.org/10.1109/ACCESS.2017.2780324

44. Campbell, S.: Beatrice Helen Worsley: Canada's female computer pioneer. IEEE Ann. Hist. Comput. **25**(4), 51–62 (2003). https://doi.org/10.1109/MAHC.2003.1253890

45. Campbell-Kelly, M., Aspray, W., Ensmenger, N., Yost, J.R.: Computer: A History of the Information Machine, 3rd edn. Westview Press, Boulder (2014)

46. Carroll, L.: The Game of Logic. Macmillan & Co., London (1886). http://archive.org/details/gameoflogic00carrrich

47. Carus, P.: Formal thought the basis of kenlore. The Monist **20**(4), 574–584 (1910). https://doi.org/10.5840/monist191020428

48. Cerf, V.: The man behind the machine. Physics World, pp. 38–39 (2018). http://physicsworld.com/a/the-man-behind-the-machine/

49. Collins, R.: Steve Jobs review: 'manically entertaining'. The Telegraph, 12 November 2015. http://www.telegraph.co.uk/film/steve-jobs/review

50. Cooper, S.B.: Turing's titanic machine? Commun. ACM **55**(3), 74–83 (2012). https://doi.org/10.1145/2093548.2093569

51. Cooper, S.B.: The Alan Turing Year: A Centenary Celebration of the Life and Work of Alan Turing. School of Mathematics, University of Leeds, UK (2012). http://www.turingcentenary.eu

52. Cooper, S.B., van Leeuwen, J. (eds.): Alan Turing: His Work and Impact. Elsevier Science (2013)

53. Copeland, B.J. (ed.): Colossus: The Secrets of Bletchley Park's Codebreaking Computers. Oxford University Press, Oxford (2006)

54. Copeland, B.J. (ed.): The Essential Turing. Oxford University Press, Oxford (2004)

55. Copeland, B.J.: Artificial intelligence. In: Copeland, B.J. (ed.) [54], pp. 353–361 (2004)

56. Copeland, B.J.: Turing: Pioneer of the Information Age. Oxford University Press, Oxford (2012)

57. Copeland, B.J.: Alan Turing: The codebreaker who saved 'millions of lives'. BBC News, 19 June 2012. http://www.bbc.co.uk/news/technology-18419691

58. Copeland, B.J., Bowen, J.P., Sprevak, M., Wilson, R., et al.: The Turing Guide. Oxford University Press, Oxford (2017)

59. Copeland, B.J., Posy, C.J., Shagrir, O.: Computability: Turing, Gödel, Church, and Beyond. MIT Press, Cambridge (2013)

60. Copeland, B.J., Proudfoot, D.: The Turing Archive for the History of Computing. http://www.alanturing.net

61. Dahl, O.-J., Dijkstra, E.W., Hoare, C.A.R.: Structured Programing. Academic Press, Cambridge (1972)

62. Dasgupta, S.: It Began with Babbage: The Genesis of Computer Science. Oxford University Press, Oxford (2014)
63. Davis, M.: Turing's vision and deep learning. In: Manea, F., Miller, R.G., Nowotka, D. (eds.) CiE 2018. LNCS, vol. 10936, pp. 146–155. Springer, Cham (2018). https://doi.org/10.1007/978-3-319-94418-0_15
64. Dawkins, R.: The God Delusion, p. 289. Bantam Press, London (2006)
65. Daylight, E.G.: Towards a historical notion of 'Turing–the father of computer science'. Hist. Philos. Logic **36**(3), 205–228 (2015). https://doi.org/10.1080/01445340.2015.1082050
66. De Mol, L.: Turing machines. In: Zalta, E.N. (ed.) Stanford Encyclopedia of Philosophy. Stanford University, USA, 24 September 2018. http://plato.stanford.edu/entries/turing-machine
67. Deutsch, D.: Quantum theory, the Church-Turing principle and the universal quantum computer. Proc. R. Soc. London A **400**, 97–117 (1985). https://doi.org/10.1098/rspa.1985.0070
68. Dijkstra, E.W.: A Discipline of Programming. Prentice Hall, Upper Saddle River (1976)
69. Dunham, W.: Euler: The Master of Us All. Mathematical Association of America (1999)
70. Dyson, G.: Darwin Among the Machines. The Penguin Press (1997)
71. Edwards, J.R.: An early history of computing at Princeton. Priceton Alumni Weekly, 4 April 2012. http://paw.princeton.edu/article/early-history-computing-princeton
72. Eperson, D.B: The Lewis Carroll Puzzle Book: Containing over 1,000 posers from Alice in Wonderland and other books by Lewis Carroll. Appeal Office (1948)
73. Evans, C.: The Mighty Micro: The Impact of the Computer Revolution. Victor Gollancz (1979)
74. Feigenbaum, E.A., McCorduck, P.: The Fifth Generation: Artificial Intelligence and Japan's Computer Challenge to the World. Addison Wesley, Boston (1983)
75. Floyd, R.W.: Assigning meaning to programs. In: Schwartz, S.T. (ed.) Mathematical Aspects of Computer Science. American Mathematical Society (1967). https://doi.org/10.1007/978-94-011-1793-7_4
76. Frith, H.: Unraveling the tale behind the Apple logo. CNN, 7 October 2011. http://edition.cnn.com/2011/10/06/opinion/apple-logo
77. Giannini, T., Bowen, J.P.: Life in code and digits: when Shannon met Turing. In: Bowen, J.P., Diprose, G., Lambert, N. (eds.) EVA London 2017: Electronic Visualisation and the Arts, pp. 51–58. BCS, Electronic Workshops in Computing (eWiC) (2017). https://doi.org/10.14236/EVA2017.9
78. Google: Alan Turing. Google Scholar. http://scholar.google.com/citations?user=VWCHlwkAAAAJ
79. Grattan-Guinness, I.: Turing's mentor, Max Newman. In: Copeland, B.J., et al. [58], chap. 40, pp. 437–442 (2017)
80. Gray, P.: Computer scientist: Alan Turing. Time **153**(12) (1999). http://content.time.com/time/subscriber/article/0,33009,990624-2,00.html
81. Gries, D.: The Science of Programming. Texts and Monographs in Computer Science. Springer, New York (1981). https://doi.org/10.1007/978-1-4612-5983-1
82. Han, B.: 枷锁与馈赠|认识真实的图灵，一位如谜的解谜者 [trans.: Shackles and gifts – Know the real Turing, a mystery puzzler]. WeChat, 3 April 2018. http://mp.weixin.qq.com/s/JcdromoslivadmFmEf8SVQ

83. Harel, D.: Computers Ltd.: What They Really Can't Do. Oxford University Press, Oxford (2000)
84. Hayes, P.J., Morgenstern, L.: On John McCarthy's 80th birthday, in honor of his contributions. AI Mag. **28**(4), 93–102 (2007). https://doi.org/10.1609/aimag.v28i4.2063
85. Heilbron, J.L. (ed.): The Oxford Companion to the History of Modern Science. Oxford University Press, Oxford (2003)
86. Hickey, S.: Alan Turing notebook sells for more than $1m at New York auction. The Guardian, 13 April 2015
87. Highfield, R.: Codebreaker wins Great Exhibition Award. Science Museum, London, 17 December 2012. http://blog.sciencemuseum.org.uk/codebreaker-wins-great-exhibition-award
88. Highfield, R.: What to think about machines that think. Science Museum, London, 11 December 2015. http://blog.sciencemuseum.org.uk/what-to-think-about-machines-that-think
89. Hillis, D., et al.: In honor of Marvin Minsky's contributions on his 80th birthday. AI Mag. **28**(4), 103–110 (2007). https://doi.org/10.1609/aimag.v28i4.2064
90. Hilton, P.: Meeting a genius. In: Copeland, J., et al. [58], chap. 3, pp. 31–34 (2017)
91. Hinchey, M.G., Bowen, J.P., Olderog, E.-R. (eds.): Provably Correct Systems. NASA Monographs in Systems and Software Engineering. Springer, Cham (2017). https://doi.org/10.1007/978-3-319-48628-4
92. Hinchey, M.G., Coyle, L. (eds.): Conquering Complexity. Springer, London (2012). https://doi.org/10.1007/978-1-4471-2297-5
93. Hoare, C.A.R.: An axiomatic basis for computer programming. Commun. ACM **12**(10), 576–580 (1969). https://doi.org/10.1145/363235.363259
94. Hoare, C.A.R., et al.: Laws of programming. Commun. ACM **30**(8), 672–686 (1987). https://doi.org/10.1145/27651.27653
95. Hoare, C.A.R., He, J.: Unifying Theories of Programming. Prentice Hall International Series in Computer Science (1998)
96. Hodges, A.: Alan Turing: The Enigma. Burnett/Simon and Schuster (1983); Centenary edition, Princeton University Press (2012)
97. Hodges, A.: Oration at Alan Turing's birthplace. Alan Turing: The Enigma, 23 June 1998. http://www.turing.org.uk/publications/oration.html
98. Hodges, A.: Alan Turing: The Enigma. http://www.turing.org.uk
99. IMDb: The Imitation Game. IMDb (2014). http://www.imdb.com/title/tt2084970
100. Isaacson, W.: Steve Jobs, p. xvi. Simon & Schuster/Little, Brown (2011)
101. Jones, A.: Five 1951 BBC broadcasts on automatic calculating machines. IEEE Ann. Hist. Comput. **26**(2), 3–15 (2004). https://doi.org/10.1109/MAHC.2004.1299654
102. Jones, A.: Brains, tortoises, and octopuses: postwar interpretations of mechanical intelligence on the BBC. Inf. & Cult. **51**(1), 81–101 (2016). https://doi.org/10.7560/IC51104
103. Jones, C.B: Systematic Software Development Using VDM. Prentice Hall International Series in Computer Science (1986)
104. Jones, C.B.: Turing's "checking a large routine". In: Cooper, S.B., van Leeuwen, J. (eds.) Alan Turing - His Work and Impact, pp. 455–461. Elsevier (2013)
105. Jones, C.B.: Turing and Software Verification. Technical report CS-TR-1441, Newcastle University, December 2014. http://homepages.cs.ncl.ac.uk/cliff.jones/publications/NU-TRs/CS-TR-1441.pdf

106. Jones, C.B.: Turing's 1949 paper in context. In: Kari, J., Manea, F., Petre, I. (eds.) CiE 2017. LNCS, vol. 10307, pp. 32–41. Springer, Cham (2017). https://doi.org/10.1007/978-3-319-58741-7_4

107. Jones, C.B.: The Turing guide. Formal Aspects Comput. **29**, 1121–1122 (2017). https://doi.org/10.1007/s00165-017-0446-y

108. Kettle, S.: Alan Turing. http://www.stephenkettle.co.uk/turing.html

109. King's College: The Turing Digital Archive. King's College, Cambridge, UK. http://www.turingarchive.org

110. Lavington, S.: The ACE, the 'British National Computer'. Early British Computers, chap. 5, pp. 23–30. Manchester University Press (1980)

111. Lavington, S. (ed.): Alan Turing and his Contemporaries: Building the World's First Computers. BCS, The Chartered Institute for IT (2012)

112. Lavington, S: Hindsight and foresight: the legacy of Turing and his contemporaries. In: Lavington, S., (ed.) [111], chap. 8, pp. 79–84 (2012)

113. Lewin, R.: Ultra Goes to War, p. 64. Grafton (1978)

114. Manchester University: Lost Turing letters give unique insight into his academic life prior to death. Discover/News. The University of Manchester, UK, 25 August 2017. http://www.manchester.ac.uk/discover/news/

115. McCarthy, J.: A basis for a mathematical theory of computation. In: Braffort P., Hirschberg, D. (eds.) Computer Programming and Formal Systems, pp. 33–70. North-Holland (1963). https://doi.org/10.1016/S0049-237X(08)72018-4

116. McKay S.: The Secret Life of Bletchley Park. Aurum (2011)

117. McKay, S.: How Alan Turing's secret papers were saved for the nation. The Telegraph, 30 July 2011

118. MGP: Alan Mathison Turing. Mathematics Genealogy Project. Department of Mathematics, North Dakota State University, USA. http://www.genealogy.ams.org/id.php?id=8014

119. Millican, P.J.A., Clark, A. (eds.): The Legacy of Alan Turing. Oxford University Press. Volume I: Machines and Thought; Volume II: Connectionism, Concepts and Folk Psychology (1996)

120. Ministry of Justice, Gyimah, S.: Thousands officially pardoned under 'Turing's Law'. UK Government, 31 January 2017. http://www.gov.uk/government/news/thousands-officially-pardoned-under-turings-law

121. Morgan, C.C.: Programming from Specifications. Prentice Hall International Series in Computer Science (1990). 2nd edition (1994)

122. Morris, F.L., Jones, C.B.: An early program proof by Alan Turing. IEEE Ann. Hist. Comput. **6**(2), 139–143 (1984). https://doi.org/10.1109/MAHC.1984.10017

123. Nature: Alan Turing at 100. Nature **482**, 450–465 (2012). http://www.nature.com/news/specials/turing

124. Naur, P.: Proof of algorithms by general snapshots. BIT **6**, 310–316 (1966). https://doi.org/10.1007/BF01

125. Newman, M.H.A.: Alan Mathison Turing, 1912–1954. Biogr. Mem. Fellows R. Soc. **1**, 253–263 (1955). https://doi.org/10.1098/rsbm.1955.0019

126. Newman, W.: Max Newman-Mathematician, codebreaker, and computer pioneer. In: Copeland, B.J. (ed.) [53], chap. 14, pp. 176–188 (2006)

127. O'Connor, J.J., Robertson, E.F.: Donald Birkby Eperson. MacTutor. School of Mathematics and Statistics, University of St Andrews, Scotland, May 2017. http://www-history.mcs.st-and.ac.uk/Biographies/Eperson.html

128. Page, C., Richards, M.: A letter from Christopher Strachey. Resurrection: J. Comput. Conserv. Soc. **73**, 22–24 (2016). http://www.computerconservationsociety.org/resurrection/res73.htm#d

129. Palfreman, J., Swade, D.: The Dream Machine: Exploring the Computer Age. BBC Books (1991)
130. Penrose, R.: The Emperor's New Mind: Concerning Computer, Minds, and the Laws of Physics. Oxford University Press, Oxford (1989)
131. Penrose, R.: Shadows of the Mind: A Search for the Missing Science of Consciousness. Oxford University Press, Oxford (1994)
132. Petrocelli, C.: The Turing Guide, by Jack Copeland, Jonathan Bowen, Mark Sprevak, and Robin Wilson. Nuncius **33**(1), 166–168 (2018). https://doi.org/10.1163/18253911-03301015
133. Princeton: Alan M. Turing. Office of the Executive Vice President, Princeton University, USA (2018). http://evp.princeton.edu/people/alan-m-turing
134. Randell, B.: On Alan Turing and the origins of digital computers. In: Meltzer, B., Michie, D. (eds.) Machine Intelligence, vol. 7, pp. 3–20. Edinburgh University Press (1972). http://www.cs.ncl.ac.uk/research/pubs/books/papers/126.pdf
135. Rendell, P.: Game of Life - Universal Turing Machine, YouTube (2010, uploaded 2012). http://www.youtube.com/watch?v=My8AsV7bA94
136. Robinson, A.: Sudden Genius: The Gradual Path to Creative Breakthroughs. Oxford University Press, Oxford (2010)
137. Robinson, A. (ed.): The Scientists: An Epic of Discovery. Thames& Hudson (2012)
138. Robinson, A.: Film: reality and check. The Lancet **386**, 2048 (2015)
139. Robinson, A.: The Turing Guide: last words on an enigmatic codebreaker? New Sci. **3107**, 42–43 (2017). http://www.newscientist.com/article/mg23331072-700
140. Rooney, D.: Codebreaker - Alan Turing's life and legacy. Science Museum, London. YouTube, 19 June 2012. http://www.youtube.com/watch?v=I3NkVMHh0_Q
141. Rooney, D.: Mathematics: How it Shaped our World. Scala Arts & Heritage Publishers (2016)
142. Russell, B.: What is logic. In: The Collected Papers of Bertrand Russell, vol. 6: Logical and Philosophical Papers, 1909–13. Part I: Logic and the Philosophy of Mathematics. Routledge (1912)
143. Shallis, M.: The Silicon Idol: The Micro Revolution and its Social Implications. Oxford University Press, Oxford (1984)
144. Singh, S.: The Code Book: The Science of Secrecy from Ancient Egypt to Quantum Cryptography. Forth Estate, London (1999)
145. Smith, C.N., et al.: Form IV b (i), Name Turing, Average Age 14.6, Age 14.8. School report. Sherborne School, UK (1927)
146. Soare, R.I.: History of computability. In: Soare, R.I. (ed.) Turing Computability. TAC, pp. 227–249. Springer, Heidelberg (2016). https://doi.org/10.1007/978-3-642-31933-4_17
147. Srinivasan, A. (ed.): Donald Michie: On Machine Intelligence. Biology & More. Oxford University Press, Oxford (2009)
148. Stoy, J.E.: Denotational Semantics: The Scott-Strachey Approach to Programming Language Theory. MIT Press, Cambridge (1977)
149. Sumner, J.: Turing today. Notes Rec. R. Soc. Lond. **66**(3), 295–300 (2012). http://www.jstor.org/stable/41723310
150. Swinford, S.: Alan Turing granted Royal pardon by the Queen. The Telegraph, 24 September 2013
151. Time: The great minds of the century. Time **153**(12) (1999). http://content.time.com/time/magazine/article/0,9171,990608,00.html

152. Gonzalez, T., Diaz-Herrera, J., Tucker, A.B. (eds.): Computing Handbook, 3rd edn. Volume I: Computer Science and Software Engineering. Chapman and Hall/CRC Press (2014)
153. Turing, A.M.: Précis of the Theory of Relativity by Albert Einstein. In: The Turing Digital Archive [109], AMT/K/2 (1927). http://www.turingarchive.org/viewer/?id=449&title=1
154. Turing, A.M.: On computable numbers with an application to the Entscheidungsproblem. Proc. Lond. Math. Soc. (Ser. 2) **42**(1), 230–265 (1936). https://doi.org/10.1112/plms/s2-42.1.230
155. Turing, A.M.: The purpose of ordinal logics. Ph.D. thesis, Princeton University, USA (1938)
156. Turing, A.M.: Checking a large routine. In: Report of a Conference on High Speed Automatic Calculating Machines, pp. 67–69. Mathematical Laboratory, University of Cambridge, UK (1949). http://www.turingarchive.org/browse.php/b/8
157. Turing, A.M.: Computing machinery and intelligence. Mind **59**(236), 433–460 (1950). https://doi.org/10.1093/mind/LIX.236.433
158. Turing, A.M.: Can digital computers think? In: The Turing Digital Archive [109], AMT/B/5, May 1951. http://www.turingarchive.org/viewer/?id=449&title=1 (see also 2018 transcription under http://aperiodical.com/wp-content/uploads/2018/01/Turing-Can-Computers-Think.pdf)
159. Turing, A.M.: The chemical basis of morphogenesis. Philos. Trans. R. Soc. Lond. **237**(641), 37–72 (1952). https://doi.org/10.1098/rstb.1952.0012
160. Turing, A.M., Braithwaite, R.B., Jefferson, G., Newman, M.: Can automatic calculating machines be said to think? (1952). In: Copeland, B.J. (ed.) [54], chap. 14, pp. 487–506 (2004)
161. Turing, D.: Prof Alan Turing Decoded: A Biography. The History Press (2015)
162. Turing, S.: Alan M. Turing: Centenary Edition. Cambridge University Press, Cambridge (2012)
163. Uhlig, R.: Genius of Britain: The Scientists who Changed the World. HarperCollins (2010)
164. van Doren, C.: A History of Knowledge: Past, Present, and Future. Ballantine Books (1991)
165. Vardi, M.Y.: Would turing have won the turing award? Commun. ACM **60**(11), 7 (2017). https://doi.org/10.1145/3144590
166. Veblen, O.: Letter to M. H. A. Newman, esq. Janus Catalogue Item 2-1-13. The Max Newman Digital Archive, University of Brighton, UK, 4 May 1928. http://www.cdpa.co.uk/Newman/MHAN
167. Wikipedia: List of things named after Alan Turing. Wikipedia, Wikimedia Foundation. http://en.wikipedia.org/wiki/List_of_things_named_after_Alan_Turing
168. Wilkes, M.V.: Automatic calculating machines. J. R. Soc. Arts **100**(4862), 56–90 (1951). http://www.jstor.org/stable/41365298
169. Wolfram, S.: A New Kind of Science. Wolfram Media (2002)
170. Worsley, B.H.: Serial programming for real and idealised digital calculating machines. Ph.D. thesis, University of Cambridge, UK, May 1952. Also. In: Archives Center, National Museum of American History, Smithsonian Institution, USA. http://sova.si.edu/details/NMAH.AC.0237#ref29
171. Yates, D.M.: Turing's Legacy: A history of computing at the National Physical Laboratory 1945–1995. Science Museum, London (1997)

Author Index

Printed in the United States
By Bookmasters